TIME FOR KIDS

ALMANAC 2006

with FACT MONSTER

Beth Rowen
Editor

Curtis Slepian
Managing Editor

TIME FOR KIDS ALMANAC 2006 with FACT MONSTER

INFORMATION PLEASE

EDITOR: Beth Rowen
CONTRIBUTORS: Borgna Brunner, Sean Dessureau, Christine Frantz, Holly Hartman
FACT-CHECKING AND PROOFREADING: Christine Frantz
DESIGNER: Sean Dessureau
INDEXING: Marilyn Rowland
EDITORIAL DIRECTOR: Borgna Brunner
VICE PRESIDENT AND GENERAL MANAGER: George Kane

TIME FOR KIDS ALMANAC

MANAGING EDITOR: Curtis Slepian
COPY EDITOR: Peter McGullam
PHOTOGRAPHY EDITOR: Sandy Perez
MAPS: Joe Lertola
ART DIRECTION AND DESIGN: R studio T, NYC: Raul Rodriguez/Rebecca Tachna
COVER DESIGN: Anna Varshavsky
EDITORIAL DIRECTOR: Keith Garton

TIME INC. HOME ENTERTAINMENT

PUBLISHER: Richard Fraiman
EXECUTIVE DIRECTOR, MARKETING SERVICES: Carol Pittard
DIRECTOR, RETAIL & SPECIAL SALES: Tom Mifsud
MARKETING DIRECTOR, BRANDED BUSINESSES: Swati Rao
ASSISTANT FINANCIAL DIRECTOR: Steven Sandonato
PREPRESS MANAGER: Emily Rabin
BOOK PRODUCTION MANAGER: Jonathan Polsky
MARKETING MANAGER: Kristin Walker
RETAIL MANAGER: Bozena Bannett
ASSOCIATE PREPRESS MANAGER: Anne-Michelle Gallero
ASSISTANT MARKETING MANAGER: Candice Ogarro

SPECIAL THANKS: Alexandra Bliss, Bernadette Corbie, Peter Harper, Suzanne Janso, Robert Marasco, Brooke McGuire, Sarah, Maya and Jayce Rowen

SPECIAL THANKS TO IMAGING: Patrick Dugan, Eddie Matros

Published by TIME For Kids Books
Time Inc.
1271 Avenue of the Americas
New York, New York 10020

ISSN: 1534-5718
ISBN: 1-932994-34-3

We welcome your comments and suggestions about TIME For Kids Books. Please write to us at:
TIME For Kids Books
Attention: Book Editors
PO Box 11016
Des Moines, IA 50336-1016

If you would like to order any of our hardcover Collector's Edition books, please call us at 1-800-327-6388 (Monday through Friday, 7:00 a.m.–8:00 p.m. or Saturday, 7:00 a.m.–6:00 p.m. Central Time).

Contents

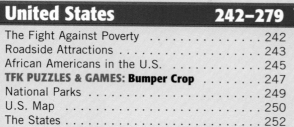

Homework Tip!
Find information for school assignments in your
TIME For Kids 2006 Almanac

go ▐ **Learn about tsunamis and how you can help
tsunami victims at timeforkids.com/tsunami**

After the Waves

At 7:58 a.m. on December 26, 2004, the Earth's crust trembled. An undersea quake set off shock waves that were felt more than 3,000 miles away. Walls of water called a tsunami swept across the Indian Ocean. The tsunami killed more than 280,000 people along the coast of South Asia and in parts of East Africa.

Responding to the devastation, volunteers flew to the affected areas. They passed out water, medical supplies and clothing. Doctors set up temporary outdoor hospitals to treat wounded survivors. Dozens of countries—led by Australia, Germany, Japan and the United States— pledged nearly $4 billion in aid.

Up to 5 million victims lacked the basic necessities to stay alive. Doctors and nurses treated thousands in hastily built camps. They also worked to prevent the spread of disease. Dirty water and food can make people sick, and disease often spreads quickly under these circumstances.

International organizations such as Doctors Without Borders, UNICEF and the International Red Cross set up aid centers to provide emergency help.

President George W. Bush sent money and troops to help. He also enlisted former Presidents Bill Clinton and George H.W. Bush to encourage private donations. In addition, the President sent then Secretary of State Colin Powell to the region.

"I've been in war and I've been through a number of hurricanes, tornadoes and other relief operations, but I've never seen anything like this," said Powell.

Remarkably, another huge earthquake struck the region in March 2005, killing hundreds of people in Indonesia.

Bush's New Term Begins

On January 20, 2005, thousands of Americans gathered outside the U.S. Capitol building in Washington, D.C. People had come to see George W. Bush sworn in for his second term as President.

Surrounded by family—his wife, Laura, and twin daughters, Jenna and Barbara—Bush placed one hand on a family Bible. Supreme Court Justice William Rehnquist administered the oath of office as thousands of police and security officers patrolled the area.

Vice President Dick Cheney was sworn in moments before the President.

After the ceremony, Bush addressed the nation. "I am grateful for the honor of this hour," he said. The President promised to continue to work for freedom throughout the world. "We go forward with complete confidence in the eventual triumph of freedom," he said.

 Visit TFK's Inauguration site at timeforkids.com/inauguration

A Historic Day of Voting in Iraq

After months of nervous anticipation, Election Day arrived in Iraq in January 2005. In spite of terrorists' threats to attack voting places, 8.5 million Iraqis—estimated at 58% of those eligible—voted for new leaders. Many first-time voters danced in the streets and proudly showed off fingers dyed with purple ink to prove that they had cast ballots. "As we worked together to finish dictatorship, let us work together toward a bright future," said Iyad Allawi, Iraq's interim Prime Minister. Despite tight security, more than 40 Iraqis were killed in attacks on 100 voting centers.

An alliance of Shiites, the United Iraqi Alliance, came out on top in the elections, winning 140 seats in the 275-member National Assembly. Its members will help write a constitution that will be put to a national vote.

Titan Up Close

In 2005 the *Huygens* (hoy-gunz) space probe safely landed on Saturn's largest moon, Titan. It had taken seven years to get there.

Huygens was attached to the *Cassini* spacecraft. After *Cassini* entered Saturn's orbit, *Huygens* separated from the spacecraft. It traveled more than 2 million miles to reach Titan. Scientists believe that Titan's atmosphere is similar to that of early Earth.

Huygens entered Titan's atmosphere and fell at a rate of about 11,000 miles per hour. Parachutes slowed the probe. It landed with a splat, probably on wet mud or clay.

Huygens's camera took about 350 pictures of Titan's landscape. Some images suggest the moon is covered by a thin fog. Others show rock-shaped objects that might be chunks of ice. "Titan is a world that is quite active," says David Grinspoon, a planet expert. Titan will surely give scientists plenty to study and celebrate for years.

go → For more about space exploration go to: www.factmonster.com/spexplore

The World Mourns

One of the world's most beloved religious leaders, Pope John Paul II, died on April 2, 2005, at his home in the Vatican. He was 84. The pope led the world's 1 billion Catholics for 26 years.

The pope was very popular not only with Catholics but also with people of other religions and with leaders all over the world. The most widely traveled pope in history, he was known for always seeking contact with ordinary people. The pope worked tirelessly to improve relations between people of all religions.

In the U.S., President Bush led the nation in remembering the pope. "The world has lost a champion of human freedom," Bush said.

The World's Biggest Plane

Now that's a jumbo jet! In 2005, Airbus, a company in Europe, announced the birth of the world's biggest commercial airplane—the A380. The new seven-story-high plane can hold up to 800 passengers. It has a wingspan of more than 260 feet. Each plane will cost about $280 million.

The gigantic jets are scheduled to carry their first passengers in 2006 for Singapore Airlines. Other airlines, including Air France, plan to use the planes for international flights.

Federal Express and United Parcel Service each ordered 10 of the planes to use for deliveries. "It will have far-reaching effects on the efficiency of world trade," FedEx chief Fred Smith said of the A380.

Two Daring Young Men

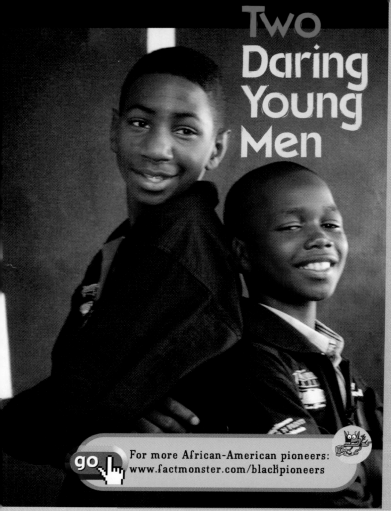

They're flying high. Kenny Roy (far left) and Jimmy Haywood made history by flying round-trip between Compton, California, and Vancouver, Canada. The 20-hour flight landed both boys in the record books. Jimmy, 11, became the youngest African-American pilot to make an international flight. Kenny, 14, is the youngest African-American pilot licensed to fly solo. Kenny took his flight test and got his license in Canada. Kids can't get their pilots' wings until age 16 in the United States.

"It's exciting," says Kenny. "I set an example for other kids."

go For more African-American pioneers:
www.factmonster.com/blackpioneers

KING OF THE MOUNTAINS

Bode Miller is going downhill fast—very fast! In 2005, Bode, 27, showed the world who rules the slopes. He won the overall World Cup title in Lenzerheide, Switzerland, becoming the first American to do so in 22 years. At the Alpine World Ski Championships in Bormio, Italy, Bode earned a gold medal in the downhill, a feat not accomplished by an American male since 1994. Earlier that winter, Miller won six of 10 international ski competitions. Look for the native of Franconia, New Hampshire, to be a star of the 2006 Winter Olympic Games in Turin, Italy.

Flash of the Future

Michelle Kwan made history in 2005 with her ninth win at the U.S. Figure Skating Championships, but daring Kimmie Meissner almost stole the show.

At the competition, held at the Rose Garden arena in Portland, Oregon, Meissner, 15, earned the loudest roar from the crowd.

The 5-foot-tall native of Baltimore didn't beat Kwan, but Meissner did land a triple axel. She became the first U.S. woman in 14 years to land that difficult jump in competition. Although too young to compete in the 2005 world ice-skating championships, this talented skater will have her chance to win championships in years to come.

A Whole Lotta Puppy Love

In England in 2004, Tia, a Neapolitan mastiff pooch, gave birth to a world-record litter of 24 puppies. Four died, but the remaining 20 are doing well. The owners, Damian Ward and Anne Kellegher, have had their hands full, bottle-feeding the pups nonstop. "We are exhausted, but excited," Ward told TFK.

So Raven, So Talented

She stars in a hit TV show, Disney Channel's *That's So Raven.* She has been in many movies, including *The Princess Diaries 2: Royal Engagement.* And her third CD, *This Is My Time,* was a big hit. For Raven-Symone, 19, life couldn't be better. "I am so excited!" she told TFK.

What are the goals of this multi-talented star? "I want to go to culinary school in Paris. I also want to have a company that thrives on helping girls become more confident and creating things just for us."

go **Read TFK's interview with Raven at timeforkids.com/raven**

POTTER POWER!

The year 2005 was a magic one for Harry Potter. J.K. Rowling published *Harry Potter and the Half-Blood Prince,* the sixth book in her popular series. Loyal fans eagerly read the story of Harry's sixth year at Hogwarts School of Witchcraft and Wizardry. In this installment, the battle between good and evil makes life very tough for Harry and his friends—and great fun for readers.

go **Play Potter games and see Potter pictures at timeforkids.com/potter**

In 2002, *American Idol* debuted on TV and quickly became a huge hit in the United States. Millions of people have not only watched the show since the first season but have also voted for their favorite singers. In the fourth season, more than 100,000 singers auditioned in seven cities to win the approval of judges Paula Abdul, Randy Jackson and Simon Cowell. For many TV viewers, *American Idol* remains "note"-worthy.

Still in Tune

Hideous Hits

When Hollywood looks for monster hits, they often look for . . . monsters! One of 2005's biggest movie monsters was *King Kong*. Peter Jackson, director of *The Lord of the Rings,* filmed a remake of the story about a giant ape.

The monstrous-looking Thing (Michael Chiklis) is a star of *Fantastic Four*, the movie version of the Marvel comic book. The other members of the foursome are the Invisible Woman (Jessica Alba), Mr. Fantastic (Ioan Gruffudd) and the Human Torch (Chris Evans).

Some people think Darth Vader is a monster. Young Darth appears in *Star Wars: Episode III—Revenge of the Sith.* George Lucas's final prequel reveals how Anakin ended up in that scary black mask.

NOWHERE TO ROAM

Wildlife parks alone cannot keep lions safe. Will new efforts to protect the cats succeed?

These lions roam the 45,000-acre Mugie Ranch. Herders there are learning nonviolent ways to protect their livestock from the big cats.

In the golden light of a setting African sun, three young lions are feasting on a baby giraffe. A mature lioness approaches. One of the lions tries to scare her off with a snarl. But she lunges at him, and he slinks off into the sunset. The lioness takes his place at the feast.

On the plains of Africa, the killing of prey by big cats is part of the rhythm of life. But with wilderness areas shrinking, lions and other predators are finding it harder and harder to survive. Ten years ago, the species was thought to number as many as 100,000. But a new survey indicates that only 23,000 wild lions are left. More than half of them live in protected areas, such as national parks. Outside these big parks, lions seem to be in alarming decline.

WAYS TO SHARE THE LAND

Conservationists are now trying new strategies to save lions. Mugie Ranch, in Kenya, is conducting an important experiment. The ranch, which raises livestock to sell as food, holds 10 lions.

Livestock owners usually kill predators. But Mugie Ranch is part of the Laikipia Predator Project, run by wildlife biologist Laurence Frank. The project aims to save large carnivores by seeking ways for big cats and humans to live together.

"To many Africans, lions are simply pests," says Frank. But Mugie's lions have begun to attract tourists. If the lions bring tourist dollars to the ranch, then both humans and lions come out ahead.

THE BIG-CAT CRISIS

Most of the world's big cats—tigers, cheetahs, snow leopards, jaguars—are in trouble. Surviving as a top cat in a world ruled by humans is tough. Big cats need big spaces. When they leave a park's boundaries, they find themselves in battles for land claimed by humans.

Even inside a wildlife sanctuary, lions are not always secure. In 1994, one-third of the lions in Serengeti National Park in Tanzania died from viruses.

Conservationists are convinced that the only way to save big cats is to let them live among us. Lions should roam from protected areas through land that is shared by humans, they say.

Still, there is no simple way to meet the needs of both humans and big cats. Whenever a choice has to be made, the needs of humans will come before those of the cats. Even on Mugie Ranch, where lions are prized, ranch manager Klaus Mortensen had

Herders at Mugie look out for lions. This herder carries a bow and arrow. Others have rifles.

to shoot a female lion. She had taken to killing sheep. "If you don't move quickly, they teach the other lions [to do the same]," Mortensen explains.

—*By Terry McCarthy*

LIONS IN THE WILD

Length: 54 inches to 86 inches, excluding tail

Maximum weight:
Males, 496 pounds
Females, 370 pounds

Estimated population: 23,000

Status: Vulnerable

Threats: Livestock owners, who kill to protect herds

Habitat: Grassy plains, dry forests, scrub, semideserts

Man-eaters: Yes

ASIA

AFRICA

Kenya

Tanzania

■ Where they now live
■ Where they once lived*

*Shows where lions are believed to have roamed. The area did not change much until the past 200 years.

Sources: Justina Ray, Wildlife Conservation Society; IUCN, Cat Specialist Group

- The lion's roar is louder than a jackhammer.
- Lions are the only big cats to live and hunt in family groups, called prides. Lions sleep as much as 19 hours a day.
- Once found in Europe, Asia and the Americas, the only wild lions outside Africa, in India's Gir Forest sanctuary, now number 300.

go Learn about animals in africa at timeforkids.com/africananimals

Classifying Animals

There are billions of different kinds of living things (organisms) on Earth. To help study them, biologists have created ways of naming and classifying them according to their similarities and differences. The system most scientists use puts each living thing into seven groups, organized from most general to most specific. Therefore, each kingdom is composed of phylums, each phylum is composed of classes, each class is composed of orders, and so on.

Kingdoms are huge groups, with millions of kinds of organisms in each. All animals are in one kingdom (called Kingdom Animalia); all plants are in another (Kingdom Plantae). It is generally agreed that there are five kingdoms: Animalia, Plantae, Fungi, Prokarya (bacteria) and Protoctista (organisms that don't fit into the four other kingdoms, including many microscopic creatures).

Species are the smallest groups. In the animal kingdom, a species consists of all the animals of a type that are able to breed and produce young of the same kind.

From **largest** to smallest, the groups are

Kingdom
Phylum
Class
Order
Family
Genus
Species

TIP

To remember the sequence for classification, keep this sentence in mind:

King Philip came over from great Spain.

A Sample Classification:

The Gray Wolf

Kingdom: Animalia includes all animals

Phylum: Chordata includes all vertebrate, or backboned, animals

Class: Mammalia includes all mammals

Order: Carnivora includes all carnivorous, or meat-eating, mammals

Family: Canidae includes all dogs

Genus: Canis includes dogs, foxes and jackals

Species: lupus the gray wolf

Did You Know?

Taxonomy is the science of classifying organisms, such as animals.

Toxic Terrors

Sharp claws and teeth aren't the only weapons animals possess. Many creatures use poisons to attack prey or defend themselves. Some poisonous animals store toxins in their glands and inject them into their victims. Other animals produce poisons in their skin. Here are some of the most poisonous animals in the world.

POISON ARROW FROG Next time you're in the rain forests of Central or South America and you spy this little amphibian, don't pick it up: its skin contains a toxic chemical that sickens or kills any animal that touches or eats it. Two micrograms of its toxin (barely enough to fit on the head of pin) will kill a large mammal—or even a person.

Poison arrow frog

Stonefish

STONEFISH Found in the waters of the Pacific and around Australia, this homely fish looks like a rock or a piece of coral. Well camouflaged, it attacks any fish that swims nearby. A powerful toxin stored in its 13 spines can stop any predator in its tracks. In humans, the venom causes intense pain, swelling of tissue, shock and, eventually, death.

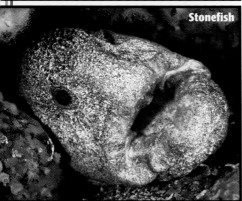

INLAND TAIPAN Native to Australia, it is considered the most poisonous snake on the planet. One bite from this shy, gentle reptile contains enough potent toxin to kill about 100 people. Its bite will stop a person from breathing.

BOX JELLYFISH Swimmers in the ocean waters in Asia and Australia should avoid touching its tentacles. Stingers on them deliver a powerful punch. In addition to causing excruciating pain that lasts for weeks, its venom can stop the heart or paralyze the lungs, as well as eat away at the skin.

BLUE-RINGED OCTOPUS The neurotoxins in its saliva work quickly. Within minutes, a person who is bitten will experience numbness and muscular weakness, and soon after, will stop breathing and die.

DEATH-STALKER SCORPION Found in North Africa and the Middle East, its name says it all. Although its stinger isn't particularly large or strong, a sting from this, the most toxic scorpion in the world, causes unbearable pain, fever, coma, convulsions, paralysis and death.

Sydney funnel-web spider

SYDNEY FUNNEL-WEB SPIDER Australia is home to many venomous creatures, and this arachnid is one of the worst. Large and aggressive, it produces toxins among the most powerful of any spider. Its fangs deliver a neurotoxin that causes great pain and can kill a person in 15 minutes.

Blue-ringed octopus

21

Fascinating ANIMAL Facts

SLOTH

GIRAFFE

Not only can a **CHAMELEON** change color to protect itself, but it can also move its eyes in two directions at the same time.

Have you noticed that **BIRDS** fly in a V formation? It helps them conserve energy. The V-shaped airstreams created by the birds in front reduce the wind resistance for the other birds. When the lead bird gets tired, another bird takes over up front.

SLOTHS spend most of their time in trees. They come down only about once a week, to relieve themselves.

The **MIDGE**, a tiny insect, beats its wings 62,000 times a minute.

Even though a **GIRAFFE** has a long neck, it has the same number of neck bones as a person: seven.

Only female **MOSQUITOES** bite. They need the protein from blood to produce their eggs.

An **ELEPHANT** eats about 250 pounds of plants and drinks about 50 gallons of water each day.

There are 200 million **INSECTS** for each person on Earth.

BABY BIRDS have an "egg tooth" (a small notch on the front of the beak) that they use to peck their way out of the egg. Once hatched, the chick loses the tooth.

An **ALBATROSS** can sleep while it flies. It dozes while cruising at speeds of up to 25 m.p.h.

AMAZON ANTS (red ants found in the Western U.S.) steal the larvae of other ants to keep as slaves. The slave ants build homes for and feed the Amazon ants, who cannot do anything but fight. They depend completely on their slaves for survival.

A **COCKROACH** can live for as much as a week without its head.

Did You Know?
Coral, which is found at the bottom of the ocean, is actually an animal.

ALBATROSS

go

For the answers to animal FAQs:
www.factmonster.com/animalfaqs

Fascinating FISH Facts

> Starfish that lose arms can grow new ones. In addition, an entire animal can sometimes grow from a single lost arm.

> The largest fish in the world is the whale shark, which grows to more than 50 feet in length and may weigh several tons. The smallest is the tiny goby, which lives in lakes in Luzon, the Philippines. It seldom is longer than a half inch at adulthood.

> Although not all fish sleep, most fish do rest. Usually they just do what we might call daydreaming. Some float in place, some wedge themselves into a spot in the mud or the coral, and some even build themselves a nest.

> Sharks continually replace lost teeth. A shark may grow 24,000 teeth in a lifetime.

> Fish that give live birth are called viviparous fishes. Sea perches of the Pacific Coast, for example, give birth to living young.

> Fish breathe oxygen, but not via the lungs as mammals do. As water passes over a fish's extremely fine gill membranes, its body is able to absorb the water's oxygen content. Gills contain a network of tiny blood vessels (capillaries) that take up the oxygen and spread it to all the muscles.

> Fish swim by contracting bands of muscles on both sides of their body so that the tail is whipped very fast from side to side. They use their vertical fins mainly to keep stable. Their pectoral and pelvic fins help them to hover and to move forward quickly.

 go For the lowdown on sharks: www.factmonster.com/sharks2

 **Puzzles & Games**

Give That Dog a Bone

Use the clues to find the dog in this picture that was named Best in Show. Clues: the Best in Show winner is not white. The Best in Show winner is sitting down. The Best in Show winner is not wearing a collar. The Best in Show winner is wagging its tail.

(See Answer Key that begins on page 342.)

Animal Groups

Almost all animals belong to one of two groups, **VERTEBRATES** or **INVERTEBRATES.** Adult vertebrates have a spinal column, or backbone, running the length of their bodies; invertebrates do not. Vertebrates are often larger and have more complex bodies than invertebrates. However, there are many more invertebrates than vertebrates.

Vertebrates

Platypuses are mammals.

Crocodiles are reptiles.

REPTILES are cold-blooded and breathe with lungs. They have thick, scaly skin, and most lay eggs. Reptiles include turtles and tortoises, crocodiles and alligators, snakes and lizards.

FISH breathe through gills and live in water. Most are cold-blooded and lay eggs (although sharks give birth to live young). Fish eggs, however, don't have shells. Most fish are covered with scales.

MAMMALS are warm-blooded and are nourished by their mothers' milk. Most live on land, but whales and dolphins, which breathe with lungs, live in water. Most are born live, but the platypus and echidna are hatched from eggs. Most mammals also have body hair.

DINOSAURS were reptiles, although some scientists believe that some dinosaurs were warm-blooded.

BIRDS are warm-blooded animals with feathers, wings and lightweight bones. They lay eggs, and most birds can fly. Some, including penguins and ostriches, cannot fly. All birds breathe with lungs.

AMPHIBIANS are cold-blooded and live both on land (breathing with lungs) and in water (breathing through gills) at different times of their lives. Three types of amphibians are caecilians, salamanders, and frogs and toads. Caecilians are primitive amphibians that resemble earthworms. They are found in the tropics.

Invertebrates

SPONGES are the most primitive of animal groups. They live in water, are sessile (do not move from place to place) and filter tiny organisms out of the water for food.

ECHINODERMS, including starfish, sea urchins and sea cucumbers, live in seawater and have external skeletons.

WORMS come in many varieties and live in all sorts of habitats—from the bottom of the ocean to the insides of other animals. They include flatworms (flukes), roundworms (hookworms), segmented worms (earthworms) and rotifers (philodina).

MOLLUSKS are soft-bodied animals, some of which live in hard shells. They include snails, slugs, octopuses, squid, mussels, oysters, clams, scallops and cuttlefish.

ARTHROPODS are the largest and most diverse of all animal groups. They have segmented bodies supported by a hard external skeleton (or exoskeleton). Arthropods include insects, arachnids (spiders and their relatives) and crustaceans (such as shrimp and crabs).

COELENTERATES are also very primitive. Their mouths, which take in food and get rid of waste, are surrounded by stinging tentacles. Jellyfish, corals and sea anemones are coelenterates.

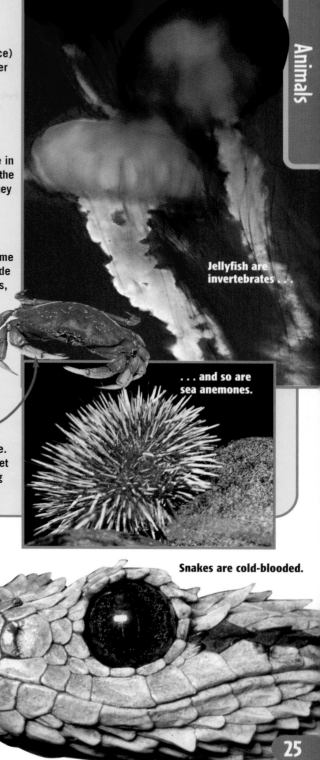

Jellyfish are invertebrates . . .

. . . and so are sea anemones.

Warm-Blooded and Cold-Blooded Animals

Warm-blooded animals regulate their own body temperatures; their bodies use energy to maintain a constant temperature. Cold-blooded animals depend on their surroundings to establish their body temperatures.

Snakes are cold-blooded.

25

Extinct, Endangered and Threatened Species

Sperm whale

Many species are disappearing from our planet. Sadly, by 2025, as much as one-fifth of the world's species may be gone. **EXTINCT** means that the entire species has died out and can never return. **ENDANGERED** animals are those in immediate danger of becoming extinct. **THREATENED** species are likely to become endangered in the future.

Humans are largely responsible when animals become extinct, endangered or threatened. Here are some of the things that can lead animals to become endangered.

DESTRUCTION OF HABITAT Humans destroy precious habitat—the natural environment of a living thing—when they fill swamps and marshes, dam rivers and cut down trees to build homes, roads and other structures or developments.

POLLUTION Oil spills, acid rain and water pollution have been devastating for many species of fish and birds.

HUNTING AND FISHING Many animals are overhunted because their meat, fur and other parts are very valuable.

INTRODUCTION OF EXOTIC SPECIES When foreign animals or plants are introduced into a new habitat, they sometimes bring diseases that the native species can't fight. Though "exotic" species can prey on the native species, they often have no natural enemies.

Green sea turtle

There are 1,072 endangered and threatened species of animals in the world. The list includes:

- 342 species of mammals, such as the red wolf, the sperm whale and the mountain gorilla.

- 273 species of birds, such as the California condor, the whooping crane and the northern spotted owl.

- 126 species of fish, such as coho salmon.

- 115 species of reptiles, such as the green sea turtle.

- 48 species of insects, including the mission blue butterfly.

- 30 species of amphibians, including the Houston toad.

Peregrine falcon

TFK Top 5

Heaviest Land Mammals

African elephants can eat up to 600 pounds of food in one day! That might be why they're the largest and heaviest mammals on land. Here's how the "heavies" of the animal kingdom stack up.

1. Elephant up to 14,000 pounds
2. Hippopotamus up to 8,000 pounds
3. Rhinoceros up to 5,000 pounds
4. Giraffe up to 4,200 pounds
5. Water buffalo up to 2,600 pounds

Source: Tthe San Diego Zoo

Fast Tracks

Forget about challenging a cheetah to a race. The fastest human sprinter only reaches a speed of about 28 m.p.h.

ANIMAL	SPEED (M.P.H.)
PEREGRINE FALCON	200+
CHEETAH	70
LION	50
ZEBRA	40
GREYHOUND	39
DRAGONFLY	36
RABBIT	35
GIRAFFE	32
GRIZZLY BEAR	30
CAT	30
ELEPHANT	25
SQUIRREL	12
MOUSE	8
SPIDER	1
GARDEN SNAIL	0.03

Source: James G. Doherty, general curator, Wildlife Conservation Society

Animal Gestation & Longevity

Here's a look at the average gestation (the time an animal spends inside its mother) and longevity (life span) of certain animals.

ANIMAL	GESTATION (DAYS)	LONGEVITY (YEARS)
CAT	52–69	10–12
COW	280	9–12
DOG	53–71	10–12
HAMSTER	15–17	2
HORSE	329–345	20–25
KANGAROO	32–39	4–6
LION	105–113	10
PIG	101–130	10
PIGEON	11–19	10–12
RABBIT	30–35	6–8
WOLF	60–63	10–12

Source: James G. Doherty, general curator, Wildlife Conservation Society

Cheetah

Did You Know?

No one knows for sure how many species of animals there are on Earth. Most scientists agree there are about 1 million species of animals and at least 20,000 species of fish. More than 10,000 new animal species are discovered each year.

For the speeds of other animals:
www.factmonster.com/animalspeeds

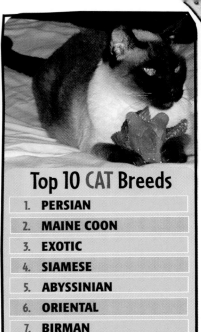

Top 10 DOG Breeds

1.	LABRADOR RETRIEVER
2.	GOLDEN RETRIEVER
3.	GERMAN SHEPHERD
4.	BEAGLE
5.	DACHSHUND
6.	YORKSHIRE TERRIER
7.	BOXER
8.	POODLE
9.	CHIHUAHUA
10.	SHIH TZU

Source: The American Kennel Club

Top 10 CAT Breeds

1.	PERSIAN
2.	MAINE COON
3.	EXOTIC
4.	SIAMESE
5.	ABYSSINIAN
6.	ORIENTAL
7.	BIRMAN
8.	AMERICAN SHORTHAIR
9.	TONKINESE
10.	BURMESE

Source: Cat Fanciers' Association

Animal Expression

People aren't the only creatures who "talk" to each other. Like people, animals use body language as well as sound and smell to communicate.

- Many animals release pheromones (airborne chemicals) to send messages to others. Pheromones play an important part in reproduction and other social behavior. Insects, wolves, deer and even humans use pheromones.

- Bees dance when they have found nectar. The scout bee will dance in the hive, and the dance directs other bees to the nectar.

- Chimpanzees greet each other by touching hands.

- Male fiddler crabs wave their giant claw to attract females.

- White-tailed deer show alarm by flicking up their tails.

- Dogs stretch their front legs out in front of them and lower their bodies when they want to play.

- Elephants show affection by entwining their trunks.

- Giraffes press their necks together when they are attracted to each other.

- Gorillas stick out their tongues to show anger.

DOG Days?

Think you're ready to expand your family with a furry friend? Owning a dog is a wonderful experience, one that brings lots of fun and companionship. But it also requires lots of time and responsibility.

Before you decide to get a dog, you should make sure you and your home are ready. Dogs, especially young ones, need lots of attention and commitment. While housebreaking your dog, plan to take it out every hour. Housebreaking can take up to six months.

Don't let a young dog roam freely around your house. Otherwise, you'll lose shoes, toys, rugs and possibly furniture to the canine's eager teeth. Dogs also need to exercise twice a day. That doesn't mean a leisurely stroll around the block. We're talking vigorous exercise.

A fenced yard with a doghouse is a good idea, especially for large and active dogs, but dogs should never be left outside alone for a long time. They crave and require company, and they should stay inside with the family whenever possible.

When you take your dog for a walk or run, always keep it on a leash and off other people's property. You are responsible for any damage, accidents and bites caused by your dog. You should always pick up after your dog, regardless of where it "does its business."

One of the most important things to do is to have your dog spayed or neutered—an operation that prevents it from having puppies. More than 4 million dogs and cats must be humanely destroyed each year because there aren't enough homes for them all.

Of course, you'll have to make sure your dog has all its shots and has regular checkups with a veterinarian.

Respect your new companion, and it will respect and protect you. There's truth to the saying, "Dogs are man's best friend!"

go Check out dog safety tips at
timeforkids.com/dogsafety

TFK Mystery Person

CLUE 1: I was born in San Francisco in 1932 and was interested in animals my whole life.

CLUE 2: On a trip to Africa, I became fascinated by mountain gorillas. Starting in 1967, I lived for nearly 18 years among gorillas in Rwanda and learned much about their behavior. I worked hard to stop poachers from killing these peaceful animals.

CLUE 3: A book I wrote about my experiences in Rwanda, *Gorillas in the Mist*, became a movie.

WHO AM I?

(See Answer Key that begins on page 342.)

Museums on

Through the ages, members of royalty, universities and monasteries have collected art. But the public was not invited to view these collections until the last few centuries. Now art museums are open to everyone. Take a quick tour of some of the best.

METROPOLITAN MUSEUM OF ART, New York City This, the greatest collection of art in the U.S., was founded in 1870. In addition to displaying American and European paintings, "the Met" has medieval art and armor, masks from Africa, mummies from Egypt, Aztec gold sculpture, as well as treasures from ancient Greece and Rome.

⭐ *TOP ART: Death of Socrates* (Jacques-Louis David), *Self-Portrait* (Rembrandt), *Cypresses* (Vincent van Gogh), *Midnight Ride of Paul Revere* (Grant Wood), *Young Woman with a Water Jug* (Jan Vermeer)

HERMITAGE, St. Petersburg, Russia It looks like a palace—because it was one. Established in the 18th century as a private collection of Empress Catherine II, it contains artwork collected by the Russian czars. The Hermitage became a public museum in the 19th century. Its six buildings hold more than 3 million items from Russia, including jeweled **EASTER EGGS** created by Carl Fabergé.

Hermitage

⭐ *TOP ART: Madonna with a Flower* (Leonardo da Vinci), *Dance* (Henri Matisse), *Woman with a Fruit* (Paul Gauguin)

LOUVRE, Paris, France Once one of the world's largest palaces, it is now one of the world's largest art museums—and maybe the most famous one. Since 1793, the Louvre has been gathering an incredible collection of ancient and Western art, including 6,000 European paintings dating from the 13th century to the middle of the 19th century. It could take visitors days to explore all the museum's long halls.

Louvre

⭐ *TOP ART: **MONA LISA** (Leonardo da Vinci), Slaves* (Michelangelo), *Embarkation for Cythera* (Jean-Antoine Watteau), *The Raft of the Medusa* (Théodore Géricault), *Venus de Milo, Victory of Samothrace*

PRADO, Madrid, Spain Finished in 1819, it originally held the paintings owned by the royal family. In 1868, it became a national museum. It is famous for its collection of Spanish, Flemish and Venetian paintings. The Prado owns more than 10,000 works of art.

⭐ *TOP ART: Naked Maja* (Goya), *Maids of Honor* (Diego Velázquez), *Adam and Eve* (Albrecht Dürer), *Garden of Earthly Delights* (Hieronymus Bosch)

Display

UFFIZI GALLERY, Florence, Italy The museum was originally a palace built in the 16th century for Cosimo I de' Medici. In 1591, the public was allowed to view the artworks inside, making the Uffizi the first public art museum in the world. Today, the Uffizi's 45 rooms hold the world's best collection of Renaissance art.

★ *TOP ART:* *Primavera* and *Birth of Venus* (Sandro Botticelli), *Annunciation* (Leonardo da Vinci), *Holy Family* (Michelangelo), *Judith Beheading Holofernes* (Artemesia Gentileschi), *Venus of Urbino* (Titian)

NATIONAL GALLERY OF ART, Washington, D.C. Part of the Smithsonian Institution, it opened in 1941. Though it holds great paintings, photographs, furniture and sculpture from all over the world, the museum focuses on American art, including portraits of the Presidents and Native Americans, as well as 20,000 drawings and watercolors that span the history of American art.

★ *TOP ART:* *Street in Venice* (John Singer Sargent), *Breezing Up* (Winslow Homer), *Watson and the Shark* (John Singleton Copley), *George Washington* (Gilbert Stuart), *Jack in the Pulpit No. IV* (Georgia O'Keeffe)

National Gallery

NATIONAL GALLERY, London, England It opened in 1824 with 38 paintings. Today, the National Gallery is a monumental museum located in Trafalgar Square. It holds one of the world's greatest collections of European art: more than 2,300 paintings that date from 1250 to 1900, many of which are masterpieces.

★ *TOP ART:* *The Virgin of the Rocks* (Leonardo da Vinci), *The Arnolfini Portrait* (Jan van Eyck), *Boating on the Seine* (Pierre-Auguste Renoir), *The Hay Wain* (John Constable)

J. PAUL GETTY MUSEUM AT THE GETTY CENTER, Brentwood, Calif. The Getty Museum has grown from a single house into six buildings that overlook Los Angeles. The collection centers on European paintings, drawings, sculpture, illuminated manuscripts and decorative arts.

J. Paul Getty Museum at the Getty Center

★ *TOP ART:* *Irises* (Vincent van Gogh), *Still Life with Fish* (Jean-Siméon Chardin), *The Supper at Emmaus* (follower of Caravaggio), *Christ on the Cross* (El Greco)

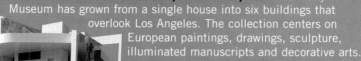

go 👆 **Read kids' reviews of websites about art at timeforkids.com/finearts**

The Color Wheel

YELLOW

YELLOW-
ORANGE

YELLOW-
GREEN

ORANGE

GREEN

RED-
ORANGE

BLUE-
GREEN

RED

BLUE

RED-VIOLET

BLUE-
VIOLET

VIOLET

A color wheel shows how colors are related.

● **Red, yellow** and **blue** are the **PRIMARY** colors. Primary colors are the most basic colors. You can't make them by mixing any other colors.

● **Orange, green** and **violet** are the **SECONDARY** colors. A secondary color is made by mixing two primary colors. For instance, if you mix red and yellow, you get orange. That is why orange is between red and yellow on the color wheel.

● What goes between primary and secondary colors? **INTERMEDIATE,** or tertiary, colors, which are made by mixing a primary color and a secondary color. **Red-orange, yellow-orange** and **yellow-green** are some intermediate colors.

VALUES The lightness or darkness of a color is called its value. You can find the values of a color by making its tints and shades.

● **TINTS** are light values that are made by mixing a color with white. Pink is a tint of red.

● **SHADES** are dark values that are made by mixing a color with black. Maroon is a shade of red.

TFK Top 5

Most Expensive Paintings by Women

PAINTING	ARTIST	PRICE
1. *Calla Lilies with Red Anemone*	Georgia O'Keeffe	**$5,600,000**
2. *The Conversation*	Mary Cassatt	**$4,100,000**
3. *Cache-cache*	Berthe Morisot	**$4,000,000**
4. *Marche' au Minho*	Sonia Delaunay	**$3,887,013**
5. *Black Cross with Stars and Blue*	Georgia O'Keeffe	**$3,700,000**

Source: *Top 10 of Everything 2005,* DK

GEORGIA
O'KEEFFE

ART movements

BAROQUE A form of art and architecture that was popular in Europe in the 17th and early 18th centuries, Baroque art was very ornate, dramatic and realistic. Peter Paul Rubens and Rembrandt were Baroque painters.

Edvard Munch's *The Scream*

IMPRESSIONISM Impressionism developed in France during the late 19th century. Impressionists tried to capture an immediate visual interpretation of their subjects by using color rather than lines. Claude Monet and Edgar Degas were Impressionist painters.

POST-IMPRESSIONISM Popular in the late 19th century and early 20th century, Post-Impressionists rebelled against the reality of Impressionism and created emotional, personal works. Vincent van Gogh and Paul Gauguin were Post-Impressionist painters.

EXPRESSIONISM Expressionist painters interpreted things around them in exaggerated, distorted and emotional ways. **Edvard Munch** was one of the best-known Expressionist painters.

CUBISM Cubism is a modern style of art that stresses basic abstract geometric forms and often presents the subject from many angles at the same time. Pablo Picasso was a Cubist painter.

ABSTRACT EXPRESSIONISM Developed in the mid-20th century, this style emphasizes form and color rather than an actual subject. **Jackson Pollock** was an Abstract Expressionist.

POP ART Pop art emerged after 1950. Pop artists use materials from the everyday world, such as comic strips and canned goods. Andy Warhol and Roy Lichtenstein were Pop artists.

Painting (1948) by Jackson Pollock

TFK Mystery Person

CLUE 1: Some consider me one of modern art's greatest innovators. I was born in 1911 in North Carolina.

CLUE 2: I'm best known for my collages. I cut up drawings and photos, then rearranged them on a canvas to create scenes that show the richness of African-American life.

CLUE 3: I wrote and illustrated a children's book called *Li'l Dan, the Drummer Boy: A Civil War Story*.

WHO AM I?

(See Answer Key that begins on page 342.)

go For the types of painting: www.factmonster.com/painting

FROM **TFK** MAGAZINE

How a Book Is Made

It usually takes at least two years for an idea to go from an author's head to a published book. Bet you'd never guess how many steps are involved! Rachel Orr, an editor at the publishing house HarperCollins, tells you how it's done.

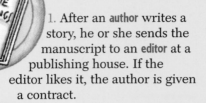

1. After an **author** writes a story, he or she sends the manuscript to an **editor** at a publishing house. If the editor likes it, the author is given a contract.

2. Next, the editor and **designer** search for an **illustrator** who is perfect for the story. Usually the author and the illustrator never even meet!

3. Whether a manuscript is three pages or 203 pages, it takes a lot of time to edit. The author and editor work hard to make sure every word is just right.

4. Editors help with the main concepts, but **copy editors** are the kings and queens of grammar. They will catch spelling and usage mistakes even your computer will miss.

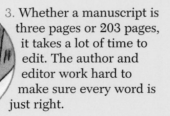

5. Meanwhile, the illustrator has been working hard on the sketches. Sometimes many pictures are revised. It's an exciting day when the final art arrives!

6. The designer scans the art onto the pages and places in the text. These unbound pages are called **galleys**. The author, editor and designer make corrections and changes on galleys.

7. The corrected galleys, in the form of computer files, go to the printer. The printer makes a version of the book called **proofs**. These pages are checked to see that the printed colors match the original art.

8. The last chance to make changes in the book is in **blues**. These pages are like blueprints—they show how the book will look when printed.

9. Once the blues are approved, the proofs are folded together into unfinished books. The publicity department uses them to spread the word about the book.

10. Last, the finished books are bound and shipped to the warehouse. From there, they are sent to stores and libraries across the country.

BOOK AWARDS

THE CALDECOTT MEDAL honors an outstanding American picture book.

2005 WINNER:
Kitten's First Full Moon, Kevin Henkes

THE NEWBERY MEDAL honors an outstanding example of children's literature. The Newbery winner is not a picture book.

2005 WINNER:
Kira-Kira, Cynthia Kadohata

2004 NATIONAL BOOK AWARD FOR YOUNG PEOPLE'S LITERATURE

Godless, Peter Hautman

THE CORETTA SCOTT KING AWARDS recognize black authors and illustrators whose works have promoted an understanding and appreciation of all cultures.

2005 WINNERS:

WRITER: Toni Morrison, *Remember: The Journey to School Integration*

ILLUSTRATOR: Kadir Nelson, *Ellington Was Not a Street*

2004 BOSTON *GLOBE* HORN BOOK AWARD

NONFICTION: *An American Plague: The True and Terrifying Story of the Yellow Fever Epidemic of 1793,* Jim Murphy

PICTURE BOOK: *The Man Who Walked Between the Towers,* Mordicai Gerstein

FICTION AND POETRY: *The Fire-Eaters,* David Almond

 Learn about the winning books at timeforkids.com/bestbooks

REFERENCE BOOKS: You Could Look It Up

Atlas
A book of maps with or without text
EXAMPLE: *TIME For Kids World Atlas*

Biographical Index
A book of information about people who are well known in a particular field
EXAMPLE: *Who's Who in America*

Dictionary
Definitions, spellings and pronunciations of words, arranged in alphabetical order
EXAMPLE: *The Merriam-Webster Collegiate Dictionary*

Encyclopedia
Information on just about every subject, arranged in alphabetical order
EXAMPLE: *Encyclopædia Britannica*

Guidebook
Information and directions, often for travelers
EXAMPLE: *The Rough Guide to Cambodia*

Thesaurus
Synonyms, or near synonyms, for words as well as related terms
EXAMPLE: *Roget's Thesaurus*

Yearbook/Almanac
Current information on a wide range of topics. You're reading one now!

 For more book awards: www.factmonster.com/bookawards

Classic Classics

Although there are thousands of exciting new books published each year, sometimes it's fun to dust off the books that your parents—or even grandparents—enjoyed when they were kids. Check out these classics that have endured the test of time.

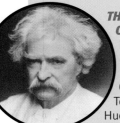

THE ADVENTURES OF TOM SAWYER
by Mark Twain
Tom lives in a small town on the Mississippi River. Clever and adventurous, Tom and his friend, Huckleberry Finn, get into one scrape after another in the days of the Old South.

THE BOOK OF THREE by Lloyd Alexander
When evil threatens the mythical land of Prydain, a young pig-keeper named Taran must face the monstrous Horned King. This is the first book in the Chronicles of Prydain series.

CHARLOTTE'S WEB
by E.B. White
Charlotte is a spider who lives in a barn above the pen of Wilbur, a lonely young barn pig. The plucky Charlotte saves Wilbur's life by writing messages in her web.

THE CRICKET IN TIMES SQUARE
by George Selden
Adventures abound when Tucker Mouse and Harry Cat, street-smart residents of a New York sewer, befriend a musical country cricket from Connecticut named Chester.

FROM THE MIXED-UP FILES OF MRS. BASIL E. FRANKWEILER
by E.L. Konigsburg
Sick of being told what to do at home, Claudia Kincaid runs away to the Metropolitan Museum of Art in New York City. Her brother Jamie joins her on the adventure that leads them to the home of Mrs. Basil E. Frankweiler.

ISLAND OF THE BLUE DOLPHINS
by Scott O'Dell
After enduring a series of heart-wrenching tragedies, 12-year-old Karana bravely survives alone on an island for 18 years. The book is based on a true story.

LITTLE HOUSE ON THE PRAIRIE
by Laura Ingalls Wilder
In a series of memoirs, Wilder vividly chronicles the triumphs and tragedies her family experienced as pioneers in the Midwest during the 19th century.

LORD OF THE FLIES
by William Golding
A group of English schoolboys stranded on a deserted island must fend for themselves. At first the boys work together to make shelters, light fires and hunt for food. But everything falls apart when some decide they would rather play than work.

MRS. FRISBY AND THE RATS OF NIMH
by Robert C. O'Brien
While trying to save her home and children from a farmer's plow, Mrs. Frisby, a field mouse, meets a colony of lab rats with humanlike intelligence. The rats devise a solution to Mrs. Frisby's problem.

Mrs. Frisby and the Rats of NIMH
Robert C. O'Brien

NANCY DREW SERIES
by Carolyn Keene
Amateur detective Nancy Drew tackles her own cases and often helps her father, a district attorney, with his. Her curiosity and clear thinking always prove successful.

The Nancy Drew Files
Case 79
No Laughing Matter
Carolyn Keene

PIPPI LONGSTOCKING SERIES by Astrid Lindgren
Pippilotta Provisionia Gaberdina Dandeliona Ephraimsdaughter Longstocking lives in the Villa Villekula with her purple-spotted horse. Pippi's spunk and whimsy lead her into many fantastic adventures.

A WRINKLE IN TIME
by Madeleine L'Engle
Otherworldly visitors guide Meg and her brother Charles on a journey through time and space as they search for their father who disappeared while doing secret work for the govenment. This is the first of a five-book series.

Types of Literature

Here are examples of different styles of fiction (made-up stories) and nonfiction (books about real-life events and people).

An **autobiography** is the story of a person's life written or told by that person.
EXAMPLE:
26 Fairmount Avenue
by Tomie dePaola

A **biography** is the story of a person's life written or told by another person.
EXAMPLE:
Snowflake Bentley
by Jacqueline Briggs Martin

A **fable** is a story that teaches a moral or a lesson. It often has animal characters.
EXAMPLE:
"The Country Mouse and the City Mouse"

A **folktale** is a story that has been passed down, usually orally, within a culture. It may be based on superstition and may feature supernatural characters.
EXAMPLE: "Hansel and Gretel"

A **legend** is a story that has been handed down over generations and is believed to be based on history, though it typically mixes fact and fiction.
EXAMPLE:
Robin Hood

A **myth** is a traditional story that a particular culture or group once accepted as sacred and true. It may center on a god or supernatural being and typically explains how something came to be.
EXAMPLE: The story of the Trojan War

Fantasy novels are often set in worlds much different from our own, and they usually include magic, sorcery and mythical creatures.
EXAMPLE: The Harry Potter series
by J.K. Rowling

Science Fiction stories examine how science and technology affect the world. The books often involve fantastic inventions that someday may be a reality.
EXAMPLE:
The Left Hand of Darkness
by Ursula K. Le Guin

Children as Authors

many children have written books that have been published. One of the first kid authors was **FRANCIS HAWKINS.** In 1641, when he was 8 years old, he wrote a book of manners called *Youths Behaviour.* Here are some others.

KATHARINE HULL, 15, and **PAMELA WHITLOCK,** 16, wrote a book about children and for children. *The Far-Distant Oxus* was published in 1937 and was praised by critics in both Europe and the U.S.

Anne Frank

ANNE FRANK'S diary was published in English in 1952 as *The Diary of a Young Girl.* She describes how her family hid during World War II because they were Jewish. After two years of hiding in the attic of a warehouse in Amsterdam, Holland, the family was discovered by the Nazis and taken to a concentration camp.

S.E. (SUSAN ELOISE) HINTON started her first novel, *The Outsiders,* at age 15. It took her a year and a half to complete the book about youth gangs and their battles. More than a million copies have been sold, and the book was made into a film.

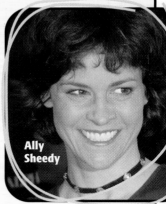

Ally Sheedy

ALEXANDRA (ALLY) ELIZABETH SHEEDY published *She Was Nice to Mice* in 1975, when she was 12 years old. It is the story of Esther Esther, an extraordinary mouse who travels back in time to the days of William Shakespeare. Sheedy is now an actress.

GORDON KORMAN wrote his first book, *This Can't Be Happening at Macdonald Hall!,* as a seventh-grader. By the time he graduated from high school, Korman had published five more books, including *Go Jump in the Pool!* and *Beware the Fish.*

When **JASON GAES** was stricken with Burkitt's lymphoma, a rare form of cancer, at age 7, he wrote *My Book for Kids with Cansur.* His twin brother **TIM** and 10-year-old brother **ADAM** illustrated the book. It provides comfort and inspiration to people of all ages.

TFK Top 5 — All-Time Best-Selling Books

Book, Author	Date first published	Approximate number of copies sold
1. *The Bible*	ca. *1451–1455*	more than 6,000,000,000
2. *Quotations from the Works of Mao Tse-Tung*	*1966*	900,000,000
3. *The Lord of the Rings,* J.R.R. Tolkien	*1954–1955*	more than 100,000,000
4. *American Spelling Book,* Noah Webster	*1783*	100,000,000
5. *The Guinness Books of Records* (now *Guinness World Records*)	*1955*	more than 95,000,000*

*Includes all annual sales and translations   Source: *Top 10 of Everything 2005,* DK

A Writer of Wrongs
Lemony Snicket tells the terrible truth

Daniel Handler tries to hide his true identity.

Snicket's books are for you. But don't harbor the hope that the orphans' fate will somehow change. Don't dream that Count Olaf will one day care for the orphans rather than continue his mission to steal their parents' fortune. That, my friends, is the stuff of fairy tales.

"The books that I write tell stories that are true, as far as I know," says Snicket. "If I encounter a story that has a happy ending, I will certainly write it down."

—By Brenda Iasevoli

Turn the page this instant! Otherwise, you might learn about Lemony Snicket, the author of *A Series of Unfortunate Events.*

Snicket, also known as Daniel Handler, chronicles the lives of the Baudelaire orphans: Violet, Klaus and Sunny. It is his dreadful duty to tell of their quest to escape their crooked uncle, Count Olaf. But Snicket advises readers to feel free to read something pleasant—if they prefer that sort of thing.

"It is my solemn vow to make these stories available to the general public," Snicket told TFK. "Though sometimes, it's difficult to rouse myself from weeping."

His latest book, *The Grim Grotto,* is the 11th book in the Unfortunate Events series. Snicket says he hopes no one will read the book or "learn any of the secrets it contains."

If you enjoy stories with unhappy beginnings, unhappy endings and hardly any happy things in between, then

Books

TFK Mystery Person

CLUE 1: I was an author, a poet and a playwright. I was born in Spain on September 29, 1547.

CLUE 2: In 1605, I created one of the most popular characters in literature, Don Quixote, who dared to follow his dreams.

CLUE 3: My book *Don Quixote de la Mancha* has been translated into more than 60 languages.

WHO AM I?

(See Answer Key that begins on page 342.)

go

Read more about Lemony Snicket:
www.factmonster.com/lemonysnicketpage

FROM TFK **MAGAZINE**

Rock formations inspired the limestone building.

A PLACE OF HONOR

A new museum celebrates the history, arts and lives of Native Americans

Native Americans stood tall in lush robes, feather headdresses and nut necklaces. The smell of burning herbs sweetened the air. The ground shook as drums pounded, bells jingled and shells rattled. In the fall of 2004, Washington, D.C., was a scene of celebration and pride. The National Museum of the American Indian (NMAI), the newest addition to the Smithsonian Institution, opened its doors.

"This monument to the first Americans is long overdue," said Senator Daniel K. Inouye (in-*oh*-way) of Hawaii at the museum's dedication. Inouye helped establish the museum in 1989. It cost $219 million to build.

Inouye had been disappointed that not one of 400 monuments in the nation's capital was dedicated to Native Americans, whose history on this land goes as far back as 35,000 years. About 4.3 million Native people now live in the U.S.

Native Point of View
What makes the NMAI unique is the way its stories are told. Instead of giving a history lesson loaded with

Cheyenne chiefs and thousands of Native Americans marched across the National Mall.

names and dates, the museum aims to echo the emotions of many tribes. "Communities across the hemisphere have been involved in the design," says Clare Cuddy, the museum's education manager. Not just a museum, the NMAI is also a symbol of Native culture.

The building faces east to greet the sunrise, as many Native structures do. The honey-colored walls of the museum curve like the wind-shaped mesas of the West. Nature is important to Native Americans, so 150 species of trees and shrubs surround the building. There are also plantings of corn, beans and squash.

The NMAI does not ignore American Indians' sometimes painful past, including wars and prejudice. But visitors also learn modern tales. The museum is as much about today as it is about yesterday. "While there are some harsh stories told," Cuddy says, "there are a lot of joyful stories too."

—By Nicole Iorio

Buildings & Landmarks

BRIDGING THE GAPS

Bridges have come a long way since ancient times, when people used logs or woven vines to cross streams. In fact, bridges have become an art form. Common types of modern bridges include: beam, truss, arch, cable-stay and suspension bridges.

BEAM BRIDGE, the simplest type of bridge, is made of long beams of wood, metal or concrete that are supported at each end by piers.

In a **TRUSS BRIDGE,** the beams are arranged in a lattice (criss-cross) pattern. Many railroad bridges are truss bridges.

ARCH BRIDGES are made of steel, concrete or masonry. Roads are built on top of arches. The Natchez Trace Bridge in Franklin, Tennessee, is an arch bridge.

SUSPENSION BRIDGES are usually longer than other types of bridges. The road is suspended in the air on long cables that extend from one end of the bridge to the other. The cables sit atop tall towers and are secured on both sides by anchorages. The Golden Gate Bridge in San Francisco is a suspension bridge.

CABLE-STAYED BRIDGES look a lot like suspension bridges, but the cables are attached directly to supporting towers and are secured to the roadway. The Leonard Zakim Bridge in Boston is an example of a cable-stayed bridge.

Golden Gate Bridge

Tallest Buildings

WORLD BUILDING	LOCATION	STORIES	HEIGHT (FT)
1. Taipei 101	Taipei, Taiwan	101	1,670
2. Petronas Towers 1 and 2	Kuala Lumpur, Malaysia	88	1,483
3. Sears Tower	Chicago	110	1,450
U.S.			
1. Sears Tower	Chicago	110	1,450
2. Empire State Building	New York	102	1,250
3. Aon Centre	Chicago	80	1,136

Tallest Towers

	TOWER	LOCATION	HEIGHT (FT)
WORLD:	Canadian National (CN) Tower	Toronto, Canada	1,815
U.S.:	LORAN-C Tower	Port Clarence, Alaska	1,350

go For a list of the world's 100 tallest buildings: www.factmonster.com/tallestbuildings

Seven Wonders of the Ancient World

Since ancient times, people have put together many "seven wonders" lists. Below are the structures that most likely were on the original list.

Homework Tip!

Set up a quiet, comfortable place to do your homework each day. Avoid places with loud music, television or other noise.

1. Pyramids of Egypt A group of three pyramids located at Giza, Egypt, was built around 2680 B.C. Of all the Ancient Wonders, only the pyramids still stand.

2. Hanging Gardens of Babylon These terraced gardens were located in what is now Iraq. They are said to have been built by Nebuchadnezzar II around 600 B.C. to please his queen.

3. Statue of Zeus (Jupiter) at Olympia The sculptor Phidias (fifth century B.C.) built this 40-foot-high statue in gold and ivory. It was located in Olympia, Greece.

4. Temple of Artemis (Diana) at Ephesus This beautiful marble structure was begun about 350 B.C. in honor of the goddess Artemis. It was located in Ephesus, Turkey.

5. Mausoleum at Halicarnassus This huge above-ground tomb was erected in Bodrum, Turkey, by Queen Artemisia in memory of her husband, who died in 353 B.C.

6. Colossus at Rhodes This bronze statue of Helios (Apollo) was about 105 feet high. It was the work of the sculptor Chares. Rhodes is a Greek island in the Aegean Sea.

7. Pharos of Alexandria The Pharos (lighthouse) of Alexandria was built during the third century B.C. off the coast of Egypt. It stood about 450 feet high.

For more about famous structures around the world: www.factmonster.com/structures

The SEVEN Wonders of the MODERN World

This "seven wonders" list celebrates monumental engineering and construction feats of the 20th century. It was made by the American Society of Civil Engineers.

EMPIRE STATE BUILDING Finished in 1931, it towers 1,250 feet over New York City. Until the first tower of the World Trade Center was finished in 1972, it was the world's tallest building.

ITAIPÚ DAM Built by Brazil and Paraguay on the Parana River, it is the world's largest hydroelectric power plant. Completed in 1991, it took 16 years to build this series of dams whose length totals 25,406 feet. It required 15 times more concrete than the Channel Tunnel *(see below)*.

CN TOWER In 1976, it became the world's tallest freestanding structure. It looms about one-third of a mile high (1,815 feet) above Toronto, Canada. A glass floor on the observation deck lets you look 1,122 feet to the ground. Don't worry: the glass is strong enough to hold 14 hippos!

PANAMA CANAL It took 34 years to create this 50-mile-long canal across the Isthmus of Panama. The amount of digging required and the size of its locks helped make it the most expensive project in American history at the time. It was also the most deadly: more than 30,000 people died during construction (many from disease).

CHANNEL TUNNEL Known as the Chunnel, it links France and England. It is 31 miles long, and 23 of those miles are 150 feet beneath the seabed of the English Channel. High-speed trains whiz through its side-by-side tubes.

NORTH SEA PROTECTION WORKS Because the Netherlands is below sea level, a series of dams, floodgates and surge barriers have been built to keep the sea from flooding the country during storms. The biggest part of the project, completed in 1986, was a 2-mile-long moveable surge barrier across an estuary. It is made of 65 concrete piers, each weighing 18,000 tons. It has been said that the entire project is nearly equal in scale to the Great Wall of China.

GOLDEN GATE BRIDGE For many years, this suspension bridge that connects San Francisco and Marin County was the longest in the world. Experts thought that winds, ocean currents and fog would make it impossible to build. Construction began in 1933, and it took about four years to complete the beautiful 1.2 mile-long bridge. It is held by 80,000 miles of steel wire. The two towers are linked by cables. Each cable weighs two tons, has a diameter of 36.5 inches and contains 25,572 separate wires.

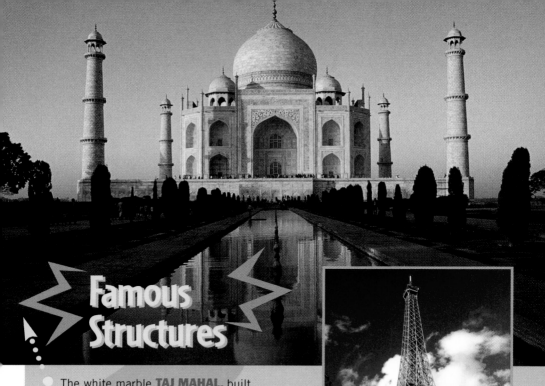

Famous Structures

The white marble **TAJ MAHAL,** built 1632–1650 at Agra, India, was a tomb for Shah Jahan's wife.

The **PARTHENON OF GREECE,** built on the Acropolis in Athens, was the chief temple to the goddess Athena. It is believed to have been completed by 438 B.C.

The **EIFFEL TOWER** in Paris was built in 1889. It is 1,056 feet high, including the television tower.

The **PANTHEON** at Rome was begun in 27 B.C. It has served for 20 centuries as a place of worship.

The **TOWER OF LONDON** is a group of buildings covering 13 acres. The central White Tower was begun in 1078. It was once a royal residence.

The **VATICAN** is a group of buildings in Rome that includes the residence of the Pope. The Basilica of St. Peter, the largest church in the Christian world, was begun in 1450.

The **COLOSSEUM OF ROME,** the largest and most famous of the Roman amphitheaters, was opened for use in A.D. 80.

● The **PALACE OF VERSAILLES** in France was built during the reign of Louis XIV in the 17th century and served as the royal palace until 1793. ● ● ● ● ● ● ● ● ● ● ● ● ● ● ●

● The 12th century temples at **ANGKOR WAT** in Cambodia are surrounded by a moat and have walls decorated with sculpture.

● The **GREAT WALL OF CHINA** (begun 228 B.C.), designed as a defense against nomadic tribes, is so big and long that it can be seen from orbit!

 **Mystery Person**

CLUE 1: I was born in 1959.

CLUE 2: When I was a 21-year-old student at Yale University, my design for the Vietnam Veterans Memorial in Washington, D.C., was chosen from more than 1,400 others.

CLUE 3: The memorial, a black granite slab near the Washington Monument, lists the names of 58,000 U.S. soldiers who died in the Vietnam War.

WHO AM I?

(See Answer Key that begins on page 342.)

● **MACHU PICCHU** is an Inca fortress in the Andes Mountains of Peru. It is believed to have been built in the mid-15th century.

● The **BROOKLYN BRIDGE,** built between 1869 and 1883, was the achievement of engineer John Roebling. It was the first steel-wire suspension bridge in the world.

2006

January
S	M	T	W	T	F	S
1	2	3	4	5	6	7
8	9	10	11	12	13	14
15	16	17	18	19	20	21
22	23	24	25	26	27	28
29	30	31				

1 New Year's Day
10 Eid al-Adha*
16 Martin Luther King Jr.'s Birthday observed
29 Chinese New Year
31 First day of Muharram*

February
S	M	T	W	T	F	S
			1	2	3	4
5	6	7	8	9	10	11
12	13	14	15	16	17	18
19	20	21	22	23	24	25
26	27	28				

14 Valentine's Day
20 Washington's Birthday

March
S	M	T	W	T	F	S
			1	2	3	4
5	6	7	8	9	10	11
12	13	14	15	16	17	18
19	20	21	22	23	24	25
26	27	28	29	30	31	

1 Ash Wednesday
14 Purim*
17 St. Patrick's Day
20 Spring begins

April
S	M	T	W	T	F	S
						1
2	3	4	5	6	7	8
9	10	11	12	13	14	15
16	17	18	19	20	21	22
23	24	25	26	27	28	29
30						

2 Daylight Saving Time begins
13 First day of Passover*
16 Easter

May
S	M	T	W	T	F	S
	1	2	3	4	5	6
7	8	9	10	11	12	13
14	15	16	17	18	19	20
22	23	23	24	25	26	27
28	29	30	31			

14 Mother's Day
29 Memorial Day observed

June
S	M	T	W	T	F	S
				1	2	3
4	5	6	7	8	9	10
11	12	13	14	15	16	17
18	19	20	21	22	23	24
25	26	27	28	29	30	

2 First day of Shavuot*
18 Father's Day
21 Summer begins

July
S	M	T	W	T	F	S
						1
2	3	4	5	6	7	8
9	10	11	12	13	14	15
16	17	18	19	20	21	22
23	24	25	26	27	28	29
30	31					

4 Independence Day

August
S	M	T	W	T	F	S
		1	2	3	4	5
6	7	8	9	10	11	12
13	14	15	16	17	18	19
20	21	22	23	24	25	26
27	28	29	30	31		

September
S	M	T	W	T	F	S
					1	2
3	4	5	6	7	8	9
10	11	12	13	14	15	16
17	18	19	20	21	22	23
24	25	26	27	28	29	30

4 Labor Day
23 First day of Rosh Hashanah*
23 Autumn begins
24 Ramadan* begins

October
S	M	T	W	T	F	S
1	2	3	4	5	6	7
8	9	10	11	12	13	14
15	16	17	18	19	20	21
22	23	24	25	26	27	28
29	30	31				

2 Yom Kippur*
7 First day of Sukkot*
9 Columbus Day
14 Simchat Torah*
24 Ramadan ends (Eid al-Fitr)*
29 Daylight Saving Time ends
31 Halloween

November
S	M	T	W	T	F	S
			1	2	3	4
5	6	7	8	9	10	11
12	13	14	15	16	17	18
19	20	21	22	23	24	25
26	27	28	29	30		

11 Veterans Day
23 Thanksgiving

December
S	M	T	W	T	F	S
					1	2
3	4	5	6	7	8	9
10	11	12	13	14	15	16
17	18	19	20	21	22	23
24	25	26	27	28	29	30
31						

16 First day of Hanukkah*
22 Winter begins
25 Christmas
26 Kwanzaa begins

* All Jewish and Islamic holidays begin at sundown the day before listed here. For a description of the religious holidays, see page 207.

Calendars & Holidays

Federal Holidays

New Year's Day
January 1

New Year's Day has its origin in ancient Roman times, when sacrifices were offered to Janus, the two-faced Roman god who looked back on the past and forward to the future.

Martin Luther King Jr. Day
Third Monday in January

This holiday honors the civil rights leader. It has been a federal holiday since 1986.

Washington's Birthday
Third Monday in February

Although this holiday is sometimes called Presidents' Day to honor both George Washington and Abraham Lincoln, the federal holiday is officially Washington's Birthday.

Memorial Day
Last Monday in May

Memorial Day originated in 1868 as a day when the graves of Civil War soldiers would be decorated. Later, it became a holiday dedicated to the memory of all war dead.

Independence Day
July 4

The Declaration of Independence was adopted on July 4, 1776. It declared that the 13 colonies were independent from Britain.

Labor Day
First Monday in September

Labor Day, a day set aside in honor of workers, was first celebrated in New York City in 1882 under the sponsorship of the Central Labor Union.

Columbus Day
Second Monday in October

Columbus Day honors Christopher Columbus's landing in the New World in 1492.

Veterans Day
November 11

Veterans Day honors all men and women who have served America in its armed forces.

Thanksgiving
Fourth Thursday in November

The first American Thanksgiving took place in 1621 to celebrate the harvest reaped by the Plymouth Colony after it survived a harsh winter.

Christmas Day
December 25

The most popular holiday of the Christian year, Christmas is a celebration of the birth of Jesus.

Thousands watch the lighting of the Christmas tree at Rockefeller Center in New York City.

go For national holidays around the world: www.factmonster.com/holidays

Other FUN Holidays

Groundhog Day
February 2
Legend has it that on this morning if a groundhog can see its shadow, there will be six more weeks of winter.

Mardi Gras
Last day before Lent
Mardi Gras, or "Fat Tuesday," is a time of carnivals and parades before Ash Wednesday starts the penitent Christian season of Lent.

Valentine's Day
February 14
Named for the third-century martyr St. Valentine, this day is celebrated with candy, cards and other tokens of love.

Mother's Day
Second Sunday in May
Having a day to honor mothers goes back at least as far as 17th century England, when Mothering Sunday began.

Father's Day
Third Sunday in June
This U.S. holiday honoring fathers began in 1910 in Spokane, Washington.

Halloween
October 31
Halloween is celebrated with jack-o-lanterns, costumes, trick-or-treating and the telling of spooky stories.

Kwanzaa
December 26 through January 1
Kwanzaa, an African-American holiday, honors the values of ancient African cultures.

TFK Puzzles & Games

Tour the Emerald Isle
Celebrate St. Patrick's Day by visiting Ireland. Along the way, visit these sites: the Opera House in Belfast; Dublin Castle; Waterford (where crystal is made); the Blarney Stone and the Aran Islands (known for their wool sweaters). Start in Belfast. Finish in Tipperary.
Remember: It's a long way to Tipperary, so don't retrace your steps!

(See Answer Key that begins on page 342.)

RAT	OX	TIGER	RABBIT	DRAGON	SNAKE

The Chinese Calendar
In the Chinese calendar, each year is named after one of 12 animals. **The Chinese New Year** is celebrated at the second new moon after the winter solstice and falls between January 21 and February 19 on the western calendar.

Chinese New Year Dates
2006 (Year of the Dog) January 29
2007 (Year of the Pig) February 18

HORSE	GOAT	MONKEY	ROOSTER	DOG	PIG

Celebrations Around the World

❀Diwali❀

Diwali, the Hindu festival of lights, is the best known of Hindu celebrations and certainly the brightest. Amid the darkest skies of autumn, lights brighten homes throughout India—a sign of welcome to the gods Rama and Lakshmi. Families get together and celebrate with gifts and feasts. Many families decorate their homes with flowers and draw a colorful *rangoli*, an intricate pattern made in rice flour, at the entrance of the home.

❀Hina Matsuri❀

Each year, Japanese girls eagerly await **Hina Matsuri,** or Doll's Festival, celebrated on the third of March. In Japanese, *hina* means "small doll." Girls display their most precious dolls on a seven-tiered platform in their home. Families visit shrines and pray for the health and happiness of their girls.

Japan also celebrates a special day for boys, called **Kodomono-hi.** On May 5, families with boys fly spectacular kites shaped like carp, a fish known for its strength and determination. Families also decorate their homes with figures of traditional warriors to inspire the boys to be strong and brave. Boys dress up in a kimono and often take baths with iris leaves, which are believed to keep them healthy and strong.

Did You Know?

On June 19, 1865, a Union general rode into Galveston, Texas, to announce the Civil War had ended two months earlier, and the last 250,000 slaves in the U.S. were finally freed. June 19—which was shortened to Juneteenth—is an official holiday in Texas and is celebrated throughout the United States.

❀N'cwala❀

Each February in Africa, the Ngoni people of Zambia's Eastern Province celebrate the first harvest of the year with an **N'cwala** ceremony. Twelve local chiefs and their best dancers travel to a village called Mutenguleni to perform a warrior dance for the chief. The dancers wear outfits and headdresses made from animal furs. The chief chooses the best group of dancers. The villagers feast on beef stew and corn.

❀Eid al-Fitr❀

More than a billion Muslims around the world observe Ramadan ("month of blessing") with prayer, fasting and charity. They celebrate the end of Ramadan with a three-day festival called **Eid al-Fitr,** which means "breaking of the fast." It's one of the most important holidays in Islam. (Islam is the name of the religion practiced by Muslims.) During Eid al-Fitr, people dress in their finest clothes, decorate their homes, give treats to children and visit with friends and family.

go ► For more international festivals: www.factmonster.com/festivals

Measuring Years

The calendar most Americans use is called the Gregorian calendar. In an ordinary year this calendar has 365 days, which is about the amount of time it takes the Earth to make one trip around the Sun.

Earth's journey actually takes slightly more than a year. It takes 365 days, 5 hours, 48 minutes and 46 seconds. Every fourth year these extra hours, minutes and seconds are added up to make another day. When this happens, the year has 366 days and is called a **leap year**.

Groups of Years

- **Olympiad: 4 years**
- **Decade: 10 years**
- **Century: 100 years**
- **Millennium: 1,000 years**

Seasons

In the Northern Hemisphere, the year is divided into four seasons. **Each season begins at a solstice or an equinox.**

In the Southern Hemisphere, the dates (and the seasons) are reversed. The summer solstice (still the longest day of the year) falls around December 21, and the winter solstice is around June 21. So when it's summer in North America, it's winter in South America (and vice versa).

- **The spring equinox brings the start of spring, around March 21. At the equinox, day and night are of about equal length.**

- **The summer solstice, which happens around June 21, has the longest daylight time. It's also the first day of summer.**

- **Fall begins at the fall equinox, around September 21. Day and night are of about equal length.**

- **The winter solstice, around December 21, has the shortest daylight time and officially kicks off winter.**

Months

Months are based roughly on the cycles of the moon. A lunar (moon) month is 29½ days, or the time from one new moon to the next.

But 12 lunar months add up to just 354 days—11 days fewer than are in our calendar year. To even things out, these 11 days are added to months during the year. As a result, most months have 30 or 31 days.

To figure out how many days are in a month, remember: "30 days have September, April, June and November. All the rest have 31, except February, which has 28."

TFK Top 5

Halloween Costumes

They're creepy and they're kooky, mysterious and spooky. Halloween costumes make the autumn holiday lots of fun. More than 6,000 Americans answered questions about how they plan to dress up. Here are the most popular choices.

1. TV or movie character **28%**
2. Witch **15%**
3. Angel **12%**
4. Pirate **9%**
5. Prince or Princess **8%**

Source: Shopping in America, 2004

Find out if you are a Halloween expert at timeforkids.com/tricky

Days

A day is measured by how long it takes Earth to rotate once—24 hours. The names of the days are based on seven celestial bodies—the Sun (Sunday), the Moon (Monday), Mars (Tuesday), Mercury (Wednesday), Jupiter (Thursday), Venus (Friday) and Saturn (Saturday). The ancient Romans believed these bodies revolved around Earth and influenced its events.

BIRTHSTONES

MONTH	STONE
JANUARY	GARNET
FEBRUARY	AMETHYST
MARCH	AQUAMARINE or BLOODSTONE
APRIL	DIAMOND
MAY	EMERALD
JUNE	PEARL, ALEXANDRITE or MOONSTONE
JULY	RUBY or STAR RUBY
AUGUST	PERIDOT or SARDONYX
SEPTEMBER	SAPPHIRE or STAR SAPPHIRE
OCTOBER	OPAL or TOURMALINE
NOVEMBER	TOPAZ OR CITRINE
DECEMBER	TURQUOISE, LAPIS LAZULI, BLUE ZIRCON or BLUE TOPAZ

Did You Know?

The Egyptians were the first to come up with the idea of adding a leap day once every four years to keep the calendar in sync with the solar year. Later, the Romans adopted this solution for their calendar, and they became the first to designate February 29 as the leap day.

TFK Mystery Person

CLUE 1: I was born in Pennsylvania on September 13, 1857.

CLUE 2: In 1903, I built a factory near my hometown to make 5¢ chocolate bars. Named after me, it became one of the largest candy factories in the world.

CLUE 3: Thanks to me, there are a lot more kisses on Valentine's Day every year.

WHO AM I?

(See Answer Key that begins on page 342.)

Test your holiday smarts at timeforkids.com/holidaytrivia

Recognition Factor

New biometric technology is helping to keep us more secure

Guy Scott proudly displays a bit of gray film the size of a postage stamp. It doesn't look like much, but he says it will change the way people do business.

The New Zealand–born engineer has created a groundbreaking device called the Authorizer. The film, a piece of plastic-coated ceramic one ten-thousandth of an inch thick, fits in the Authorizer's touch pad. The pad sits in a cellphone. To make a credit-card purchase, a buyer presses his finger to the touch pad. The ceramic film vibrates, creating an ultrasound image of the person's fingerprint. That image is converted to a digital image, which is compared against a database of fingerprint images. If the print matches, the credit-card charge goes through. It can also be used by ATM machines and other devices. The Authorizer and machines like it may one day create a world that doesn't use any cash.

The Authorizer is one of a new breed of biometric devices. These are machines that can identify a person by measuring body features, such as fingerprints or facial patterns. Biometric identification systems are being developed to make financial transactions more secure. They are also helping to fight terrorism. For example, U.S. Customs recently began using a fingerprinting scanner on all foreign visitors arriving at airports and seaports and traveling on visas. A computer instantly matches a person's fingerprints against those contained in a database.

Facing Facts

Face recognition is also a growing area of biometric technology. Many visitors to the U.S. are required to present passports imprinted with bar codes that contain a facial biometric. A computer compares this information with a digital photo taken upon entry into the U.S. Our passports may soon have embedded chips that contain a facial biometric and personal data.

Besides mapping the features of the face, the next-generation software will add a new dimension: skin texture. This will make the results far more accurate. "The canvas of the human skin is as unique as a fingerprint," says Joseph Atick, a physicist who is a pioneer in the technology. The software will map areas of skin, noting the size and position of tiny features like pores. The result, says Atick, will allow money transactions to take place far more securely. In other words, it will be possible to know whether you have a face that can be trusted.

—*By Elaine Shannon*

TFK Top 5

Sites Kids Visit Most

Millions of kids surf the Internet every day. Most kids log on to sites for help with homework. Others look for fun stories or news about their favorite TV shows. Here are the websites kids visited the most in one typical month.

	Site	kid visitors
1	Yahoo.com	7,619,000
2	AOL.com	6,389,000
3	MSN.com	6,332,000
4	Google.com	4,511,000
5	Ebay.com	3,762,000

Source: comScore Media Metrix

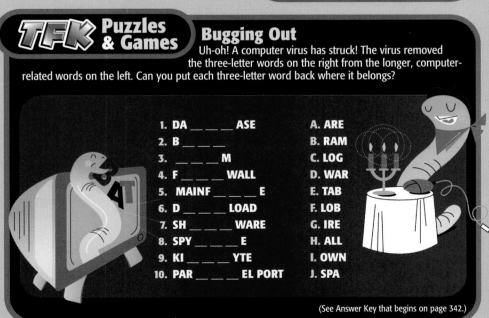

TFK Puzzles & Games

Bugging Out

Uh-oh! A computer virus has struck! The virus removed the three-letter words on the right from the longer, computer-related words on the left. Can you put each three-letter word back where it belongs?

1. DA __ __ __ ASE
2. B __ __ __ __
3. __ __ __ M
4. F __ __ __ WALL
5. MAINF __ __ __ __ E
6. D __ __ __ __ LOAD
7. SH __ __ __ WARE
8. SPY __ __ __ E
9. KI __ __ __ YTE
10. PAR __ __ __ EL PORT

A. ARE
B. RAM
C. LOG
D. WAR
E. TAB
F. LOB
G. IRE
H. ALL
I. OWN
J. SPA

(See Answer Key that begins on page 342.)

Fact Monster's
Internet
Research Guide

The Internet has become a convenient tool for finding information on just about anything. Here are some important things to keep in mind when you're doing research on the Internet.

> **Be as specific as possible with search terms.** If, for example, you heard that scientists have discovered that Jupiter has more moons than previously thought, include all the information you know when doing your search. If you simply search *Jupiter*, you'll get too much general information. But if you type in *Jupiter, moon* and *new*, chances are you'll find out what you want much more quickly.

> **If you're searching for a specific phrase, put the words in quotes.** The search engine will only look for the exact term that's inside the quotes. For example, if you want information on the Vietnam War, type *"Vietnam War."*

> **Use the word AND (in uppercase letters) to indicate that you want two or more terms to appear in the search results.** For example, if you're looking for hurricanes that occurred in Bermuda, you'd type *Bermuda AND hurricanes*. Similarly, you can use the word *NOT* (in uppercase letters) to eliminate a term from the search. For instance, by typing *Bermuda NOT shorts*, you are telling the search engine that you are not interested in Bermuda shorts. You can also use the plus sign (+) and minus sign (-) in place of *AND* and *NOT*. Don't put a space between the sign and the search term.

> **If you're not having luck with your search term, try using a synonym.** Instead of typing *Revolutionary War*, try *American Revolution*. Or instead of *9/11*, try *September 11*.

> **When searching for a biography, it helps to type the word *biography* after the person's name in the search engine.** That weeds out some irrelevant search results. Biographies on the web are sometimes unreliable, so it's very important to check dates and other facts against other biographies—in books, say—to make sure they are accurate.

> **Go directly to a site if you know it will help you.** For example, if you're looking for information on Saturn, you might try NASA's site first. You can type the URL directly in the address bar of your web browser. If you don't know the URL, you can search for the site using a search engine.

> **Try different search engines if one isn't producing results.** Google, Ask Jeeves and Alta Vista are some reputable search engines.

> **Know your source!** Anybody can put up information on the Internet and claim to be an expert. The information you read on someone's home page may be incorrect. The websites of government sources, schools and publishers of magazines and newspapers are more accurate. If you use other sources, verify the information in a book or on another website.

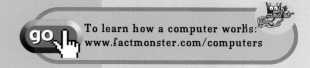

go To learn how a computer works:
www.factmonster.com/computers

Internet Resource Guide

Here's a list of especially useful and informative websites.

Animals
>American Zoo and Aquarium Association:
  www.aza.org
>Animals A-Z:
  www.oaklandzoo.org/atoz/atoz.html
>The Dinosauria: www.ucmp.berkeley.edu/
  diapsids/dinosaur.html
>Kid's Planet: www.kidsplanet.org
>National Wildlife Federation: www.nwf.org/kids

Art
>Metropolitan Museum of Art, New York City:
  www.metmuseum.org/explore/museum
  kids.html
>National Gallery of Art for Kids:
  www.nga.gov/kids
>Smithsonian Institution, Washington, D.C.:
  www.mnh.si.edu

Geography
>Atlapedia Online: www.atlapedia.com
>CIA World Factbook:
  www.cia.gov/cia/publications/factbook
>50 States.com: www.50states.com

Government and Politics
>Congress for Kids: www.congressforkids.net
>Kids in the House:
  clerkkids.house.gov
>State and Local Governments:
  www.lcweb.loc.gov/global/state/stategov.html
>White House: www.whitehouse.gov/kids/

News
>The Internet Public Library:
  www.ipl.org/div/news/
>New York Times: www.nytimes.com
>Scholastic News:
  www.teacher.scholastic.com/
  scholasticnews
>TIME For Kids: www.timeforkids.com/TFK

Reference
>Fact Monster: www.factmonster.com
>Internet Public Library: www.ipl.org
>Kids Zone: www.lycoszone.lycos.com
>Refdesk: www.refdesk.com

Science and Math
>Ask Dr. Math: mathforum.org/dr.math
>Astronomy for Kids: www.frontiernet.net/
  ~kidpower/astronomy.html
>BAM! Body and Mind: www.bam.gov
>Bill Nye the Science Guy: www.billnye.com
>Cool Science for Curious Kids:
  www.hhmi.org/coolscience
>FunBrain: www.funbrain.com
>NASA Kids: kids.msfc.nasa.gov
>Space Kids: www.spacekids.com

Search
>Ask Jeeves Kids: ajkids.com
>Google: www.google.com
>Yahooligans!: www.yahooligans.com

How Big Is a Bit?

A bit is short for "binary digit." A bit is the smallest piece
of computer information. Most computers use combinations
of eight bits, called bytes, to represent one character of data.
For example, the word *cat* has three characters, and
it would be represented by three bytes.

   A kilobyte (K or KB) is equal to 1,024 bytes.
   A megabyte (MB) is equal to 1,048,576 bytes, but it is usually
rounded off to one million bytes.
   A gigabyte is one thousand megabytes.
   Computer memory is usually measured in megabytes or gigabytes. This describes how
much information your computer can store.

go Get tips for safe Internet surfing at
timeforkids.com/safesurf

COOL Computer Software

CLUEFINDERS SEARCH & SOLVE (The Learning Company)

Leave your fears behind as you venture into a haunted amusement park to solve a mind-bending mystery. Use treasure maps, create coded messages and fend off creepy characters on your quest for answers.

I SPY FANTASY (Scholastic)

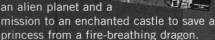

Fans of the *I Spy* books will love this game, which takes players on a treasure hunt, an expedition to an alien planet and a mission to an enchanted castle to save a princess from a fire-breathing dragon.

LEARN TO PLAY CHESS WITH FRITZ AND CHESSTER (Viva Media)

Bored with checkers? Then check out this game. Fritz and an adorable rat named Chesster guide you through an amusing array of arcade games, mazes and other adventures (including an area where you smash toilets) as they explain chess pieces, moves and strategies.

MATH MISSIONS: THE AMAZING ARCADE (Scholastic)

It's up to you to stop Randall Underling from shutting down all the stores in Spectacle City and taking over the metropolis. As you conquer challenges and save stores, you're rewarded with money that you can use to open and run fun-filled arcades.

NANCY DREW: THE SECRET OF SHADOW RANCH (Her Interactive)

As plucky supersleuth Nancy Drew, you travel to a ranch out West to figure out if a phantom horse is causing devastating accidents. The game is based on the best-selling Nancy Drew book of all time.

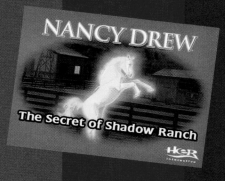

Top Video Games of 2004

	TITLE	PLATFORM
1.	Grand Theft Auto: San Andreas	PlayStation 2
2.	Halo 2	Xbox
3.	Madden NFL 2005	PlayStation 2
4.	ESPN NFL 2K5	PlayStation 2
5.	Need for Speed: Underground 2	PlayStation 2

Source: The NPD Group / NPD Funworld®

Homework Tip!

Pace yourself with large projects by breaking them down into small pieces, such as "research," "write draft" and "print out final copy." Keep track of your progress on projects with "to-do" lists typed in a word-processing program on your computer.

go ▸ Read kids' reviews of computer and technology websites at timeforkids.com/computers

Top Things People Do on the Internet

1. SEND E-MAIL
2. USE A SEARCH ENGINE TO FIND INFORMATION
3. SEARCH FOR A MAP OR DRIVING DIRECTIONS
4. DO AN INTERNET SEARCH TO ANSWER A SPECIFIC QUESTION
5. RESEARCH A PRODUCT OR SERVICE BEFORE BUYING IT
6. LOOK FOR INFORMATION ON A HOBBY OR AN INTEREST
7. CHECK THE WEATHER
8. GET NEWS
9. SURF THE WEB FOR FUN
10. GET TRAVEL INFORMATION
    LOOK FOR HEALTH OR MEDICAL INFORMATION
    LOOK FOR INFORMATION FROM A GOVERNMENT WEBSITE (TIE)

Source: Pew Internet & American Life Project tracking surveys

TFK Mystery Person

Countries with the Most Internet Users

COUNTRY	NUMBER OF USERS
1. U.S.	160,700,000
2. JAPAN	64,800,000
3. CHINA	54,500,000
4. GERMANY	30,350,000
5. UNITED KINGDOM	27,150,000
6. SOUTH KOREA	26,900,000
7. ITALY	20,850,000
8. CANADA	17,830,000
9. FRANCE	16,650,000
10. INDIA	16,580,000

Source: Computer Industry Almanac, Inc.

CLUE 1: In 1992, as a student at the University of Illinois, I developed Mosaic. It was the first Web browser to have hyperlinks and to allow images and text to appear on the same page. Mosaic made the Web easier to use and much more popular.

CLUE 2: I started my own company and developed a new browser called Netscape.

CLUE 3: I gave away Netscape for free on the Internet in the mid-1990s, and it soon became the favorite browser of Web users.

WHO AM I?

(See Answer Key that begins on page 342.)

go For a history of the Internet: www.factmonster.com/Internet

When Did Dinosaurs Live?

Iguanodon

JURASSIC 208 to 146 million years ago

- The supercontinent Pangaea continued to break apart.
- Dinosaurs ruled the land and flourished during the period.
- Herbivores and carnivores increased in size; some of the largest dinosaurs emerged during the Jurassic Period.
- Birdlike dinosaurs first appeared.
- Flowering plants began to appear late in the period.
- The Jurassic Period also ended with an extinction, but it was not as extensive as the one in the Triassic Period. Only a few types of dinosaurs died out.

Jurassic dinosaurs include:

Allosaurus "different lizard"

Apatosaurus (formerly called *Brontosaurus*) "deceptive lizard"

Archaeopteryx "ancient wing"

Brachiosaurus "armed lizard"

Compsognathus "pretty jaw"

Diplodocus "double-beamed"

Mamenchisaurus "Mamenchin lizard"

Stegosaurus "plated lizard"

Megaraptor

Pteranodon

Dinosaurs

Dinosaurs lived throughout the **MESOZOIC ERA,** which began 245 million years ago and lasted for 180 million years. It is sometimes called the Age of Reptiles. The era is divided into **THREE PERIODS,** shown here: the Triassic, the Jurassic and the Cretaceous.

TRIASSIC 245 to 208 million years ago

- During the Triassic Period, all land on Earth existed as one enormous mass. It was called Pangaea. The supercontinent slowly began to break up during the Triassic Period.
- Some reptiles, frogs, turtles and crocodiles existed earlier, but dinosaurs didn't appear until late in the Triassic Period.
- The period marked the rise of small, lightly built dinosaurs.
- The first mammals evolved during the Triassic Period.
- Most of the plants that existed were evergreens.

- The period ended with a mass extinction that wiped out most animals and reptiles. The dinosaurs that survived flourished in the next period, the Jurassic.

Triassic dinosaurs include:

Coelophysis "hollow form"
Desmatosuchus "link crocodile"
Eoraptor "dawn thief"
Ichthyosaurus "fish lizard"
Iguanodon "iguana teeth"
Plateosaurus "flat lizard"
Saltopus "leaping foot"

Stegosaurus

Brachiosaurus

CRETACEOUS 146 to 65 million years ago

- Pangaea continued to separate into smaller continents.
- A wide variety of dinosaurs roamed the land.
- Birds flourished and spread all over the globe.
- Flowering plants developed.
- Mammals thrived.
- Dinosaurs became extinct by the end of the period. The extinction, the second largest of all time, marked the end of the Age of Reptiles and the beginning of the Age of Mammals.

Cretaceous dinosaurs include:

Ankylosaurus "crooked lizard"
Hadrosaurus "bulky lizard"
Megaraptor "huge robber"
Pteranodon "winged and toothless"
Seismosaurus "quake lizard"
Triceratops "three-horned face"
Troödon "wounding tooth"
Tyrannosaurus rex "tyrant lizard"

For the Birds?

Did birds evolve from dinosaurs? Two recent discoveries add evidence to scientists' theory that they did. The dinosaur fossils were unearthed in Liaoning (lee-ow-ning) province, in China.

Mark Norell, a paleontologist from the American Museum of Natural History in New York City, and dinosaur experts from China named one fossil *Dilong paradoxus*. It is about 130 million years old and a close relative of the fierce *Tyrannosaurus rex*. *Dilong* is the first dinosaur in *T. rex*'s group found with a featherlike covering. This suggests that some tyrannosaurs—even *T. rex* babies—were soft and fluffy.

The second find, which the scientists named *Mei long*, is the first dinosaur fossil found in a sleeping position. With its head tucked between its elbow and body and its tail wrapped around itself to keep warm, the dinosaur looks like a resting bird. Researchers believe that some dinosaurs were warm-blooded, like birds. Norell told TFK that the recent finds "show just how birdlike many dinosaurs were."

A sleeping *Mei long* may have looked like this.

Is this what *Dilong* looked like? The feathered dinosaur was about six feet long.

Fossils

Fossils are the remains or imprints of prehistoric plants or animals. They are found in sedimentary rock (formed from sand and mud), coal, tar, volcanic ash or fossilized tree sap. Usually only the hard parts of plants and animals, like their bones and teeth, become fossils.

How Fossils Form

Most animals that became fossils either lived in water or were washed into a body of water. After an animal died, its soft parts, such as its fur, skin, muscles and organs, decomposed. The hard parts that remained were buried under moist layers of mud or sand, where there was no oxygen or bacteria to cause them to decay. Over time, many of these bodies of water dried up. The sediment that covered the bones eventually turned into solid rock. Over millions of years, minerals in the surrounding rock partly or completely replaced the original animal material and formed a fossil.

Sometimes water seeped into the rocks and dissolved the animal remains. When this happened, the outline of the animal remained intact between the layers of rock, leaving a fossil in the form of a natural mold.

Paleontologists, or scientists who study dinosaurs, use fossils to learn about the creatures who roamed Earth millions of years ago.

Dinosaur Hall of Fame

Largest
SEISMOSAURUS "quake lizard"

Cretaceous Period

Found in New Mexico

It measured about 120 feet (36 m) from head to tail and stood about 18 feet (5.5 m) tall.

Smallest
COMPSOGNATHUS "delicate jaw"

Jurassic Period

Found in Germany, France and Portugal

This tiny creature was about the size of a chicken and weighed about 6.5 pounds (3 kg).

Fastest
ORNITHOMIMUS "bird mimic"

Cretaceous Period

Found in the Western U.S. and Mongolia

This dinosaur, which looked like an ostrich, could run about 40 to 50 m.p.h. (64 to 80 km per hour).

Smartest
TROÖDON "wounding tooth"

Cretaceous Period

Found in North America and Asia

Troödon had the largest brain-to-body ratio of all known dinosaurs. It's believed to have been as smart as modern-day birds.

Dumbest
STEGOSAURUS "plated lizard"

Jurassic Period

Found in the U.S., Europe, India, China and Africa

This giant's brain was the size of a walnut. If brain-to-body ratio indicates intelligence (or lack of it!), then this 3-ton herbivore was certainly not a mental giant.

Most Famous
TYRANNOSAURUS REX "tyrant lizard"

Cretaceous Period

Found in North America and Asia

T. rex ran the show during the Cretaceous Period and still dominates the popular imagination.

TFK Mystery Person

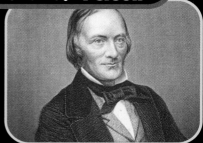

CLUE 1: Born in England in 1804, I became a famous zoologist and founded the British Natural History Museum.

CLUE 2: I studied fossils of several huge animals found in England. I theorized that they were all from an extinct group of reptiles.

CLUE 3: In 1841, I coined the term dinosaur to describe these ancient animals.

WHO AM I?

(See Answer Key that begins on page 342.)

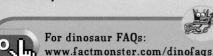

For dinosaur FAQs:
www.factmonster.com/dinofaqs

A Survival MINI MANUAL

You never know when disaster will strike. If it does, it's important to be prepared. Your life—or the lives of others—may depend on knowing how to get out of a jam. Here are some tricks that experts say will increase a person's chances of surviving a sticky situation.

You are bitten by a snake

Even if you saw it done in a movie, don't try to suck the venom and spit it out. This will make you absorb even more venom. Remain calm. Most snake bites aren't fatal, and panic will only make your heart beat faster, speeding the spread of the venom through your body. Clean the wound the way you would treat any other type of cut. Then tie a band between the wound and your heart to keep the venom from spreading too quickly. Don't make the band as tight as a tourniquet. Seek medical attention right away. If you are in the woods and can't easily get to a doctor, find a road and wave down a car.

You are in water with sharks

Try to keep still, to keep the shark from noticing you. If you think it's attacking, hit it in the eyes or gills with your fists or any hard object. (Punch the nose only if you can't reach the eyes or gills.) Sharks aren't interested in going after prey that fights back, so it will probably swim away. To avoid this frightening encounter, don't swim alone far from the ocean's shore or during the twilight or evening. Stay out of the water if you have an open wound, because the blood will attract sharks.

You are attacked by a bear

Don't turn your back on the bear and run away. The bear will think you are prey and chase you. There's no way you can outrun a bear. Nor can you outclimb one. Bears will chase you up a tree, where there's no escape. Your best option is to lie down and play dead. The bear might come over and inspect you, maybe even swipe at you with its claws. With any luck, it will lose interest and leave.

You are caught in an avalanche

Get out of its way by running from its path. Close your mouth to keep it free of snow. When the snow hits, try to stay on its surface. Do this by moving your arms as if you're swimming. If this doesn't work, try to grab a tree or some other stationary object as you move by. If you get buried, create an air pocket around your nose or mouth by cupping your hands. It will allow you to breathe until you are rescued.

Disasters

You are stuck in quicksand

Just remember: don't struggle wildly. Thrashing around will make you sink faster. Quicksand is sand saturated with underground water. Like regular water, you can float on its surface. Try shifting your body until you're lying on your back. Now you can float on the quicksand as if you were in a swimming pool. Maneuver yourself to the edge of the quicksand and escape.

You are in a lightning storm

It's not what you do—it's what you shouldn't do. Don't stay in high places or on open ground. Don't stand under a tree or a flagpole or in a picnic area, baseball dugout or bleachers. Don't go near metal fences or any body of water. It's better to stand inside a large building than a small one. Once inside, don't touch anything leading to the outside that conducts electricity, such as metal window frames, showers or pipes. Don't use a telephone, computer or TV. If you're inside a car, roll up the windows and try not to touch anything that can conduct electricity.

Your car is sinking

First, open the car windows. You want water to fill the car so the pressure on the inside and outside of the car is equal. Now you will be able to open the doors. Get out of the car as quickly as possible. If you can't open the windows, try to break them. If that doesn't work, wait as water coming through the trunk and engine slowly fills the car. Once the water has reached your head, the water pressure should be equalized. Hold your breath, open the door and swim out.

Your tongue is stuck to a cold pole

This isn't life-threatening, but it is painful and embarrassing. The best advice is to not put your tongue on a freezing pole in the first place. But if you do, don't try to quickly pull your tongue off the pole—you may rip it! Instead, move your hands (they should be in gloves!) over the pole near your tongue. This should warm the pole enough to let you slowly pull your tongue off. If warm water is nearby, splash it over your tongue to thaw it. Don't put cool water or your saliva over the area: they will both freeze, making the situation even stickier.

Homework Tip!
Ask questions to avoid a homework disaster! If you don't understand an assignment, speak up. Chances are your classmates don't understand it either.

Source: worstcasescenarios.com

63

Disastrous Events
THAT MADE HISTORY

The Chicago fire left 100,000 people homeless.

The Chicago Fire
October 8, 1871
The legendary fire consumed 17,450 buildings, killed 250 people and caused $196 million in damage.

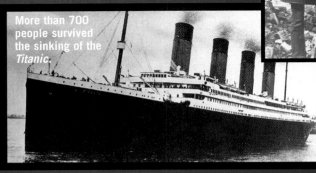

More than 700 people survived the sinking of the *Titanic*.

A *Titanic* Disaster
April 15, 1912
They called it "unsinkable." But on its maiden voyage, the British luxury steamship *Titanic* collided with a massive iceberg southeast of Newfoundland. The ship began to fill with icy water. Less than three hours later, the 883-foot-long *Titanic* turned on end and then slipped into the ocean. More than 1,500 people died.

The Fall of the *Hindenburg*
May 6, 1937
The German blimp, or airship, *Hindenburg* burst into flames 200 feet over its intended destination at New Jersey's Lakehurst Naval Air Station. Thirty-five people on board the flight were killed, along with one crewman on the ground. The majestic ship landed in a ball of flames on the ground in only 34 seconds.

The *Hindenburg* was 804 feet long.

Nuclear Disaster at Chernobyl
April 26, 1986
In the worst nuclear disaster in history, a reactor blew at a nuclear power plant in Chernobyl, Ukraine. The explosion released eight tons of radioactive material over part of the Soviet Union, Eastern Europe, Scandinavia and later Western Europe. Total casualties are unknown, but estimates run into the thousands.

Two jets struck the Twin Towers within 15 minutes of each other.

The *Exxon Valdez* Oil Spill
March 24, 1989

The *Exxon Valdez* oil tanker hit an undersea reef and tore open, spilling 11.2 million gallons of crude oil into Alaska's Prince William Sound. The worst oil spill in U.S. history, it killed millions of birds, fish and other wildlife. Cleanup efforts began late and ended up costing billions of dollars.

Terrorist Attack Against the U.S.
September 11, 2001

One of the worst disasters of all time was the September 11, 2001, terrorist attack against the U.S. Hijackers who were members of the al-Qaeda terrorist group crashed two commercial jets into the Twin Towers of the World Trade Center in New York City. Another hijacked plane crashed into the Pentagon in Washington, D.C., and a fourth into a field in rural Pennsylvania. The total number of people who died in the attack reached 2,995, including the hijackers. That's more than the number of people who died in the Japanese attack on Pearl Harbor in 1941.

Space Shuttle Tragedies
February 1, 2003
and
January 28, 1986

The *Columbia* space shuttle broke up as it was preparing to land at the Kennedy Space Center in Florida in February 2003. All seven astronauts aboard the shuttle died, including six Americans and Israel's first astronaut. As the shuttle was re-entering Earth's atmosphere, hot gases filled the wing, leading to the destruction of the spacecraft.

The *Challenger* flew nine successful missions before its final one.

Seventeen years earlier, the *Challenger* had exploded 73 seconds after liftoff. All seven people aboard the shuttle died, including six NASA astronauts and Christa McAuliffe, a schoolteacher who was to be the first civilian in space. A booster fuel leak had ignited, causing the tragedy.

Disasters Near and Far

Disasters can be natural occurrences, such as floods; human mistakes, such as shipwrecks; or acts of violence, such as terrorism. Here's a look at some of the worst disasters of all time.

Epidemics

An epidemic occurs when a disease affects a large number of people in one area or when a disease spreads to areas that are not usually associated with the disease.

- **What:** Bubonic plague, also called Black Death
- **Where:** Europe
- **When:** 1347–1351
- The disease spread rapidly throughout Europe. About 25 million people, or about one-quarter of Europe's population, died of bubonic plague.

- **What:** Spanish influenza
- **Where:** United States and other countries
- **When:** March–November 1918
- An outbreak of Spanish influenza killed more than 500,000 people. It was the single worst U.S. epidemic. Worldwide, the outbreak killed between 20 million and 40 million people.

Droughts and Famines

Droughts are long periods of insufficient rain that can ruin crops and deplete water supplies. Droughts may lead to famines—extreme food shortages that cause people to die of starvation.

- **Where:** Many states in the U.S.
- **When:** 1930s
- About 80% of the population was affected by drought. An enormous "dust bowl" covered about 50 million acres of the Great Plains. During 1934, dry areas stretched from New York to the California coast.

- **Where:** Northern China
- **When:** 1959–1961
- The world's deadliest famine killed about 30 million people in China.

Devastating Floods

A flood happens when a body of water rises and overflows onto dry land. Floods are most often caused by heavy rain, melting ice and snow, or a combination of these.

- **Where:** Pennsylvania
- **When:** 1889
- The Johnstown Flood is one of the worst disasters in U.S. history. After a rainstorm, a dam 74 miles upriver from Johnstown broke. One out of 10 people in the path of the flood died. Approximately 2,000 people were killed in less than an hour.

- **Where:** Italy
- **When:** 1966
- After heavy rain, the Arno River overflowed, flooding the streets of Florence. Art in the city's famous museums was damaged. In two days, more than 100 people died, and the city was covered with half a million tons of mud, silt and sewage.

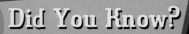

Did You Know?

People often get rowdy at sporting events, but sometimes the revelry can turn deadly. In 1964 in Lima, Peru, more than 300 people were killed and 500 injured in riots that followed an unpopular ruling by a referee in a Peru vs. Argentina soccer game.

The Arno flood destroyed ancient books and precious paintings.

To the Rescue

When disasters occur in the U.S., the Federal Emergency Management Agency (FEMA) steps in to help victims find a place to live if their homes are damaged or destroyed. FEMA also helps to repair homes and public buildings that have been damaged. The agency is part of the Executive Branch of the government.

FEMA also teaches people how to prepare for natural calamities and offers tips for people to make their homes as safe and as disaster-resistant as possible. Here are some ways to make disasters less disastrous.

Assemble a Disaster Kit

Your disaster kit should include:

- first-aid kit and essential medications.
- canned food and a can opener.
- at least three gallons of water for each person in the house.
- warm clothing, rainwear and bedding or sleeping bags.
- a battery-powered radio, a flashlight and extra batteries.
- special items for babies, the elderly or disabled family members.
- written instructions for how to turn off the electricity, gas and water in your home.
- several places to meet if told to evacuate.

Be Prepared for a Fire

- Install a smoke alarm outside each bedroom and on each level of your home. Test the batteries monthly and replace them twice a year.
- Make sure you have at least one fire extinguisher in your home.
- Plan two ways to escape from each room.
- Choose a place for family members to meet outside.
- Practice "stop, drop and roll"—which you do if your clothing catches fire.

TFK Mystery Person

CLUE 1: I was born in 1900 in Ohio. I started my career as a physicist but switched to seismology—the study of earthquakes.

CLUE 2: At the California Institute of Technology, I came up with a system of measurement that describes the magnitude, or energy, of a quake. Until then, quakes had been measured by the amount of destruction they caused.

CLUE 3: The earthquake scale I invented is named after me.

WHO AM I?

(See Answer Key that begins on page 342.)

Water Troubles

Earth's most valuable resource is at risk. Can we keep it flowing?

UNICEF is helping to install clean-water systems and hand pumps, like this one, in East Timor's poorest villages.

Not long ago, Cormelia Gogu and other students in her small town in Romania didn't have any clean water at their school. Old pipes made it dangerous for kids to drink the water or even to wash their hands.

These days, things are improving at Cormelia's school. A Romanian aid group is rebuilding the school's pipes and bathrooms. "Now we can drink water during our breaks," Cormelia, 12, told TFK. She knows that water is a precious gift. But many people in the U.S. and other wealthy nations don't.

Eighty of the world's 193 countries suffer from serious water shortages. Problems are the greatest in the developing nations of Africa, Asia and Latin America.

In recent years, the United Nations and other international groups have pumped up their efforts to protect the world's water and to deliver it to those who need it most. As a result, many of the world's poorest communities now have access to updated, more efficient water systems. Still, 1.1 billion people lack access to safe drinking water.

Two major problems are causing this: an increase in water pollution and a drastic growth in water use. Water use increased at twice the rate that the world's population grew during the past century. In parts of China, India, Pakistan, some African countries and even the United States, wells that bring people groundwater for drinking and crop irrigation are drained faster than they can refill.

Expanding desert regions and unpredictable rainfall levels are parching some places on Earth. Countries in the Middle East, parts of Asia, and east and southern Africa are suffering from years of drought.

It won't be easy to quench the world's thirst. But as Cormelia and her neighbors found out, it can be done.

—By Kathryn Satterfield

Environment & Energy

Are You Doing Your Share?

Recycling is a great way to conserve resources and help the environment. Remember the three Rs:

REDUCE: Reducing waste is the best way to help the environment. Buy large containers of food whenever possible. For example, buy a 32-ounce container of yogurt rather than four 8-ounce cups.

REUSE: Instead of throwing things away, find new ways to use them again. Use food containers for paint cups or to store toys or art supplies. Cut old clothes into pieces and use them for rags.

RECYCLE: Recycled items are new products made out of the materials from old ones. Recycle all of your used paper and your aluminum, plastic and glass containers.

RECYCLE THESE FACTS!

- Recycling one ton of paper saves 17 trees and 7,000 gallons of water.
- Recycling one aluminum can saves enough electricity to run a TV for three hours.
- Recycling one glass bottle or jar saves enough electricity to light a 100-watt bulb for four hours.
- More than 30 million trees are cut down to produce a year's supply of newspapers.
- Waste decomposes slowly. A Styrofoam cup takes about 500 years to decompose, an orange peel six months and a newspaper two to five months.

Change Those Wasteful Ways

Do you ever take a really long shower on a cold morning? Or turn up the heat rather than put on a sweater? If you do, you're wasting precious resources. Follow these guidelines to conserve our natural resources. Every bit counts!

- Turn off the lights and television when you leave a room.
- Set your computer to the "sleep mode." It darkens the screen when it's not in use.
- Turn off or turn down the heat or air conditioner when you go to bed or when you leave your home for a long time.
- Get your parents to fix drafty windows and doors.
- Encourage your parents to buy appliances that have an Energy Star label. The label has the word *energy* and a picture of a star with a rainbow.
- Walk or ride your bike rather than having your parents drive you places.
- Turn off the water while brushing your teeth and lathering up.
- Run dishwashers only when they are fully loaded. The light-wash feature uses less water.
- Dripping faucets need to be fixed. One drop per second wastes 540 gallons of water per year!
- Don't use water toys that require a constant flow of water.
- Don't water your lawn too much. Grass only needs to be watered about once a week in the summer. Lawns can go two weeks without water after a heavy rain.

Take our quiz about protecting our environment at timeforkids.com/eq

ENERGY and the EARTH

Energy is the power we use for transportation, for heat and light in our homes, and for the manufacture of all kinds of products. Energy comes in two types of sources: nonrenewable and renewable.

Nonrenewable Sources of Energy

Most of the energy we use comes from fossil fuels, such as coal, natural gas and petroleum. Once these natural resources are used up, they are gone forever. Uranium, a metallic chemical element, is another nonrenewable source, but it is not a fossil fuel. Uranium is converted to a fuel and used in nuclear power plants.

The process of gathering these fuels can be harmful to the environment. In addition, to produce energy, fossil fuels are put through a process called combustion. Combustion releases pollution, such as carbon monoxide and sulfur dioxide, and may contribute to acid rain and global warming.

Renewable Sources of Energy

Wind turbines in New Mexico create electricity.

Renewable sources of energy can be used over and over again. Renewable resources include solar energy, wind, geothermal energy, biomass and hydropower. They generate much less pollution—both in gathering and production—than nonrenewable sources.

- **SOLAR ENERGY** comes from the Sun. Some people use solar panels on their homes to convert sunlight into electricity.
- **WIND TURBINES,** which look like giant windmills, generate electricity.
- **GEOTHERMAL ENERGY** comes from the Earth's core. Engineers extract steam or very hot water from the Earth's crust and use the steam to generate electricity.
- **BIOMASS** includes natural products such as wood, manure and corn. These materials are burned and used for heat.
- Dams and rivers generate **HYDROPOWER.** When water flows through a dam, it activates a turbine, which runs an electric generator.

TFK Top 5

Cities Whose Air Is Riskiest for Children

1. Mexico City, Mexico
2. Beijing, China
3. Shanghai, China
4. Tehran, Iran
5. Calcutta, India

Source: World Health Organization

Homework Tip!

Make a list of the phone numbers and e-mail addresses of students you can call to find out what assignments you missed when you were absent. Those students can also help you if you're having trouble with an assignment.

For a list of pollutants: www.factmonster.com/pollutants

U.S. ENERGY SOURCES

HERE'S A BREAKDOWN OF THE SOURCES OF ENERGY IN THE UNITED STATES:

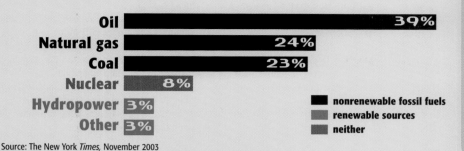

Source	Percentage
Oil	39%
Natural gas	24%
Coal	23%
Nuclear	8%
Hydropower	3%
Other	3%

■ nonrenewable fossil fuels
■ renewable sources
■ neither

Source: The New York *Times*, November 2003

What Americans Throw Away . . .

Paper products and cardboard	36%
Yard waste	20%
Food waste	9%
Metals	9%
Glass	8%
Plastics	7%
Rubber and leather goods	3%
Other	8%

. . . And Where It Goes

Most trash ends up in landfills, better known as dumps. Landfills are shallow holes that are often lined with plastic to prevent toxic substances from seeping into the soil or water supply. The country's landfills are quickly filling up, and cities and towns are faced with a big problem, since most people oppose plans to open landfills in their neighborhoods.

Sometimes garbage is burned in incinerators, or large furnaces. The good thing about incinerators is that the trash is gone once it's burned. The downside is that the ash and smoke released in the burning process sometimes contain harmful chemicals.

Did You Know?

Fossil fuels are called fossil fuels because over many millions of years, heat from the Earth's core and pressure from rock and soil have reacted with the fossils (or remains) of dead plants and animals to form fuel.

Environmental DANGERS

Human-caused pollution may be making the world a warmer place, a process called GLOBAL WARMING. Scientists think pollution could contribute to a rise in the Earth's surface temperature over the next 100 years. A warmer world could mean big trouble. Hotter temperatures are causing some ice at the North and South Poles to melt and the oceans to rise. The warmer climate is changing our weather patterns and could result in dangerous tornadoes or droughts.

The Earth stays warm the same way a greenhouse does. Gases in the atmosphere, such as carbon dioxide, methane and nitrogen, act like the glass of a greenhouse: they let in the Sun's light and warmth, but they keep the Earth's heat from escaping. This is known as the GREENHOUSE EFFECT. Scientists think that if too many of these greenhouse gases are released into the atmosphere, from pollution, for example, the gases can trap too much heat, causing temperatures to rise.

The OZONE LAYER, a thin sheet of an invisible gas called ozone, surrounds Earth about 15 miles above its surface. Ozone protects us from the Sun's harmful rays. In recent years, the amount of ozone in the atmosphere has decreased, probably due to human-made gases called chlorofluorocarbons (CFCs). As the ozone level decreases, the Sun's rays become more dangerous to humans.

POLLUTION is the contamination of air or water by harmful substances. One source of pollution is HAZARDOUS WASTE—anything thrown away that could be dangerous to the environment, such as paint and pesticide. These materials can seep into water supplies and contaminate them.

ACID RAIN occurs when rainwater is contaminated with pollutants like nitrogen oxide and sulfur dioxide. These gases come from fuels being burned at high temperatures, as in car exhausts. When acid rain falls, it can damage wildlife and erode buildings.

 **TFK Puzzles & Games**

What a Waste

The people in this house use much more than their share of water. Help them use this natural resource wisely. Circle nine examples of wasteful behavior.

(See Answer Key that begins on page 342.)

GREEN or Mean?

The ACEEE's Green Book® is a buyer's guide that rates cars according to their emissions and fuel consumption. Each year it publishes a list of the greenest (the least polluting) and meanest (the most polluting) cars.

GREEN Cars of 2004

MAKE AND MODEL

1. HONDA CIVIC GX
2. HONDA INSIGHT
3. TOYOTA PRIUS
4. HONDA CIVIC HYBRID
5. TOYOTA ECHO
6. NISSAN SENTRA
7. HONDA CIVIC HX
8. MAZDA 3
9. TOYOTA COROLLA
10. HYUNDAI ELANTRA

Honda Insight

Mean Cars of 2004

MAKE AND MODEL

1. VOLKSWAGEN TOUAREG
2. LAND ROVER RANGE ROVER
3. FORD EXCURSION
4. DODGE RAM PICKUP 1500
5. LEXUS LX 470
6. TOYOTA LAND CRUISER
7. HUMMER H2
8. GMC YUKON XL K2500
9. CHEVROLET SUBURBAN K2500
10. TOYOTA SEQUOIA

The Future Is Now

Most people couldn't live without cars and trucks, but the vehicles have become very expensive to run and harmful to the environment. Gas prices are high, and carbon-dioxide emissions from cars pollute the environment and contribute to global warming. As a result, hybrid cars and electric cars are becoming economical and Earth-friendly alternatives to conventional vehicles.

HYBRID CARS

Hybrid vehicles combine two sources of energy, such as a battery-powered electric motor and a regular gasoline-fueled internal-combustion engine. Short jaunts to the grocery store could use the electric motor, while long trips may require the internal-combustion engine. The Honda Insight and the Toyota Prius are popular hybrid cars. In late 2004, Ford introduced the first hybrid SUV, the Escape.

ELECTRIC CARS

Electric cars run on rechargeable batteries rather than fuel. The best thing about them is they cause about 97% less pollution than regular cars. But there are some downsides. The battery runs out of juice after driving between 100 and 140 miles. Electric cars also are expensive. Their batteries cost $2,000 and wear out in just a few years.

Ford's Think City electric car

73

Major BIOMES of the WORLD

Have you visited any biomes lately? A biome is a large community of plants and animals that is supported by a certain type of climate.

Gra
wolve

Arctic Tundra

WHERE: The Arctic tundra is a cold, treeless area of low, swampy plains in the far north around the Arctic Ocean.

SPECIAL FEATURES: This is Earth's coldest biome. The Arctic tundra's frozen subsoil, called permafrost, makes it impossible for trees to grow.

WHAT LIVES THERE? Animals that live in this biome include polar bears, Arctic foxes, caribou and gray wolves. Plants that you might find include small shrubs and the lichen that covers the tundra's many rocks.

Desert

WHERE: About one-fifth of Earth's land surface is desert. Deserts are found on every continent except Europe. There are two kinds: hot and dry (such as the Sahara) and cold and dry (such as Antarctica).

SPECIAL FEATURES: Lack of water and intense heat or cold make this biome unfriendly for most life forms.

WHAT LIVES THERE? Most of the plants you'll see in the hot desert are types of cactuses. A few animals—mainly reptiles, such as snakes and lizards, and amphibians, such as frogs and toads—are adapted to the hot desert. Another famous hot-desert animal is the camel. Emperor penguins are well-known animals that live at the edge of the Antarctic desert.

Coniferous Forest

WHERE: The coniferous-forest biome is south of the Arctic tundra. It stretches from Alaska across North America and across Europe and Asia.

SPECIAL FEATURES: These forests consist mainly of cone-bearing trees such as spruce, hemlock and fir. The soil is not very fertile, because there are no leaves to decompose and enrich it.

WHAT LIVES THERE? Some animals that thrive in this biome are ermine, moose, red fox, snowshoe rabbits and great horned owls.

Deciduous Forest

WHERE: This biome is in the mild-temperate zone of the Northern Hemisphere. Major regions are found in eastern North America, Europe and eastern Asia.

SPECIAL FEATURES: Deciduous trees lose their leaves in fall. The natural decaying of the fallen leaves enriches the soil and supports plant and animal life.

Woodpecker

WHAT LIVES THERE? Oak, beech, ash and maple trees are typical, and many types of insect and animal life abound. In the U.S., the deciduous forest is a home to many animals including deer, American gray squirrels, rabbits, raccoons and woodpeckers.

Did You Know?

An ecosystem is a community of plants and animals in an environment that supplies them with the raw materials they need, such as nutrients and water. An ecosystem may be as small as a puddle or as large as a forest.

Grasslands

WHERE: Grasslands are known throughout the world by different names. In the U.S. they are called prairies.

SPECIAL FEATURES: Grasslands are places with hot, dry climates that are perfect for growing food. This inland biome includes vast areas of grassy fields. It receives so little rain that very few trees can grow.

WHAT LIVES THERE? The U.S. prairies are used to graze cattle and to raise cereal crops. There is little variety of animal life. Today, common grassland animals include the prairie dog and the mule deer in North America, the giraffe and the zebra in Africa and the lion in Africa and Asia.

Mountains

WHERE: Mountains exist on all the continents. Many of the world's mountains lie in two great belts. The Circum-Pacific chain runs from the West Coast of the Americas through New Zealand and Australia, and through the Philippines to Japan. The Alpine-Himalayan system stretches from the Pyrenees in Spain and France through the Alps, and on to the Himalayas before ending in Indonesia.

SPECIAL FEATURES: A mountain biome is very cold and windy. The higher the mountain, the colder and windier the environment. There is also less oxygen at high elevations.

WHAT LIVES THERE? Mountain animals that have adapted to the cold, the lack of oxygen and the rugged landscape include the mountain goat, sheep and puma. Lower elevations are often covered by forests, while very high elevations are usually treeless.

Puma

Rain Forests

WHERE: Tropical rain forests are found in Asia, Africa, South America, Central America and on many Pacific islands. Brazil has the largest area of rain forest in the world—almost a billion acres.

SPECIAL FEATURES: Tropical rain forests receive at least 70 inches of rain each year and have more species of plants and animals than any other biome. The thick vegetation absorbs moisture, which then evaporates and falls as rain.

A rain forest grows in three levels. The canopy, or tallest level, has trees between 100 and 200 feet tall. The second level, or understory, contains a mix of small trees, vines and palms, as well as shrubs and ferns. The third and lowest level is the forest floor, where herbs, mosses and fungi grow.

WHAT LIVES THERE? The combination of heat and moisture makes the tropical rain forest the perfect environment for more than 15 million plants and animals. Some of the animals of the tropical rain forest are the jaguar, orangutan, sloth and toucan. Among the many plant species are bamboo, banana trees and rubber trees.

go For an environment glossary: www.factmonster.com/envterms

TFK Mystery Person

CLUE 1: In 1998, a lumber company threatened to cut down an ancient redwood tree in California. To protest, I lived for two years in the tree, 180 feet above the ground.

CLUE 2: I climbed down only when the lumber company spared the tree and the forest around it.

CLUE 3: I continue to work to save forests and help the environment. I am the youngest person to be elected to the Ecology Hall of Fame.

WHO AM I?

(See Answer Key that begins on page 342.)

75

FASHION MILESTONES

1930

1874	Levi Strauss begins selling blue jeans for $13.50 per dozen.
1896	Brooks Brothers introduces buttoned-down collars.
1913	Gabrielle "Coco" Chanel opens a boutique in France. Her chic suits usher in the era of modern fashion.
1916	An American company makes the country's first sneakers, called Keds.
1923	The U.S. Attorney General declares it legal for women to wear pants.
1926	Knee-length hemlines mark a new high in women's dresses.
1930	Tennis star René Lacoste designs a tennis shirt with a crocodile embroidered on the chest. It's believed to be the first time a designer logo appears on clothing.
1938	Nylon stockings are invented. They go on sale in 1940.
1946	The bikini bathing suit debuts in Paris.
1947	Christian Dior's "New Look" features tight waists and billowing skirts. The feminine look ends a time of simple, wartime attire.
1950	Kiss-proof lipstick hits the shelves.
1955	Jeans become a big hit with teens after the release of the film *Rebel Without a Cause*.
	London designer Mary Quant opens Bazaar, a boutique on Carnaby Street. Her miniskirts, tights and crocheted tops define the youth culture look.
1967	San Francisco's "hippie look" catches on throughout the country.
1969	The Gap opens in San Francisco.
1972	Nike begins to manufacture sneakers.
1977	The release of the film *Saturday Night Fever* sparks the disco craze. Polyester leisure suits, pant suits and shirts are all the rage.
1978	Gloria Vanderbilt introduces the first designer jeans.
1995	"Casual Fridays" become popular in the U.S. Companies allow employees to wear more casual clothes, such as khakis, sweaters and polo shirts, instead of suits.
2000s	Celebrities such as P. Diddy and Jennifer Lopez develop and sell their own line of clothing.

1874

1972

2000s

1967

76

go

Play our Fashion Flashback game at
timeforkids.com/style

Color Code

Red
The Aztecs of Mexico taught Spaniards how to make red dye by crushing insects called cochineals. Deep red looks bold, while pale red (pink) looks gentle. Pink is now associated with girls. Before 1920, it was considered a boys' color.

Yellow
Want to be noticed? Then wear yellow, an attention-getting color. In ancient Rome, yellow was the most popular wedding color. Yellow is sometimes worn for safety reasons—a yellow raincoat can be seen easily.

Blue
Blue is the most common color—especially since blue jeans are everywhere! Blue has a calming effect. U.S. police officers traditionally wear blue because it also symbolizes loyalty.

Green
Green is the easiest color on the eye. Perhaps hospital uniforms are often green because the color relaxes patients. Green is also associated with nature. During the Middle Ages, brides in Europe wore green to symbolize fertility.

Purple
Purple has always been considered the color of royalty, because it is rare in nature. Purple suggests luxury, wealth and sophistication. It is also feminine and romantic.

Black
Black is generally considered a serious color. In the West, black is traditional for both funeral dress and eveningwear. It is popular in fashion because it makes people appear thinner. It is also stylish and timeless.

White
Beginning in the 20th century, Western brides have worn white to symbolize purity. In China, however, white is the color of mourning.

TFK Mystery Person

CLUE 1: I am considered one of the world's foremost fashion designers.

CLUE 2: I was born in the Bronx in 1939. I went from selling ties to designing them. In 1968, I started my own clothing company, Polo Fashions.

CLUE 3: My version of an affluent American lifestyle can be seen in the clothes and home furnishings that I sell.

WHO AM I?

(See Answer Key that begins on page 342.)

Food History

The history of a food is often as interesting as the chow itself. Take a nibble at the origins of these delicious dishes.

Beef Wellington

A British hero for defeating Napoleon at Waterloo in 1815, Arthur Wellesley was made the first Duke of Wellington. His favorite dish—beef, mushrooms, truffles, Madeira wine and paté cooked in pastry—was named in his honor.

Caesar salad

In the 1920s, Caesar Cardini, owner of an Italian restaurant in Mexico, invented a salad of romaine lettuce, anchovies, egg, lemon juice, Parmesan cheese and croutons tossed with a garlic vinaigrette. He later named the dish after himself.

Eggs Benedict

Mr. and Mrs. LeGrand Benedict were regulars at New York City's Delmonico's Restaurant. They complained that the menu never changed and asked for something new. The chef served up a muffin layered with eggs and ham and covered in Hollandaise sauce. The rich breakfast entrée was named for them.

Peach Melba

Famed chef Auguste Escoffier created a dessert of poached peach halves, vanilla ice cream and raspberry sauce in honor of Australian opera singer Dame Nellie Melba.

Waldorf salad

In 1896, Oscar Tschirky, the maître d'hôtel of the famed Waldorf-Astoria Hotel in New York City, created a salad of apples, celery and mayonnaise. The salad was an immediate hit, and the new dish was called Waldorf salad.

KEEPING EVIL AWAY

Did You Know?

On special occasions, the Bedouin tribes of the Middle East stuff a fish with eggs and put it inside a chicken. The chicken is put inside a sheep, the sheep is put inside a camel, and the entire mix is roasted.

- The ancient Egyptians thought onions kept evil spirits away. When they took an oath, they placed one hand on an onion.

- The custom of throwing rice at weddings goes back to the time when people thought rice, a symbol of health and prosperity, would appease evil spirits so they would not bother the couple.

- In Japan, during the festival of Setsuben, beans are scattered in dark corners and at the entrances of the home to drive out evil spirits.

Feast and Fast

People often celebrate holidays with special foods or meals. Others observe holidays, usually religious ones, by fasting. When people fast, they either don't eat at all or they avoid certain foods for a period of time.

Feasts

Christmas
Christmas dinner in Denmark is traditionally roast goose. In Greece, it's roast leg of lamb, and in Hungary, it's chicken *paprikash* (paprika-flavored).

Hanukkah
This eight-day Jewish festival of lights is celebrated with doughnuts or potato pancakes (latkes) fried in oil. This is a reminder of the oil that burned in the temple's lamps for eight days.

Kwanzaa
Kwanzaa is an African-American celebration that runs from December 26 to January 1. Sweet potatoes and banana custard with raisins are traditional fare.

The New Year
People in Madrid, Spain, count down the last minutes of the old year by popping grapes into their mouths.

In the southern part of the U.S., black-eyed peas are eaten on New Year's Day for good luck.

The Buddhist New Year is celebrated in Tibet with a dish called *guthok*, which is made of nine special ingredients, including a piece of charcoal. The person who gets the charcoal is said to have an evil heart.

St. Lucia
On December 13, people in Sweden celebrate the festival of St. Lucia. In many homes, a girl gets up early in the morning and serves her family warm *lussekatt* buns for breakfast. The buns, shaped like the number eight, are usually flavored with saffron and topped with raisins or nuts.

Fasts

MUSLIMS fast from dawn to sunset during the holy month of Ramadan. Before dawn they eat a meal called *suhur*. After sunset they eat a meal called *iftar*.

JEWS fast on the holy day of Yom Kippur to atone for their sins. From sunset to sunset—one full day—they do not eat or drink anything, not even water.

CHRISTIANS fast during Lent, 40 days that commemorate the 40 days Jesus fasted in the desert. At one time bread and water were the only foods allowed during Lent. Later, the only forbidden food was meat. Today, people often give up their favorite foods during Lent.

He's Cooking!

Alex Brown, 16, really gets things cooking! Alex is a chef's apprentice at Marcel's, a popular French restaurant in Washington, D.C. Alex prepares salads and appetizers, but he plans to move up to the main dishes on the menu. "It is difficult living up to Marcel's high standards," Alex told TFK. "But I'm loving the discipline, organization and energy."

Alex first got a taste for cooking three years ago, baking chocolate-chip cookies and crepes. He loved it so much, he started classes at a nearby culinary school. After touring Marcel's kitchen for his 14th birthday, he returned on his 15th birthday—to work! Alex says he wants to continue cooking after finishing high school: "It's a hard career, but it's satisfying."

A World of Food

Next time your mom asks you what you want for dinner, impress her with your knowledge of international cuisine.

BOBOTIE (SOUTH AFRICAN) This popular meal is made of minced lamb or beef; bread, rice or mashed potatoes; onions; and spices. The ingredients are mixed with egg and milk and baked.

CASSOULET (FRENCH) This casserole is made of white beans, sausage, bacon, tomatoes, carrots, herbs and other vegetables and is simmered and baked.

DIM SUM (CHINESE) This meal is usually eaten as breakfast or lunch at a restaurant. Waiters push around trays loaded with meat, noodles, dumplings and vegetables. Diners eat bite-sized portions from bamboo cups.

ENCHILADA (MEXICAN) In this rich dish, a soft corn tortilla is stuffed with shredded cheese, onions, chilies and some-times meat. It's either broiled or fried and topped with salsa and cheese.

FEIJOADA (BRAZIL) This is the national dish of Brazil. It's a stew of black beans, pork and spices. Pigs' feet and ears are sometimes included in the mix.

Moussaka

MOUSSAKA (GREEK) Considered Greece's signature dish, this casserole is made of lamb, eggplant, tomatoes and spices.

PAD THAI (THAI) This Thai staple features rice noodles stir-fried with peanuts, eggs, vegetables and usually tofu, chicken or fish.

Samosas

SAMOSAS (INDIAN) These snacks are made of meat, potatoes, vegetables and spices stuffed inside pastry dough and fried in oil.

SUYA (NIGERIAN) This spicy dish is made of cubed chicken or beef marinated in ground peanuts, hot pepper, ginger, garlic and other spices and grilled on skewers.

Enchilada

Healing Foods

According to folklore, these foods are good for you. Now some scientists agree.

CRANBERRY JUICE is good for urinary-tract infections. The juice inhibits a type of bacteria that clings to the wall of the bladder and causes infection.

CARROTS are good for your eyes. Carrots and some other fruits and vegetables contain beta-carotene, which can reduce the chance of eye disease. One carrot a day can help prevent macular degeneration, which eventually leads to blindness.

CHICKEN SOUP fights congestion that comes with a cold. Chicken has an amino acid that thins the mucous lining of the sinuses, relieving stuffiness.

GARLIC and **ONIONS** can kill flu and cold viruses.

FISH is good for your brain. The mineral zinc is found in fish and shellfish. Studies show that even a small deficiency of zinc impairs thinking and memory.

BLUEBERRIES fight the bacteria that causes diarrhea.

BANANAS are a natural antacid. They soothe heartburn.

SPINACH is good for your spirits. It contains lots of folic acid. If your body doesn't have enough folic acid, you may feel depressed.

Eat **ONIONS** to fight insomnia. Onions contain a mild natural sedative called quercetin that will help you fall asleep.

ZZZZZZ

TFK Top 5

Best-Selling Girl Scout Cookies

About 200 million boxes of Girl Scout cookies are sold in the U.S. each year. Here are the best sellers (some go by more than one name).

Other 23%

1. Thin Mints 25%

2. Samoas/ Caramel deLites 19%

3. Peanut Butter Patties/Tagalongs 13%

4. Peanut Butter Sandwich/Do-si-dos 11%

5. Trefoils/ Shortbread 9%

Source: GIRL SCOUTS OF THE U.S.A.

TFK Mystery Person

CLUE 1: I was a chef, an author and a star of television cooking shows. I was born in Pasadena, California, in 1912.

CLUE 2: I moved to Paris in 1948 to attend the famous Cordon Bleu cooking school.

CLUE 3: My TV kitchen is on display at the Smithsonian's National Museum of American History in Washington, D.C.

WHO AM I?

(See Answer Key that begins on page 342.)

FROM
TFK
MAGAZINE

A Sleeping Giant Awakes

Mount Saint Helens heated up 24 years after its last big explosion

Steam and ash pour out of the volcano.

With a rumble and a roar, lava rocketed up to the top of Mount Saint Helens in Washington in 2004. The volcano had been bursting with activity for a month, when thousands of little earthquakes hit. The 8,634-foot mountain continued to heat up, spewing steam and ash.

Scientists are measuring the volcano's every shudder. Waves of hot molten rock, or magma, have pushed upward toward the mountaintop. Lava, which is what magma is called when it reaches the Earth's surface, has been collecting steadily on the crater floor inside the volcano. The lava's temperature reaches nearly 1,700°F. Enough new rock is forming from the lava to fill an Olympic-size swimming pool every 15 minutes!

The last time the volcano erupted violently was on May 18, 1980. Tens of thousands of acres of forests were destroyed, and 57 people were killed. No one is allowed within about 10 miles of the volcano. "Volcanic activity is an inevitable part of the world we live in," says Jeff Wynn, the chief volcanologist for the U.S. Geological Survey. "But we're doing everything we can to make sure we're all safe this time."

DETECTING DANGER

Volcanoes can "rest" for years, then explode with sudden violence. Because these giants are unpredictable, studying them is a dangerous profession. Many scientists have lost their lives investigating volcanoes. But now advanced technology can detect changes in volcanic behavior without endangering human lives.

New tools allow volcanologists to keep track of nearly any change in or around a volcano. Tiny microphones set up around Mount Saint Helens record even the smallest surface explosions, so scientists can tell whether it is acting up. Helicopters equipped with instruments fly over the volcano's crater and collect gases.

Geography

STEAM AND ASH

CRATER Measures more than a mile across

LAVA DOME This cap of cooled magma is fixed like a cork in a bottle. When the pressure gets too high, the mountaintop pops.

ICE

BOILING OVER Steam and other gases are released at the top of the dome. Heat from the magma below also melts the snow in the crater and creates even more steam.

SHAKING UP Pressure from magma and hot gases cracks the mountain's rocks. The magma's heat boils groundwater, creating steam.

TIGHT FIT The magma from Mount Saint Helens is squeezed upward like thick toothpaste through a narrow tube. When it gets to the top, it can burst out as lava.

UP AND OUT As magma rises, it creates more and more pressure and upward movement, pushing rocks aside and building toward eruption.

Magma, or molten rock, collects underground before it is forced to the surface.

Did You Know?

Many of the world's volcanoes are lined up along the Ring of Fire, a belt that encircles the Pacific Ocean. This region experiences frequent earthquakes and volcanic activity. Mount Saint Helens is located in the ring. So are about 75% of the world's volcanoes!

Volcanologists study the gases for hints about what might be brewing inside the mountain. Tiny global positioning system devices measure the volcano's movements. That helps scientists figure out if magma is putting pressure on the mountaintop and pushing aside the surface (see diagram above).

For thousands of years, the volcano has alternated between bursts of violent activity and slumber. "It's like there's a giant on-and-off switch," says Wynn.
—By Jeremy Caplan

TFK Top 5

Tallest Mountains in the U.S.
Alaska is home to the 16 highest mountains in the U.S. Here are the nation's tallest towering peaks.

1. Mt. McKinley	20,320 feet
2. Mt. Saint Elias	18,008 feet
3. Mt. Foraker	17,400 feet
4. Mt. Bona	16,500 feet
5. Mt. Blackburn	16,390 feet

Source: U.S. Geological Survey

The Seven Continents

CONTINENT	APPROX. AREA	HIGHEST POINT	LOWEST POINT
Africa	11,608,000 square miles (30,065,000 sq km)	Mount Kilimanjaro, Tanzania: 19,340 feet (5,895 m)	Lake Assal, Djibouti: 512 feet (156 m) below sea level
Antarctica	5,100,000 square miles (13,209,000 sq km)	Vinson Massif: 16,066 feet (4,897 m)	Ice covering: 8,327 feet (2,538 m) below sea level
Asia (includes the Middle East)	17,212,000 square miles (44,579,000 sq km)	Mount Everest, China/Nepal: 29,035 feet (8,850 m)	Dead Sea, Israel/Jordan: 1,349 feet (411 m) below sea level
Australia (includes Oceania)	3,132,000 square miles (8,112,000 sq km)	Mount Kosciusko, Australia: 7,316 feet (2,228 m)	Lake Eyre, Australia: 52 feet (16 m) below sea level
Europe (Ural Mountains divide Europe from Asia)	3,837,000 square miles (9,938,000 sq km)	Mount Elbrus, Russia/Georgia: 18,510 feet (5,642 m)	Caspian Sea, Russia/Kazakhstan: 92 feet (28 m) below sea level
North America (includes Central America and the Caribbean)	9,449,000 square miles (24,474,000 sq km)	Mount McKinley, Alaska, U.S.: 20,320 feet (6,194 m)	Death Valley, California, U.S.: 282 feet (86 m) below sea level
South America	6,879,000 square miles (17,819,000 sq km)	Mount Aconcagua, Argentina: 22,834 feet (6,960 m)	Valdes Peninsula, Argentina: 131 feet (40 m) below sea level

Source: WorldAtlas.com

The Five Oceans

In 2000, the International Hydrographic Organization delimited (marked the boundaries of) a fifth ocean. The new ocean, called the Southern Ocean, surrounds Antarctica and extends north to 60 degrees south latitude. It is the fourth-largest ocean, bigger only than the Arctic Ocean.

OCEAN	AREA	AVERAGE DEPTH
Pacific Ocean	60,060,700 square miles (155,557,000 sq km)	13,215 feet (4,028 m)
Atlantic Ocean	29,637,900 square miles (76,762,000 sq km)	12,880 feet (3,926 m)
Indian Ocean	26,469,500 square miles (68,556,000 sq km)	13,002 feet (3,963 m)
Southern Ocean	7,848,300 square miles (20,327,000 sq km)	13,100–16,400 feet* (4,000–5,000 m)
Arctic Ocean	5,427,000 square miles (14,056,000 sq km)	3,953 feet (1,205 m)

*Official depths of the Southern Ocean are in dispute.

go
For facts about changes to Earth:
www.factmonster.com/earthchanges

Earth on the Move

If you look at a map of the world, you'll see that the continents look as if they are pieces of a big puzzle. If you pushed South America and Africa into each other, they would fit together as one land mass. Many scientists believe that until about 200 million years ago, the world was made up of a single supercontinent called Pangaea. It eventually separated and drifted apart into the seven continents we have today. This movement is called **continental drift.**

According to the theory of **plate tectonics,** the Earth's lithosphere—the crust and the outer part of the mantle—is not one giant piece of rock. Instead, it's broken into several moving slabs, or plates. These plates slide above a hot layer of the mantle. The plates move as much as a few inches every year. The oceans and the continents sit on top of the plates and move with them.

Greenland

North America

North American Plate

Pacific Plate

Nazca Plate

South America

South American Plate

The white lines show the plate borders. The arrows show the directions the plates move.

Earthquakes

There are thousands of earthquakes each year. Most of them are so weak that we don't even realize that they occurred. But we can usually expect one exceptionally big earthquake each year.

An earthquake is a trembling movement of Earth's rocky outer layer, called the crust. The crust is divided into several plates that are slowly and continuously shifting. Most earthquakes occur along a fault—a crack in the crust between two plates—when two plates crash together or move in opposite directions. A quake begins at a point called the focus.

The most devastating earthquake in history hit Shansi, China, in 1556. About 830,000 people died in the disaster.

A tsunami is a series of giant sea waves that follows an earthquake or a volcanic eruption. The waves can be up to 50 feet (15 m) tall and move at about 600 miles per hour (965 km/hour). The waves can cause massive destruction when they break on land. In late 2004, a giant tsunami devastated parts of Asia and killed more than 280,000 people.

Did You Know?
The most widely used scale to measure the intensity of an earthquake is moment magnitude. It is based on the size of the fault on which an earthquake occurs and the amount of land that slips during an earthquake.

An earthquake in Ojiya, Japan, in 2004 damaged houses.

go ►
For the deadliest earthquakes:
www.factmonster.com/deadlyquakes

85

The Lines on a Map

The equator divides Earth into halves, or **HEMISPHERES.** The Northern Hemisphere is the half of Earth between the North Pole and the equator. The Southern Hemisphere is the half between the South Pole and the equator.

Earth can also be divided into the Eastern and Western Hemispheres. The Western Hemisphere includes North and South America. The Eastern Hemisphere includes Asia, Africa, Australia and Europe.

LATITUDE measures distance from the equator. Latitude is measured in degrees and shown on a map by lines that run east and west. Lines of latitude are also called parallels.

LONGITUDE measures distance from the prime meridian, an imaginary line on a map that runs through Greenwich, England. It is measured in degrees and shown on a map by lines that run north and south. Lines of longitude are also called meridians.

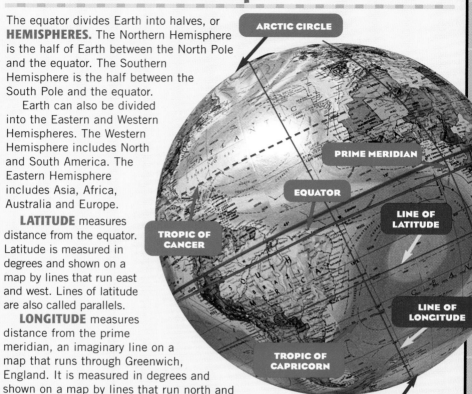

ARCTIC CIRCLE

PRIME MERIDIAN

EQUATOR

LINE OF LATITUDE

TROPIC OF CANCER

LINE OF LONGITUDE

TROPIC OF CAPRICORN

ANTARCTIC CIRCLE

 **Puzzles & Games**

The Four-Color Rule

For years, mapmakers claimed that any map could be drawn using just four colors, with bordering regions or countries in different colors. Mathematicians, using a computer, have proved that the theory is true. At right is a design that represents a map of 13 countries. Can you fill in the regions using no more than four colors? **Remember this important mapmaking rule:** regions that share a border can't be the same color.

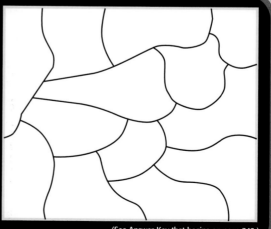

(See Answer Key that begins on page 342.)

86

IMPORTANT EXPLORERS

1000 Leif Eriksson (Viking) explored Labrador and Newfoundland in Canada.

1271 Marco Polo (Italian) explored China.

1492

1325–1349 Ibn Batuta (Arab) explored Africa, the Middle East, Europe, parts of Asia.

1488 Bartholomeu Dias (Portuguese) rounded South Africa's Cape of Good Hope.

1492 Christopher Columbus (Italian) arrived in the West Indies.

1498 Vasco da Gama (Portuguese) explored the coast of India.

1513 Ponce de León (Spanish) reached Florida.

1519–1521 Hernando Cortés (Spanish) conquered Mexico.

1519–1522 The expedition led by Ferdinand Magellan (Portuguese) circled the globe.

1535-36

1532–1533 Francisco Pizarro (Spanish) conquered Peru.

1535–1536 Jacques Cartier (French) sailed up Canada's St. Lawrence River.

1539–1542 Hernando de Soto (Spanish) explored the southeastern U.S.

1607 John Smith (British) settled Jamestown, Virginia.

1609–1610 Henry Hudson (British) explored the river, strait and bay that bear his name.

1769 James Cook (British) explored New Zealand.

1804–1806 Meriwether Lewis and William Clark (American) explored the northwest U.S.

1909 Robert E. Peary (American) reached the North Pole.

1911 Roald Amundsen (Norwegian) reached the South Pole.

1909

For myths about explorers:
www.factmonster.com/explorermyths

Record Breakers

LARGEST LAKE: CASPIAN SEA
152,239 square miles (394,299 sq km)

LONGEST RIVER: THE NILE
4,180 miles (6,690 km)

SHORTEST RIVER: THE ROE
Montana, U.S., 201 feet (61 m)

LARGEST ISLAND: GREENLAND
839,999 square miles (2,175,600 sq km)

LONGEST MOUNTAIN RANGE:
THE ANDES South America, more than 5,000 miles (8,000 km)

HIGHEST WATERFALL: ANGEL (SALTO ANGEL) Venezuela, 3,212 feet (979 m) high

BIGGEST DESERT: SAHARA
3.5 million square miles (9.1 million sq km)

TFK Mystery Person

CLUE 1: I was born in Ireland in 1874. I grew up near London, England, and became a famous explorer of Antarctica.

CLUE 2: I led three expeditions seeking to reach the South Pole. In 1909, I traveled to within 111 miles of the Pole—the closest anyone had come at the time.

CLUE 3: My most famous trip began in 1914 on board the *Endurance*. We failed to cross Antarctica, but our journey became one of the greatest tales of survival ever told.

WHO AM I?

(See Answer Key that begins on page 342.)

The
Constitution

★ ★ ★ ★ ★

I n 1787 leaders of the states gathered to write the Constitution—a set of principles that described how the new nation would be governed. The Constitution went into effect in 1789. The Constitution begins with a famous section called the preamble. The preamble says that the U.S. government was created by the people and for the benefit of the people:

We the people of the United States, in order to form a more perfect Union, establish justice, insure domestic tranquility, provide for the common defense, promote the general welfare and secure the blessings of liberty to ourselves and our posterity, do ordain and establish this Constitution for the United States of America.

The leaders of the states wanted a strong and fair national government. But they also wanted to protect individual freedoms and prevent the government from abusing its power. They believed they could do this by having three separate branches of government: the Executive, the Legislative and the Judicial. This separation is described in the first three articles, or sections, of the Constitution.

The Constitution was originally made up of **seven** articles.

ARTICLE I Creates the Legislative Branch—the House of Representatives and the Senate—and describes its powers and responsibilities.

ARTICLE II Creates the Executive Branch, which is led by the President, and describes its powers and responsibilities.

ARTICLE III Creates the Judicial Branch, which is led by the Supreme Court, and describes its powers and responsibilities.

ARTICLE IV Describes the rights and powers of the states.

ARTICLE V Explains how amendments (changes or additions) can be made to the Constitution.

ARTICLE VI Says the Constitution is "the supreme law of the land."

ARTICLE VII Tells how the Constitution would be ratified (approved and made official) by the states.

 go For the complete Constitution, including all the amendments: www.factmonster.com/constitution

Government

As Article V shows, the authors of the Constitution expected from the beginning that amendments would be made to the document. There are now **27 Amendments.**

The first 10 Amendments are known as the Bill of Rights. They list individual freedoms promised by the new government. The Bill of Rights was approved in 1791.

The Bill of Rights

AMENDMENT I Guarantees freedom of religion, speech and the press.

AMENDMENT II Guarantees the right of the people to have firearms.

AMENDMENT III Says that soldiers may not stay in a house without the owner's permission.

AMENDMENT IV Says that the government cannot search people and their homes without a strong reason.

AMENDMENT V Says that every person has the right to a trial and to protection of his or her rights while waiting for a trial. Also, private property cannot be taken without payment.

AMENDMENT VI Says that every person shall have the right to "a speedy and public trial."

AMENDMENT VII Guarantees the right to a trial in various types of legal cases.

AMENDMENT VIII Outlaws all "cruel and unusual punishment."

AMENDMENT IX Says that people have rights in addition to those listed in the Constitution.

AMENDMENT X Says that the powers the Constitution does not give to the national government belong to the states and to the people.

Other Notable Amendments

AMENDMENT XIII (approved 1865) Declares slavery illegal.

AMENDMENT XIX (approved 1920) Grants women the right to vote.

AMENDMENT XXII (approved 1951) Says that a President may serve no more than two four-year terms.

AMENDMENT XXIV (approved 1964) Forbids poll taxes—money paid for the right to vote—in national elections.

Unusual Amendments

Since **1789,** members of Congress have proposed about 10,000 amendments to the Constitution. These are just a few that Congress did not approve.

1893: To rename the U.S. the "United States of the Earth"

1914: To make divorce illegal

1916: To put all acts of war to a national vote. Those who vote "yes" must register for military service.

1933: To limit personal wealth to $1 million

1971: To give Americans the right to a pollution-free environment

The
Legislative Branch

★ ★ ★ ★ ★ ★ ★

The Legislative Branch is made up of the two houses of Congress—the **Senate** and the **House of Representatives.** The most important duty of the Legislative Branch is to make laws. Laws are written, discussed and voted on in Congress.

There are **100 Senators** in the Senate, two from each state. Senators are elected by their states and serve six-year terms. The Vice President of the U.S. is considered the head of the Senate but does not vote in the Senate unless there is a tie. The President Pro Tempore of the Senate presides over the chamber in the absence of the Vice President. The Senator in the majority party who has served the longest is usually elected to the position.

The Senate approves nominations made by the President to the Cabinet, the Supreme Court, federal courts and other posts. The Senate must ratify all treaties by a two-thirds vote.

There are **435 Representatives** in the House of Representatives. The number of

Representatives each state gets is based on its population. For example, California has many more Representatives than Montana has. When Census figures determine that the population of a state has changed significantly, the number of Representatives in that state may shift proportionately. Representatives are elected by their states and serve two-year terms. The Speaker of the House, elected by the Representatives, is considered the head of the House.

Both parties in the Senate and the House of Representatives elect leaders. The leader of the party that controls the house is called the majority leader. The other party leader is called the minority leader.

Both houses of Congress elect whips. The whips keep track of votes on bills, try to persuade party members to vote along the party line and make sure lawmakers show up for votes. "Whip" comes from the British word for the person who whips dogs to keep them running with the pack during a fox hunt.

CONGRESS

SENATE	HOUSE OF REPRESENTATIVES
100 members (2 from each state) 6-year terms	435 members (number from each state is based on its population) 2-year terms

President Pro Tempore	Senate Majority Leader	Senate Minority Leader	Speaker of the House	House Majority Leader	House Minority Leader
Ted Stevens (R)	Bill Frist (R)	Harry Reid (D)	Dennis Hastert (R)	Tom DeLay (R)	Nancy Pelosi (D)

go Find and contact your Representative and Senator in Congress at timeforkids.com/congress

The Executive Branch

★ ★ ★ ★ ★ ★ ★

he President is the head of the Executive Branch, which makes laws official. The President is elected by the entire country and serves a four-year term. The President cannot serve more than two four-year terms. He or she approves and carries out laws passed by the Legislative Branch, appoints or removes Cabinet members and officials, negotiates treaties and acts as head of state and Commander-in-Chief of the armed forces.

The Executive Branch also includes the **Vice President** and other officials, such as members of the **Cabinet.** The Cabinet is made up of the heads of the 15 major departments of the government.

The Cabinet gives advice to the President about important matters.

THE PRESIDENT

GEORGE W. BUSH

THE VICE PRESIDENT

RICHARD CHENEY

THE CABINET

Secretary of Agriculture	Secretary of Commerce	Secretary of Defense	Secretary of Education	Secretary of Energy
Mike Johanns	Carlos Gutierrez	Donald Rumsfeld	Margaret Spellings	 Spencer Abraham

Secretary of Health and Human Services	Secretary of Housing and Urban Development	Secretary of the Interior	Attorney General	Secretary of Labor
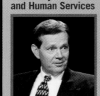 Michael O. Leavitt	Alphonso Jackson	 Gale Norton	Alberto Gonzales	Elaine Chao

Secretary of State	Secretary of Transportation	Secretary of the Treasury	Secretary of Veterans Affairs	Secretary of Homeland Security
Condoleezza Rice	Norman Mineta	John W. Snow	Anthony Principi	 Michael Chertoff

go For more information on the President's cabinet: www.factmonster.com/cabinet

91

The Judicial Branch

★ ☆ ★ ☆ ★ ☆ ★

The Judicial Branch oversees the court system of the U.S. Through court cases, the Judicial Branch explains the meaning of the Constitution and laws passed by Congress. **The Supreme Court** is the head of the Judicial Branch. Unlike a criminal court, the Supreme Court rules whether something is constitutional or unconstitutional—that is, whether or not it is permitted under the Constitution.

On the Supreme Court there are **nine Justices,** or judges: eight associate Justices and one Chief Justice. The judges are nominated by the President and approved by the Senate. They have no term limits.

The Supreme Court is the highest court in the land. Its decisions are final, and no other court can overrule those decisions. Decisions of the Supreme Court set precedents—new ways of interpreting the law.

Justices of the Supreme Court, from left: Antonin Scalia, Ruth Bader Ginsburg, John Paul Stevens, David Souter, Chief Justice William Rehnquist, Clarence Thomas, Sandra Day O'Connor, Stephen Breyer and Anthony Kennedy.

Significant Supreme Court Decisions

1803 *Marbury v. Madison*
The first time a law passed by Congress was declared unconstitutional

1857 *Dred Scott v. Sanford*
Declared that a slave was not a citizen, and that Congress could not outlaw slavery in U.S. territories

1896 *Plessy v. Ferguson*
Said that racial segregation was legal

1954 *Brown v. Board of Education*
Made racial segregation in schools illegal

1966 *Miranda v. Arizona*
Stated that criminal suspects must be informed of their rights before being questioned by police

2003 *Grutter v. Bollinger* and *Gratz v. Bollinger*
Ruled that colleges can, under certain conditions, consider race and ethnicity in admissions

go For other Supreme Court cases:
www.factmonster.com/courtdecisions

Checks and Balances

The system of checks and balances is an important part of the Constitution. With checks and balances, each of the three branches of government can limit the powers of the others. This way, no one branch becomes too powerful. Each branch "checks" the power of the other branches to make sure that the power is balanced among them. How does this system of checks and balances work?

The process of making laws *(see following page)* is a good example of checks and balances in action. First, the **Legislative Branch** introduces and votes on a bill. If the bill passes, it then goes to the **Executive Branch,** where the President decides whether the bill is good for the country. If so, the bill is signed and becomes a law.

If the President does not believe the bill is good for the country, it does not get signed. This is called a veto. But the Legislative Branch gets another chance. With enough votes, the Legislative Branch can override the Executive Branch's veto, and the bill becomes a law.

Once a law is in place, the people of the country can test it through the court system, which is under the control of the **Judicial Branch.** If someone believes a law is unfair, a lawsuit can be filed. Lawyers then make arguments for and against the case, and a judge decides which side has presented the most convincing arguments. The side that loses can choose to appeal to a higher court, and the case may eventually reach the highest court of all, the Supreme Court.

If the Legislative Branch does not agree with the way in which the Judicial Branch has interpreted the law, it can introduce a new piece of legislation, and the process starts all over again.

Senate

White House

Supreme Court

How a
Bill Becomes a Law

★ ★ ★ ★ ★ ★ ★

1. A member of Congress introduces the bill.

When a Senator or Representative introduces a bill, it is sent to the clerk of the Senate or House, who gives it a number and title. Next, the bill goes to the appropriate committee.

2. Committees review and vote on the bill.

Committees specialize in different areas, such as foreign relations or agriculture, and are made up of small groups of Senators or Representatives.

The committee may reject the bill and "table" it, meaning it is never discussed again. Or the committee may hold hearings to listen to facts and opinions, make changes in the bill and cast votes. If most committee members vote in favor of the bill, it is sent back to the Senate and the House for debate.

3. The Senate and the House debate and vote on the bill.

Separately, the Senate and the House debate the bill, offer amendments and cast votes. If the bill is defeated in either the Senate or the House, the bill dies.

Sometimes, the House and the Senate pass the same bill, but with different amendments. In these cases, the bill goes to a conference committee made up of members of both houses of Congress. The conference committee works out differences between the two versions of the bill.

Then the bill goes before all of Congress for a vote. If a majority of both the Senate and the House votes for the bill, it goes to the President for approval.

4. The President signs the bill—or not.

If the President approves the bill and signs it, the bill becomes a law. However, if the President disapproves, he or she can veto the bill by refusing to sign it.

Congress can try to overrule a veto. If both the Senate and the House pass the bill by a two-thirds majority, the President's veto is overruled and the bill becomes a law.

You're Grounded

The President, the Vice President and other U.S. officials can be impeached—that is, formally charged with "high crimes and misdemeanors," which include bribery, perjury, treason and abuse of power.

Under the Constitution, only the House of Representatives has the power to impeach a federal official. If a majority of the House votes for impeachment, then the Senate holds a trial and votes on whether to convict the official. If two-thirds of the Senate votes for conviction, the official will be removed from office.

Only two Presidents have been impeached: Andrew Johnson and Bill Clinton. However, neither was convicted by the Senate.

★ ☆ ★ ☆ ★ ☆ ★

Once voters decide on a candidate, how do they actually make their choice official? Americans vote in five different ways. Here's a look at the voting systems used around the country, listed in order of how common they are.

★ **Optical-Scan Systems** This method is similar to the one used for standardized tests. Voters fill in a small bubble by a candidate's name. The paper is later scanned by a machine that adds up the votes.

★ **Electronic Machines** Like ATMs, these gadgets let voters touch a screen to select the name of their chosen candidate.

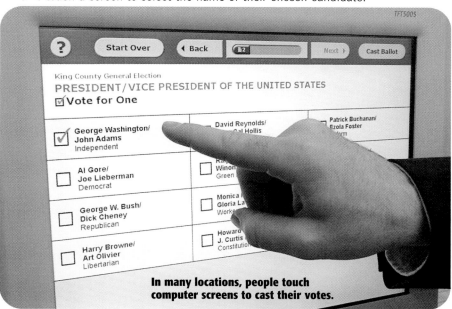

TFT5005

| ? | Start Over | ◀ Back | ◀ 12 | Next ▶ | Cast Ballot |

King County General Election
PRESIDENT/VICE PRESIDENT OF THE UNITED STATES
☑ **Vote for One**

☑ George Washington/ John Adams — Independent
David Reynolds/ Cal Hollis
Patrick Buchanan/ Ezola Foster — Reform

☐ Al Gore/ Joe Lieberman — Democrat
☐ Ralph Nader/ Winona — Green

☐ George W. Bush/ Dick Cheney — Republican
☐ Monica Gloria La — Worke

☐ Harry Browne/ Art Olivier — Libertarian
☐ Howard J. Curtis — Constitution

In many locations, people touch computer screens to cast their votes.

★ **Punch Cards** To select a candidate this way, voters use a special hole puncher to mark a spot by the name of the person they want to elect.

★ **Lever Machines**
Voters pull a lever next to the name of the nominee they support. Their vote is recorded on a wheel behind the machine.

★ **Paper Ballots**
Voters place a piece of paper marked with their preferred candidate's name in a sealed box. The papers are later counted by hand.

Homework Tip!
Bring all the supplies you will need to the library, including your assignment, books, pens, paper and change for the photocopier. Remember to ask the librarian if you need help finding resources.

How the
President Gets Elected

★ ★ ★ ★ ★ ★

Step by Step on the Campaign Trail

1. Candidate announces plan to run for office.

This announcement launches the candidate's official campaign. Speeches, debates and baby kissing begin.

2. Candidate campaigns to win delegate support.

The first stage of a presidential campaign is the nomination campaign. At this time the candidate is competing with other candidates in the same party, hoping to get the party's nomination. The candidate works to win delegates—representatives who pledge to support the candidate's nomination at the national party convention—and to persuade potential voters in general.

3. Caucuses and primary elections take place in the states.

Caucuses and primaries are ways for the general public to take part in nominating presidential candidates.

At a caucus, local party members gather to nominate a candidate. A caucus is a lively event at which party leaders and activists debate issues and consider candidates. The rules governing caucus procedures vary by party and by state.

A primary is more like a general election. Voters go to the polls to cast their votes for a presidential candidate (or delegates who will represent that candidate at the party convention). A primary election is the main way voters choose a nominee.

4. Nominee for President is announced at national party convention.

There are two primary political parties in the U.S.—the Democratic Party and the Republican Party. The main goal of a national party convention is to unify party members. Thousands of delegates gather to rally support for the party's ideas and to formally nominate party candidates for President and Vice President.

After the convention, the second stage of the presidential campaign begins: the election campaign. In this stage, candidates from different parties compete against each other as they try to get elected President.

5. Citizens cast their votes.

Presidential elections are held every four years on the Tuesday after the first Monday of November.

Many Americans think that when they cast their ballot, they are voting for their chosen candidate. Actually, they are selecting groups of electors in the Electoral College.

 Follow the path from getting nominated to getting elected at timeforkids.com/presidency

6. The Electoral College casts its votes.

Some Founding Fathers wanted Congress to elect the President. Others wanted the President to be elected by popular vote. The Electoral College represents a compromise between these ideas.

Every state has a number of electors equal to its number of Senators and Representatives. In addition, there are three electors for the District of Columbia. Laws vary by state, but electors are usually chosen by popular vote. An elector may not be a Senator, Representative or other person holding a national office.

In most cases, the electoral votes from a particular state go to the candidate who leads the popular vote in that state. (Only Maine and Nebraska divide electoral votes among candidates.)

This "winner takes all" system can produce surprising results; in the elections of 1824, 1876, 1888 and 2000, the candidate who had the greatest popular vote did not win the greatest Electoral College vote and so lost the presidency.

On the first Monday after the second Wednesday in December, the electors cast their ballots. At least 270 electoral votes are required to elect a President. If this majority is not reached, the House of Representatives chooses the President.

7. The President is inaugurated.

On January 20, the President enters office in a ceremony that is known as the Inauguration and takes the presidential oath: "I do solemnly swear (or affirm) that I will faithfully execute the office of President of the United States, and will to the best of my ability, preserve, protect and defend the Constitution of the United States."

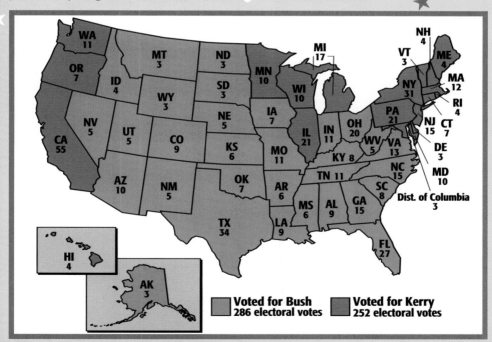

Voted for Bush 286 electoral votes
Voted for Kerry 252 electoral votes

Electoral votes by state in the 2004 election.

Play election games and learn about the 2004 presidential election at timeforkids.com/election04

The Presidential Succession

Who would take over if the President died, resigned or was removed from office? The list of who is next in line is known as presidential succession.

★ Vice President
★ Speaker of the House
★ President Pro Tempore of the Senate
★ Secretary of State
★ Secretary of the Treasury
★ Secretary of Defense
★ Attorney General
★ Secretary of the Interior
★ Secretary of Agriculture
★ Secretary of Commerce
★ Secretary of Labor
★ Secretary of Health and Human Services
★ Secretary of Housing and Urban Development
★ Secretary of Transportation
★ Secretary of Energy
★ Secretary of Education
★ Secretary of Veterans Affairs
★ Secretary of Homeland Security

Who on the current Cabinet was not born in the U.S. and therefore cannot become President?

(See Answer Key that begins on page 342.)

Did You Know?

Democrats and Republicans have long used animals to represent their parties. The Democratic donkey symbolizes intelligence and bravery, while the Republican elephant indicates strength and dignity.

TFK Puzzles & Games

Hear! Hear!

Circle the words from the list at left that appear in the puzzle. The leftover letters spell the answer to this riddle:

What do government officials want to hear? Answer: _ _ _ _   _ _ _ _ _

DEMOCRACY
COMPROMISE
ELECT
HOUSE
SENATE
LEGISLATE
LAWS
OPEN MIND
LEAD
POLICY
BILLS
DEBATE
IDEAS
STATE
YOU
TERM
ISSUES

Y	S	E	N	A	T	E	Y	S	E
O	C	Y	B	E	O	C	W	S	H
U	U	A	R	I	I	A	I	T	O
R	S	M	R	L	L	M	V	A	U
T	A	O	O	C	O	L	I	T	S
C	E	P	C	R	O	E	S	E	E
E	D	O	P	E	N	M	I	N	D
L	I	M	E	T	A	B	E	D	A
E	O	I	S	S	U	E	S	D	E
C	E	T	A	L	S	I	G	E	L

(See Answer Key that begins on page 342.)

Franks, Pork, a Dirty Trick and Other Trivia

⭐ Members of Congress don't need postage stamps for their official mail—they just need a frank. No, not a hot dog! It's their signature on the outside of envelopes that contain letters mailed to constituents. Franks can't be used for personal business or for political campaigns.

⭐ The sound of carriages and carts passing on cobblestone streets outside the Pennsylvania State House distracted the delegates to the Constitutional Convention, who were busy writing the Constitution. They solved the problem by hiring people to shovel dirt onto the street to muffle the noise.

⭐ The youngest people working in Congress are pages. These high-school juniors carry legislative documents between the House of Representatives and the Senate. They also help answer phones in the party cloakrooms and deliver messages to members of Congress.

⭐ The Republican Party has been known as the G.O.P., or Grand Old Party, since around 1880. Although no one knows the exact origin of the moniker, many people think it was taken from the nickname of British Prime Minister William Gladstone. He was known as the Grand Old Man, or G.O.M.

⭐ Only John Hancock and Charles Thomson, secretary of the Continental Congress, signed the first copy of the Declaration of Independence. The men could have been jailed or killed by the British for putting their names to the document. The other Founding Fathers waited about six weeks before adding their names to the Declaration.

⭐ "Pork-barrel legislation" refers to bills introduced by members of Congress that only benefit people in their home states. The phrase refers to a time before the Civil War, when plantation owners gave salt pork from barrels to their slaves as a treat.

TFK Mystery Person

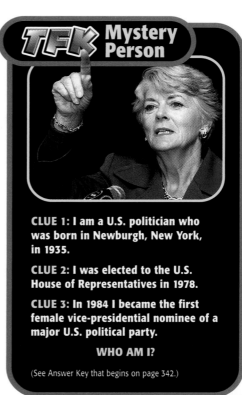

CLUE 1: I am a U.S. politician who was born in Newburgh, New York, in 1935.

CLUE 2: I was elected to the U.S. House of Representatives in 1978.

CLUE 3: In 1984 I became the first female vice-presidential nominee of a major U.S. political party.

WHO AM I?

(See Answer Key that begins on page 342.)

< King students dig the school garden.

Food for Thought

School gardens teach kids to take better care of themselves and the planet

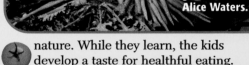

"Every time I go see the kids, I know the program is a good idea," says Alice Waters.

It's science class for some eighth-graders at Martin Luther King Jr. Middle School in Berkeley, California. But the students aren't sitting at their desks. Instead, they are harvesting fava beans and planting corn in their school's garden. Everything in the garden—from broccoli to oranges—is grown organically without the use of harmful chemicals.

King students have been digging into learning this way since 1997. That's when Alice Waters, a famous chef, started a program called the Edible Schoolyard at their school. Teachers and kids incorporate the organic garden into many lessons. In math class, they measure vegetable beds; in art, they draw the wonders of nature. While they learn, the kids develop a taste for healthful eating.

North Country School in Lake Placid, New York, is another school with deep roots in garden-based learning. For almost 75 years, lessons at the boarding school have been connected to raising livestock and tending gardens. Kids take part in everything from from planting and harvesting to preparing and eating. Much of the food served at North Country is homegrown, even the maple syrup. "Knowing you helped produce it makes it [taste] so much better," says Anthony Edwards, 12.

THE SEEDS OF LEARNING

According to the National Gardening Association, about 25,000 schools in the U.S. involve students in gardening, and the numbers are growing like weeds! Waters hopes that these schools will set an example. Her goal is to turn lunch into an academic subject. Students would get a grade for helping to prepare locally grown organic foods.

—By Elizabeth Winchester

North Country students collect sap to make syrup.

Health & Body

The Doctor's In

Fact Monster asked pediatrician BRIAN ORR to answer some questions kids frequently ask about their bodies.

Is a healthy person's temperature always 98.6°F?

Healthy or sick, our temperatures change in a rhythm throughout the day. When we are healthy, our average temperature is 98.6°F, but even when we are healthy our temperature could go up to 99°F or down to 97°F. When we are sick, our temperatures rise to higher points. Someone has a fever when their body temperature is over 100.5°F, so a temperature of 99°F is not a reason to stay home from school!

Are low-carbohydrate diets good for kids?

No diet is good for kids. You may have heard about some fad diets, such as the Atkins Diet or the South Beach Diet. Adults follow these diets to lose weight. As for kids, no diet is as effective as eating sensibly. You also need to exercise each day to stay healthy and trim. So turn off the TV, get moving and eat your fruits and vegetables.

Why do some people have "innie" belly buttons and others have "outies"?

Many mothers ask me if their babies will have an "innie" or an "outie." Babies whose skin grows out from the umbilical cord end up with "outies" when the cord falls off. Those whose skin doesn't grow out toward the umbilical cord are left with very little extra skin on their belly button, an "innie." Do you have an "innie" or an "outie"?

When I get a sore throat, why does the doctor stick that wood thing down my throat?

Doctors use the stick to push your tongue down (and have you say "ahh") so we have a better view of your throat. We're looking for redness and white patches on the tonsils, which could be sign of a bacteria called streptococcus, the cause of "strep" throat. Sometimes it's hard to tell if you have strep by just looking, so the doctor swabs your throat to remove some of the infection. We check the sample in the office and at a lab to determine if you have strep. It's important to treat the infection so it doesn't spread to other parts of your body—like your heart.

Why do we blink?

Blinking protects our eyes from foreign objects, sweeps up dirt that gets in our eyes and lubricates our eyes by spreading tears across the surface. Don't you think that is a lot to accomplish with the "blink of an eye"?

Dr. What?

- A cardiologist treats the heart.
- A dermatologist treats the skin and hair.
- A neurologist specializes in disorders affecting the nervous system (see page 107).
- An obstetrician specializes in obstetrics, the branch of medicine that deals with human birth.
- An ophthalmologist diagnoses and treats eye problems and performs eye surgery.
- An orthopedist is trained to treat the entire skeletal system.
- An otologist specializes in the treatment of the ear.
- A psychiatrist treats people with emotional problems.
- A radiologist specializes in making and explaining x rays and other pictures that show areas inside the body.

Healthy Habits

Recent statistics have highlighted an alarming trend: the number of overweight and obese Americans—including children—is rapidly increasing. The Centers for Disease Control and Prevention estimates that 15% of kids ages 6 to 19 are obese and 20% are overweight. Obesity can lead to serious health problems, such as heart disease, stroke, diabetes and high blood pressure.

Exercise: It's Good for You

Not only is exercise fun, but it also helps your mind, body and overall well-being. Kids who exercise regularly often do better in school, sleep better, are less likely to be overweight or obese, and are stronger than less-active kids. Exercise can also relieve stress and improve your mood.

Federal health officials recently reported that most kids spend a shocking 4 ½ hours each day watching TV, using a computer or playing video games! They recommend that kids exercise for about an hour almost every day of the week. So get up and get moving!

There are two types of exercise, **AEROBIC** and **ANAEROBIC.** When you do aerobic exercises, such as running, swimming, biking and playing soccer, you increase your heart rate and the flow of oxygen-rich blood to your muscles. Aerobic exercise also builds endurance and burns fat and calories. Anaerobic exercise, such as weightlifting, involves short bursts of effort. It also helps to build strength and muscle mass.

Playing on a team is a great way to exercise and meet new friends, but it's not for everyone. If you prefer to work out alone, try dancing, jumping rope, jogging, swimming or roller skating.

Don't let bad weather stop you from working up a sweat. Run up and down the stairs in your house or set up an indoor obstacle course. Head to your local YMCA for a swim or a game of hoops.

THE RIGHT STUFF

Nutritionist Jeffrey S. Hampl of Arizona State University has these tips for eating smart:

Encourage your family to keep fresh vegetables and dried fruits on hand. Baby carrots, dried apricots and apples make great snacks, and they're loaded with vitamins.

Go nuts! Peanuts and almonds are easy to eat on the run. They are high in fat, but some of the fat is actually good for you!

Milk is a great source of calcium. Cheese, yogurt and orange juice with calcium added are also good choices.

Most fast food is fattening. If you eat at a fast-food place, don't load up on greasy stuff. Order a salad or some frozen yogurt instead of fries. Try to choose the smallest burger. Don't supersize!

Watch how much soda you drink. It's full of sugar and has no calcium or vitamins. If you drink more than a can a day, try bubbly or flavored water.

Don't eat while watching TV. You don't realize how much you are eating.

Keeping Healthy
The New Guidelines

In 1992, the Department of Health and Human Services and the Department of Agriculture created the food pyramid. It recommended the number of servings of each food group a person should eat daily to stay healthy. The food groups in the pyramid include: grains, vegetables, fruits, dairy, meat, and fats and oils. Today, more than two-thirds of Americans are overweight or obese. So in 2005, the government issued new, tougher guidelines on how to keep healthy and fit. Here are the highlights:

What to Eat and Do

FRUITS AND VEGETABLES Five servings of fruits and vegetables a day–the old standard–aren't enough anymore to maintain good nutrition and prevent disease. The new goal is nine servings of about half a cup each, split between four servings of fruit per day and five of vegetables or legumes, such as beans, peas and lentils.

WHOLE GRAINS Look for whole kernels of wheat or other grains in your bread and cereals. Whole-grain goods are packed with more nutrients than bagels, white bread or cakes and muffins made from refined flours.

EXERCISE For those who have been inactive, try walking briskly or rollerskating for at least 30 minutes most days of the week.

What to Avoid

SODIUM For the first time, the government recommends a target for salt intake–no more than 1 teaspoon of salt a day–to keep blood pressure from rising.

FATS Limit your total fat to 35% or less of daily calories, and keep consumption of trans fats (found in processed foods) to a minimum.

SUGAR It's everywhere, but especially in sodas. In another first, the guidelines suggest that in addition to cutting back on sweet sodas, people should switch to low-fat milk, water or any other beverage that is low in sugar.

Counting Calories

A calorie is a type of measurement that indicates how much energy we get from food. Nutrition labels tell you how many calories a food contains. In general, kids ages 7 to 12 should take in about 2,200 calories each day. Teenage girls also need about 2,200 calories, while teenage boys require about 2,800.

Calorie Consumption

Here's a look at how many calories you can burn per hour for certain activities.

ACTIVITY	CALORIES BURNED
DANCING	210
DOWNHILL SKIING	288
HIKING	288
JOGGING (6 M.P.H.)	790
PLAYING BASKETBALL	380
PLAYING SOCCER	360
ROLLER SKATING (9 M.P.H.)	336
SLEEPING	90

Your Body

If you could peek inside your own body, what would you see? Hundreds of bones, miles of blood vessels and trillions of cells, all of which are constantly working together.

Skin

MAIN JOB: To protect your internal organs from drying up and to prevent harmful bacteria from getting inside your body
HOW MUCH: The average person has about six pounds of skin.

MAIN LAYERS:
- **Epidermis:** Outer layer of skin cells, hair, nails and sweat glands
- **Dermis:** Inner layer of living tissue, containing nerves and blood vessels

Ligaments

MAIN JOB: To hold joints together. These bands of tough tissue are strong and flexible.

Joints

MAIN JOB: To allow bones to move in different directions
DID YOU KNOW? Bones don't bend. Joints allow two bones next to each other to move.

Tendons

MAIN JOB: To hold your muscles to your bones
DID YOU KNOW? Tendons look like rubber bands.

Cells

MAIN JOB: To perform the many jobs necessary to stay alive, such as moving oxygen around your body, taking care of your energy supply and waste removal
DID YOU KNOW? There are 26 billion cells in a newborn baby and 50 trillion cells in an adult.

SOME DIFFERENT CELLS
- **Bone cells** help to build your skeleton by producing the fibers and minerals from which bone is made.
- **Fat cells** contain fat, which is burned to create energy.
- **Muscle cells** are organized into muscles, which move body parts.
- **Nerve cells** pass nerve messages around your body.
- **Red blood cells** carry oxygen around your body.

Muscles

MAIN JOB: To make body movement possible
HOW MANY: Your body has more than 650 muscles.

KINDS OF MUSCLES
- **Skeletal muscles** help the body move. You have about 400 skeletal muscles.
- **Smooth muscles** are located inside organs, like the stomach.
- **Cardiac muscle** is found only in the heart.

Bones

MAIN JOB: To give shape and support to your body
HOW MANY: At birth you had more than 300 bones in your body. As an adult you'll have 206, because some bones fuse together.
DID YOU KNOW? The largest bone in the body is the femur, or thighbone. In a 6-foot-tall person, it is 20 inches long. The smallest is the stirrup bone in the ear. It is one-tenth of an inch long.

KINDS OF BONES

- **Long bones** are thin; they are found in your legs, arms and fingers.
- **Short bones** are wide and chunky; they are found in your feet and wrists.
- **Flat bones** are flat and smooth, like your shoulder blades.
- **Irregular bones**, like the bones in your inner ear and the vertebrae in your spine, come in many different shapes.

Glands

MAIN JOB: To manufacture substances that help your body to function

KINDS OF GLANDS

- **Endocrine glands** make hormones, which tell the different parts of your body when to work.
- **Oil glands** keep your skin from drying out.
- **Salivary glands** make saliva, which helps you to digest and swallow food.
- **Sweat glands** make perspiration, which regulates your body temperature.

Viscera

This term refers to the organs that fill your body's chest and abdominal cavity.
MAIN JOB: To provide your body with food and oxygen and to remove waste
HOW MANY: The viscera include the trachea (windpipe), lungs, liver, kidneys, gallbladder, spleen, stomach, large intestine, small intestine and bladder.

Blood Types

Everyone's blood may look the same, but there are different types of blood. Human blood is grouped into four types: A, B, AB and O. The letters stand for two antigens, or proteins, on the surface of red blood cells. The antigens are A and B.

- **GROUP A** blood has only the A antigen.
- **GROUP B** has only the B antigen.
- **GROUP AB** has both.
- **GROUP O** has neither.

Each blood type is also grouped by its Rhesus factor, or Rh factor. Blood is either Rh positive (Rh+) or Rh negative (Rh−). About 85% of Americans have Rh+ blood.

Giving Blood

You can't donate or receive red blood cells from just anyone. Blood groups need to be matched.

YOUR TYPE	YOU CAN GIVE BLOOD TO	YOU CAN RECEIVE BLOOD FROM
A	TYPE A OR AB	TYPE A OR O
B	TYPE B OR AB	TYPE B OR O
AB	TYPE AB	ANY TYPE OF BLOOD
O	ANY TYPE OF BLOOD	TYPE O

Homework Tip!

Like exercise, doing homework takes energy. Do the assignments that you find most difficult first, when you have more energy. Avoid doing homework when you're tired.

Your Body's Systems

Circulatory System

The circulatory system transports blood throughout the body. The heart pumps the blood and the arteries and veins transport it. Blood is carried away from the heart by arteries. The biggest artery, called the aorta, branches from the left side of the heart into smaller arteries, which then branch into even smaller vessels that travel all over the body. When blood enters the smallest of these vessels, which are called capillaries, it gives nutrients and oxygen to cells and takes in carbon dioxide, water and waste. The blood then returns to the heart through veins. Veins carry waste products away from cells and bring blood back to the heart, which pumps it to the lungs to pick up oxygen and eliminate waste carbon dioxide.

Digestive System

The digestive system breaks down food into protein, vitamins, minerals, carbohydrates and fats, which the body needs for energy, growth and repair. After food is chewed and swallowed, it goes down a tube called the esophagus and enters the stomach, where it is broken down by powerful acids. From the stomach the food travels into the small intestine, where it is broken down into nutrients. The food that the body doesn't need or can't digest is turned into waste and eliminated from the body through the large intestine.

Endocrine System

The endocrine system is made up of glands that produce hormones, the body's long-distance messengers. Hormones are chemicals that control body functions, such as metabolism and growth. The glands, which include the pituitary gland, thyroid gland, adrenal glands, pancreas, ovaries and testes, release hormones into the bloodstream, which then transports the hormones to organs and tissues throughout the body.

Immune System

The immune system is our body's defense system against infections and diseases. It works to respond to dangerous organisms, such as viruses or bacteria, and substances that may enter the body. There are three types of response systems in the immune system:

- **The anatomic response physically prevents dangerous substances from entering your body. The anatomic system includes the skin and the mucous membranes.**
- **The inflammatory system eliminates the invaders from your body. Sneezing and fever are examples of the inflammatory system at work.**
- **The immune response is made up of white blood cells, which fight infection by gobbling up toxins, bacteria and other threats.**

Muscular System

The muscular system is made up of fibrous tissues that work with the skeletal system to control movement of the body. Some muscles—like the ones in your arms, legs, mouth and tongue—are voluntary, meaning that you decide when to move them. Other muscles, like the ones in your stomach, heart, blood vessels and intestines, are involuntary. This means that they're controlled by the nervous system and hormones, and you often don't even realize they're at work.

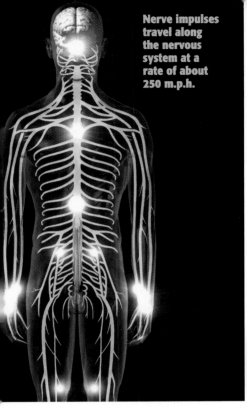

Nerve impulses travel along the nervous system at a rate of about 250 m.p.h.

Respiratory System

The respiratory system brings air into the body and removes carbon dioxide. It includes the nose, trachea (windpipe) and lungs. When you inhale, air enters your nose and goes down the trachea. The trachea branches into two bronchial tubes, which go to the lungs. These tubes branch off into even smaller bronchial tubes, which end in air sacs. Oxygen follows this path and passes through the air sacs and blood vessels and enters the bloodstream. At the same time, carbon dioxide passes into the lungs and is exhaled.

Skeletal System

The skeletal system is made up of bones, ligaments and tendons. It shapes the body and protects organs. The skeletal system works with the muscular system to help the body move.

Nervous System

The nervous system is made up of the brain, the spinal cord and nerves. The nervous system sends and receives nerve impulses that tell your muscles and organs what to do. There are three parts of your nervous system that work together.

- The central nervous system consists of the brain and spinal cord. It sends out nerve impulses and receives sensory information, which tells your brain about things you see, hear, smell, taste and feel.
- The peripheral nervous system includes the nerves that branch off from the brain and the spinal cord. It carries the nerve impulses from the central nervous system to the muscles and glands.
- The autonomic nervous system regulates involuntary action, such as heartbeat and digestion.

TFK Mystery Person

CLUE 1: A pioneer in the medical profession, I was born in England in 1821 and moved to the U.S. when I was 11.

CLUE 2: In 1849, I became the first woman to graduate from medical school. That made me the first female doctor in modern history.

CLUE 3: Hospitals refused to hire a woman physician, so I treated women and children in private practice. Later, I became the first registered female doctor in Britain.

WHO AM I?

(See Answer Key that begins on page 342.)

The Fremont decorated pottery (above left) and etched animals, human figures and spirals on rock panels (above).

Canyon of Treasures

Researchers unearth ancient ruins in Utah

The red dirt of a Utah ranch has been keeping a secret for centuries. In recent years, archaeologists have been uncovering an almost perfectly preserved picture of ancient American-Indian life in Range Creek, a remote canyon located in east-central Utah. "It's like a brand-new library that nobody's ever looked at before," says Kevin Jones, an archaeologist for the state of Utah.

Range Creek holds evidence of the Fremont culture. The Fremont were farmers and hunter-gatherers who lived in the area about 1,000 years ago. Researchers have found more than 300 village sites. They believe that the remote canyon may hold thousands more. "The most astounding thing we've discovered so far in Range Creek is that the

Waldo Wilcox stands at the remains of an ancient American-Indian house.

sites are in fantastic condition," says Jones. "They haven't been damaged."

Time, looters and vandals have taken a heavy toll on other American-Indian sites. But Range Creek's treasures are amazingly well preserved. Archaeologists have found stone pit houses that the Fremont partially dug into the ground. The houses kept people warm in the winter and cool in the summer. High on cliff sides, the Fremont built stone granaries to store grain and corn. Pottery shards and arrowheads are scattered about the area. Researchers have unearthed human bones at four village sites.

SECRET RUINS REVEALED

Waldo Wilcox, a rancher, owned Range Creek for more than 50 years. He kept the historical treasures a secret. "I didn't want people to destroy it," he told TFK. In 2001, he sold the ranch to a conservation group. The group transferred the land to the Bureau of Land Management, which then turned it over to Utah. Range Creek's ruins remained hidden until 2004, when archaeologists revealed the site to reporters.

Now the challenge is to protect the site. "We need to allow people to see it and learn from it in a way that doesn't wreck it," Jones says.

—By Jennifer Marino

History

A Shaken City

On April 18, 1906, a large swath of California rocked—literally. Almost 300 miles of the San Andreas fault shifted, causing an enormous earthquake in San Francisco. The quake lasted only 47 seconds, but it was felt hundreds of miles away.

More than 500 people died in what was then the nation's most destructive natural disaster. Fires, mainly caused by broken gas mains, raged throughout the city for three days after the earthquake. The earthquake also broke water lines, making it very difficult for firefighters to battle the blazes. The infernos devastated 490 city blocks and a total of 25,000 buildings and left about 250,000 people homeless. The earthquake and the fires nearly destroyed the city.

San Francisco and its brave residents recovered quickly from the tragedy. The city grew into a leading transportation, industrial and cultural center.

The earthquake caused more than $350 million worth of damage.

TFK Puzzles & Games

Freedom Fighters

Many leaders have worked hard for the fair treatment of African Americans. Unscramble the name of the hero in each sentence.

1. RRIETHA BUTNAM helped slaves escape the South in the 1800s.

2. KICERFDER SSDUOLAG fought for the rights of blacks in the 1800s.

3. In 1955, SARO KRPAS refused to give up her bus seat to a white man.

4. In 1947, CKAIEJ BONRISNO was the first black to play modern Major League Baseball.

5. EJSSE AONCKJS ran for President twice in the 1980s.

(See Answer Key that begins on page 342.)

TFK Mystery Person

CLUE 1: I was the original Dracula. I was born in Transylvania in 1431. Transylvania is now part of Romania.

CLUE 2: I belonged to a club called the Order of the Dragon. That's how I got my nickname, Dracula. It comes from *draco*, which is Latin for "dragon."

CLUE 3: People feared me. I was a cruel leader. But I wasn't a vampire!

WHO AM I?

(See Answer Key that begins on page 342.)

Ancient HISTORY

3000–2000 B.C.

600–500 B.C.

10,000–4000 B.C. In Mesopotamia, settlements develop into cities, and people learn to use the wheel.

4500–4000 B.C Earliest known civilization arises in Sumer.

3000–2000 B.C. The rule of the pharaohs begins in Egypt. King Khufu completes construction of the Great Pyramid at Giza (ca.* 2680 B.C.), and King Khafre builds the Great Sphinx of Giza (ca. 2540 B.C.).

3000–1500 B.C. The Indus Valley civilization flourishes in what is today Pakistan. In Britain, Stonehenge is erected.

1500–1000 B.C. Moses leads the Israelites out of Egypt and delivers the Ten Commandments. Chinese civilization develops under the Shang Dynasty.

1000–900 B.C. Hebrew elders begin to write the books of the Hebrew Bible.

900–800 B.C Phoenicians establish Carthage (ca. 810 B.C.). The *Iliad* and the *Odyssey* are composed, probably by the Greek poet Homer.

800–700 B.C. The first recorded Olympic games (776 B.C.) take place.

700–600 B.C Lao-tse, Chinese philosopher and founder of Taoism, is born (604 B.C.).

600–500 B.C Confucius (551–479 B.C.) develops his philosophy in China. Buddha (ca. 563–483 B.C.) founds Buddhism in India.

800–700 B.C.

500–400 B.C. Greek culture flourishes during the age of Pericles (450–400 B.C.). The Parthenon is built in Athens as a temple of the goddess Athena (447–432 B.C.).

400–300 B.C. Alexander the Great (356–323 B.C.) destroys Thebes (335 B.C.), conquers Tyre and Jerusalem (332 B.C.), occupies Babylon (330 B.C.) and invades India.

300–250 B.C. The Temple of the Sun is built at Teotihuacán, Mexico (ca. 300 B.C.).

250–200 B.C. The Great Wall of China is built (ca. 215 B.C.).

250–200 B.C.

100–31 B.C. Julius Caesar (100–44 B.C.) invades Britain (55 B.C.) and conquers Gaul (France) (ca. 50 B.C.). Cleopatra rules Egypt (51–31 B.C.).

44 B.C. Julius Caesar is murdered.

*ca. is an abbreviation for circa, which means around.

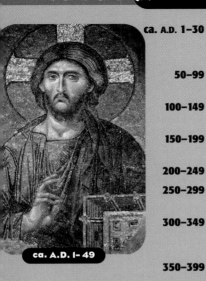

ca. A.D. 1–49

ca. A.D. 1–30	Life of Jesus Christ (ca. A.D. 1–30). Emperor Kuang Wu Ti founds Han dynasty in China. Buddhism introduced to China.
50–99	Jews revolt against the Romans; Jerusalem destroyed (A.D. 70).
100–149	The great Emperor Hadrian rules Rome. (A.D. 117–138).
150–199	The earliest Mayan temples are built in Central America.
200–249	Goths invade Asia Minor (ca. A.D. 220).
250–299	Mayan civilization (A.D. 250–900) has advances in art, architecture and science.
300–349	Constantine the Great (rules A.D. 312–337) unites eastern and western Roman empires, with new capital at Constantinople (A.D. 330).
350–399	Huns (Mongols) invade Europe (ca. A.D. 360).
400–449	St. Patrick returns to Ireland (A.D. 432) and brings Christianity to the island.
450–499	Vandals destroy Rome (A.D. 455).
500–549	Arthur, king of the Britons, is killed around 537.
550–599	After killing about half the European population, plague subsides (594).
600–649	Muhammad, founder of Islam, flees from Mecca to Medina (the Hegira, 622). Arabs conquer Jerusalem (637) and destroy the Alexandrian library (641).
650–699	Arabs attack North Africa (670) and destroy Carthage (697).
700–749	Arab empire extends from Lisbon to China (by 716).
750–799	City of Machu Picchu flourishes in Peru.
800–849	Charlemagne is crowned first Holy Roman Emperor in Rome (800).
850–899	Russian nation is founded by Vikings under Prince Rurik (855–879).
900–949	Vikings discover Greenland (ca. 900). Arab Spain under Abd al-Rahman III becomes center of learning (912–961).
950–999	Erik the Red establishes first Viking colony in Greenland (982).

600–649

900–949

ca. 1000–1300

ca. 1000–1300	The Pueblo period of Anasazi culture flourishes; cliff dwellings are built.
ca. 1000	Viking raider Leif Eriksson reaches North America.
ca. 1008	Murasaki Shikibu finishes *The Tale of Genji*, the world's first novel.
1066	William of Normandy invades England; is crowned William I "the Conqueror."
1096	Pope Urban II launches the First Crusade, one of at least eight European military campaigns between 1095 and 1291 to take the Holy Land from the Muslims.
ca. 1150	The temple complex of Angkor Wat is completed in Cambodia.
1211	Genghis Khan invades China, captures Peking (1214), conquers Persia (1218) and invades Russia (1223).
1215	Britain's King John is forced by barons to sign the Magna Carta, limiting royal power.
1231	The Inquisition begins as the Roman Catholic Church fights heresy; torture is used.
1251	Kublai Khan governs China.
1271	Marco Polo of Venice travels to China; visits court of Kublai Khan (1275–1292).
1312–1337	The Mali Empire reaches its height in Africa under King Mansa Musa.
ca. 1325	Aztecs establish Tenochtitlán on the site of modern Mexico City.
1337–1453	In the Hundred Years' War, English and French kings fight for control of France.
1347–1351	At least 25 million people die in Europe's Black Death (bubonic plague).
1368	The Ming Dynasty begins in China.
ca. 1387	Geoffrey Chaucer writes *The Canterbury Tales*.
1428	Joan of Arc leads the French against the English.
1438	The Incas rule in Peru.
1450	Florence, Italy, becomes the center of Renaissance art and learning.
1453	The Turks conquer Constantinople, thus beginning the Ottoman Empire.
1455	Johannes Gutenberg invents the printing press.
1462	Ivan the Great rules Russia until 1505 as first czar.
1492	Christopher Columbus reaches the New World.

1271

1492

ca. 1503

1501	The first African slaves in America are brought to the Spanish colony of Santo Domingo.
ca. 1503	Leonardo da Vinci paints the *Mona Lisa*.
1509	Henry VIII takes the English throne. Michelangelo begins painting the ceiling of the Sistine Chapel.
1517	Martin Luther objects to wrongdoing in the Catholic Church; start of Protestantism.
1519	Hernando Cortés conquers Mexico for Spain.
1520	Suleiman I "the Magnificent" becomes Sultan of Turkey.
1522	Portuguese explorer Ferdinand Magellan's expedition circumnavigates the globe.
1543	Copernicus publishes his theory that Earth revolves around the Sun.
1547	Ivan IV "the Terrible" is crowned czar of Russia.
1588	The Spanish Armada is defeated by the English.
1609	Galileo makes the first astronomical observations using a telescope.

1620

1618	Thirty Years' War begins. European Protestants revolt against Catholic oppression.
1620	Pilgrims, after a three-month voyage aboard the *Mayflower*, land at Plymouth Rock.

1789

1775	The American Revolution begins with the Battle of Lexington and Concord.
1776	The U.S. Declaration of Independence is signed.
1783	The American Revolution ends with the Treaty of Paris.
1789	The French Revolution begins with the storming of the Bastille.
1819	Simón Bolívar leads wars for independence throughout South America.
1824	Mexico becomes a republic, three years after declaring independence from Spain.
1846	Failure of potato crop causes famine in Ireland.
1861	The U.S. Civil War begins as attempts to reach a compromise on slavery fail.
1865	The U.S. Civil War ends.
1884	The Berlin West Africa Conference is held; Europe colonizes the African continent.
1893	New Zealand becomes the first country in the world to give women the right to vote.
1898	The Spanish-American War begins.

1909

1903 The Wright brothers fly the first powered airplane at Kitty Hawk, North Carolina.

1904 The Russo-Japanese War begins, as competition for Korea and Manchuria heats up.

1909 U.S. explorers Robert E. Peary and Matthew Henson reach the North Pole. The National Association for the Advancement of Colored People (NAACP) is founded in New York City.

1912 The *Titanic* sinks on its maiden voyage; more than 1,500 drown.

1914 World War I begins.

1917 U.S. enters World War I. Russian Revolution begins.

1918 World War I fighting ends. A worldwide flu epidemic strikes; by 1920, about 20 million are dead.

1919 Mahatma Gandhi begins his nonviolent resistance against British rule in India.

1924 Joseph Stalin begins his rule as Soviet dictator, which lasts until his death in 1953.

1929 In the U.S., stock market prices collapse and the Depression begins.

1933 Adolf Hitler is appointed German Chancellor; Nazi oppression begins. Franklin Delano Roosevelt is inaugurated U.S. President; he launches the New Deal.

1937 The Nazis open their first concentration camp (Buchenwald); by 1945, the Nazis had murdered some 6 million Jews in what is now called the Holocaust.

1939 World War II begins.

1941 A Japanese attack on the U.S. fleet at Pearl Harbor in Hawaii (December 7) brings U.S. into World War II. Manhattan Project (atom bomb research) begins.

1945 War ends in Europe on V-E Day (May 8). The U.S. drops the atom bomb on Hiroshima, Japan (August 6), and Nagasaki, Japan (August 9). The war ends in the Pacific on V-J day (September 2).

1947 The U.S. Marshall Plan is proposed to help Europe recover from the war. India and Pakistan gain independence from Britain.

1948 The existence of the nation of Israel is proclaimed.

1949 The North Atlantic Treaty Organization (NATO) is founded. Communist People's Republic of China is proclaimed by Chairman Mao Zedong. South Africa sets up apartheid (a policy of discrimination against nonwhites).

1950 Korean War begins when North Korean Communist forces invade South Korea. It lasts three years.

1957 Russians launch *Sputnik I*, the first Earth-orbiting satellite; the space race begins.

1945

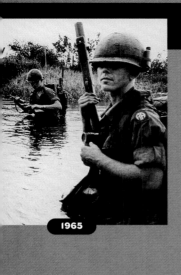

1979

1965

2003

1963 Martin Luther King Jr. delivers his "I have a dream" speech in Washington, D.C. President John F. Kennedy is killed by a sniper in Dallas.

1965 U.S. planes begin combat missions in Vietnam War.

1967 Israeli and Arab forces battle; Six-Day War ends with Israel occupying Sinai Peninsula, Golan Heights, Gaza Strip and part of the Suez Canal.

1969 *Apollo 11* astronauts take man's first walk on the Moon.

1973 Vietnam War ends with the signing of peace pacts. The Yom Kippur War begins as Egyptian and Syrian forces attack Israel.

1979 Muslim leader Ayatollah Khomeini takes over Iran; U.S. citizens seized and held hostage.

1981 Scientists identify the AIDS virus.

1989 Thousands rallying for democracy are killed in Tiananmen Square, China. After 28 years, the Berlin Wall that divided Germany is torn down.

1990 South Africa frees Nelson Mandela, who was imprisoned 27 years. Iraqi troops invade Kuwait, setting off nine-month Persian Gulf War.

1991 The Soviet Union breaks up after President Mikhail Gorbachev resigns. In Yugoslavia, Slovenia and Croatia secede; a four-year war with Serbia begins.

1994 South Africa holds first interracial national election; Nelson Mandela is elected President.

2000 Elections in Yugoslavia formally end the brutal rule of Slobodan Milosevic.

2001 On Sept. 11, hijackers crash two jetliners into New York City's World Trade Center, another into the Pentagon and a fourth in rural Pennsylvania. In response, U.S. and British forces attack the Taliban government and bomb al-Qaeda terrorist camps in Afghanistan.

2003 The U.S. and Britain lead an invasion of Iraq. Their forces topple Saddam Hussein's government within weeks. U.S. troops capture the former dictator.

2004 The U.S. transfers power of Iraq to an interim Iraqi government. Hamid Karzai is elected president of Afghanistan. An underwater earthquake in the Indian Ocean causes a raging tsunami that devastates several Asian countries and parts of East Africa; more than 280,000 people die in the disaster.

2005 Iraq holds democratic elections for the first time in 50 years.

1991

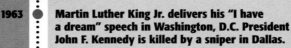

115

1773

1607	Jamestown, the first permanent English settlement in America, is established in Virginia.
1620	After a three-month voyage aboard the *Mayflower*, the Pilgrims land at Plymouth in Massachusetts.
1770	In the Boston Massacre, British troops fire into a mob, killing five men.
1773	A group of colonists dump tea into Boston Harbor to protest the British tea tax. The event becomes known as the Boston Tea Party.
1775	The American Revolution begins with the Battle of Lexington and Concord.
1776	The Continental Congress adopts the Declaration of Independence; the United States is born.
1783	The American Revolution officially ends with the signing of the Treaty of Paris.
1787	Delegates from 12 of the original 13 colonies meet in Philadelphia to draft the U.S. Constitution.
1789	George Washington is unanimously elected President of the U.S. The U.S. Constitution goes into effect.
1791	The first 10 Amendments to the Constitution, known as the Bill of Rights, are ratified.
1803	The U.S. purchases the Louisiana Territory from France; this nearly doubles the size of the U.S.
1804	Meriwether Lewis and William Clark set out from St. Louis, Missouri, to explore the West and to find a route to the Pacific Ocean.
1805	Lewis and Clark reach the Pacific Ocean.
1812	The U.S. declares war on Britain for interfering with American shipping and westward expansion. It becomes known as the War of 1812.
1814	Francis Scott Key writes the "Star-Spangled Banner." The Treaty of Ghent ends the War of 1812.
1819	The U.S acquires Florida from Spain.
1823	President Monroe declares in the Monroe Doctrine that the Americas are to be off-limits for further colonization by European powers.

1814

1836 Texas declares its independence from Mexico. All the Texan defenders of the Alamo are killed in a siege by the Mexican Army.

1838 More than 15,000 Cherokee Indians are forced to march from Georgia to Indian Territory in present-day Oklahoma. About 4,000 die from starvation and disease along the "Trail of Tears."

1845 Texas becomes a state.

1846 The U.S. declares war on Mexico to gain territory in the Southwest.

1848 The Mexican War ends; the U.S. gains territory comprising present-day California, Nevada, Utah, most of New Mexico and Arizona and parts of Colorado and Wyoming.

1849 Gold is discovered at Sutter's Mill in California.

1854 Congress establishes the territories of Kansas and Nebraska. Tensions rise between those who want them to be free states and those who want them to be slave states.

1857 Abolitionist John Brown and 21 followers try to spark a slave revolt by capturing a government arms depot in Harpers Ferry, West Virginia.

1838

1857

1860 Following the election of Abraham Lincoln as President, South Carolina secedes from the U.S.

1861 More Southern states secede from the U.S. and form the Confederate States of America, with Jefferson Davis as President. The Civil War, a conflict between the North (the Union) and the South (the Confederacy) over the expansion of slavery, begins when the Confederates attack Fort Sumter in Charleston, South Carolina.

1863 Lincoln issues the Emancipation Proclamation, freeing slaves in the Confederate states.

1865 The Civil War ends with the surrender of Confederate general Robert E. Lee to Union general Ulysses S. Grant. Lincoln is assassinated by John Wilkes Booth. The 13th Amendment to the Constitution is ratified, prohibiting slavery.

1867 The U.S. purchases Alaska from Russia.

1869 The Central Pacific and Union Pacific railroads are joined at Promontory, Utah, creating the first transcontinental (cross-country) railroad.

1869

1919

1945

1890	The last major battle of the Indian Wars occurs at Wounded Knee in South Dakota.
1898	The U.S.S. *Maine* is blown up in Havana harbor, which leads the U.S. to declare war on Spain. As a result of winning the Spanish-American War, the U.S. acquires Puerto Rico, Guam and the Philippines.
1917	The U.S. enters World War I by declaring war on Germany and Austria-Hungary.
1920	The 19th Amendment to the Constitution is ratified, giving women the right to vote.
1929	The U.S. stock market crashes, and the Great Depression begins.
1933	President Franklin Roosevelt's economic recovery measures, known as the New Deal, are enacted by Congress.
1941	Japan attacks the U.S. naval base at Pearl Harbor, Hawaii, leading to the U.S.'s entry into World War II.
1945	Germany surrenders, marking the end of World War II in Europe. The U.S. drops two atom bombs on Japan. Japan surrenders, and World War II ends in the Pacific.
1950	The Korean War begins as the U.S. sends troops to defend South Korea against communist North Korea.
1953	The Korean War ends.
1954	The Supreme Court decision *Brown v. Board of Education of Topeka, Kansas*, declares that racial segregation of schools is unconstitutional.
1955	Rosa Parks refuses to sit at the back of the bus. Martin Luther King Jr. leads a black boycott of the Montgomery, Alabama, bus system.
1963	President John F. Kennedy is assassinated in Dallas, Texas.
1965	The first U.S. combat troops arrive in South Vietnam.
1968	Martin Luther King Jr. is assassinated in Memphis, Tennessee.
1969	Astronauts Neil Armstrong and Edwin Aldrin Jr. become the first men to land on the moon.
1973	The U.S., North Vietnam, South Vietnam and the National Liberation Front (Viet Cong) sign peace pacts in Paris. The U.S. withdraws from Vietnam.

1963

1974

1974 President Nixon resigns as a result of the Watergate scandal.

1979 Iranian students storm the U.S. embassy in Tehran and hold 66 people hostage.

1981 The U.S. hostages held in Iran are released after 444 days in captivity.

1986 The space shuttle *Challenger* explodes 73 seconds after liftoff.

1991 The U.S. and its allies fight in the first Persian Gulf War, driving the Iraqis out of Kuwait.

1992 President George H.W. Bush and Russian President Boris Yeltsin formally declare an end to the cold war.

1998 The House of Representatives votes to impeach President Bill Clinton.

1999 The Senate acquits Clinton of impeachment charges.

2000 The presidential contest between Al Gore and George W. Bush is one of the closest elections in U.S. history. The U.S. Supreme Court determines the outcome, and Bush is declared the winner.

2000

2001 Hijackers crash two jetliners into New York City's World Trade Center and another into the Pentagon. A fourth hijacked plane crashes in rural Pennsylvania. President Bush declares war on terrorism, and

2001

U.S. and British forces topple the Taliban government and attack Osama bin Laden's al-Qaeda terrorist camps in Afghanistan.

2002 A wave of corporate accounting scandals rocks the U.S. economy as Enron and several other companies are investigated by federal authorities.

2003 Seven astronauts die when the space shuttle *Columbia* explodes upon re-entry into the Earth's atmosphere. The U.S. and Britain lead a war in Iraq and topple dictator Saddam Hussein. Troops capture Hussein in December.

2004 The U.S. transfers control of Iraq to an interim Iraqi government led by Prime Minister Iyad Allawi.

2003

SEPARATED AT SCHOOL

Whittier sixth-grader Consuelo Moreno in her all-girl classroom

Do boys and girls learn better apart? Under new rules, more schools may find out.

Since school started, not one boy has raised his hand in Maritza De La Pena's sixth-grade class. And during discussions, boys never speak up. Why not? Because it's a girls-only class!

Whittier Middle School is one of nine public middle schools in the San Antonio, Texas, school district that offers single-gender education. Both boys and girls go to Whittier, and the seventh- and eighth-grade students are in mixed classes. All but one group of the sixth graders are in boys- or girls-only classes.

Maritza, 11, says that she notices a big change in her classmates. "Boys want to compete and answer first," Maritza told TFK. "Girls would be quiet. Now, we're not quiet."

A UNIQUE KIND OF CLASSROOM

Ninety-three public schools in the U.S. have either all boy students, all girl students or some single-gender classes. There is not a lot of research on the topic, but there is some evidence that single-gender learning can help improve school performance. Teachers say kids are more focused and better behaved.

Officials at the U.S. Department of Education have proposed regulations that would make it easier for public-school districts to create single-gender classrooms and schools. Right now, a federal law called Title IX *(see box on page 121)* applies strict rules on single-gender schooling.

The new proposals would relax the rules. Public schools could create single-gender classes simply to provide more learning options or because their community wants such classes. And they wouldn't have to create identical programs for boys and girls.

Some critics fear that boys and girls won't learn to get along if they're separated. Others warn that the new rules violate Title IX and could lead to discrimination against girls in the classroom. "The concern we have is that it will endanger the gains that girls and women have made over the last 30 years," says Jocelyn Samuels of the National Women's Law Center.

But one supporter, Leonard Sax, a psychologist, says that it comes down to "basic science." Sax is the executive director of the National Association of Single Sex Public Education. He says that a boy's brain does not develop the same as a girl's, and the dissimilarities cause each to learn in different ways.

SO FAR, SO GOOD IN SAN ANTONIO

Peggy Stark is San Antonio's assistant superintendent of special programs. She has already heard from happy teachers in the single-sex program. "They can see real differences in the way girls respond in math and science," she says.

Are single-gender classes better? That may depend on what you want to learn. Whittier sixth-grader John Mireles, 11, would prefer a mixed class. "When it's mixed," he says, "you can learn more about the girls."

—By Kathryn Satterfield

John Mireles is in a Whittier classroom that has no girls.

What Is Title IX?

In 1972, Congress passed Title IX, a federal law that prohibits discrimination based on gender in schools that receive government funds.

Before Title IX, women and girls were treated unequally in most schools. Few colleges offered women athletic scholarships. In high schools, girls were discouraged from studying subjects like math. Title IX was passed to ensure that girls have the same opportunities as boys in the classroom and on the playing field.

Today, supporters point to Title IX's successes. For example, fewer than

Do single-gender classrooms violate Title IX?

30,000 women participated in college sports in 1972. By 2003, some 160,000 college women were competing.

Colleges must follow rules to show they offer equality in women's and men's sports. Opponents of Title IX say some successful men's teams have been eliminated by schools trying to keep things equal.

No boys are allowed in this Whittier classroom.

Facing the Blank Page

The staff members at *TIME For Kids* magazine go through the same challenges that you do as you write: finding a topic; researching facts; getting organized; writing a draft; revising; editing and proofreading. Writing is a process, and by using a series of steps you can become a better writer. Here are some of the staff members' ideas, thoughts and strategies about writing.

Getting Started: Gathering the Facts

Finding good ideas to write about can be difficult. Many writers use a variety of strategies to help them get started. You may be assigned topics to write about, or you might have to come up with ideas on your own.

EDITOR MARTHA PICKERILL tells how she starts an assignment:
"When I write a story, I begin by gathering every piece of information I think I'll need. As soon as I have gathered all of my interviews, news reports and background information from books and the Internet, I read over every bit of it at least twice. Sometimes I determine that important facts are missing, and I do a bit more research to fill in the gaps. Having all the necessary facts strengthens any writer's work.

"The shape of the story starts to come together in my head as I read over my research. For a short news story, I sort of talk myself through an outline: I'll lead with that great quote, followed by two paragraphs describing exactly what happened. Then I should have room to refer back to the last time such a thing happened, or have some other connection to put the story in context. Sometimes, I'll finish with an expert's quote saying why this event is important.

"When I cook up my plan, I mentally check off the **five Ws (WHO, WHAT, WHERE, WHY, WHEN)** and **H (HOW)** to make sure the basic questions will be covered."

making a Plan

How do you plan and organize a story? Some writers use an outline to organize the facts and details they want to include in a story. **WRITER RITU UPADHYAY** shares one way of getting organized:

"Once I've done the reporting and research, I write an outline to help me get focused. Planning ahead ensures that I get in all the major points I want to include in my story. Organizing the information into sections gives structure to the story. Of course, the outline can change once I start writing, but it's really helpful to have something to use as a guide when I begin. For example, when I wrote a story about Cleopatra's lost city, I made a quick outline."

I. Introduction
    A. Cleopatra's underwater city
    B. Who is Cleopatra?
    C. Why did the city sink?

II. The city rediscovered
    A. Recovering the artifacts
    B. The city's first complete map
        1. New view of the city
        2. Map might change

III. Other finds from the underwater city
    A. Cleopatra's personal temple
    B. Statues

IV. Recovering artifacts
    A. How it is done
    B. Future expeditions

V. Conclusion

TFK Top 5

Favorite Subjects

Can you guess which school subjects kids like best? (Recess does not count.) Researchers asked 1,016 students ages 10 to 17. More than 1 in 4 picked math. Go figure! Here are the subjects that make the grade:

1. Math—28%

2. Science—21%

3. Art—16%

4. History/Social Studies—15%

5. English—13%

Source: Peter D. Hart Research Associates for National Science Foundation, Bayer

Homework Tip!

Set up a quiet, comfortable place to do your homework each day. Avoid places with loud music, television or other distractions.

Writing a First Draft

You have an idea and a plan. Now you are ready to write the first draft. Your goal is to get all your ideas down on paper.

As **RITU UPADHYAY** wrote her story (below) on Cleopatra's lost city, she included notes on the side. They will help her to improve the next draft.

Describe how the city was preserved

More than 1,600 years ago, a royal court full of treasures was swallowed up by the sea. The island of Antirhodos, home of Cleopatra, the famous Queen of Egypt, sank after the area was hit by a huge earthquake in A.D. 335. Along with the island, part of Alexandria, Egypt's harbor city, also disappeared. For centuries, the palace buildings and statues lay 30 feet underwater, 3.5 miles off the coast of northern Egypt.

Add pronunciation guide

Put in a quote from Goddio

Add what will happen next now that the map is completed

In 1996, French explorer Franck Goddio rediscovered the fabled city. He and his team of divers have been working on excavating the site ever since. Goddio recently unveiled the first map of the old city.

Add where he made his announcement about the map

Describe Ms. Hendrickson's job

Over the past few years, the group has uncovered many artifacts. "We're looking right at statues from 2,000 years ago that look just as they did back then," says Sue Hendrickson. Along with statues, the team has found buildings and temples that are still standing underwater.

Check if the word is correct

Explain why the divers do this

The marine biologists working in Alexandria are careful not to disturb the city. "We are just mapping it, cleaning it up and leaving it all as we've found it," says Hendrickson. Sometimes the divers bring up a statue to study or photograph, but they always return it to its home underwater. Goddio's team hopes that one day the government of Egypt will allow tourists to dive down and experience the splendor of Cleopatra's palace for themselves.

Change conclusion?

Homework Tip!
If you are having trouble with homework, ask for help from friends, parents or teachers.

Writing a Paragraph

Words, sentences and paragraphs are the building blocks of writing, says **ASSOCIATE EDITOR KATHRYN R. SATTERFIELD.** A paragraph is made up of one or more sentences that support the subject or idea of the paragraph. Check out the example below.

This is the main idea of the paragraph. ⟶

This detail supports the facts. ⟶

So what's the big deal if you're a bit tired? Getting too little sleep can affect your mood, your coordination, how well you learn and even your speech. Studies of people who volunteer to go without sleep have shown that they have trouble with memory and can't concentrate well enough to do a task as simple as adding numbers. The biggest change, though, is in your mood. Exhaustion makes you grouchy and depressed.

⟵ *These facts give more information about the main idea.*

⟵ *This closing sentence ends the paragraph.*

Taking the Lead!

Kathryn explains why she works hard at writing a lead, or introduction, to a news story.

"A good introduction should grab the reader's attention by revealing something unique or exciting. When working on an introduction, I ask myself what makes the story interesting. Is there a surprising anecdote or an unusual fact that stands out? If so, introducing the information in the lead will make the reader curious.

"I wrote two introductions for a story about a Native American school. Can you see why I chose the first one to go with my story?"

Introduction 1

The kids at the Akwesane Freedom School in Rooseveltown, New York, start their day the same way lots of other kids around the U.S. do—chatting about Harry Potter, Hilary Duff, the latest Nintendo games and sports. But when class begins, their day takes on a different sound.

This introduction gives a glimpse of the Akwesane school. It shows similarities between the readers and the Akwesane students. The last sentence is a good transition sentence; it sets the tone for some new information.

Introduction 2

The kids at Akwesane Freedom School in Rooseveltown, New York, aren't allowed to speak any English in the classroom. In fact, the students won't speak a word of English until school lets out in the afternoon. Some don't even use it at home. "I never, ever speak it to my mom and dad," says Karonhiakwekon—in perfect English.

This introduction gives too much infor- mation, and that information is weaker than the first. The reader isn't yet aware that the student's difficult name is in his native language.

125

Why Revise?

Revising means making changes. Writers do a lot of revising because first drafts can always be improved. **DEPUTY EDITOR NELLIE GONZALEZ CUTLER** explains why she revises:

"Revising is one of the most important parts of the writing process. After I've written a first draft of a story, I reread it carefully. Then I mark the areas that need work.

"First, I review the overall structure of the story. Are all the paragraphs arranged in a logical order? Does the first paragraph have an idea and explain it clearly? Do the other paragraphs move the story along? If necessary, I rearrange paragraphs.

"Next, I target specific sentences. I ask myself several questions: Is the writing lively and engaging? Does the story have enough quotes? Do these quotes help tell the story? Does the last paragraph sum up or end the story?

"Finally, I reread the story again, this time circling words that I may have repeated and making sure all the sentences are in the correct tense. I also check to see that words are spelled correctly.

"After making corrections on my first draft, I write a second draft and repeat the entire process. I'll do this as many times as necessary—some stories need only one draft, others need several rewrites! Remember: write, read, revise and repeat!"

Revision Checklist

A checklist can help you remember what to look for when you revise your writing. Use this list as a guide.

Stay Focused on the Topic

❏ **Do I have a topic sentence, the main idea of my writing?**
❏ **Do I stay on my topic throughout my paper?**
❏ **Does my paper make sense?**

Support the Topic

❏ **Do I use details, facts or examples to support my main idea?**
❏ **Do I need to add more details, facts or examples?**
❏ **Do I say enough about my topic?**

Organize the Writing

❏ **Do I have an introduction that tells my reader what my story will be about?**
❏ **Do I use supporting paragraphs to build my story?**
❏ **Are my ideas in the best order?**
❏ **Do I have a conclusion that ends my story?**
❏ **Is my writing easy to follow?**

Make Needed Changes

❏ **Do I use descriptive words to explain my ideas?**
❏ **Do I use a variety of words?**

Hunting for Errors

In this stage of the writing process, TFK writers rely on copy editors to make sure their writing is free of errors.

COPY EDITOR STEVE LEVINE finds and corrects errors in usage, style and spelling. As he reads a story, he makes sure that:

- **each sentence has a subject and a verb.**
- **each sentence makes sense.**
- **each sentence begins with a capital letter.**
- **each sentence ends with a punctuation mark.**
- **words are correctly capitalized.**
- **commas are used when needed.**
- **quotation marks are used correctly.**
- **the subject and the verb agree.**
- **words are not repeated.**
- **words are spelled correctly.**

Steve reads to make sure there are no fragments or run-on sentences.

FOR EXAMPLE:

> Ran away.

This sentence is a fragment. It doesn't have a subject. To correct this fragment, Steve gives it a subject.

> The black bear ran away.

A run-on sentence never seems to end.

FOR EXAMPLE:

> The black bear ran away from the scientists they had wanted to catch the bear for a study.

To correct this run-on, he splits it into two separate sentences.

> The black bear ran away from the scientists. They had wanted to catch the bear for a study.

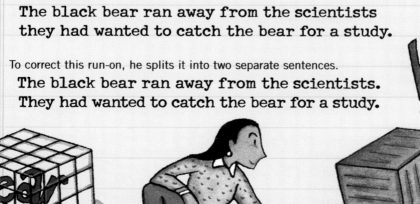

Common Editing Symbols

Editors use symbols to correct writing mistakes. These symbols let writers know what writing changes need to be made.

make an uppercase letter.

Make a **l**owercase **l**etter.

Add a comma please.

Add quotation marks.

Add a period⊙

Take it out.

Add a well⹀ placed hyphen.

¶ Start a new paragraph; the first sentence of the paragraph should be indented.

Checklist for Expository Writing

The type of writing the editors of *TIME For Kids* do is called expository writing. Expository writing is nonfiction. It gives facts and explanations. Use this checklist to be sure you have done everything you need to do for your writing assignment.

❏ My writing is organized clearly and logically.
❏ I have taken out all details that do not belong in my writing.
❏ I keep a record of all books and other sources of information.
❏ I use a consistent point of view.
❏ I use descriptive language.
❏ I use adjectives and adverbs to make my writing lively.
❏ I use figurative language, such as metaphors and similes.
❏ I use original language to create my own style.
❏ I have tried to make this writing interesting for my readers.
❏ I have made the purpose of my writing clear.
❏ I have proofread my writing.
❏ Others have read my writing (classmates or teachers, for example).
❏ I have revised my writing.
❏ My writing is the best that I can make it.

How to Write a Narrative Essay

The first important thing to remember about a narrative essay is that it tells a story. You may write about:

- an experience or event from your past.
- a recent or an ongoing experience or event.
- something that happened to somebody else, such as a parent or a grandparent.

Learning something new can be a scary experience. One of the hardest things I've ever had to do was to learn how to swim. I was always afraid of the water, but I decided that swimming was an important skill that I should learn.

The second important thing is that in a narrative essay the story should have a point. In the final paragraph, you should come to a conclusion about the story you told.

Learning to swim was not easy for me, but in the end my efforts paid off. Now when I am faced with a new situation I am not so nervous. I may feel uncomfortable at first, but I know that as my skills improve, I will feel more and more comfortable.

The conclusion is where the author reflects on the larger meaning of the experience described. In this case, the author concludes that learning to swim has helped her to feel more confident about herself in new situations. The idea that self-confidence comes from conquering your fears is something that anyone can relate to. It is the point of this essay.

GET PERSONAL!

The writing in an essay should be lively and engaging. Try to keep the reader's interest by adding details or observations. Sharing your thoughts invites the reader into your world and makes the story more personal and more interesting.

Homework Tip!

If you're conducting an interview for a research paper, avoid asking "yes" or "no" questions. You'll get much more interesting answers if your questions require an explanation.

How to Write a Persuasive Essay

The purpose of a persuasive essay is to convince the reader to agree with your viewpoint or to accept your recommendation for a course of action. For instance, you might argue that the salaries of professional athletes are too high. Or you might recommend that vending machines be banned from your school cafeteria. A successful persuasive essay will use evidence to support your viewpoint, consider opposing views and present a strong conclusion.

Some people worry that adopting a school-uniform policy would be too expensive for families. However, there are ways to lessen the cost. For example, in Seattle, Washington, local businesses pay for uniforms at South Shore Middle School. In Long Beach, California, graduating students donate or sell their old uniforms to other students.

Use evidence to support your viewpoint. Statistics, facts, quotations from experts and examples will help you build a strong case for your argument. Appeal to the reader's sense of logic by presenting specific and relevant evidence in a well-organized manner.

Homework Tip!
Make homework part of your daily schedule. If you don't get any, read or write for pleasure.

Consider opposing views. Try to anticipate the concerns and questions that a reader might have about your subject. Responding to these points will give you the chance to explain to the reader why your viewpoint or recommendation is the best one.

Present a strong conclusion. All your evidence and explanations should build toward a strong ending in which you summarize your view in a clear and memorable way. The conclusion in a persuasive essay might include a call to action.

REMEMBER: Use a pleasant, reasonable tone in your essay. Sarcasm and arrogance weaken an argument. Logic and fairness will help to keep it strong.

go **Read sample persuasive essays at timeforkids.com/persuasive**

Tackle a Descriptive Essay

The purpose of a descriptive essay is to describe a person, place or thing in such vivid detail that the reader can easily form a mental picture. You may accomplish this by using words that create a mood, making interesting comparisons and describing images that appeal to the senses.

I have always been fascinated by carnival rides. My first experience with a carnival ride was a Ferris wheel at a local fair. It was huge, smoky and noisy. Ever since that first impression years ago, these rides have reminded me of mythical beasts carrying off their screaming passengers. Even the droning sound of their engines brings to mind the great roar of a fire-breathing dragon.

Mood Words The author uses words that create excitement, like "fascinated," "great roar" and "fire-breathing dragon."

Interesting Comparisons One way the author makes his subject interesting is by comparing the Ferris wheel to a mythical beast.

Sensory Details The author uses his senses for details about how the Ferris wheel looks, sounds and feels. The ride is "huge, smoky and noisy" and its engines "drone."

Like any essay, a descriptive essay should be well organized. This essay began with a general statement—that the author has always been fascinated by carnival rides. The body is made of paragraphs that describe the subject. The conclusion restates the main idea—in this case, that the author continues to find carnival rides fascinating.

A trip on the Ferris wheel never fails to thrill me. The fascination I have for Ferris wheels comes back with each and every ride.

 Get writing, research and organizing tips and tools at timeforkids.com/homeworkhelper

How to Write a Biography

A biography is the story of a life. Biographies can be just a few sentences long, or they can fill an entire book. Biographers (people who write biographies) use primary and secondary sources.

● Primary sources convey firsthand experience. They include letters, diaries, interview tapes and other accounts of personal experience.

● Secondary sources convey secondhand experience. They include articles, textbooks, reference books and other sources of information.

To write a biography, you should:

1. Select a person you find interesting.

2. Find out the basic facts of the person's life. You might want to start by looking in an encyclopedia.

3. Think about what else you would like to know about the person.

● What makes this person special or interesting?

● What kind of effect did he or she have on the world?

● What are the adjectives you would use to describe the person?

● What examples from the person's life show those qualities?

● What events shaped or changed this person's life?

TFK Puzzles & Games

Back-to-School Maze

Joey does not want to be late on the first day of school. Help him find his class. Trace the shortest path he can take to get there.

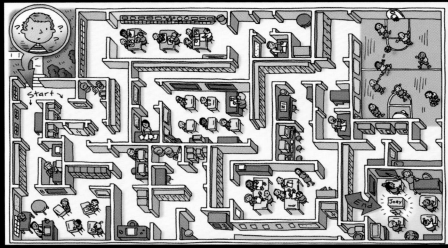

Start

Joey

(See Answer Key that begins on page 342.)

Don't Copy This!

Plagiarism **means you used someone else's work without giving them credit. In your writing, you must give credit whenever you use information that you found in a source, unless it is common knowledge** *(see below).*
Always give your source for:

- quotations (exact words).
- paraphrased information. Simply changing a few words of someone else's writing is unacceptable.
- summarized information.
- facts that are not common knowledge.
- ideas, including opinions and thoughts about what particular facts mean.
- maps, charts, graphs, data and other visual or statistical information.

Common knowledge is information that is widely available. If you saw the same fact repeated in most of your sources, and if your reader is likely to already know this fact, it is probably common knowledge. For example, the fact that Vladimir Putin was elected president of Russia in 2000 is common knowledge.

Accidental Plagiarism

Sometimes, plagiarism is obvious. Copying a lab report from another student and buying a research paper over the Internet are clear examples of plagiarism. But plagiarism can also be accidental. Close paraphrasing and misuse of credits are the most common causes of accidental plagiarism. These tips will help you avoid accidental plagiarism.

- In your research, when you copy words from a source, put quotation marks around them so that you do not forget that they were not your own words.
- When your notes include an idea, write in parentheses whether it is the source's idea or your own idea.
- Check your final text against your notes. Make sure that you did not accidentally use wording or other content without giving credit for it.

How to Write a

Book reports are a way to show how well you understood a book and to tell what you think about it. Many teachers have their own rules about what should be in a book report, so be sure to check with your teacher. Here are some general guidelines.

Introduction

The introduction starts your report and captures the reader's attention. It should include:

☞ **the title and author of the book.**

☞ **some information about the book (but don't give away the ending).**

☞ **what kind of story it is—adventure, fantasy, biography, animal, history, science fiction.**

Body

This is where you describe the main parts of the story: theme, plot, setting and characters. Then you can give your opinions about the book.

☞ The **theme** is the most important message in the story. An example might be the importance of friendship. Tell what you think the theme is and why you do. Lessons learned by the main character are often important clues to the theme.

☞ The **plot** is the main story or event in the book. In your book report, you should explain the plot's main event or conflict. What events lead up to it? What happens as a result?

Be careful not to re-tell the whole plot in detail—you will need room in your report to write about other things. Just say enough about the plot so that the rest of your report will make sense. If the plot has a big mystery or a surprise, be careful not to give away the ending.

☞ The **setting** is the time and place of the story. Is it set a long time ago, in the present or in the future? Does it take place in another country or in an imaginary place?

☞ The **characters** are people, animals and creatures in the book. The main character is called the protagonist. Who are the other characters? Do they help or hinder the protagonist?

Homework Tip!
If your home is noisy, use your school or local library to complete assignments.

Book Report

An important part of a book report is giving your opinion or telling what you thought about the book. Some questions you might want to answer are:

- ☞ **Did you like the story? Why or why not?**
- ☞ **What was the best part of the book? Why?**
- ☞ **How did the story make you feel? Did you feel different emotions at different points?**
- ☞ **Would you recommend the book to friends?**
- ☞ **Would you read other books by the author?**
- ☞ **What new things did you learn from the book?**

Conclusion

The conclusion sums up your report. It gives your overall opinion of the book and the most important thing you want readers to know about it.

Comet in Moominland:
A Fantastic Adventure

A giant comet is heading straight for Moominland. Can Moomintroll, his family and friends escape the danger? That's the question at the heart of *Comet in Moominland* by Tove Jansson. This fantasy novel describes the adventures that the creatures of Moominland encounter as they scramble to save their beloved home.

I liked this book because it tells about a scary event and because it is full of fun and surprises. For example, Moomintroll and Sniff travel into the Lonely Mountains. This is a dangerous journey, but they meet many wonderful and interesting creatures.

 See book reports, a checklist and an idea organizer at timeforkids.com/bookreport

How to Write a Research Paper

Writing a research paper involves all of the steps for writing an essay plus some additional ones. To write a research paper you must first do some research; that is, investigate your topic by reading about it in different sources, including books, magazines, newspapers and on the Internet. The information you gather is used to support the points you make in your paper.

Writing a research paper also involves documenting your sources of information in footnotes or endnotes. This way, the reader knows where you got your information and can judge if it is reliable.

EIGHT STEPS TO A GREAT RESEARCH PAPER

1. **Find your topic.** Try to pick a topic that's fun and interesting. If your topic genuinely interests you, chances are that you'll enjoy working on it.

2. **Look for sources.** Take a trip to the library. Use the electronic catalog or browse the shelves to look for books on your topic. If you find a book that is useful, check the bibliography (list of sources) in the back of that book for other books or articles on that topic. If you need help finding sources, ask a librarian.

Keep a list of all the sources that you use. Include the title of the source, the author, publisher and place and date of publication.

3. **Read your sources and take notes.** After you've gathered your sources, begin reading and taking notes. Use 3 x 5 index cards, writing one fact or idea per card. This way related ideas from different sources can be easily grouped together. Be sure to note the source and the page number on each card.

4. **Make an outline.** Organize your index cards by topic, then develop an outline to organize your ideas. An outline shows your main ideas and the order in which you are going to write about them. *(See page 123 for a sample outline.)*

Homework Tip!
Don't eat messy snacks while doing your homework.

go Check out sample research papers at timeforkids.com/research

5. **Write a first draft.** Every essay or paper is made up of three parts: the introduction, the body and the conclusion.

☛ **The introduction** is the first paragraph. It often begins with a general statement about the topic and ends with a more specific statement of your main idea.

☛ **The body** of the paper follows the introduction. It has a number of paragraphs in which you develop your ideas in detail. Limit yourself to one main idea per paragraph, and use examples and quotations to support your ideas.

☛ **The conclusion** is the last paragraph of the paper. Its purpose is to sum up your points—leaving out specific examples—and to restate your main idea.

6. **Use footnotes or endnotes.** These identify the sources of your information. If you are using footnotes, the note will appear on the same page as the information you are documenting, at the bottom (or foot) of the page. If you are using endnotes, the note will appear together with all other notes on a separate page at the end of your report, just before the bibliography. Since there are different formats, be sure to use the one your teacher prefers.

The National Beagle Club held its first show in 1891.[1]

[1] Samantha Lopez, *For the Love of Beagles* (New York: Ribbon Books, 1993), p. 24.

7. **Revise your draft.** After you've completed your first draft, you'll want to make some changes. *(See page 126 for general tips.)* Also remember that in a research paper, it's important to check that you have footnotes or endnotes wherever they are needed.

8. **Proofread your final draft.** When you are happy with your revision, print it and check spelling, punctuation and grammar. It is good to do this more than once, checking for different kinds of mistakes each time.

TFK Top 5

Biggest Elementary Schools

Most elementary schools in the United States have between 400 and 600 students. But some have almost 3,000! These U.S. elementary schools have the most kids.

1. Miles Avenue Elementary
   Huntington Park, Calif.—2,709 students

2. Ernest R. Graham Elementary
   Hialeah, Fla.—2,449

3. Hoover Street Elementary
   Los Angeles, Calif.—2,372

4. Palm Springs North Elementary
   Hialeah, Fla.—2,245

5. Public School 19 Marino P. Jeantet
   Corona, N.Y.—2,164

Source: National Center for Education Statistics

137

Giving Credit Where It Is Due:
Putting Together a Bibliography

A bibliography is a list of the sources you used to get information for your report. It is included at the end of your report. You will find it easy to prepare your bibliography if you keep track of each source you use as you are reading and taking notes.

When putting together a final bibliography, list your sources (texts, articles, interviews and so on) in alphabetical order by authors' last names. Sources that don't have authors should be alphabetized by title. There are different formats for bibliographies, so be sure to use the one your teacher prefers.

General Guide for Bibliographies

BOOK
Author (last name first). *Title of the book*. City: Publisher, Date of publication.
  Dahl, Roald. *The BFG*. New York: Farrar, Straus and Giroux, 1982.

ENCYCLOPEDIA
***Encyclopedia title*, edition, date. Volume number, "Article title," page numbers.**
  Encyclopædia Britannica, 1997. Volume 7, "Gorillas," pp. 50–51.

MAGAZINE
Author (last name first), "Article title." *Name of magazine*. Volume number, (Date): page numbers.
  Jordan, Jennifer, "Filming at the Top of the World." *Museum of Science Magazine*. Volume 47, No. 1 (Winter 1998): p. 11.

NEWSPAPER
Author (last name first), "Article title." *Name of newspaper,* city, state of publication. (Date): edition if available, section, page number(s).
  McGrath, Charles, "A Rigorous Intellectual Dressed in Glamour." The New York *Times*, New York, N.Y. (12/29/04): New England Edition, The Arts, p.B1.

PERSON
Full name (last name first). Occupation. Date of interview.
  Martin, Jayce. Police officer. April 1, 2004.

CD-ROM
***Disc title:* version, date. "Article title," pages if given. Publisher.**
  Compton's Multimedia Encyclopedia: Macintosh version, 1995.
  "Civil rights movement," p. 3. Compton's Newsmedia.

INTERNET
Author (last name first) (date). "Article title." Date work retrieved, name and URL of website.
  Brunner, Borgna (2001). "Earthquakes!" Retrieved January 27, 2003, from www.infoplease.com/spot/earthquake1.html.

And Furthermore:
Transition Words and Phrases

Transition words and phrases help establish clear connections between ideas. They also ensure that sentences and paragraphs flow together smoothly, making them easier to read. Use the following words and phrases in the circumstances below.

To indicate more information:	To indicate an example:	To indicate a cause or reason:	To indicate a result or an effect:
Besides	For example	As	Accordingly
Furthermore	For instance	Because	Consequently
In addition	In particular	Because of	Finally
In fact	Particularly	Owing to	Therefore
Moreover	Specifically	Since	Thus

The Dewey Decimal System

Imagine walking into a house where room after room is filled with shelves, all packed with books in no specific order. It would be almost impossible to find the book you want! That's what happened every day to Melvil Dewey, an American librarian who lived from 1851 to 1931. He became so unhappy trying to help people find books that he invented the Dewey Decimal System of Classification, which is still used in libraries. The system numbers books by their subject matter in the following way.

000–099	GENERAL WORKS (ENCYCLOPEDIAS, MAGAZINES, ALMANACS)
100–199	PHILOSOPHY AND PSYCHOLOGY
200–299	RELIGION AND MYTHOLOGY
300–399	SOCIAL SCIENCE
400–499	LANGUAGE
500–599	MATH AND SCIENCE
600–699	MEDICINE AND TECHNOLOGY
700–799	ARTS AND ENTERTAINMENT
800–899	LITERATURE
900–999	HISTORY AND GEOGRAPHY

How to Study for Tests

Tests are a way for you and your teacher to measure how well you have learned the material covered in class. Think of them as a challenge!

Before the Test

1. If possible, find out what material the test will cover and what type of test it will be (multiple choice, true or false, short answer or essay).

2. Study at a time when you are alert and not hungry or sleepy.

3. Don't wait until the last minute! Short, daily study sessions are better than cramming the night before the test.

4. Set a goal for each study period. If you are being tested on three chapters, set up four study sessions—one for each chapter and one for a review of all three.

5. Repeat, repeat, repeat! Read and reread your notes and the key parts of the textbook.

6. While reviewing your notes, cover them up and summarize them aloud.

Group Study

Working in a group can be a great way to study. Here's one plan for getting the most out of it.

1. First, compare your notes and review old homework.

2. Next, drill each other on facts you need to memorize. For example: What are the four stages of a butterfly's life cycle?

3. Finally, take the time to discuss "why" questions. For example: Why do monarch butterflies migrate?

Remember—be prepared!

A study group is a place to share your understanding of a subject. The other people in the group aren't there to teach you facts you should already know.

Study Tips

● Use your notes to make an **outline** of the main ideas.

● Make a **timeline** of important dates.

● Make **flashcards** for studying key events or vocabulary.

● Have someone **test** you.

10 Tips for Taking Tests

1. Read the instructions carefully. Never assume you will know what they will say! Ask the teacher if you are unsure about anything.

2. Read the entire test through before you start to answer it. Notice the point value of each section. This will help you to pace yourself.

3. Answer the easiest questions first, then the ones with the highest point value. You don't want to spend 20 minutes trying to figure out a two-point problem!

4. Keep busy! If you get stuck on a question, go back to it later. The answer might come to you while you are working on another part of the test.

5. If you aren't sure how to answer a question fully, try to answer at least part of it. You might get partial credit.

6. Need to guess on a multiple-choice test? First, eliminate the answers that you know are wrong. Then take a guess. Because your first guess is most likely to be correct, you shouldn't go back and change an answer later unless you are certain you were wrong.

7. On an essay test, take a moment to plan your writing. First, jot down the important points you want to make. Then number these points in the order you will cover them.

8. Keep it neat! If your teacher can't read your writing, you might lose points.

9. Don't waste time doing things for which you will not receive credit, such as rewriting test questions.

10. Leave time at the end to look over your work. Did you answer every question? Did you proofread for errors? It is easy to make careless mistakes while taking a test.

After the Test

☞ Read the teacher's comments carefully and try to learn from your mistakes.

☞ Save tests to review for end-of-term tests.

Homework Tip!
Keep your homework out of reach of pets and younger siblings.

How to Give an Oral Report

In many ways, planning an oral report is similar to planning a written report.

- ☛ **Choose a subject that is interesting to you.** What do you care about? What would you like to learn more about? Follow your interests, and you'll find your topic.

- ☛ **Be clear about your purpose.** Do you want to persuade your audience? Inform them about a topic? Or just tell an entertaining story?

An oral report also has the same three basic parts as a written report.

- ☛ **The introduction should "hook" your audience.** Catch their interest with a question, a dramatic tale or a personal experience that relates to your topic.

- ☛ **The body is the main part of your report and will take up most of your time.** Make an outline of the body so that you can share information in an organized way.

  - ☛ **The conclusion is the time to summarize and get across your most important point.** What do you want the audience to remember?

1. Research!

It's important to really know your subject and be well organized. If you know your material, you will be confident and able to answer questions. If your report is well organized, the audience will find it informative and easy to follow.

Think about your audience. If you were listening to a report on your subject, what would you want to know? Too much information can seem overwhelming, and too little can be confusing. Organize your outline around your key points, and focus on getting them across.

Remember—enthusiasm is contagious! If you're interested in your subject, the audience will be interested too.

2. Rehearse!

Practicing your report is a key to success. At first, some people find it helpful to go through the report alone. You might practice in front of a mirror or in front of your stuffed animals. Then try out your report in front of a practice audience—friends or family. Ask your practice audience:

- ☛ **Could you follow my presentation?**

- ☛ **Did I seem knowledgeable about my subject?**

- ☛ **Was I speaking clearly? Could you hear me? Did I speak too fast or too slowly?**

If you are using visual aids, such as posters or overhead transparencies, practice using them while you rehearse. Also, you might want to time yourself to see how long your report actually takes. The time will probably go by faster than you expect.

3. Report!

Stand up straight. Hold your upper body straight, but not stiff, and keep your chin up. Try not to distract your audience by shifting around or fidgeting.

Make eye contact. You will seem more sure of yourself, and the audience will listen better, if you make eye contact during your report.

Use gestures. Your body language can help you make your points and keep the audience interested. Lean forward at key moments, and use your hands and arms for emphasis.

Use your voice effectively. Vary your tone and speak clearly. If you're nervous, you might speak too fast. If you find yourself hurrying, take a breath and try to slow it down.

Nerves!

Almost everyone is nervous when speaking before a group. Many people say public speaking is their No. 1 fear. Being well prepared is the best way to prevent nerves from getting the better of you. Also, try breathing deeply before you begin your report, and remember to breathe during the report. Being nervous isn't all bad—it can help to keep you on your toes!

One last thing!

Have you prepared and practiced your report? Then go get 'em! Remember: you know your stuff, and your report is interesting and important.

Homework Tip!

Use Post-It Notes in books to mark down where you stopped reading. Write notes on them summarizing what you've read.

TFK Mystery Person

CLUE 1: I was born in Italy in 1870. I became internationally famous as an educator.

CLUE 2: As a teacher, I discovered that children learn best on their own, with a teacher to gently guide them in a kid-friendly environment. I also invented learning tools, such as math blocks and sandpaper letters.

CLUE 3: Today, schools that use my methods are named after me. But my ideas influence the way kids are taught everywhere.

WHO AM I?

(See Answer Key that begins on page 342.)

The Coolest Inventions of 2004

Every year, inventive minds dream up tools, toys and machines that make our lives easier, safer or at least a lot more fun. Here are some of 2004's best.

REALLY SURFING THE WEB

Intel has made the world's first Wireless Technology Surfboard. The board has a webcam to make videos and a built-in computer, which lets surfers send e-mail and surf the Web.

BRAINY SOLES

The Adidas 1 are smart sneakers. Sensors in the shoes measure how much pressure is put on the heels. A computer determines whether the cushioning level is too soft or too firm and then adjusts the sole.

SEEING IS BELIEVING

Nike's new swim goggles stay on without straps! Disposable sticky strips attach the lenses to the face and keep water out. The goggles don't drag water, so they don't slow down swimmers.

WHEELIE FUN

The Centaur is a souped-up scooter. Powered by batteries and an electric motor, it travels over rocks, grass or sand.

Inventions

SMOOTH MOVERS

The 14-inch Chroino (kro-eeno), at right, takes smooth, natural steps. So does JVC's robot, the 8-inch tall J4 (left). It can even kick a soccer ball!

← – – – → BRUSH ZAPPER

BRUSH ZAPPER

A dirty toothbrush is gross, and rinsing it does not eliminate bacteria. The Violight is a special container that stores and cleans your toothbrush. It uses ultraviolet light to kill 99.9% of the germs. One thing it can't do is remind you to brush twice a day.

VIO light

BLASTOFF!

Burt Rutan designed SpaceShip-One, the first spacecraft built by a private company. It uses rubber and a gas called nitrous oxide for fuel. In 2004, the craft made two round-trips into space. It may start carrying passengers by 2007. The price of a single ticket: $190,000.

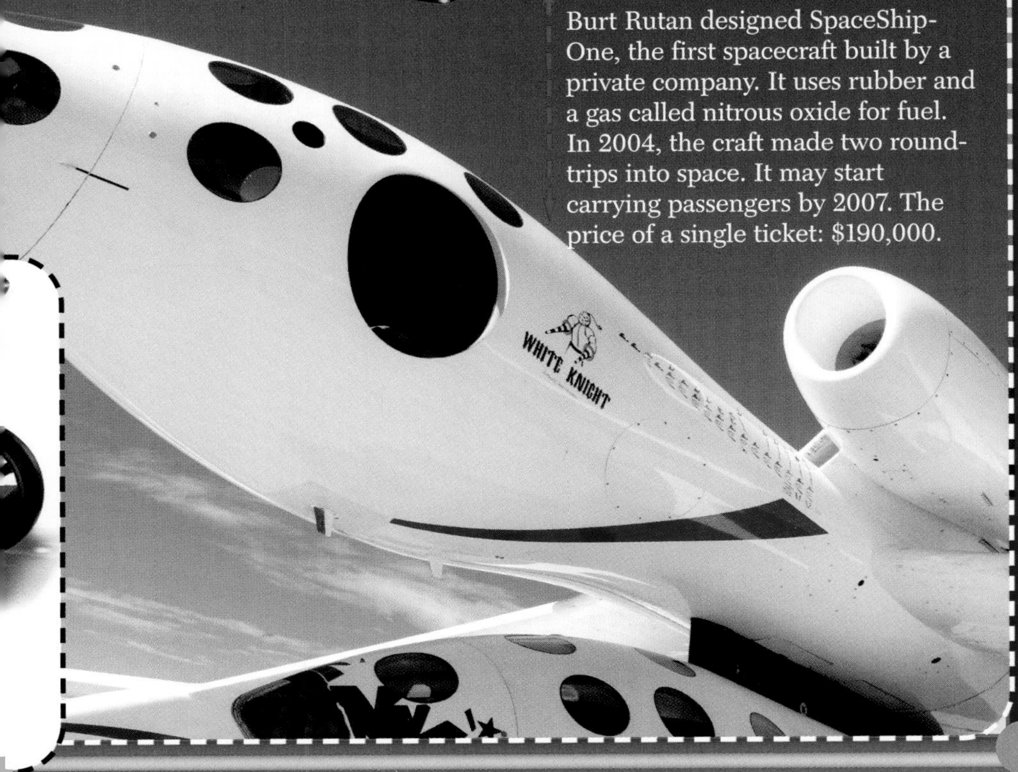

WHITE KNIGHT

ca. 3800–3600 B.C. — Wheel

ca. A.D. 100 — Paper

1608 — Telescope

1709 — Piano

1752 — Lightning rod

1753 — Hot-air balloon

1783 — Steamship

1829 — Braille

1831 — Lawn mower

1832 — Matches

1839 — Rubber

1850 — Refrigerator

1867 — Dynamite

Fluorescent lamp

Typewriter

1869 — Vacuum cleaner

1870 — Chewing gum

1876 — Telephone

1877 — Phonograph (record player)

1885 — Bicycle

1888 — Ballpoint pen

1889 — Handheld camera

1891 — Zipper

1893 — Motion pictures (movies)

1895 — X ray

1899 — Aspirin

Tape recorder

1901 — First transatlantic radio signals

1903 — First motorized plane (Wright brothers)

Windshield wipers

1904 — Ice-cream cone

1907 — Plastic

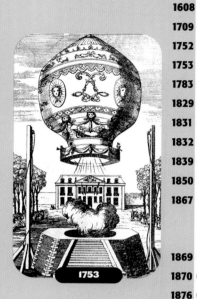

1753

1895

1709

1608

1930

1901

19

GREAT MINDS

1908	Model T car
1909	Toaster
1911	Air conditioning
1913	Moving assembly line
1927	Television
1928	Penicillin, a cure for infections
	Animated sound cartoons
1929	Scotch tape
1930	Pre-sliced bread
	Chocolate chip cookies
1933	FM radio
1939	Jet airplane
1945	Microwave oven
1946	Electronic computer
1949	Silly Putty
1950	Disposable diaper
1953	Structure of DNA (gene chemical) discovered
1955	Polio vaccine
1957	*Sputnik* satellite
1963	Home video recorder
1969	The Internet
1972	Compact disk
1979	Sony Walkman
1980	Rollerblades
	Post-It Notes
1981	Space shuttle
1983	Cellular telephones
1988	Facsimile (fax) machine
1991	World Wide Web
1994	Digital camera
1995	DVD (digital video disk)
1997	Dolly the sheep—first animal made by cloning adult cells
2000	Human-genome map
2004	First privately built spacecraft

1949

1981

1995

TFK Mystery Person

CLUE 1: I was born in Waterville, New York, in 1854. In 1889, I invented roll film and a handheld box camera. It was the very first Kodak camera.

CLUE 2: In 1900, I introduced a camera for kids, called the Brownie. It sold for $1.

CLUE 3: My inventions helped make photography easier. Taking pictures became a popular hobby.

WHO AM I?

(See Answer Key that begins on page 342.)

Kids Protect the Planet

The United Nations holds an all-kids conference on the environment

Kids discuss the issues at the U.

Kids from nearly 100 countries recently met in Connecticut to learn about the environment and to discuss ways to protect it. The Tunza International Children's Conference on the Environment is the largest United Nations event bringing kids from all over the world together. Kids ages 10 to 13 discussed four main environmental issues: oceans, rivers and waterways; extinction and biodiversity; indigenous healing; and energy.

At the conference, the kids attended educational sessions, took field trips to museums and heard presentations from other kids. They talked about different problems in their countries and how to solve them. One of the things they talked about was how to preserve water quality by enforcing laws against dumping waste into water sources.

KIDS TAKE CHARGE

The topics that are discussed at the conference are selected by a group of 10 kids from around the world who make up the Junior Board. In 2004 the board had members from Australia, Ghana, Canada, Colombia, Kenya and the United States. Since members live all over the world, the board held meetings over the Internet before meeting in person a week before the conference began.

One Junior Board member was Adrian Mahoney, 13, from the U.S. Mahoney attends conferences and goes to protests to let other people know how important it is to protect the environment. Mahoney sometimes meets people who don't care about the environment, but he attempts to get them to care. "I tell people that even small things count, so they should keep on trying," Mahoney said.

—*By Elexis Silverman*

TFK Mystery Person

CLUE 1: I was born in Ghana, a nation in Africa, in 1989.

CLUE 2: My family moved to Maryland when I was 8. I live with my mother and am a typical American teenager in every way except one.

CLUE 3: I am the youngest—and highest paid—player in Major League Soccer. Many consider me the best young soccer player in the world.

WHO AM I?

(See Answer Key that begins on page 342.)

Kids of the World

China

Location: East Asia

SCHOOL

- Most schools in China run from about 7:30 a.m. to 5:00 p.m., including a two-hour break for lunch. Uniforms are usually required.

- Besides subjects such as language and math, schools teach moral education— values and attitudes that are believed to be important for all citizens.

PLAY

- *Tiaoqi* (Chinese checkers) and *Xiangqi* (Chinese chess) are favorite board games.

- Soccer, basketball and Ping-Pong are popular.

FAMILY

- About half of the children in cities live mainly with their grandparents while their parents work.

- Since 1979, China has had a "one-child policy." Families with more than one child risk paying steep fines to the government.

FAVORITE FOOD

- Congee, a soupy rice porridge that's eaten at any time of day. It can include fish, yams or beans.

Did You Know? China has the largest population of any nation, with about 1.3 billion people. One in five people in the world is Chinese.

France

Location: Europe

SCHOOL

- The school day usually runs from 8:00 a.m. to 4:00 p.m., with a two-hour lunch break. Schools close Wednesday and Sunday, and open for half a day on Saturday.

- There are no uniforms in public schools.

PLAY

- Escargot (snail), or *la marelle ronde*, is a traditional hopscotch game that uses a spiral shape and only one foot. Many traditional card games are also played.

- Soccer, bicycling and tennis are favorite sports. In some areas, *pelote*, a traditional handball game, is popular.

FAMILY

- Most French mothers work; the majority of preschool children attend state-run day-care centers known as crèches.

- France has laws about naming children. Until 1993, all names had to be chosen from an official list. Today, public prosecutors can still reject a newborn's name.

FAVORITE FOOD

- *Clafouti*, a dessert made of fruit, such as cherries or peaches, topped with a rich cake batter and then baked

Did You Know? There are more than 350 kinds of cheese in France. The average French person eats about 50 pounds of cheese per year.

149

Turn the page for more countries ➜

Brazil

Location: North Eastern South America

SCHOOL

- The school year runs from February through December. Kids attend school for about four hours in the morning or the afternoon. Most schools require uniforms.

- An estimated one-quarter of children, especially in Brazil's cities, do not attend school at all, but work instead.

PLAY

- A traditional pastime is *queimada*, a game of tag that is played in two teams. Jump rope, card games and checkers are other favorites.

- Soccer is the national pastime. Brazil's beautiful beaches also make swimming and volleyball popular.

FAMILY

- Brazilian families are often large. Many kids have five or six siblings. Nearly one-third of the population is under age 18!

- Most Brazilians live in cities. About a quarter of city dwellers live in hillside shantytowns called favelas.

FAVORITE FOOD

- *Feijoada*, a stew of black beans and different meats, traditionally served with rice and oranges

Did You Know? Almost half of Brazil is rain forest. The rain forest includes over a million insect species and tens of thousands of plant species.

Egypt

Location: North Africa/Middle East

SCHOOL

- School attendance is required for six years, generally beginning at age 6 or 7. However, many kids do not attend. Literacy in Egypt is less than 60%.

- Besides lessons in reading and writing, the school week includes religious education. Muslim and Christian children receive separate instruction.

PLAY

- Shooting marbles is a popular activity that—like tic-tac-toe—may have been passed down from ancient Egypt.

- Soccer is the No. 1 sport. Tennis, squash and wrestling are also favorites.

FAMILY

- Egyptian kids generally live with their parents, but close to extended family. In cities, related families may live in the same building.

- In most families, girls help with indoor chores, like laundry, while boys help with outdoor chores, like shopping.

FAVORITE FOOD

- *Fool madames*, a dish of seasoned fava beans. The most popular dish in Egypt, it has been eaten since ancient times.

Did You Know? Egypt is home to the Nile, the world's longest river. About 200 species of fish, 350 species of birds and the Nile crocodile depend on this river.

India

Location: Southern Asia

SCHOOL
- The school year begins in April in most of the north and east, and in June in most of the south and west.
- Barely half the children in India finish primary school. Dropout rates are higher for girls; only about 40% of adult women in India can read.

PLAY
- *Pachisi* (Parcheesi) has been called India's "national game." Kite flying is also a widespread passion.
- Hockey, cricket and soccer are very popular. *Kabaddi*, a fast-paced team sport that has its roots in India, is now played throughout Asia.

FAMILY
- The "joint family" system is a common tradition, in which the families of several relatives (usually brothers) live together.
- Tens of millions of children in India—more than in any other country—work to help support their families.

FAVORITE FOOD
- India's famous chutneys—fresh or cooked relishes—are used at almost every meal. Nuts, chili peppers, fruits and spices are common chutney ingredients.

Did You Know? Two of the world's major religions, Hinduism and Buddhism, were founded in India.

Nigeria

Location: Western Africa

SCHOOL
- The school year in Nigeria runs from January through December. Typically, there are three semesters, with a month off after each one.
- Most schools have strict dress codes. Uniforms are required and there are rules about hairstyles and jewelry.

PLAY
- A game called *ayo*, played by two people using seeds and a board that has 12 cups, is popular. So are checkers and hand-clapping games.
- Soccer is a national craze in Nigeria, as in much of Africa. Volleyball, wrestling and boxing are also popular.

FAMILY
- Age earns respect in many families. As a mark of honor, an older sibling may be addressed as "Senior Brother" or Senior Sister."
- Most Nigerians live in extended families, either within the same home or in separate homes clustered close together.

FAVORITE FOOD
- Plantains (a member of the banana family), which can be fried, stewed with meat, toasted or made into pastries

Did You Know? Nigeria is diverse, with more than 250 ethnic groups. The largest are the Yoruba, the Hausa and Fulani and the Ibo (Igbo).

FROM *TFK* MAGAZINE

WORD WIZARDS

It's bee season! Sensational spellers win their way to the 2004 final.

The moment had arrived. After hundreds of hours spent studying thousands of words, only six letters stood between Erik Zyman-Carrasco, 12, and a third trip to the Scripps National Spelling Bee.

After a deep breath, Erik spelled z-e-p-h-y-r, then pumped his fists with joy. Erik's win, in New York City, enabled him to join 263 other regional champs who would compete at the 77th annual nationals in Washington, D.C., in 2004.

"There won't be much pressure, because being there means you're already a champion," Erik told TFK. Even so, his goal was to win the $12,000 first prize.

Erik's dream, alas, did not come true. The 2004 winner was David Tidmarsh, 14, from Indiana. David won by correctly spelling the word *autochthonous* (native).

Erik and David are two of more than 10 million kids nationwide who take part in spelling bees every year. At the national bee, super spellers in eighth grade or lower represent Jamaica, Mexico, Puerto Rico, the Bahamas and every U.S. state except Vermont. The finalists compete in front of 1,000 people and an ESPN television audience of millions.

Spelling champs study an average of five to 15 hours a week. Some of that time is spent mastering lists of difficult words. But most spellers also practice word sleuthing. That means they learn to use language clues to figure out the spelling of unfamiliar words.

Jonathan Cohen, 11, of Rhode Island, enjoys the language detective work. He won his school bee as a fourth-grader in 2003. He says, "I really like how there are so many different ways to spell a word. That challenge is what makes it fun."

—By Jeremy Caplan

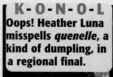

K - O - N - O - L
Oops! Heather Luna misspells *quenelle*, a kind of dumpling, in a regional final.

152

Language

The World's 10 Most Spoken Languages

1. Chinese (Mandarin)
2. English
3. Hindustani
4. Spanish
5. Russian
6. Arabic
7. Bengali
8. Portuguese
9. Malay-Indonesian
10. French

Source: Ethnologue

TFK Top 5

Languages Spoken in the U.S.

These are the most common languages spoken in the United States, after English:

1. Spanish
2. Chinese
3. French
4. German
5. Tagalog (Spoken by Philippine-born people)

Source: U.S. Census Bureau

Winning Words

Kids have taken part in the National Spelling Bee since 1925. Here are some tongue-twisting words that made students into national champs.

1990	fibranne	1998	chiaroscurist
1991	antipyretic	1999	logorrhea
1992	lyceum	2000	demarche
1993	kamikaze	2001	succedaneum
1994	antediluvian	2002	prospicience
1995	xanthosis	2003	pococurante
1996	vivisepulture	2004	autochthonous
1997	euonym		

TFK Puzzles & Games

Language Laughs

Can you answer these mind-bending questions?

1. The sentence below is a pangram. By looking carefully at the sentence, can you guess what a pangram is?

    A quick brown fox jumps over the lazy dog.

2. The **UNITED ARAB EMIRATES** is a small country in the Middle East. Can you guess why the name of this nation is a big deal to word lovers?

3. The word **HIDEOUS** has three syllables. Can you replace one letter to form a new word with only two syllables?

4. What is the one letter that doesn't appear in the name of any state in the U.S.?

5. The word **THEREIN** contains only seven letters. But it contains other words that can be formed using consecutive letters. Can you find at least eight of them? (Hint: Check the dictionary to make sure you've found a real word.)

6. Some people consider **SMILES** to be the longest word in the English language. Why?

(See Answer Key that begins on page 342.)

 Hear foreign languages spoken at timeforkids.com/goplaces

Latin and Greek Word ELEMENTS

LATIN ROOT	BASIC MEANING	EXAMPLES
-dict-	to say	dictate, predict
-ject-	to throw	eject, projectile
-port-	to carry	portable, transport
-scrib-, -script-	to write	scribble, description
-vert-	to turn	convert, vertical

Many English words and word elements can be traced back to Latin and Greek. A word root is a part of a word. It contains the core meaning of the word, but it cannot stand alone.

LATIN PREFIX	BASIC MEANING	EXAMPLES
co-	together	coordinate, cohost
inter-	between, among	international, interject
re-	again; back, backward	rebuild, recall
sub-	under	submarine, subway
trans-	across, beyond, through	transatlantic, transport

A prefix is placed at the beginning of a word to change its meaning.

A suffix is placed at the end of a word to change its meaning.

LATIN SUFFIX	BASIC MEANING	EXAMPLES
-able, -ible	capable or worthy of	likable, flexible
-ation	forms nouns from verbs	create, creation; civilize, civilization
-fy, -ify	to make or cause to become	purify, humidify
-ment	forms nouns from verbs	entertain, entertainment; amaze, amazement
-ty, -ity	forms nouns from adjectives	cruel, cruelty; sane, sanity

GREEK ROOT	BASIC MEANING	EXAMPLES
-anthrop-	human	philanthropy, anthropology
-chron-	time	synchronize, chronicle
-dem-	people	demography, undemocratic
-path-	feeling, suffering	pathetic, sympathy
-phon-	sound	phonograph, cacophony

GREEK PREFIX	BASIC MEANING	EXAMPLES
anti-, ant-	opposite; opposing	antiwar, antagonize
auto-	self, same	autobiography, automatic
bio-	life, living organism	biology, biopsy
neo-	new, recent	neophyte, neonatal
thermo-, therm-	heat	thermometer, thermal

GREEK SUFFIX	BASIC MEANING	EXAMPLES
-ism	the act, state or theory of	capitalism, criticism
-ist	a person who practices or believes something	cyclist, conformist
-logue, -log	speech, discourse; to speak	dialogue, monologue
-logy	talk, theory, study	dermatology, geology
-meter, -metry	measuring device; measure	chronometer, kilometer

"Onyms"

Acronyms	are words or names formed by combining the first letters of words in a phrase. For example, **SCUBA** comes from **s**elf-**c**ontained **u**nderwater **b**reathing **a**pparatus.
Antonyms	are words with opposite meanings. **Sweet** and **bitter** are antonyms.
Eponyms	are words based on or derived from a person's name. For example, the word **diesel** was named after Rudolf **Diesel,** who invented the **diesel** engine.
Heteronyms	are words with identical spellings but different meanings and pronunciations. For example, **bow** and arrow, and to **bow** on stage.
Homonyms	are words that sound alike (and are sometimes spelled alike) but name different things. **Die** (to stop living) and **dye** (color) are homonyms.
Pseudonyms	are false names or pen names used by an author. The word comes from the Greek **pseud** (false) and **onym** (name). Mark Twain is a pseudonym for Samuel Langhorne Clemens.
Synonyms	are words with the same or similar meanings. **Cranky** and **grumpy** are synonyms.

SAY WHAT?

You may have heard these foreign words and phrases. Here's what they mean.

AD NAUSEAM to a sickening degree: "The politician made one promise after another ad nauseam."

BONA FIDE authentic: "After clearly explaining the complicated theory, she proved that she was a bona fide expert in physics."

CARTE BLANCHE unrestricted power to act on one's own: "I may have carte blanche at my grandparents' house, but at home I must follow strict rules."

FAUX PAS a social blunder: "Her friend blushed in embarrassment when she realized she had made yet another faux pas."

MEA CULPA I'm to blame: "His mea culpa was so sincere, I knew he felt truly sorry."

PRO BONO done or donated without charge: "The penniless man was lucky to find a lawyer who agreed to represent him in court pro bono."

QUID PRO QUO an equal exchange: "Tom let his sister borrow one of his CDs when she agreed to lend him a video game as a quid pro quo."

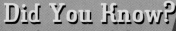

Did You Know?

Homophones are words that are pronounced the same but have different spellings and meanings. For example, *fare* and *fair* and *dear* and *deer* are homophones.

American Sign Language (ASL) and the American Manual Alphabet

American Sign Language (ASL) was developed at the American School for the Deaf, which was founded in 1817 in Hartford, Connecticut. Teachers at the school created ASL by combining French Sign Language with several American visual languages. ASL includes signs, gestures, facial expressions and the **American Manual Alphabet** shown below. Today, it is the fourth most-used language in the U.S.

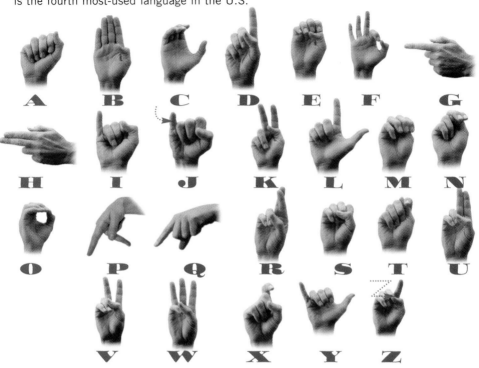

PALINDROMES

A **palindrome** is a word, phrase or sentence that reads the same forward and backward.
Here are some examples of palindromes.

A daffodil slid off Ada.
Boston did not sob.
Dee saw a seed.
Dennis and Edna sinned.
Kayak
Ma is as selfless as I am.
Never odd or even.
Rise to vote, sir.
Step on no pets.

Can you think of other palindromes?

WORDS TO THE WISE

Here are the surprising origins of some everyday words and phrases.

ON CLOUD NINE This expression means to feel exhilarated. It came from the National Weather Bureau, which ranks clouds according to their height. Since the highest rating for a cloud is nine, people on cloud nine couldn't feel higher.

BIG APPLE Years ago, musicians called the small towns they visited "little apples." The musicians called New York City "the big apple" because it was the biggest city in the U.S.

SIDEBURNS General Ambrose Burnside, a Union general during the Civil War, famously wore huge muttonchop whiskers. After a while, people began calling those whiskers "burnsides," which became "sideburns."

GOD BLESS YOU In medieval times, people believed that when a person sneezed, the soul left the body and was stolen by the devil. The blessing was supposed to save the soul until it returned to the sneezer.

APPLE OF ONE'S EYE In olden times, people thought the eyeball's pupil looked like an apple. Since the pupil is very precious, the expression came to mean something that is valuable.

IN THE DOGHOUSE This refers to a person who is out of favor. In the book *Peter Pan*, the father mistreated the family dog, and his punishment was to spend time in the pooch's doghouse.

WHOLE HOG Today, "going whole hog" means going to the limit. In the 17th century, a hog was slang for a valuable type of coin. A person who spent a whole hog had invested a lot of money.

Source: *Morris Dictionary of Word and Phrase Origins*

Most Common Words

Here are the 50 words used most often in English.

the	on	by	your
of	are	one	which
and	as	had	their
a	with	not	said
to	his	but	if
in	they	what	do
is	at	all	will
you	be	were	each
that	this	when	about
it	from	we	how
he	I	there	up
for	have	can	
was	or	an	

Source: *American Heritage Word Frequency Book*

TFK Mystery Person

CLUE 1: A scientist and scholar, I was born in England in 1779.

CLUE 2: In 1852, I published a book that made it easy to find synonyms—words of similar meanings—for thousands of entries.

CLUE 3: This *Thesaurus of English Words and Phrases* is still being published and continues to bear my name.

WHO AM I?

(See Answer Key that begins on page 342.)

Metric Weights and Measures

Most of the world uses the metric system. The only countries not on this system are the U.S., Myanmar (formerly called Burma) and Liberia.

The metric system is based on 10s. For example, 10 decimeters make a meter.

Length

UNIT	VALUE
millimeter (mm)	0.001 meter
centimeter (cm)	0.01 meter
decimeter (dm)	0.1 meter
meter (m)	1 meter
dekameter (dam)	10 meters
hectometer (hm)	100 meters
kilometer (km)	1,000 meters

Metric Conversions

MULTIPLY	BY	TO FIND
centimeters	.3937	inch
feet	.3048	meter
gallons	3.7853	liters
grams	.0353	ounce
inches	2.54	centimeters
kilograms	2.2046	pounds
kilometers	.6214	mile
liters	1.0567	quarts
liters	.2642	gallon
meters	3.2808	feet
meters	1.0936	yards
miles	1.6093	kilometers
ounces	28.3495	grams
pounds	.4536	kilogram
quarts	.946	liter
square kilometers	.3861	square mile
square meters	1.196	square yards
square miles	2.59	square kilometers
square yards	.8361	square meter
yards	.9144	meter

Mass & Weight

UNIT	VALUE
milligram (mg)	0.001 gram
centigram (cg)	0.01 gram
decigram (dg)	0.10 gram
gram (g)	1 gram
dekagram (dag)	10 grams
hectogram (hg)	100 grams
kilogram (kg)	1,000 grams
metric ton (t)	1,000,000 grams

Capacity

UNIT	VALUE
milliliter (ml)	0.001 liter
centiliter (cl)	0.01 liter
deciliter (dl)	0.10 liter
liter (l)	1 liter
dekaliter (dal)	10 liters
hectoliter (hl)	100 liters
kiloliter (kl)	1,000 liters

U.S. Weights and Measures

Measuring Length

12 inches	= 1 foot
3 feet	= 1 yard
$5\frac{1}{2}$ yards	= 1 rod
40 rods	= 1 furlong
8 furlongs	= 1 mile

Measuring Area

144 square inches	= 1 square foot
9 square feet	= 1 square yard
$30\frac{1}{4}$ square yards	= 1 square rod
160 square rods	= 1 acre
640 acres	= 1 square mile

Measuring Weight

16 ounces	= 1 pound
2,000 pounds	= 1 ton

Measuring Liquid

2 cups	= 1 pint
2 pints	= 1 quart
4 quarts	= 1 gallon
8 ounces	= 1 cup
16 ounces	= 1 pint

Cooking Measures

3 teaspoons	= 1 tablespoon
4 tablespoons	= $\frac{1}{4}$ cup
5 tablespoons + 1 teaspoon	= $\frac{1}{3}$ cup
16 tablespoons	= 1 cup

Did You Know?

A **cardinal number** shows quantity—it tells how many.

- 8 puppies
- 10 friends

In the United States, we use the U.S. customary system to measure things. Here are some of the units of measurement in the system.

LENGTH	WEIGHT	CAPACITY
mile (mi.)	ton (t. or tn.)	gallon (gal.)
yard (yd.)	pound (lb.)	quart (qt.)
foot (ft.)	ounce (oz.)	pint (pt.)
inch (in.)	dram (dr.)	cup (c.)

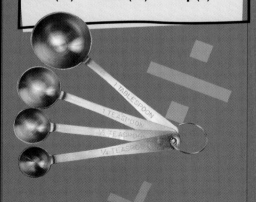

go For more about measurement tables:
www.factmonster.com/measurement

Integers

Integers are **whole numbers.** They include positive numbers, negative numbers and zero, but **not** fractions, decimals, percents or exponents. Here are some rules to remember when you add, subtract, multiply and divide integers.

★ **Adding a negative number is the same as subtracting a positive number.**
$$3 + (-4) = 3 - 4$$

★ **Subtracting a negative number is the same as adding a positive number. The two negatives cancel out each other.**
$$3 - (-4) = 3 + 4$$

★ **If you multiply or divide two positive numbers, the result will be positive.**
$$6 \times 2 = 12$$

★ **If you multiply or divide a positive number with a negative number, the result will be negative.**
$$6 \times (-2) = -12$$

★ **If you multiply or divide two negative numbers, the result will be positive—the two negatives cancel out each other.**
$$(-6) \times (-2) = 12$$

Famous math minds

Imagine solving difficult math problems before there were computers! Many of the world's most famous mathematicians came up with complicated theories and inventions well before high-tech tools were developed.

ARCHIMEDES Many people think Archimedes is one of the most influential mathematicians of all time—amazing, considering he was born around 287 B.C.! He discovered buoyancy (he's said to have yelled "Eureka"—which means "I found it!"—in delight when he figured out why some things float), as well as many weapons of war, several formulas for measuring capacity and pi.

CHARLES BABBAGE Born in England in 1791, Babbage devoted most of his life to inventing mechanical calculating machines. Around 1830, he designed a machine that would perform simple mathematical calculations. Next, he tried to make a device that used cards with holes to compute complicated functions at great speed. Although both contraptions were too advanced for their time, the designs became the basis for modern computers.

ALBERT EINSTEIN Probably the most famous genius of all time, Einstein changed history when he scribbled E=mc² in 1905. His theory of relativity says that the speed of light inside a vacuum is the fastest speed in the universe. Einstein's discoveries became the foundation for much of modern science. Einstein was born in Germany in 1879 and became a U.S. citizen in 1940.

SIR ISAAC NEWTON Considered one of the greatest mathematicians and physicists in history, Newton was born in England in 1643. He discovered the mathematical laws of gravity and solved difficult problems in geometry. Newton also invented a type of math called calculus.

BLAISE PASCAL Born in 1623, this French philosopher and mathematician was a math expert by age 12, and he invented the first calculator when he was only 19. He also invented the barometer, the hydraulic press and the syringe.

Rounding numbers

Arounded number **has about the same value as the number you start with, but it is less exact. For example, 341 rounded to the nearest hundred is 300. That is because 341 is closer in value to 300 than to 400.**

Rules for Rounding

Here are the general rules for rounding:

- **If the number you are rounding ends with 5, 6, 7, 8 or 9, round the number up.**

  Example: **38 rounded to the nearest 10 is 40.**

- **If the number you are rounding ends with 0, 1, 2, 3 or 4, round the number down.**

  Example: **33 rounded to the nearest 10 is 30.**

What Are You Rounding To?

When rounding a number, ask: What are you rounding it to? Numbers can be rounded to the nearest 10, the nearest 100, the nearest 1,000 and so on.

Consider the number 4,827:

- **4,827 rounded to the nearest 10 is 4,830.**

- **4,827 rounded to the nearest 100 is 4,800.**

- **4,827 rounded to the nearest 1,000 is 5,000.**

Rounding and Decimals

Rounding decimals works exactly the same way as rounding whole numbers. The only difference is that you round to tenths, hundredths, thousandths and so on.

- **7.8899 rounded to the nearest tenth is 7.9.**

- **1.0621 rounded to the nearest hundredth is 1.06.**

- **3.8792 rounded to the nearest thousandth is 3.879.**

Did You Know?

When rounding long decimals, look only at the number in the place you are rounding to and the number that follows it. For example, to round 5.3874791 to the nearest hundredth, just look at the number in the hundredths place—8—and the number that follows it—7. Then you can easily round it up to 5.39.

Fractions, Decimals

How to Reduce a Fraction

Divide the numerator (the top part) and the denominator (the bottom part) by their greatest common factor (GCF), which is the largest whole number that can be divided evenly into each of the numbers.

Example: $6/15$
The greatest common factor is 3, so
$(6 ÷ 3) / (15 ÷ 3) = 2/5$

Or

Divide the numerator and the denominator by a common factor. A factor is any number that divides a number evenly without a remainder. Keep dividing until you can no longer divide either the numerator or the denominator evenly by the common factor.

Example: $8/20$, using 2 as the factor:
$(8 ÷ 2) / (20 ÷ 2) = 4/10 =$
$(4 ÷ 2) / (10 ÷ 2) = 2/5$

To change

A fraction to a decimal:
Divide the numerator by the denominator.

$1/4 = 1.00 ÷ 4 = 0.25$

A fraction to a percent:
Multiply the fraction by 100 and reduce it. Then, attach a percent sign.

$1/4 \times 100/1 = 100/4 = 25/1 = 25\%$

A decimal to a fraction:
Starting from the decimal point, count the decimal places. If there is one decimal place, put the number over 10 and reduce. If there are two places, put the number over 100 and reduce. If there are three places, put it over 1,000 and reduce, and so on.

$0.25 = 25/100 = 1/4$

A decimal to a percent:
Move the decimal point two places to the right. Then, attach a percent sign.

$0.25 = 25\%$

A percent to a decimal:
Move the decimal point two places to the left. Then, drop the percent sign.

$25\% = 0.25$

A percent to a fraction:
Drop the percent sign. Put the number over 100 and reduce.

$25\% = 25/100 = 1/4$

Homework Tip!
Do math assignments in pencil, and keep an eraser handy! It's okay to try different methods.

162

& Percents

Common Fractions with Decimal and Percent Equivalents

Here's a list of some common fractions and what they look like written as decimals and percents.

Fraction	Decimal	Percent
1/3	0.333 . . .	33.333 . . .%
2/3	0.666 . . .	66.666 . . .%
1/4	0.25	25%
1/2	0.5	50%
3/4	0.75	75%
1/5	0.2	20%
2/5	0.4	40%
3/5	0.6	60%
4/5	0.8	80%
1/6	0.1666 . . .	16.666 . . .%
5/6	0.8333 . . .	83.333 . . .%
1/8	0.125	12.5%
3/8	0.375	37.5%
5/8	0.625	62.5%
7/8	0.875	87.5%
1/10	0.1	10%
1/12	0.08333 . . .	8.333 . . .%
1/16	0.0625	6.25%
1/32	0.03125	3.125%

Decimal Places

One decimal place to the left of the decimal point is the ones place.
One decimal place to the right of the decimal place is the tenths place.

Keep your eye on the 9 to see where the decimal places fall.

millions	9,000,000.0
hundred thousands	900,000.0
ten thousands	90,000.0
thousands	9,000.0
hundreds	900.0
tens	90.0
ones	9.0
tenths	0.9
hundredths	0.09
thousandths	0.009
ten-thousandths	0.0009
hundred-thousandths	0.00009
millionths	0.000009

To add or subtract decimals, line up the decimal points and use zeros to fill in the blanks:

$$9 - 2.67 =$$

$$
\begin{array}{r}
9.00 \\
-2.67 \\
\hline
6.33
\end{array}
$$

9.0

multiplication Table

To find the answer to a multiplication problem, pick one number from the top of the box and one number from the left side. Follow each row into the center. The place where they meet is the answer.

X	0	1	2	3	4	5	6	7	8	9	10	11	12
0	0	0	0	0	0	0	0	0	0	0	0	0	0
1	0	1	2	3	4	5	6	7	8	9	10	11	12
2	0	2	4	6	8	10	12	14	16	18	20	22	24
3	0	3	6	9	12	15	18	21	24	27	30	33	36
4	0	4	8	12	16	20	24	28	32	36	40	44	48
5	0	5	10	15	20	25	30	35	40	45	50	55	60
6	0	6	12	18	24	30	36	42	48	54	60	66	72
7	0	7	14	21	28	35	42	49	56	63	70	77	84
8	0	8	16	24	32	40	48	56	64	72	80	88	96
9	0	9	18	27	36	45	54	63	72	81	90	99	108
10	0	10	20	30	40	50	60	70	80	90	100	110	120
11	0	11	22	33	44	55	66	77	88	99	110	121	132
12	0	12	24	36	48	60	72	84	96	108	120	132	144

Prime Numbers

A prime number is a number that can be divided, without a remainder, only by itself and by 1. For example, 17 is a prime number. It can be divided only by 17 and by 1.

Some facts:

● The only even prime number is 2. All other even numbers can be divided by 2.

● No prime number greater than 5 ends in a 5. Any number greater than 5 that ends in a 5 can be divided by 5.

● Zero and 1 are not considered prime numbers.

● Except for 0 and 1, a number is either a prime number or a composite number. A composite number is any number greater than 1 that is not prime.

To prove whether a number is a prime number, first try dividing it by 2, and see if you get a whole number. If you do, it can't be a prime number. If you don't get a whole number, next try dividing it by 3, then by 5, then by 7 and so on, always dividing by a prime number.

Here's a list of prime numbers between 1 and 100: 2, 3, 5, 7, 11, 13, 17, 19, 23, 29, 31, 41, 43, 47, 53, 59, 61, 67, 71, 73, 79, 83, 89 and 97.

Squares and Square Roots

A square of a number is that number times itself.
For example:

$4^2 = 16: 4 \times 4 = 16$

$6^2 = 36: 6 \times 6 = 36$

Finding a square root is the **inverse operation** of squaring. Inverse operations are two operations that do the opposite, such as multiplication and division. The square root of 4 is 2, or:

$\sqrt{4}$ is 2: $2 \times 2 = 4$

$\sqrt{9}$ is 3: $3 \times 3 = 9$

Here's a table of squares and square roots for numbers from 1 to 20.

Number	Square	Square Root
1	1	1.00
2	4	1.414
3	9	1.732
4	16	2.000
5	25	2.236
6	36	2.449
7	49	2.646
8	64	2.828
9	81	3.000
10	100	3.162
11	121	3.317
12	144	3.464
13	169	3.606
14	196	3.742
15	225	3.873
16	256	4.000
17	289	4.123
18	324	4.243
19	361	4.359
20	400	4.472

The easiest way to find a square root is to use a calculator, but you can do it without one. Here's one way, using 12 as an example of the squared number:

1. Pick a number that when squared comes close to (but is less than) the number whose square root you're finding: $3 \times 3 = 9$. This is a better choice than 4: $4 \times 4 = 16$

2. Divide the number you're finding the square root of (12) by the number you squared (3) in step 1: $12 \div 3 = 4$

3. Average the closest square root (3) and the answer of step 2 (4): $3 + 4 = 7.\ 7 \div 2 = 3.5$

4. Square the average to see how close the number is to 12:

$3.5 \times 3.5 = 12.25$—Close, but not close enough!

Repeat steps 2 and 3 until the number squared is very close to 12:

Divide: $12 \div 3.5 = 3.43$

Average: $3.5 + 3.43 = 6.935$

$6.935 \div 2 = 3.465$

$3.465 \times 3.465 = 12.006$, close enough!

Did You Know?

A nominal number identifies or names something:

- Jersey number 2
- ZIP code 01966

An ordinal number shows rank—the order of a thing in a set.

- 3rd fastest
- 10th in line

Numerical Prefixes

A prefix is an element at the beginning of a word. A numerical prefix lets you know how many there are of a particular thing. You can use these prefixes to figure out how many sides a figure has. For example, a hexagon has six sides, and a heptagon has seven.

PREFIX	MEANING	EXAMPLE
uni-	1	unicorn: mythical creature with one horn
mono-	1	monorail: train that runs on one track
bi-	2	bicycle: two-wheeled vehicle
tri-	3	triceratops: three-horned dinosaur
quadr-	4	quadruped: four-footed animal
quint-	5	quintuplets: five babies born at a single birth
penta-	5	pentagon: figure with five sides
hex-	6	hexapod: having six legs—an insect, for example
sex-	6	sextet: group of six musicians
hept-	7	heptathlon: athletic contest with seven events
sept-	7	septuagenarian: a person between ages 70 and 80
octo-	8	octopus: sea creature with eight arms
nove-	9	novena: prayers said over nine days
deka- or deca-	10	decade: a period of 10 years
cent-	100	century: a period of 100 years
hecto-	100	hectogram: 100 grams
milli-	1,000	millennium: a period of 1,000 years
kilo-	1,000	kilogram: 1,000 grams
mega-	1,000,000	megaton: 1 million tons
giga-	1,000,000,000	gigabyte: 1 billion bytes

More Than a Million

Numbers don't stop at the millions, billions or trillions. In fact, they go on and on and on. Here's what some really big numbers look like:

10 million	10,000,000
100 million	100,000,000
billion	1,000,000,000
trillion	1,000,000,000,000
quadrillion	1,000,000,000,000,000
quintillon	1,000,000,000,000,000,000
sextillion	1,000,000,000,000,000,000,000
septillion	1,000,000,000,000,000,000,000,000
octillion	1,000,000,000,000,000,000,000,000,000
nonillion	1,000,000,000,000,000,000,000,000,000,000
googol	1 followed by 100 zeroes
centillion	1 followed by 303 zeroes
googolplex	1 followed by a googol of zeroes

Find the best math sites on the web with TFK's Homework Helper at timeforkids.com/research

Polygons: How Many Sides?

A geometrical figure with three or more sides is called a **polygon** or a **polyhedron.** Here are the names of some polygons.

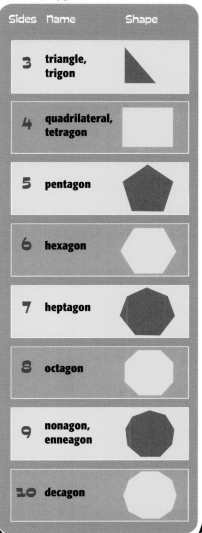

Sides	Name	Shape
3	triangle, trigon	
4	quadrilateral, tetragon	
5	pentagon	
6	hexagon	
7	heptagon	
8	octagon	
9	nonagon, enneagon	
10	decagon	

For more tables and formulas: www.factmonster.com/formulas

Common Formulas

Finding Area

Area is the amount of surface within fixed lines.

SQUARE
Multiply the length of the side by itself. (For example, if the side is 6 inches long, multiply 6 x 6.)

side / side

RECTANGLE
Multiply the base by the height.

height / base

CIRCLE
Multiply the radius by itself, then multiply the result by 3.1416.

radius

TRAPEZOID
Add the two parallel sides, multiply by the height and divide by 2.

height / parallel side / parallel side

TRIANGLE
If you know the base and the height, multiply them and then divide by 2.

height / base

Finding Circumference and Perimeter

The circumference of a circle is the complete distance around it. To find the circumference of a circle, multiply its diameter by 3.1416.

diameter

The perimeter of a geometrical figure is the complete distance around that figure. To find the perimeter, simply add up the lengths of the figure's sides.

side / side

ROMAN NUMERALS

The ancient Romans gave us this numbering system. The year 2006 in Roman numerals is **MMVI**.

One	I
Two	II
Three	III
Four	IV
Five	V
Six	VI
Seven	VII
Eight	VIII
Nine	IX
Ten	X
Eleven	XI
Twelve	XII
Thirteen	XIII
Fourteen	XIV
Fifteen	XV
Sixteen	XVI
Seventeen	XVII
Eighteen	XVIII
Nineteen	XIX
Twenty	XX
Thirty	XXX
Forty	XL
Fifty	L
Sixty	LX
Seventy	LXX
Eighty	LXXX
Ninety	XC
One hundred	C
Five hundred	D
One thousand	M

RULES FOR ROMAN NUMERALS

- A letter repeats its value that many times (XXX = 30, CC = 200). A letter can only be repeated three times in a row.

- If one or more letters are placed after another letter of greater value, add that amount.

  VI = 6 (5 + 1 = 6)

  LXX = 70 (50 + 10 + 10 = 70)

- If a letter is placed before another letter of greater value, subtract that amount.

  IV = 4 (5 − 1 = 4)

  XC = 90 (100 − 10 = 90)

- A bar placed on top of a letter or string of letters increases the numeral's value 1,000 times.

  XV = 15, $\overline{XV}$ = 15,000

There are several rules for subtracting amounts from Roman numerals:

- Only subtract powers of 10 (I, X, or C, but not V or L).

  For 95, do NOT write VC (100 − 5).
  DO write XCV (XC + V or 90 + 5).

- Only subtract one number from another.
  For 13, do NOT write IIXV (15 − 1 − 1).
  DO write XIII (X + I + I + I or 10 + 3).

- Do not subtract a number from one that is more than 10 times greater (that is, you can subtract 1 from 10 [IX] but not 1 from 20—there is no such number as IXX).
  For 99, do NOT write IC
  (C − I or 100 − 1).
  DO write XCIX (XC + IX or 90 + 9).

Homework Tip!
Take advantage of any help or tutoring teachers offer on a difficult subject, like math.

Powers & Exponents

A power is the product of multiplying a number by itself.

Usually, a power is represented with a **base number** and an **exponent**. The **base number** tells **what number is being multiplied**. The exponent, a small number written above and to the right of the base number, tells how many times the base number is being multiplied.

For example, "6 to the 5th power" may be written as 6^5. Here, the base number is 6 and the exponent is 5. This means that 6 is being multiplied by itself 4 times:

$$6 \times 6 \times 6 \times 6 \times 6$$

$$6 \times 6 \times 6 \times 6 \times 6 = 7{,}776 \text{ or } 6^5 = 7{,}776$$

BASE NUMBER	2ND POWER	3RD POWER	4TH POWER	5TH POWER
1	1	1	1	1
2	4	8	16	32
3	9	27	81	243
4	16	64	256	1,024
5	25	125	625	3,125
6	36	216	1,296	7,776
7	49	343	2,401	16,807
8	64	512	4,096	32,768
9	81	729	6,561	59,049
10	100	1,000	10,000	100,000

Math

TFK Puzzles & Games

COMPUTING PIE

Try to cut this pizza into eight pieces. Problem is, you can only use three cuts. Hints: The pieces don't have to be the same size. And one of the cuts isn't a straight line.

(See Answer Key that begins on page 342.)

TFK Mystery Person

CLUE 1: I was born in West Virginia in 1928.

CLUE 2: While at Princeton University, I made an important mathematical discovery about game theory (the study of how players in a game make decisions). This theory has had an impact on politics, law, war and economics—which is why I won the Nobel Prize for Economics in 1994.

CLUE 3: Russell Crowe played me in the Oscar-winning movie about my life, *A Beautiful Mind*.

WHO AM I?

(See Answer Key that begins on page 342.)

AMERICA'S WARS

From the American Revolution to the war in Iraq, the U.S. has fought in 12 major conflicts. Do you know their names, where they were fought and why, and who won? Here's a quick look.

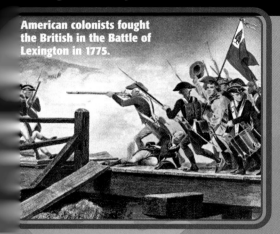

American colonists fought the British in the Battle of Lexington in 1775.

The War of 1812
1812-1815

CAUSE: The British obstructed American trade overseas and forced American sailors to serve on British ships. Some members of Congress, called "war hawks," encouraged the war because they hoped to gain some of Britain's territory in North America.

OUTCOME: Trade issues between the two countries remained unresolved, but Britain gave up claims to some of its land on the continent.

The American victory at Fort McHenry near Baltimore inspired Francis Scott Key to write the words for our national anthem, "The Star-Spangled Banner."

The American Revolution
1775-1783

CAUSE: Great Britain forced its 13 American colonies to pay taxes but did not give them any representation in the British Parliament. "Taxation without representation" and other injustices led the colonies to seek independence.

OUTCOME: The U.S. declared its independence on July 4, 1776. It achieved formal recognition when the Treaty of Paris was signed with Britain in 1783.

At the Battle of Bunker Hill, colonial officer William Prescott ordered, "Do not fire until you see the whites of their eyes!" His troops had the courage and discipline to hold their fire until the enemy was near, an early sign that the ragtag American army had a chance of defeating the well-trained, well-armed British troops.

During the War of 1812, the British set fire to Washington, D.C.

The Mexican War
1846-1848

CAUSE: Mexico was angered by the U.S.'s annexation of Texas, which had belonged to Mexico. The U.S. wanted to gain more of Mexico's land, especially California.

Military & War

More than 620,000 people died in the Civil War. That was 2% of the U.S. population.

OUTCOME: Mexico was forced to give up two-fifths of its territory and received $15 million from the U.S. in damages. This land eventually became the states of California, Nevada, Arizona, New Mexico and Utah.

The war was fought in the name of "manifest destiny," the belief that the U.S. should possess the entire continent from the Atlantic Ocean to the Pacific Ocean.

The Civil War
1861-1865

CAUSE: The Northern states (the Union) and the Southern states (the Confederacy) fought over slavery and states' rights. Eleven states (South Carolina, Mississippi, Florida, Alabama, Georgia, Louisiana, Texas, Arkansas, North Carolina, Virginia and Tennessee) seceded from the Union to form a separate nation called the Confederate States of America.

OUTCOME: The Union victory led to the reunification of the country and ended slavery.

More than 180,000 black soldiers fought in the Union Army. By the end of the war, they made up 10% of the Union troops. Both free African Americans and runaway slaves volunteered as soldiers.

The Spanish-American War
1898

CAUSE: The U.S. supported Cuba's desire for independence from Spanish rule. It saw the war as an opportunity to expand its own power in other parts of the world.

OUTCOME: Cuba was freed from Spanish rule, and the U.S. gained several former Spanish territories: Puerto Rico, Guam and the Philippines.

Before the war began, an explosion in Havana Harbor sank the U.S. battleship *Maine*, killing 260 crew members. "Remember the *Maine*!" became the war's most famous slogan.

World War I
1914-1918

CAUSE: Rivalries over power, territory and wealth led to the Great War. The U.S. joined the Allies (Britain, France, Russia, Italy and Japan), who were at war with the Central Powers (Germany, Austria-Hungary, Bulgaria and Turkey), after German submarines began sinking unarmed ships—notably the *Lusitania*.

OUTCOME: About 10 million soldiers died and 20 million were wounded. Germany was forced to admit guilt for the war, pay the other countries for the damage it caused and return territory it claimed during the war.

World War I was characterized by trench warfare. Each army dug protective trenches—long, deep rows of ditches in the ground. The troops slept, ate and fought against the enemy in these trenches.

World War II
1939–1945

CAUSE: The Axis powers—Hitler's Germany, along with the dictatorships of Italy and Japan—attempted to dominate the world. The Allies (the U.S., Britain, France, the U.S.S.R. and others) fought to stop them.

OUTCOME: Germany surrendered in 1945, and Japan surrendered later that year, after the U.S. dropped atom bombs on the cities of Hiroshima and Nagasaki.

One of the most horrific chapters of the war was the Holocaust, the systematic annihilation of about 6 million Jews as well as millions of others who did not conform to Nazi Germany's racist ideals.

The Korean War
1950–1953

CAUSE: Communist North Korea, supported by China, invaded non-communist South Korea. U.N. forces, mostly made up of U.S. troops, fought to protect South Korea.

OUTCOME: South Korea maintained its independence from North Korea.

The Korean War was the first armed conflict in the global struggle between democracy and communism—the "cold war."

The Vietnam War
1955–1975

CAUSE: Communist North Vietnam invaded noncommunist South Vietnam in an attempt to unify the country and impose communist rule. The United States fought on the side of South Vietnam to keep it independent.

OUTCOME: The United States withdrew its combat troops in 1973. In 1975, North Vietnam succeeded in taking control of South Vietnam.

Vietnam was the longest conflict the U.S. ever fought and the first war it lost.

Persian Gulf War
1991

CAUSE: Iraq invaded the country of Kuwait. The U.S., Britain and other countries came to Kuwait's aid.

OUTCOME: Iraq withdrew from Kuwait.

In a brilliant, lightning-fast campaign, U.S. and coalition ground troops defeated President Saddam Hussein's troops in just four days.

Overshadowed by World War II and Vietnam, the Korean War is sometimes called the Forgotten War.

U.S. troops met resistance from Iraqi insurgents in 2003's war in Iraq.

Afghanistan War
2002

CAUSE: Afghanistan's Taliban government harbored Osama bin Laden and members of the al-Qaeda terrorist group, who were responsible for the September 11, 2001, attacks on the U.S. After they refused to turn over bin Laden, the U.S. and U.N. coalition forces attacked.

OUTCOME: The Taliban government was ousted, and many terrorist camps in Afghanistan were destroyed.

 The Taliban surrendered within two months, much earlier than expected.

Iraq War
2003

CAUSE: Dictator Saddam Hussein's supposed possession of illegal weapons of mass destruction and Iraq's suspected ties to terrorism prompted the U.S. and Britain to invade and topple his government.

OUTCOME: Saddam Hussein was removed from power. American troops remained in Iraq, fighting and rebuilding.

 In December 2003, U.S. troops captured Saddam Hussein. They found him hiding in an eight-foot hole on a farm near his hometown of Tikrit. He had been on the run for nearly nine months.

American soldiers must be prepared for different climate conditions.

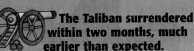

Did You Know?

There are more than 1,400,000 troops and officers in the U.S. Army, Navy, Air Force and Marines. Of those, only 35 have reached the highest rank of general or admiral.

Bobby Hearne, a project volunteer

Military Memories

Every Veterans Day, November 11, Americans honor the men and women who served in the armed forces. There are parades and speeches. But **Bobby Hearne,** 14, has a different way of celebrating veterans' contributions. Bobby interviewed veterans at the National World War II Reunion in Washington, D.C. He was one of 400 volunteers participating in the Veterans History Project, a national effort sponsored by the Library of Congress.

The project collects and records the wartime stories of American men and women who served in the military. The experiences of those outside the military who helped in war efforts, such as medical volunteers, are also included. The collection holds recorded interviews as well as letters, diaries and photos.

Many veterans don't like to talk about the hardships of war. Still, Bobby found that veterans warmed up to him: "I just acted as if I were talking to my grandpa, just asking him questions." Bobby heard firsthand accounts from men who had fought overseas and from women who had gone to work in factories. "I got to learn a lot about World War II from people who were actually in the war," he says.

Those people were happy to share their experiences. Lieutenant Commander John LaMontagne, 85, is a veteran of World War II and the Korean War. He says that the Veterans History Project is about the future, not just the past. "Young folks have to learn about these wars so they don't repeat our mistakes," he told TFK. The project has collected more than 20,000 stories about American heroes. To learn more about the project, go to *www.loc.gov/folklife/vets.*

—By Elizabeth Hira

The collection includes such items as a World War II photo (above) and a soldier's prisoner-of-war papers (left).

Terms of War

COLLATERAL DAMAGE A term used to indicate that civilians died in a military operation.

DECAPITATION STRIKE A military attack intended to remove a regime or a country's leadership. The U.S. military attempted a decapitation strike against Saddam Hussein at the beginning of the war in Iraq.

EMBEDDED REPORTER A journalist who travels with troops and reports from the battlefield. The 2003 Iraq war was the first time "embeds" were used.

IMPROVISED EXPLOSIVE DEVICE (IED) A homemade explosive device used by terrorists.

REGIME CHANGE The overthrow of a government.

SMART BOMBS Bombs that are guided to their targets by Global Positioning Satellites.

WEAPONS OF MASS DESTRUCTION (WMD) Chemical, biological and nuclear weapons that are designed to kill many people, usually over a large area. Chemical weapons include poisons, gases and other manufactured substances. Biological weapons are germs, bacteria and other microorganisms that are used to kill people or make them seriously ill. Anthrax is an example. Nuclear weapons create massive explosions that release radioactive chemicals into the air.

The Branches of the Military

There are five branches of the U.S. military: the **AIR FORCE, ARMY, COAST GUARD, MARINE CORPS** and **NAVY.** Each branch, except the Coast Guard, is part of the Department of Defense. The Coast Guard falls under the Department of Homeland Security.

An Air Force fighter jet patrols the skies.

> **AIR FORCE** The U.S. Air Force, the newest branch, was created in 1947. Its main function is to protect the country from the air and space. It uses fighter, bomber and transport aircraft as well as helicopters. The Air Force also controls the country's nuclear missiles.

> **ARMY** The U.S. Army, the oldest and largest branch, was created in 1775 by the Continental Congress. It is a ground force, meaning it operates only on land. Its main role is to protect and defend the country, using troops, tanks and artillery (large guns and other heavy weapons).

> **COAST GUARD** The U.S. Coast Guard was originally established in 1790 as the Revenue Cutter Service. In 1915, it was reorganized as the Coast Guard. During peacetime, the Coast Guard enforces the laws of the sea and rescues people and vessels in trouble. During war, the President of the United States can transfer Coast Guard resources to the Navy.

> **MARINE CORPS** The U.S. Marine Corps was organized in 1775 to help the Navy. It became its own branch in 1798. The Marine Corps is amphibious—it has responsibilities both on land and in the sea. During wartime, the Marine Corps carries out operations that clear the way for attacks by other branches, usually the Navy. Recently, Marines have expanded their role in ground operations. The Marine Corps has its own tanks and other armor, artillery and aircraft.

> **NAVY** The U.S. Navy was also created in 1775 by the Continental Congress. Its main role is to make sure the United States has access to the sea when and where necessary. The Navy also has a fleet of aircraft that it sends from its largest ships, called aircraft carriers, to areas where there are no available runways. Navy boats and submarines are used to attack the enemy.

TFK Mystery Person

CLUE 1: I was one of the greatest military leaders in world history. I was born in 356 B.C. My father was King Philip II of Macedon, a part of present-day Greece.

CLUE 2: By the time I took over my father's throne at age 20, I had commanded his troops in battle.

CLUE 3: Leading a small army, I conquered Greece and most of the known world, including Persia (Iran), Egypt, Central Asia and northern India. My personality and military feats made me a legend.

WHO AM I?

(See Answer Key that begins on page 342.)

U.S. Currency

The U.S. Mint and the Bureau of Engraving and Printing (BEP) are parts of the U.S. Treasury Department. Congress created the Mint in 1792. It makes all of the country's coins. The BEP was established in 1861. It designs and prints U.S. bills. It also prints U.S. postage stamps.

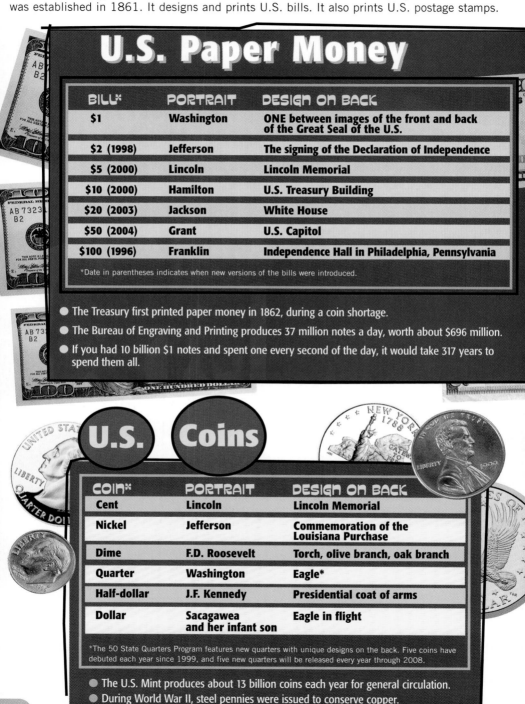

U.S. Paper Money

BILL*	PORTRAIT	DESIGN ON BACK
$1	Washington	ONE between images of the front and back of the Great Seal of the U.S.
$2 (1998)	Jefferson	The signing of the Declaration of Independence
$5 (2000)	Lincoln	Lincoln Memorial
$10 (2000)	Hamilton	U.S. Treasury Building
$20 (2003)	Jackson	White House
$50 (2004)	Grant	U.S. Capitol
$100 (1996)	Franklin	Independence Hall in Philadelphia, Pennsylvania

*Date in parentheses indicates when new versions of the bills were introduced.

- The Treasury first printed paper money in 1862, during a coin shortage.
- The Bureau of Engraving and Printing produces 37 million notes a day, worth about $696 million.
- If you had 10 billion $1 notes and spent one every second of the day, it would take 317 years to spend them all.

U.S. Coins

COIN*	PORTRAIT	DESIGN ON BACK
Cent	Lincoln	Lincoln Memorial
Nickel	Jefferson	Commemoration of the Louisiana Purchase
Dime	F.D. Roosevelt	Torch, olive branch, oak branch
Quarter	Washington	Eagle*
Half-dollar	J.F. Kennedy	Presidential coat of arms
Dollar	Sacagawea and her infant son	Eagle in flight

*The 50 State Quarters Program features new quarters with unique designs on the back. Five coins have debuted each year since 1999, and five new quarters will be released every year through 2008.

- The U.S. Mint produces about 13 billion coins each year for general circulation.
- During World War II, steel pennies were issued to conserve copper.
- "In God we trust" first appeared on U.S. coins in 1864, on the two-cent coin.

Countering Counterfeiters

Funny money is no joke. Millions of dollars worth of counterfeit money is circulating in the U.S. The Bureau of Engraving and Printing has made life tougher for counterfeiters by printing bills on special material—cotton and linen rag, with tiny red and blue fibers. This material is hard to reproduce and illegal to make. Counterfeiters also have trouble making images and numbers as crisp and distinct as they are on real money. But copying machines and electronic scanners have made it easier for forgers to create realistic bills. To fight back, the government constantly adds anti-forging features to bills. Here are some of them:

- **SECURITY THREAD** A plastic strip is placed in a different spot for each denomination. To see the thread, hold the bill up to a bright light. Under ultraviolet light, the strip of each denomination glows a different color.

- **WATERMARK** A different picture of the person on the bill is visible when the bill is held up to the light.

- **PORTRAIT** There is much more detail of the Presidents, making it harder to fake.

- **COLOR-SHIFTING INK** The number in the lower right-hand corner of the bill looks green when seen straight on. But at an angle it looks black.

- **MICROPRINTING** A magnifying lens is needed to see this tiny printing. It becomes blurred when copied.

- **FINE-LINE PRINTING PATTERNS** These tiny patterns appear in the backgrounds of portraits and buildings and are tough for computer scanners to reproduce.

- **SERIAL NUMBER** No two bills of the same denomination and series (the year the note was produced) have the same serial numbers. Many counterfeiters run off batches of bills with the same serial number.

- **COLORS** In the past, bills were printed only in black and green. Now other colors are being used. A new series of $20 bills, for example, is being printed in blue, peach and yellow.

Larger and more lifelike face

To Catch a Crook

If you receive a counterfeit note, follow the advice of the Secret Service:

1. Hold onto it.

2. Try to remember who passed you the fake note.

3. Write your initials and date on the edge of the bill.

4. Try not to handle the note; place it in a plastic bag or envelope, so you won't erase fingerprints.

5. Have your parents contact the police department or bring the bill to a local bank.

Source: U.S. Secret Service

"The United States of America" microprinted on oval

Clean, fine-line printing patterns

Security thread glows green

Old Money

- Before coins existed, the ancient Greeks used iron nails as money, the ancient Britons used sword blades and the ancient Chinese used swords and knives. The Hercules coin was introduced by Alexander the Great in 325 B.C.

- Cowrie shells have been used as money in many cultures.

- Some American colonists used wampum as money. Wampum was beautiful strands of beads made by Native Americans for ceremonial purposes. Our founding fathers also used livestock and produce as currency.

- Chinese coins had holes in the center so they could be strung together like beads. This made carrying them easier.

- A Roman coin shows the double-faced god Janus. It dates from 240–220 B.C.

- People used banks even before they used paper money and coins! In ancient Mesopotamia, grains and other valuable trade goods were stored in palaces and temples for safekeeping.

A cowrie-shell belt (top) is used as money on an Indonesian island. A Chinese coin (above). A wampum belt (right).

Average Allowances

Here are the average weekly allowances for kids, based on a survey done by Kids' Money.

Age	Average Allowance
4	$2.85
5	$3.15
6	$3.85
7	$4.10
8	$4.32
9	$5.52
10	$7.18
11	$7.92
12	$9.58
13	$9.52
14	$13.47
15	$15.57
16	$17.84
17	$30.66
18	$40.10

Source: www.kidsmoney.org

Make Your Own Budget

Grownups aren't the only people who have to worry about making ends meet. Say you'd like to buy a new videogame, but you don't have any money saved. Make a budget to see if you can afford to save a few dollars each week for the new game.

Here's how to make your own budget: write down every single item you spend money on each week and how much it costs. Your list may include movies, CDs and food. Now add up how much you earn each week from an allowance, baby-sitting or a paper route. Subtract the money you spend from the money you earn. You have a budget surplus if there's money left over. You have a deficit if there's no money left or you come up with a negative number. In that case, look at each item on your "spend" list to see if there's anything that you can cut.

Use TFK's Budget Blaster to see how you're handling your money at timeforkids.com/budget

TFK Mystery Person

CLUE 1: I am an actress and host of a popular TV talk show.

CLUE 2: I formed my own entertainment production company, called HARPO Productions, in 1986, and became the first woman to own and produce her own TV show.

CLUE 3: I was named one of the 100 Most Influential People of the 20th Century by TIME magazine. I am the first African-American woman to become a billionaire.

WHO AM I?

(See Answer Key that begins on page 342.)

179

Animation's Fast Track

The Polar Express takes moviemaking technology into the future

Fans of Tom Hanks were thrilled when *The Polar Express* chugged into theaters. Hanks played a train conductor, a boy, the boy's father, a hobo and Santa Claus. The actor nailed each performance without ever changing his costume or makeup. In fact, he didn't wear either!

So how did he do it? *The Polar Express*, based on the book by Chris Van Allsburg, is the first film made with a technique called performance capture. The process allows film-makers to build an animated character based on an actor's performance.

The ability to capture, or record, full-body movement is nothing new. A similar process has been used to make video games. But performance capture is more advanced. It records lifelike movements and human emotions. "The breakthrough is that we're able to record facial movements in extremely high detail," says Steve Starkey, one of the film's producers.

Hanks and the other actors in

the movie wore nearly 200 sensors, or reflective dots, on their faces and bodies. The cast worked on a nearly empty stage, without sets or costumes that could block the sensors. Cameras recorded each performance in a three-dimensional format. The 3-D image was then inserted into a virtual set in a computer program.

"All I saw were white dots dancing around on a black screen," Hanks told TFK in an interview. "But I knew it was [actor] Peter Scolari. I could tell his face, his posture."

It took Hanks only 40 days to make *The Polar Express*. He hopes the film leaves the audience with a sense of magic and wonder. "I'd like them to say, 'If a train pulled up in my yard on some late December evening, I'd like to get on board because it looks as if it would be as wonderful as that one [the Polar Express] was.'"
—*By Kathryn Satterfield*

The conductor's expressions and motions match Hanks's. Reflective dots on him help capture the performance.

Movies & TV

Top Kids Movies of All Time*

MOVIE	MONEY EARNED IN THE U.S.
1. *Star Wars*	$460,998,007
2. *Shrek 2*	436,471,036
3. *E.T.–The Extra-Terrestrial*	434,949,459
4. *Star Wars : Episode I–The Phantom Menace*	431,088,295
5. *Spider-Man*	403,706,375
6. *Spider-Man 2*	373,377,893
7. *Jurassic Park*	357,067,947
8. *Finding Nemo*	339,714,978
9. *The Lion King*	328,539,505
10. *Harry Potter and the Sorcerer's Stone*	317,575,550

Source: Exhibitor Relations Co., Inc.
*Through January 2, 2005

Top Animated Films of All Time*

MOVIE	MONEY EARNED IN THE U.S.
1. *Shrek 2*	$436,471,036
2. *Finding Nemo*	339,714,978
3. *The Lion King*	328,539,505
4. *Shrek*	267,665,011
5. *Monsters, Inc.*	255,870,172
6. *The Incredibles*	251,657,004
7. *Toy Story 2*	245,852,179
8. *Aladdin*	217,350,219
9. *Toy Story*	191,780,865
10. *Ice Age*	176,387,405

Source: Exhibitor Relations Co., Inc.
*Through January 2, 2005

Japan's Disney

Howl's Moving Castle is Miyazaki's latest movie.

Hayao Miyazaki is called the Walt Disney of Japan. His animated movies, which include *Howl's Moving Castle* and *Spirited Away*, have brought him international fame.

Miyazaki writes, animates and directs his films. His artistry doesn't come out of a computer—his films are mostly drawn by hand. Although he has a large staff of artists, Miyazaki is involved in every aspect of the animation process. In *Princess Mononoke*, for example, he personally looked at 80,000 of the 140,000 frames that made up the movie.

Born in Tokyo, Japan, in 1941, Miyazaki started his career creating *manga* (comic books). Later he turned to creating *anime*, or animated features. Miyazaki creates fantasy worlds that seem astonishingly real. He accomplishes this by paying careful attention to detail. Whether he draws clouds, flying machines, butterflies or robots, everything looks believable. Few animators can match his films' vivid colors and convincing texture, dimension and depth.

Although Miyazaki draws objects with great precision, he is most concerned with the world of nature. His peaceful, beautiful landscapes teach us that people should live in harmony with nature rather than try to dominate it.

Big Feat

Each winter, Hollywood stars get decked out in glamorous gowns and suits, jewelry and hairstyles for film's biggest extravaganza of the year—the Academy Awards, also known as the Oscars.

The Academy Awards honor the best in moviemaking. Winning an Oscar, a golden statue handed out by the Academy of Motion Picture Arts & Sciences, is considered the highest honor for moviemakers, actors and actresses.

Although adults dominate the list of nominees and winners, kids have made their mark in Oscar history. Check out these young Oscar contenders. (People whose names are in white won an Oscar.)

High Honors

ACTOR	AGE	FILM	YEAR
Justin Henry	8	Kramer vs. Kramer	1979
Jackie Cooper	9	Skippy	1931
Mary Badham	10	To Kill a Mockingbird	1962
Quinn Cummings	10	The Goodbye Girl	1977
Patty McCormack	10	The Bad Seed	1956
Tatum O'Neal	10	Paper Moon	1973
Brandon De Wilde	11	Shane	1953
Haley Joel Osment	11	The Sixth Sense	1999
Anna Paquin	11	The Piano	1993
Keisha Castle-Hughes	13	Whale Rider	1999
Patty Duke	16	The Miracle Worker	1962
Jack Wild	16	Oliver!	1968

To Kill a Mockingbird

The Miracle Worker

These kids' movies were nominated for Best Picture Oscars. The titles in red won the statue.

The Wizard of Oz (1939)

The Yearling (1946)

Mary Poppins (1964)

Doctor Dolittle (1967)

E.T.—The Extra-Terrestrial (1982)

Babe (1995)

Did You Know?

In 1991, *Beauty and the Beast* became the first animated film nominated for a Best Picture Oscar. The Academy of Motion Picture Arts & Sciences created a new category, Best Animated Feature, in 2001. *Shrek* took home the trophy, beating out *Monsters, Inc.* and *Jimmy Neutron: Boy Genius*.

go
For the history of film:
www.factmonster.com/movietimeline

TFK Puzzles & Games

Made in Hollywood

You can't make a film without actors and a director. But the movie crew is also vital in producing a motion picture. Can you match each crew member to the job he or she performs?

1. **Foley artist**

2. **Rigger**

3. **Key grip**

4. **Wrangler**

5. **Gaffer**

A. This person is the chief electrician on a set and is responsible for setting up the lights and making sure that all the electrical equipment is operating safely.

B. This person adds sound effects to movies after they are filmed, such as the sound of a door closing, as well as more complicated effects like the sound of the light saber in *Star Wars*.

C. This person is in charge of the livestock and animals on the set that don't need special training and aren't dangerous.

D. This person supervises the moving and hauling of objects on a set, such as cranes, cables, backdrops and tracks for cameras, and is in charge of setting up and taking down the entire set.

E. This person comes on a set before the shooting begins and sets up or builds major pieces of construction, such as scaffolding that holds lights.

(See Answer Key that begins on page 342.)

Top Selling DVDs of 2004

1. *Shrek 2*
2. *The Lord of the Rings: The Return of the King*
3. *Star Wars* Trilogy
4. *The Passion of the Christ*
5. *Harry Potter and the Prisoner of Azkaban*
6. *Spider-Man 2*
7. *Matrix Revolutions*
8. *Elf*
9. *The Lion King 1 ¹/₂*
10. *Brother Bear*

Source: Video Business Online

Most Rented Videos of 2004

1. *Open Range*
2. *Out of Time*
3. *Radio*
4. *Cheaper by the Dozen*
5. *Something's Gotta Give*
6. *Mystic River*
7. *American Wedding*
8. *Secondhand Lions*
9. *School of Rock*
10. *The Day After Tomorrow*

Source: Video Business Online

 Read Q&A's with the kid actors in the Lemony Snicket movie at timeforkids.com/orphans

183

TV Facts and Figures

Did you ever keep track of how much time you spend in front of the television? Try it—you might be surprised or even shocked!

- The television is on an average of 7 hours 40 minutes a day in U.S. homes.

- 56% of children ages 8 to 16 have a TV in their bedroom; 36% of kids ages 6 and under have a TV in their bedroom.

- American children spend an average of 4 hours 41 minutes each day in front of a video screen of some kind.

- The average American youth watches television 1,023 hours per year.

- The average American youth spends 900 hours each year in school.

- Parents spend 38.5 minutes each week engaged in meaningful conversation with their children.

- The average American child sees 200,000 acts of violence on TV by age 18.

- 40% of Americans always or often watch television while eating dinner.

- 80% of Hollywood executives believe there is a link between TV violence and real violence.

- American children ages 2 to 17 spend 19 hours 40 minutes each week watching television.

- 91% of children polled said they felt "upset" or "scared" by violence on television.

- Ten or more hours of TV watching per week has been shown to negatively affect academic achievement.

Source: TV-Turnoff Network

Homework Tip!

Don't do your homework in a room where the TV is on. It'll distract you. Instead, choose a quiet place where you won't be disturbed.

TOP-RATED Kid Shows*

KIDS 6 TO 11

Network Shows
1. *American Idol*–Tuesday (Fox)
2. *American Idol*–Wednesday (Fox)
3. *Survivor: All-Stars* (CBS)
4. *Survivor: Pearl Islands* (CBS)
5. *Survivor: Vanuatu* (CBS)

Cable Shows
1. *SpongeBob SquarePants* (Nick-at-Nite)
2. *The Adventures of Jimmy Neutron: Boy Genius* (Nickelodeon)
3. *Casper Meets Wendy* (Disney)
4. *Fairly OddParents* (Nickelodeon)
5. *Rocket Power* (Nickelodeon)

KIDS 12 TO 17

Network Shows
1. *American Idol*–Tuesday (Fox)
2. *American Idol*–Wednesday (Fox)
3. *Survivor: All-Stars* (CBS)
4. *Survivor: Pearl Islands* (CBS)
5. *Survivor: Vanuatu* (CBS)

Cable Shows
1. *SpongeBob SquarePants* (Nick-at-Nite)
2. *The Adventures of Jimmy Neutron: Boy Genius* (Nickelodeon)
3. *Casper Meets Wendy* (Disney)
4. *Fairly OddParents* (Nickelodeon)
5. *Rocket Power* (Nickelodeon)

*September 2003–September 2004
Source: Nielsen Media Research

Movies & TV

Top-Rated Series Finales

The last episode of a popular television series has become a must-see event. These are the top-rated send-offs of all time.

Rank	Show	Date
1.	*M*A*S*H*	February 28, 1983
2.	*The Fugitive*	August 29, 1967
3.	*Cheers*	May 20, 1993
4.	*Seinfeld*	May 14, 1998
5.	*Magnum P.I.*	May 1, 1988
	Friends (tie)	May 6, 2004

*M*A*S*H*

TFK Mystery Person

CLUE 1: I'm a famous director, and one of my companies, Industrial Light and Magic, creates visual effects for movies.

CLUE 2: My first blockbuster was *American Graffiti*, a film about teenagers in California, where I grew up.

CLUE 3: My most famous movies are set a long time ago in a galaxy far, far away.

WHO AM I?

(See Answer Key that begins on page 342.)

Did You Know?

In 1927, Philo Farnsworth transmitted the first all-electronic television image. The television age began the next year, when General Electric introduced a TV set with a three-inch screen. By 1931, there were nearly 40,000 sets in the U.S.

Genres of Music

blues A style of music that evolved from southern African-American work songs and secular (nonreligious) songs. Blues influenced the development of rock, rhythm-and-blues and country music. Some blues musicians include **Bessie Smith, Muddy Waters, Robert Johnson** and **Sonny Boy Williamson.**

classical Music that is usually more sophisticated and complex than other styles of music. Many classical compositions are instrumentals, which means there are no words in the songs. Classical music has its roots in Europe. It includes symphonies, chamber music, sonatas and ballets. Some important classical-music composers are **Wolfgang Amadeus Mozart, Ludwig van Beethoven** and **Johann Sebastian Bach. Philip Glass** and **John Williams** are modern classical composers.

country-and-western music A form of American music that originated in the Southwest and the Southeast in the 1920s. Early country songs often told stories of poor people facing difficult lives. Recent country-music songs are often hard to tell apart from pop-music songs. **Johnny Cash, George Strait, Willie Nelson, Faith Hill** and **Dolly Parton** are popular country-music singers.

aith Hill

folk A style of music that has been passed down orally within cultures or regions. It is known for its simple melodies and the use of acoustic instruments. Modern folk music is based on traditional folk music and often contains political lyrics. **Bob Dylan, Pete Seeger, Woody Guthrie, Joan Baez** and the group **Peter, Paul and Mary** are folk performers.

jazz American music born in the early part of the 20th century from African rhythms and slave chants. It has spread from its African-American roots to become a worldwide style. Jazz forms include improvisation (unrehearsed playing), swing, bebop and cool jazz. **Benny Goodman, Miles Davis, Cassandra Wilson** and **Thelonius Monk** are famous jazz musicians.

pop (popular) music A genre that covers a wide range of music, is often softer than rock and is driven by melody. Pop usually appeals to a broad assortment of listeners. Some famous pop musicians include **Frank Sinatra, Avril Lavigne, Justin Timberlake** and **Beyoncé.**

Avril Lavigne

rap Urban, typically African-American music that features lyrics—usually spoken over sampled sounds or drum loops—often about social or political issues. Hip-hop, a style of music similar to rap, blends rock, jazz and soul with sampled sounds. **Jay-Z, Run-D.M.C., 50 Cent, Missy Elliott** and **Eminem** are rappers.

rock One of the most popular forms of 20th century music, which combines African-American rhythms, urban blues, folk and country music. It developed in the early 1950s and has inspired—and been inspired by—many other styles, such as grunge, ska and heavy metal. Some important rock bands are **the Beatles, the Rolling Stones, Led Zeppelin, Nirvana, R.E.M.** and **U2.**

Good Vibrations

Families of Instruments

Musical instruments are grouped into families based on how they make sounds. In an orchestra, musicians sit together in these family groupings. But not every instrument fits neatly into a group. For example, the piano has strings that vibrate and hammers that strike. Is it a stringed instrument or a percussion instrument? Some say it is both!

Brass

Brass instruments are made of brass or some other metal and make sounds when air is blown inside. The musician's lips must buzz, as though making a "raspberry" noise against the mouthpiece. Air then vibrates inside the instrument, which produces a musical sound.

Brass instruments include the trumpet, trombone, tuba, French horn, cornet and bugle.

Strings

Yes, the sounds of string instruments come from their strings. The strings may be plucked, as with a guitar or harp; bowed, as with a cello or violin; or struck, as with a piano. This creates a vibration that causes a unique sound.

Stringed instruments include the violin, viola, cello, bass, double bass, harp, lute, guitar and dulcimer.

Percussion

Most percussion instruments, such as drums and tambourines, make sounds when they are hit. Others are shaken, like maracas, and still others may be scratched, rubbed or whatever else makes the instrument vibrate and produce a sound.

Percussion instruments include drums, cymbals, triangles, chimes, bells and xylophones.

Woodwinds

Woodwind instruments produce sound when air (wind) is blown inside. Air might be blown across an edge, as with a flute; between a reed and a surface, as with a clarinet; or between two reeds, as with a bassoon. The sound happens when the air vibrates inside.

Woodwind instruments include the flute, piccolo, clarinet, recorder, bassoon and oboe.

Most Downloaded Songs of 2004

SONG	NUMBER OF DOWNLOADS
1. "THE REASON," HOOBASTANK	379,839
2. "THIS LOVE," MAROON 5	346,922
3. "LET'S GET IT STARTED," BLACK EYED PEAS	328,239
4. "HEY YA!" (RADIO MIX), OUTKAST	324,848
5. "YEAH," USHER	314,009
6. "SHE WILL BE LOVED," MAROON 5	306,550
7. "1985," BOWLING FOR SOUP	260,962
8. "TOXIC," BRITNEY SPEARS	243,873
9. "DROP IT LIKE IT'S HOT," SNOOP DOGG	234,046
10. "LOSE MY BREATH," DESTINY'S CHILD	225,204

Source: Nielsen SoundScan

Did You Know?

In 2004, music fans bought 651 million CDs and 5.5 million digital albums (downloaded from the Internet), according to Nielsen SoundScan.

Grammy Award
Winners

The new year brings lots of resolutions—and awards. More than 100 Grammy Awards are handed out each year. Here's a look at some of 2005's winners.

❖**Record of the Year**
"Here We Go Again," Ray Charles and Norah Jones

❖**Album of the Year**
Genius Loves Company, Ray Charles and various artists

❖**Song of the Year (award for the songwriter)**
"Daughters," John Mayer

❖**Best New Artist**
Maroon 5

❖**Best Female Pop Performance**
"Sunrise," Norah Jones

❖**Best Male Pop Performance**
"Daughters," John Mayer

❖**Best Pop Group Performance**
"Heaven," Los Lonely Boys

❖**Best Rock Album**
American Idiot, Green Day

❖**Best Alternative Album**
A Ghost Is Born, Wilco

❖**Best R&B Album**
The Diary of Alicia Keys

❖**Best Rap Album**
The College Dropout, Kanye West

❖**Best Dance Recording**
"Toxic," Britney Spears

❖**Best Country Album**
Van Lear Rose, Loretta Lynn

❖**Best Musical Album for Children**
cELLAbration! A Tribute to Ella Jenkins

Most Played Songs on the Radio in 2004

1.	"YEAH," USHER
2.	"THE REASON," HOOBASTANK
3.	"THIS LOVE," MAROON 5
4.	"BURN," USHER
5.	"SOMEDAY," NICKELBACK
6.	"MY IMMORTAL," EVANESCENCE
7.	"IF I AIN'T GOT YOU," ALICIA KEYS
8.	"TIPSY," J-KWON
9.	"I DON'T WANNA KNOW," MARIO WINANS
10.	"HERE WITHOUT YOU," 3 DOORS DOWN

Source: Nielsen SoundScan

Top Selling Albums of 2004

	Album	Artist	Units sold
1.	*Confessions*	Usher	7,978,594
2.	*Feels Like Home*	Norah Jones	3,842,920
3.	*Encore*	Eminem	3,517,097
4.	*When the Sun Goes Down*	Kenny Chesney	3,072,224
5.	*Here for the Party*	Gretchen Wilson	2,931,097
6.	*Live Like You Were Dying*	Tim McGraw	2,786,840
7.	*Songs About Jane*	Maroon 5	2,708,415
8.	*Fallen*	Evanescence	2,614,226
9.	*Autobiography*	Ashley Simpson	2,576,945
10.	*NOW That's What I Call Music! 16*	Various artists	2,560,316

Source: Nielsen SoundScan

Homework Tip!

Don't be impatient if you are having trouble with your work. Mistakes are normal. Take a short break, and then begin again. Ask for help if you get stuck. Even professional musicians don't always get it right on the first take!

go For inductees into the Rock and Roll Hall of Fame: www.factmonster.com/rockhall

Types of Dance

From the earliest times, people have used dance to entertain, to celebrate, to convey beliefs and feelings—and just for the fun of it.

Almost every culture in the world has used dance as a means of expression. Argentina, for example, is the home of the sultry ballroom dance called the tango.

Traditional African dances often form part of religious ceremonies or mark important events. The square dances that developed in colonial America became an opportunity for farmers to gather socially with their often far-flung neighbors.

Some of the most common forms of dance performance are ballet, modern dance and Broadway musical dance.

Ballet

was created in 16th century Italy. Each position and step is choreographed, or carefully planned. Many ballets convey a feeling of delicate beauty and lightness—ballet dancers' graceful motions seem effortless, and much of the movement is focused upward. Toe (or pointe) shoes allow ballerinas to dance on their toes and appear to defy gravity.

Modern dance,

created in the 20th century, is a rejection of many of the traditions of ballet. It goes against what some viewed as ballet's rigid steps, limited emotional expression and dainty beauty. Modern-dance steps often seem informal, and modern dancers don't mind if a step looks rough if it expresses an emotion.

The waltz

is a romantic ballroom dance in which the couple revolves in circles to a beat of three. The Viennese waltz is the most famous.

Flamenco

is a fiery, emotional dance that originated in Spain and is characterized by hand-clapping and fast, rhythmic foot-stamping.

Native-American dance

is often ceremonial or religious, traditionally calling on the spirits for help in farming or hunting or giving them thanks for rain or for victory in war.

Hip-Hop

was developed by teenagers in New York City's South Bronx in the late 1970s. It brings together driving rhythm, athletic moves and urban style.

TFK Mystery Person

CLUE 1: I am an American-Indian ballet dancer. I was born in Fairfax, Oklahoma, in 1925.

CLUE 2: I am known as one of the greatest American ballerinas ever. I was the first U.S.-born dancer to be named top ballerina at the New York City Ballet.

CLUE 3: I married the legendary choreographer George Balanchine.

WHO AM I?

(See Answer Key that begins on page 342.)

Some myths that you know today may have been around for hundreds, or even thousands, of years. Although myths are often entertaining, they did not originate just for entertainment. Unlike folklore or fables, myths were once believed to be true. Myths helped to explain human nature and the mysteries of the world.

THE OLYMPIAN GODS AND GODDESSES

In Greek mythology, 12 gods and goddesses ruled the universe from atop Greece's Mount Olympus. All the Olympians are related to one another. The Romans adopted most of these gods and goddesses, but with new names (given below in parentheses).

The most powerful of all was **Zeus (Jupiter),** god of the sky and the king of Olympus. His temper affected the weather; he threw thunderbolts when he was unhappy. He was married to Hera.

Hera (Juno) was goddess of marriage and the queen of Olympus. She was Zeus's wife and sister. Many myths tell of how she got back at Zeus for his many insults.

POSEIDON

Poseidon (Neptune) was god of the sea. He was the most powerful god after his brother, Zeus. He lived in a beautiful palace under the sea and caused earthquakes when he was in a rage.

Hades (Pluto) was king of the dead. He lived in the underworld, the heavily guarded land that he ruled. He was the husband of Persephone (daughter of the goddess Demeter), whom he kidnapped.

Aphrodite (Venus) was the goddess of love and beauty. Some people believe she was a daughter of Zeus. Others believe she rose from the sea.

Apollo (same Roman name) was the god of music and healing. He was also an archer and hunted with a silver bow.

Ares (Mars) was the god of war. He was both cruel and a coward. Ares was the son of Zeus and Hera, but neither of his parents liked him.

Hephaestus (Vulcan) was the god of fire and the forge (a furnace in which metal is heated). Although he made armor and weapons for the gods, he loved peace.

APHRODITE

Mythology

Artemis (Diana) was the goddess of the hunt and the protector of women in childbirth. She loved all wild animals.

Athena (Minerva) was the goddess of wisdom. She was also skilled in the art of war. Athena sprang full-grown from the forehead of Zeus and became his favorite child.

Hestia (Vesta) was the goddess of the hearth (a fireplace at the center of the home). She was the oldest Olympian.

Hermes (Mercury) was the messenger god, a trickster and a friend to thieves. He was the son of Zeus. The speediest of all gods, he wore winged sandals and a winged hat.

ATHENA

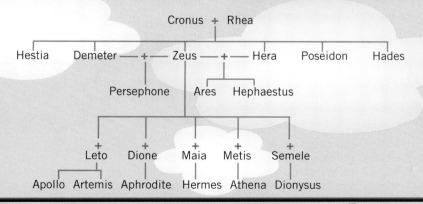

DIONYSUS

These Olympians are sometimes included in the list of rulers:

Demeter (Ceres) was the goddess of the harvest. The word *cereal* comes from her Roman name.

Dionysus (Bacchus) was the god of wine. In ancient Greece, he was honored with springtime festivals that centered on theater.

A Greek Family Tree

Zeus was the son of Cronus and Rhea. These two Titans ruled the universe before being overthrown by their children, the Olympians. Zeus was the king of Olympus, and **Hera** was the queen. Zeus was the father of many gods with his wife, Hera, and with other women. Here's the genealogy, or family tree, of the Greek gods. A plus sign (+) means that the two gods produced children. For example, Zeus + Leto indicates that they were the parents of Apollo and Artemis.

```
                    Cronus  +  Rhea
   ┌─────────┬───────────┬──────┬───────┬──────────┬─────────┐
 Hestia   Demeter ─ + ─ Zeus ─ + ─ Hera   Poseidon    Hades
              ┌────────────┴─────┬──────┐
         Persephone          Ares   Hephaestus
      ┌─────────┬─────────┬──────┬──────────┐
      +         +         +      +          +
    Leto      Dione     Maia   Metis     Semele
      │         │         │      │          │
  Apollo Artemis Aphrodite Hermes Athena  Dionysus
```

191

Gods and Goddesses Around the World

AZTEC

Coatlicue was the goddess of the earth and the mother of all the gods. She also gave birth to the moon and stars. The Aztecs carved a gigantic stone statue of her wearing a necklace made of human hearts and hands.

Huitzilopochtli was the god of the sun and of war. He was the patron god of the Aztec capital of Tenochtitlán, where Mexico City now stands. The Aztecs built a great temple there in his honor and sacrificed many humans to him.

Chicomecoatl was the goddess of corn and fertility. So important was corn to the Aztecs that she was also known as "the goddess of nourishment."

EGYPTIAN

Ra was the supreme god and the god of the sun. The early pharaohs claimed to be descended from him. He sometimes took the form of a hawk or a lion.

Nut represented the heavens and helped to put the world in order. She had the ability to swallow stars and the pharaohs and cause them to be born again. She existed before all else had been created.

Osiris was the god of the underworld and the judge of the dead. He was associated with the cycle of life and was often shown wearing mummy wrappings.

Isis invented agriculture. She was the goddess of law, healing, motherhood and fertility. She came to be seen as a Mother Earth figure.

ISIS

Horus was a sky god who loved goodness and light. The son of Osiris and Isis, he was often shown as a young child.

Thoth was the god of wisdom and magic. He was believed to have invented writing, astronomy and other arts, and served as a scribe, or writer, to the gods.

Nephthys was the goddess of the dead. She was a kind friend to the newly dead as well as to those left behind.

MAYAN

Hunahpu was a god of the sun and the father of the first humans. A great hero, with his brother he defeated the forces of death and went on to rule in the heavens.

Hurakan was the god of storms and winds. When the first humans made him angry, he swept them away in a violent flood. The word *hurricane* comes from his name.

Ixchel was the goddess of the moon and the protector of pregnant women. She was often shown as an old woman wearing a full skirt and holding a serpent.

Chac was the god of agriculture and a great friend to humans. He brought them rain and used his huge tail and fangs to protect planted fields.

CHAC

Itzamna was the official god of the Mayan empire and the founder of its people. Corn, chocolate, writing and calendars were among his many gifts to them.

African Myths

Africa is rich in stories and myths. These are just a few of them. The tribe or culture from which the myth originated is listed in parentheses.

The origin of the world and people (Yoruba)

Before there was land, there was only the sky and water. The god Obatala wanted to cover the water with land, where people would live. He hung a gold chain from the sky and climbed down it, toward the waves crashing beneath him. He poured sand into the waves and then dropped a hen onto the sand. The hen kicked the sand all around, and the sand became land.

Obatala lived on the land and planted a tree. Other plants and trees soon began sprouting from the ground. Lonely, Obatala made figures of people out of mud and clay. Olorun, the ruler of the sky, gave life to Obatala's figures.

How the ostrich got its long neck (Kikuyu)

Ostriches didn't always have such long necks. Exhausted from sitting on her eggs for weeks, a female ostrich was happy when her husband relieved her. That night, the male heard his wife laughing with another male ostrich. He wanted to check things out, but he couldn't leave the nest. Instead, he strained his neck to try to see what was going on. He did this all night, and in the morning he discovered that his neck had been permanently stretched.

Hare clears his land (West Africa)

Hare wanted to get married, but he needed to plant crops to feed his wife. Overwhelmed by his overgrown fields, the lazy hare challenged a hippopotamus to a tug-of-war. Sensing an easy win, the hippo agreed. The hare tied a rope around the hippo and hopped off into the woods, where an elephant took him up on the same offer. The elephant and hippo struggled all day, both shocked that a hare could be so strong. By the end of the day, the two animals had flattened and softened the hare's fields, making them ready for planting.

TFK Mystery Person

CLUE 1: I was born in Oxford, England, in 1919. As a child, I enjoyed mythology.

CLUE 2: My granduncle, Nerny Madan, suggested that Mars's moons be named Deimos and Phobos.

CLUE 3: When I was 11 years old, I came up with the name Pluto—the Greek god of the underworld—for a newly discovered planet. The Lowell Observatory officially named the planet Pluto.

WHO AM I?

(See Answer Key that begins on page 342.)

1 GEORGE WASHINGTON (SERVED 1789–1797)

Born: Feb. 22, 1732, in Virginia; died: Dec. 14, 1799
Political Party: None
Vice President: John Adams
DID YOU KNOW? **Washington was the only President unanimously elected. He received all 69 electoral votes.**
FIRST LADY: **Martha Dandridge Custis**

2 JOHN ADAMS (SERVED 1797–1801)

Born: Oct. 30, 1735, in Massachusetts; died: July 4, 1826
Political Party: Federalist
Vice President: Thomas Jefferson
DID YOU KNOW? **Adams was the first President to live in the White House.**
FIRST LADY: **Abigail Smith**

3 THOMAS JEFFERSON (SERVED 1801–1809)

Born: April 13, 1743, in Virginia; died: July 4, 1826
Political Party: Democratic-Republican
Vice Presidents: Aaron Burr, George Clinton
DID YOU KNOW? **In signing the 1803 Louisiana Purchase, Jefferson nearly doubled the size of the U.S.**
FIRST LADY: **Martha Wayles Skelton**

4 JAMES MADISON (SERVED 1809–1817)

Born: March 16, 1751, in Virginia; died: June 28, 1836
Political Party: Democratic-Republican
Vice Presidents: George Clinton, Elbridge Gerry
DID YOU KNOW? **Madison was the only President to have two Vice Presidents die in office. Clinton died in 1812 and Gerry died in 1814.**
FIRST LADY: **Dorothy "Dolley" Payne Todd**

5 JAMES MONROE (SERVED 1817–1825)

Born: April 28, 1758, in Virginia; died: July 4, 1831
Political Party: Democratic-Republican
Vice President: Daniel D. Tompkins
DID YOU KNOW? **The Monroe Doctrine forbade foreign countries like Spain and Russia from expanding into North and South America.**
FIRST LADY: **Elizabeth "Eliza" Kortright**

6 JOHN QUINCY ADAMS (SERVED 1825–1829)

Born: July 11, 1767, in Massachusetts; died: Feb. 23, 1848
Political Party: Democratic-Republican
Vice President: John C. Calhoun
DID YOU KNOW? **In 1843, Adams became the first President to have his photograph taken.**
FIRST LADY: **Louisa Catherine Johnson**

Presidents

7 ANDREW JACKSON (SERVED 1829–1837)
Born: March 15, 1767, in South Carolina; died: June 8, 1845
Political Party: Democratic
Vice Presidents: John C. Calhoun, Martin Van Buren
DID YOU KNOW? **Jackson took several bullets while fighting in duels—an activity for which he was famous.**
FIRST LADY: **Rachel Donelson Robards**

8 MARTIN VAN BUREN (SERVED 1837–1841)
Born: Dec. 5, 1782, in New York; died: July 24, 1862
Political Party: Democratic
Vice President: Richard M. Johnson
DID YOU KNOW? **Van Buren was the first President born a U.S. citizen rather than a British subject.**
FIRST LADY: **Hannah Hoes**

9 WILLIAM HENRY HARRISON (SERVED 1841)
Born: Feb. 9, 1773, in Virginia; died: April 4, 1841
Political Party: Whig
Vice President: John Tyler
DID YOU KNOW? **Harrison had the shortest presidency: he died after only a month in office.**
FIRST LADY: **Anna Tuthill Symmes**

10 JOHN TYLER (SERVED 1841–1845)
Born: March 29, 1790, in Virginia; died: Jan. 18, 1862
Political Party: Whig
Vice President: None
DID YOU KNOW? **Tyler was the first President to marry in office. He was also the President with the most children (15).**
FIRST LADY: **Letitia Christian (d. 1842); Julia Gardiner**

11 JAMES KNOX POLK (SERVED 1845–1849)
Born: Nov. 2, 1795, in North Carolina; died: June 15, 1849
Political Party: Democratic
Vice President: George M. Dallas
DID YOU KNOW? **Polk's inauguration was the first one to be reported by telegraph.**
FIRST LADY: **Sarah Childress**

 Read about a reporter who covered nine U.S. Presidents at timeforkids.com/presidents

12 ZACHARY TAYLOR (SERVED 1849–1850)

Born: Nov. 24, 1784, in Virginia; died: July 9, 1850
Political Party: Whig
Vice President: Millard Fillmore
DID YOU KNOW? **Taylor never voted until he was 62 years old.**
FIRST LADY: **Margaret Mackall Smith**

★

13 MILLARD FILLMORE (SERVED 1850–1853)

Born: Jan. 7, 1800, in New York; died: March 8, 1874
Political Party: Whig
Vice President: None
DID YOU KNOW? **Fillmore and his first wife, Abigail, started the White House Library.**
FIRST LADY: **Abigail Powers (d. 1853); Caroline Carmichael McIntosh**

★

14 FRANKLIN PIERCE (SERVED 1853–1857)

Born: Nov. 23, 1804, in New Hampshire; died: Oct. 8, 1869
Political Party: Democratic
Vice President: William R. King
DID YOU KNOW? **Pierce was the only elected President not re-nominated by his party for a second term.**
FIRST LADY: **Jane Means Appleton**

★

15 JAMES BUCHANAN (SERVED 1857–1861)

Born: April 23, 1791, in Pennsylvania; died: June 1, 1868
Political Party: Democratic
Vice President: John C. Breckinridge
DID YOU KNOW? **Buchanan was the only President to remain a bachelor—he never married.**
FIRST LADY: **None**

★

16 ABRAHAM LINCOLN (SERVED 1861–1865)

Born: Feb. 12, 1809, in Kentucky; died: April 15, 1865
Political Party: Republican
Vice Presidents: Hannibal Hamlin, Andrew Johnson
DID YOU KNOW? **Lincoln's Gettysburg Address and Second Inaugural Address are among the greatest presidential speeches.**
FIRST LADY: **Mary Todd**

★

17 ANDREW JOHNSON (SERVED 1865–1869)

Born: Dec. 29, 1808, in North Carolina; died: July 31, 1875
Political Party: Democratic
Vice President: None
DID YOU KNOW? **Johnson was the first President to be impeached. The Senate found him not guilty, however, and he remained President.**
FIRST LADY: **Eliza McCardle**

18 ULYSSES S. GRANT (SERVED 1869–1877)

Born: April 27, 1822, in Ohio; died: July 23, 1885
Political Party: Republican
Vice Presidents: Schuyler Colfax, Henry Wilson
DID YOU KNOW? **Grant's much-praised *Memoirs* has been in print since 1885.**
FIRST LADY: **Julia Boggs Dent**

19 RUTHERFORD B. HAYES (SERVED 1877–1881)

Born: Oct. 4, 1822, in Ohio; died: Jan. 17, 1893
Political Party: Republican
Vice President: William A. Wheeler
DID YOU KNOW? **The first telephone was installed in the White House while Hayes was President.**
FIRST LADY: **Lucy Ware Webb Hayes**

20 JAMES A. GARFIELD (SERVED 1881)

Born: Nov. 19, 1831, in Ohio; died: Sept. 19, 1881
Political Party: Republican
Vice President: Chester A. Arthur
DID YOU KNOW? **Garfield was the first President who campaigned in two languages—English and German.**
FIRST LADY: **Lucretia Rudolph**

21 CHESTER A. ARTHUR (SERVED 1881–1885)

Born: Oct. 5, 1829, in Vermont; died: Nov. 18, 1886
Political Party: Republican
Vice President: None
DID YOU KNOW? **A stylish dresser, Arthur was nicknamed "Gentleman Boss" and "Elegant Arthur."**
FIRST LADY: **Ellen Lewis Herndon**

22 GROVER CLEVELAND (SERVED 1885–1889)

Born: March 18, 1837, in New Jersey; died: June 24, 1908
Political Party: Democratic
Vice President: Thomas A. Hendricks
DID YOU KNOW? **Cleveland was the only President to be defeated and then re-elected, serving two non-consecutive terms.**
FIRST LADY: **Frances Folsom**

23 BENJAMIN HARRISON (SERVED 1889–1893)

Born: Aug. 20, 1833, in Ohio; died: March 13, 1901
Political Party: Republican
Vice President: Levi P. Morton
DID YOU KNOW? **Benjamin Harrison was the only President who was a grandson of a President (William Henry Harrison).**
FIRST LADY: **Caroline Lavina Scott (d. 1892); Mary Scott Lord Dimmick**

24 GROVER CLEVELAND (SERVED 1893–1897)
Born: March 18, 1837, in New Jersey; died: June 24, 1908
Political Party: Democratic
Vice President: Adlai E. Stevenson
DID YOU KNOW? Cleveland was the only President to be married in the White House.
FIRST LADY: Frances Folsom

25 WILLIAM McKINLEY (SERVED 1897–1901)
Born: Jan. 29, 1843, in Ohio; died: Sept. 14, 1901
Political Party: Republican
Vice Presidents: Garret A. Hobart, Theodore Roosevelt
DID YOU KNOW? McKinley was one of four Presidents assassinated in office.
FIRST LADY: Ida Saxton

26 THEODORE ROOSEVELT (SERVED 1901–1909)
Born: Oct. 27, 1858, in New York; died: Jan. 6, 1919
Political Party: Republican
Vice President: Charles W. Fairbanks
DID YOU KNOW? Theodore Roosevelt was the first President to ride in an automobile, an airplane and a submarine.
FIRST LADY: Edith Kermit Carow

27 WILLIAM H. TAFT (SERVED 1909–1913)
Born: Sept. 15, 1857, in Ohio; died: March 8, 1930
Political Party: Republican
Vice President: James S. Sherman
DID YOU KNOW? Taft was the only President who went on to serve on the Supreme Court as Chief Justice.
FIRST LADY: Helen Herron

28 WOODROW WILSON (SERVED 1913–1921)
Born: Dec. 28, 1856, in Virginia; died: Feb. 3, 1924
Political Party: Democratic
Vice President: Thomas R. Marshall
DID YOU KNOW? Wilson was the first President to hold a news conference. About 125 members of the press attended the event on March 15, 1913.
FIRST LADY: Ellen Louise Axson (d. 1914); Edith Bolling Galt

29 WARREN G. HARDING (SERVED 1921–1923)
Born: Nov. 2, 1865, in Ohio; died: Aug. 2, 1923
Political Party: Republican
Vice President: Calvin Coolidge
DID YOU KNOW? Harding was a newspaper publisher before he was President.
FIRST LADY: Florence King

30 CALVIN COOLIDGE (SERVED 1923–1929)
Born: July 4, 1872, in Vermont; died: Jan. 5, 1933
Political Party: Republican
Vice President: Charles G. Dawes
DID YOU KNOW? **Coolidge was the first President to be sworn in by his father, a justice of the peace.**
FIRST LADY: Grace Anna Goodhue

★

31 HERBERT C. HOOVER (SERVED 1929–1933)
Born: Aug. 10, 1874, in Iowa; died: Oct. 20, 1964
Political Party: Republican
Vice President: Charles Curtis
DID YOU KNOW? **An asteroid, Hooveria, was named for Hoover.**
FIRST LADY: Lou Henry

★

32 FRANKLIN D. ROOSEVELT (SERVED 1933–1945)
Born: Jan. 30, 1882, in New York; died: April 12, 1945
Political Party: Democratic
Vice Presidents: John Garner, Henry Wallace, Harry S. Truman
DID YOU KNOW? **Franklin D. Roosevelt was the only President elected to four terms.**
FIRST LADY: Anna Eleanor Roosevelt

★

33 HARRY S. TRUMAN (SERVED 1945–1953)
Born: May 8, 1884, in Missouri; died: Dec. 26, 1972
Political Party: Democratic
Vice President: Alben W. Barkley
DID YOU KNOW? **Truman was a farmer, a hatmaker and a judge before entering politics.**
FIRST LADY: Elizabeth "Bess" Virginia Wallace

★

34 DWIGHT D. EISENHOWER (SERVED 1953–1961)
Born: Oct. 14, 1890, in Texas; died: March 28, 1969
Political Party: Republican
Vice President: Richard M. Nixon
DID YOU KNOW? **Eisenhower was a five-star general in World War II before becoming President.**
FIRST LADY: Marie "Mamie" Geneva Doud

★

35 JOHN F. KENNEDY (SERVED 1961–1963)
Born: May 29, 1917, in Massachusetts; died: Nov. 22, 1963
Political Party: Democratic
Vice President: Lyndon B. Johnson
DID YOU KNOW? **Kennedy was the first Roman Catholic President.**
FIRST LADY: Jacqueline Lee Bouvier

36 LYNDON B. JOHNSON (SERVED 1963–1969)
Born: Aug. 27, 1908, in Texas; died: Jan. 22, 1973
Political Party: Democratic
Vice President: Hubert H. Humphrey
DID YOU KNOW? **Lyndon Johnson was the first person to take the oath of office on an airplane. It was the presidential jet.**
FIRST LADY: **Claudia Alta "Lady Bird" Taylor**

37 RICHARD M. NIXON (SERVED 1969–1974)
Born: Jan. 9, 1913, in California; died April 22, 1994
Political Party: Republican
Vice Presidents: Spiro T. Agnew, Gerald R. Ford
DID YOU KNOW? **Nixon was the only President to resign.**
FIRST LADY: **Thelma Catherine "Pat" Ryan**

38 GERALD R. FORD (SERVED 1974–1977)
Born: July 14, 1913, in Nebraska
Political Party: Republican
Vice President: Nelson A. Rockefeller
DID YOU KNOW? **After college, Ford was a football coach, a park ranger and a male model.**
FIRST LADY: **Elizabeth "Betty" Anne Bloomer Warren**

39 JIMMY CARTER (SERVED 1977–1981)
Born: Oct. 1, 1924, in Georgia
Political Party: Democratic
Vice President: Walter F. Mondale
DID YOU KNOW? **Carter won the Nobel Peace Prize in October 2002.**
FIRST LADY: **Rosalynn Smith**

40 RONALD W. REAGAN (SERVED 1981–1989)
Born: Feb. 6, 1911, in Illinois; died: June 5, 2004
Political Party: Republican
Vice President: George H.W. Bush
DID YOU KNOW? **Reagan worked for nearly 30 years as a Hollywood actor.**
FIRST LADY: **Nancy Davis**

41 GEORGE H.W. BUSH (SERVED 1989–1993)
Born: June 12, 1924, in Massachusetts
Political Party: Republican
Vice President: J. Danforth Quayle
DID YOU KNOW? **Bush was the first President to spend a holiday with troops overseas—Thanksgiving in Saudi Arabia.**
FIRST LADY: **Barbara Pierce**

42 WILLIAM J. CLINTON (SERVED 1993–2001)

Born: Aug. 19, 1946, in Arkansas
Political Party: Democratic
Vice President: Albert Gore Jr.

DID YOU KNOW? Clinton was the second of two Presidents to be impeached. The Senate acquitted him.

FIRST LADY: Hillary Rodham

★

43 GEORGE W. BUSH (SERVED 2001–)

Born: July 6, 1946, in Connecticut
Political Party: Republican
Vice President: Richard B. Cheney

DID YOU KNOW? George W. Bush was an owner of the Texas Rangers baseball team from the late 1980s until 1998.

FIRST LADY: Laura Welch

Homework Tip!

Keep old papers, quizzes and tests. You may need them for future projects or to study for tests.

BIG HEADS

There are several presidential monuments to our former leaders. One of the most famous—and awe-inspiring—is Mount Rushmore in the Black Hills of South Dakota. During the summer, more than 20,000 people each day visit Mount Rushmore, part of the National Park System, to admire the enormous, 60-foot-high heads of Presidents Washington, Jefferson, Theodore Roosevelt and Lincoln.

Sculptor Gutzon Borglum began the project in 1927. He died in 1941, before completing the monument. His son Lincoln finished up later that year. The monument is the largest work of art in the world. Even the features are huge: each nose is 20 feet long, the mouths are 18 feet wide and each eye is 11 feet across.

go For biographies of the Presidents:
www.factmonster.com/presidents

Words of Wisdom

Here are some famous presidential quotes.

★ **George Washington** "Liberty, when it begins to take root, is a plant of rapid growth."

★ **Thomas Jefferson** "One man with courage is a majority."

★ **John Quincy Adams** "Always vote for principle, though you may vote alone, and you may cherish the sweetest reflection that your vote is never lost."

★ **William Henry Harrison** "But I contend that the strongest of all governments is that which is most free."

★ **Abraham Lincoln** "If slavery is not wrong, nothing is wrong."

★ **Ulysses S. Grant** "I have never advocated war except as a means of peace."

★ **Chester A. Arthur** "Good ballplayers make good citizens."

★ **Benjamin Harrison** "The disfranchisement of a single legal elector by fraud or intimidation is a crime too grave to be regarded lightly."

★ **Theodore Roosevelt** "Speak softly and carry a big stick."

★ **Herbert Hoover** "Peace is not made at the council table or by treaties, but in the hearts of men."

★ **Harry S. Truman** "You cannot stop the spread of an idea by passing a law against it."

★ **John F. Kennedy** "Ask not what your country can do for you; ask what you can do for your country."

★ **Jimmy Carter** "We are of course a nation of differences. Those differences don't make us weak. They're the source of our strength."

★ **Ronald Reagan** "America is too great for small dreams."

TFK Top 5

Closest Presidential Races

In the 1800 election, two candidates received the same number of electoral votes. The House of Representatives broke the tie by voting for Thomas Jefferson. Here are the closest elections and the number of electoral votes the two top candidates received.

1. 1800: Jefferson: 73 / Burr: 73

2. 1877: Hayes: 185 / Tilden: 184

3. 1796: Adams: 71 / Jefferson: 68

4. 2000: Bush: 271 / Gore: 266

5. 1916: Wilson: 277 / Hughes: 254

Source: *Top 10 of Everything*, DK

Did You Know?

President Theodore Roosevelt gave the White House its name in 1901, when he had "White House" engraved on his stationery. Until then it had been called President's Palace, President's House and Executive Mansion.

 go Learn fun facts and take a quiz about Theodore Roosevelt at timeforkids.com/bio/troosevelt

CAMP DAVID

SUMMER CAMP for Presidents

★ ★ ★ ★ ★ ★ ★ ★ ★

President Bush entertains Russian President Vladimir Putin at Camp David.

If you can't take the heat . . . head for Camp David! The summer retreat offers Presidents and special dignitaries a place to relax and escape the sweltering summers of Washington, D.C. Franklin D. Roosevelt was the first President to stay in this camp located in the Catoctin mountains of Maryland. Roosevelt called it Shangri-La, after the imaginary paradise in the novel *Lost Horizon*. President Dwight Eisenhower renamed it Camp David in honor of his grandson, David.

The public is not allowed on the grounds, which are run by the U.S. Navy and protected by the U.S. Marines. Its attractions include a pool, a putting green, a driving range, tennis courts, a gym, horseback riding and guest cabins. In this retreat, Gerald Ford snowmobiled, Jimmy Carter fished, Ronald Reagan tinkered in a woodworking shop and George H.W. Bush pitched horseshoes.

Presidents entertain visiting heads of state, conduct Cabinet meetings and brief congressional leaders at Camp David. It has been the site of such historic events as the planning of the Normandy invasion, discussions about the Bay of Pigs invasion and meetings between the leaders of Egypt and Israel held by Jimmy Carter that led to the Camp David Accords.

TFK Mystery Person

CLUE 1: I was a U.S. journalist and researcher who was born in Jefferson, Iowa, in 1901.

CLUE 2: I developed statistical methods that surveyed the public's opinion on issues. These methods are used today to predict election results.

CLUE 3: I began a polling company that bears my name.

WHO AM I?

(See Answer Key that begins on page 342.)

go For White House facts:
www.factmonster.com/whitehouse

THE FIVE MAJOR FAITHS

	JUDAISM	CHRISTIANITY
FOUNDER	The Hebrew leader Abraham founded Judaism around 2000 B.C. Moses gave the Jews the Torah around 1250 B.C.	Jesus Christ, who was crucified around A.D. 30 in Jerusalem
HOW MANY GODS	One	One
HOLY WRITINGS	The most important are the Torah, or the five books of Moses. Others include Judaism's oral tradition, which is known as the Talmud when it is written down.	The Bible is the main sacred text of Christianity.
BELIEFS	Jews believe in the laws of God and the words of the prophets. In Judaism, however, actions are more important than beliefs.	Jesus taught love of God and neighbor and a concern for justice. 
TYPES	The three main types are Orthodox, Conservative and Reform. Orthodox Jews strictly follow the traditions of Judaism. Conservative Jews follow most traditional practices, but less strictly than the Orthodox. Reform Jews are the least traditional.	In 1054 Christians separated into the Eastern Orthodox Church and the Roman Catholic Church. In the early 1500s the major Protestant groups (Lutheran, Presbyterian and Episcopalian) came into being. Dozens of other groups have since developed.
WHERE	There are large Jewish populations in Israel and in the U.S.	Through its missionary activity, Christianity has spread to most parts of the globe.

Religion

Monotheism Monotheism is the belief that there is only one god. **Judaism,** **Christianity** and **Islam** are all monotheistic faiths.

ISLAM	HINDUISM	BUDDHISM
Muhammad, who was born in A.D. 570 at Mecca, in Saudi Arabia	Hinduism has no founder. The oldest religion, it may date to prehistoric times.	Siddhartha Gautama, called the Buddha, in the 4th or 5th century B.C. in India
One	Many	None, but there are enlightened beings (Buddhas)
The Koran is the sacred book of Islam.	The most ancient are the four Vedas.	The most important are the Tripitaka, the Mahayana Sutras, Tantra and Zen texts.
The Five Pillars, or main duties, are: 1. Profession of faith 2. Prayer 3. Charitable giving 4. Fasting during the month of Ramadan 5. Pilgrimage to Mecca at least once	Reincarnation is the belief that all living things are in a cycle of death and rebirth. Life is ruled by the laws of karma, in which rebirth depends on moral behavior.	The Four Noble Truths 1. All beings suffer. 2. Desire for possessions, power and so on causes suffering. 3. Desire can be overcome. 4. The path that leads away from desire is the Eightfold path (the Middle Way).
Almost 90% of Muslims are Sunnis. Shiites are the second-largest group. The Shiites split from the Sunnis in 632, when Muhammad died.	No single belief system unites Hindus. A Hindu can believe in only one god, in many or in none.	Theravada (Way of the Elders) and Mahayana (Greater Vehicle) are the two main types.
Islam is the main religion of the Middle East, Asia and the north of Africa.	Hinduism is practiced by more than 80% of India's population.	Buddhism is the main religion in many Asian countries.

A Clash Over Symbols

In France, a Muslim woman protests the new law.

Organized Religions in the World

	RELIGION	MEMBERS	% OF WORLD POPULATION
1.	Christianity	2 billion	**33.0%**
2.	Islam	1.3 billion	**22.0**
3.	Hinduism	900 million	**15.0**
4.	Buddhism	360 million	**6.0**
5.	Sikhism	23 million	**0.4**

Source: Adherents.com

Top Religious Groups in the United States

About 140 million Americans belong to a religious group. Here's a breakdown:

Religious Body	Adherents
1. PROTESTANT	**66 MILLION**
2. CATHOLIC	**62 MILLION**
3. JEWISH	**6 MILLION**
4. MORMON	**4 MILLION**
5. MUSLIM	**1.6 MILLION**

Source: Religious Congregation and Membership

In 2004, the French government passed a law barring students from wearing head scarves and other noticeable religious symbols in public schools. The law prohibits students from wearing head scarves, called *hijab*, worn by Muslim women and girls. Students also can't wear head coverings called *kippas*, worn by Jewish men and boys, and large crosses, worn by Christians.

The goal of the law, French President Jacques Chirac said, was to make sure "our youngsters are not exposed to divisive ill winds, which drive people apart and set them against one another."

Critics of the law say wearing a head scarf in school is a personal choice and a basic right.

"The government should not be in the business of telling a woman how to dress," Salam Al-Marayati, the executive director of the California-based Muslim Public Affairs Council, told TFK. —*By Dina El Nabli*

Did You Know?

Religious sects and movements of many types arose in the United States in the 19th century. They were established for many reasons, including new interpretations of the Bible, teachings of new prophets and thinkers, and the expectation of Christ's Second Coming. The largest still in existence are: Christian Scientists, Mormons, Seventh-Day Adventists and Jehovah's Witnesses.

Religious Holidays

Christian Holidays 2006

ASH WEDNESDAY MARCH 1
The first day of Lent

EASTER APRIL 16
The resurrection of Jesus

PENTECOST JUNE 4
The feast of the Holy Spirit

FIRST SUNDAY IN ADVENT DECEMBER 3
The start of the Christmas season

CHRISTMAS DECEMBER 25
The birth of Jesus

Muslim Holidays 2006

All Muslim holidays begin at sundown the day before the dates listed here.

EID AL-ADHA JANUARY 10
The festival of sacrifice

MUHARRAM JANUARY 31
The Muslim New Year

MAWLID AL-NABI APRIL 11
The prophet Muhammad's birthday

RAMADAN SEPTEMBER 24
The month of fasting

Jewish Holidays 2006

All Jewish holidays begin at sundown the day before the dates listed here.

PURIM MARCH 14
The feast of the lots

PASSOVER APRIL 13
The feast of unleavened bread

SHAVUOT JUNE 2
The feast of first fruits

ROSH HASHANAH SEPTEMBER 23
The Jewish New Year

YOM KIPPUR OCTOBER 2
The day of atonement

SUKKOT OCTOBER 7
The feast of the tabernacles

SIMCHAT TORAH OCTOBER 14
The rejoicing of the law

HANUKKAH DECEMBER 16
The beginning of the festival of lights

 **Mystery Person**

CLUE 1: I am an important religious figure in American history. I was born in Vermont in 1805.

CLUE 2: I preached that I was chosen by God to start a new church. My followers called me a prophet.

CLUE 3: I formed and led the Church of Jesus Christ of Latter-day Saints. Members of this church are known as Mormons.

WHO AM I?

(See Answer Key that begins on page 342.)

Little Person, Big Discovery

Homo floresiensis's skull (left) is much smaller than a normal human skull (below).

Scientists find evidence of a tiny human species

Scientists are buzzing about the discovery of a tiny female fossil they say is a new human species. The species lived about 18,000 years ago on the Indonesian island of Flores. It is extremely small, about three feet tall. Scientists believe the species was stuck on the island, while modern humans were spreading across the rest of the planet.

Scientists say the new species, called *Homo floresiensis*, or Flores Man, is a relative of the modern human. They also found seven other similar individual fossil specimens. The specimens range from 95,000 to 12,000 years old.

Scientific discoveries "don't get any better" than a discovery like Flores Man, said anthropologist Bernard Wood. Wood also said that he thinks the find is the "most significant discovery concerning our own genus" in his lifetime.

Some scientists have serious questions about the discovery. A group of Indonesian scientists says that the fossil is actually no different from modern humans—it's just a great deal smaller. "The skeleton is…simply a fossil of a modern human, *Homo sapiens*, that lived about 13,000 to 18,000 years ago," said anthropologist Teuku Jacob.

WAS FLORES MAN REALLY HUMAN?

Other scientists say Flores Man is too different from modern humans and our distant cousins. If scientists decide to include the new species in the Homo family, which includes modern humans, it would be the eighth species in the family.

The Flores species has a skull that looks like the skull of *Homo erectus* but is much smaller. Scientists say Flores Man's brain was about a quarter of the size of the modern human brain, or about the size of a small grapefruit! Its front teeth are smaller than modern human teeth. Flores Man may have made and used tools, lit fires and hunted for meat in organized groups.

Geological evidence on the island leads scientists to believe that Flores Man and other species were wiped out by a volcano. Local folktales tell of a tiny people that lived in the island's forests. No one took those legends seriously—until now.

—By Dina El Nabli

The depiction is based on a fossil skeleton.

Earth's Timeline

Life on Earth began about 2 billion years ago, but there are no good fossils from before the Cambrian Period, which began 550 million years ago. The largely unknown past before then is called the Precambrian. It is divided into the Lower (older) and Upper (younger) Precambrian—also called the Archeozoic and Proterozoic Eras.

The history of Earth since the Cambrian Period began is divided into three giant chunks of time, or eras, each of which includes a number of shorter periods.

PALEOZOIC ERA
This era began 550 million years ago and lasted for 305 million years. It is sometimes called Early Life.

Period	Millions of Years Ago	Creatures That Appeared
CAMBRIAN	550–510	INVERTEBRATE SEA LIFE
ORDOVICIAN	510–439	FIRST FISH
SILURIAN	439–409	GIGANTIC SEA SCORPIONS
DEVONIAN	409–363	MORE FISH AND SEA LIFE
CARBONIFEROUS	363–290	EARLY INSECTS AND AMPHIBIANS
PERMIAN	290–245	EARLIEST TURTLES

MESOZOIC ERA
This era began 245 million years ago and lasted for 180 million years. It is sometimes called Middle Life or the Age of Reptiles.

Period	Millions of Years Ago	Creatures That Appeared
TRIASSIC	245–208	EARLY REPTILES AND MAMMALS
JURASSIC	208–146	EARLY DINOSAURS; FIRST BIRDS
CRETACEOUS	146–65	MORE DINOSAURS, BIRDS; FIRST MARSUPIALS

CENOZOIC ERA
This era began 64 million years ago and includes the geological present. It is sometimes called Recent Life or the Age of Mammals.

Period	Millions of Years Ago	Creatures That Appeared
TERTIARY	64–2	LARGER MAMMALS; MANY INSECTS; BATS
QUATERNARY	2–present	EARLY HUMANS TO MODERN HUMANS

For more about ancient ancestors:
www.factmonster.com/ancientancestors

SCIENCE FAQs

Why does a knuckleball "dance" or an airplane fly? Here are answers to some science questions kids often ask.

Why does a knuckleball seem to "dance" toward home plate?

The ball drops and soars unpredictably because it doesn't spin. The lack of rapid spin turns the seams of the baseball into tiny airfoils—surfaces that create lift and drag when they fly through the air. As the air passes over the seams, tiny swirls are created, causing pockets of low pressure around the surface of the ball. As air rushes in to fill the pockets, the ball is pushed in different directions. If the ball rotates too much, the seams will present a more consistent surface to the wind, and then the ball will follow a smoother path.

Why do leaves change color in the fall?

One sure sign of fall (besides the beginning of a new school year) is the change in color of leaves from green to yellow, orange and red. Trees are like bears—they store up food during the spring and summer and rest for the winter. Over the spring and summer, trees use a process called photosynthesis *(see page 216)* to make food and energy. A green pigment called chlorophyll makes photosynthesis happen. During the fall and winter, there isn't enough light or water for photosynthesis to occur, so the chlorophyll begins to fade way. As the green disappears, other colors begin to show. These colors have been in the leaves all along but were covered by the chlorophyll. To see the different colors in leaves, try the experiment on the next page.

Why does my hair stand on end when I take off my winter hat?

Every atom has an electrical charge, either positive or negative. The nucleus, or center, of an atom is surrounded by small particles called electrons, which carry a negative charge. When two objects are rubbed together, the electrons sometimes move from one object to the other. When you take your hat off, electrons from your hat move onto your hair. Two objects with the same charge push away from each other. Since your individual hairs now have the same charge, they move away from each other, and you look funny.

How does a plane take off and fly?

It's easy to understand how a bird can fly—it's lightweight and it has wings. But how does a huge airplane get off the ground? The plane's engines push the plane forward. As it moves, air flowing around the wings creates lift. The lift increases as the plane gathers speed. The plane takes off once there's enough lift to overcome gravity. When the plane is in the air, thrust from the engines pushes the plane forward.

How do scientists know how to make a flu vaccine if viruses can be different every year?

The flu virus changes every year. However, scientists gather information about virus mutations, or changes, before the flu-virus season begins. This lets them predict what each year's flu virus might look like. Based on that, a vaccine is made that scientists hope will be accurate enough to help people fight off major cases of the flu.

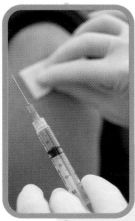

What are stem cells?

Stem cells, the basic building blocks of human development, are sometimes

called "magic seeds." That's because they can regenerate different kinds of human tissue. The use of stem cells is controversial because the best source for the cells is human embryos. Stem cells form four to five days after an egg is fertilized. These embryos must be destroyed to harvest the cells, and some people say this the same as taking human life. Others think that an embryo that is just a few days old is simply a tiny cluster of cells and not the same as a human life. They also maintain that stem cells could someday save human lives. Stem cells show promise of being able to treat and cure many medical conditions, such as

---

YOUR TURN — Leaf Chromatography

Discover what colors are in green leaves.

Materials
- 3 green leaves from 3 different kinds of trees
- 3 small glass jars
- aluminum foil
- rubbing alcohol
- coffee filter
- shallow baking pan
- hot water
- tape
- pen
- butter knife

What to do

1. Label each jar with the type of tree you took the leaf from.

2. Tear the leaves into small pieces, keeping the different types of leaves separate.

3. Cut three strips from the coffee filter and label them as you did the jars.

4. Put the leaf pieces into their corresponding jars.

5. Pour enough rubbing alcohol into the jars to just cover the leaves.

6. Use the knife to grind the leaves into a mush.

7. Pour about 1 inch of hot water into the pan.

8. Cover the jars loosely with the aluminum foil. Place them in the pan.

9. Swirl the jars every five minutes once the alcohol becomes discolored. Replace the water when it cools.

10. After about 30 minutes, remove the jars from the water.

11. Place one end of a coffee filter into the alcohol of the corresponding jar. Secure the other end to the jar with a piece of tape. Wait at about an hour (possibly longer) and watch what happens.

What happens

As the alcohol evaporates, it pulls the colors in the leaf up the coffee filter and separates them. The green you see is chlorophyll. You'll also see shades of yellow, red or orange. You only see these colors in the fall, when the chlorophyll fades, but they have always been in the leaves.

For science project tips:
www.factmonster.com/scienceprojects

LIFE-CHANGING SCIENCE DISCOVERIES

Try to imagine life with no antibiotics. Without them, we wouldn't live nearly as long as we do. Here's a look at some discoveries that have changed the world. It's impossible to rank their importance, so they're listed in the order in which they were discovered.

In 1543, while on his deathbed, Polish astronomer **NICHOLAS COPERNICUS** published his theory that the Sun is a motionless body at the center of the solar system, with the planets revolving around it. Before the Copernican system was introduced, astronomers believed Earth was at the center of the universe.

ISAAC NEWTON, an English mathematician and physicist, is

considered the greatest scientist of all time. Among his many discoveries, the most important may be the law of universal gravitation. In 1664, Newton figured out that gravity is the force that draws objects toward each other. It explained why things fall down and why the planets orbit the Sun.

MICHAEL FARADAY made two big discoveries that changed our lives. In 1821, he discovered that when a wire carrying an electric current is placed next to a single magnetic pole, the wire will rotate. This led to the development of the electric motor. Ten years later, he became the first person to produce an electric current by moving a wire through a magnetic field. Faraday's experiment created the first generator, the forerunner of the huge dynamos that produce our electricity.

When **CHARLES DARWIN,** the British naturalist, came up with the theory of evolution in 1859, he changed our idea of how life on Earth developed. Darwin argued that all organisms evolve, or change, very slowly over time. These changes are adaptations that sometimes allow a species to survive in its environment. These adaptations happen by chance. If a species doesn't adapt, it may become extinct. He called this process natural selection, but it is often called the survival of the fittest.

Before French chemist **LOUIS PASTEUR** began experimenting with bacteria in the 1860s, people did not know what caused disease. He not only

discovered that disease came from microorganisms, but he also realized that bacteria could be killed by heat and disinfectant. This idea led doctors to wash their hands and sterilize their

instruments, which has saved millions of lives.

The special theory of relativity, which **ALBERT EINSTEIN** published in 1905, explains the relationships between speed, time and distance. The complicated theory states that the speed of light always remains the same—186,000 miles per second—regardless of how fast someone or something is moving toward or away from the light's source. This theory became the foundation of much of modern science.

Nobody knows exactly how the universe came into existence, but many scientists believe that it happened about 13.7 billion years ago with a massive explosion called the Big Bang. In 1927, **GEORGES LEMAÎTRE** proposed the Big Bang theory of the universe. The theory says that all the matter in the universe was originally compressed into a tiny dot. In a fraction of a second, the dot expanded, and all the matter instantly filled what is now our universe. The event marked the beginning of time. The vast majority of scientists now accepts the theory's validity.

Danish physicist **NIELS BOHR** is considered one of the most important figures in modern physics. He won a 1922 Nobel Prize in Physics for his research on the structure of an atom and

for his work in the development of the quantum theory. Although he helped develop the atom bomb, he frequently advocated using atomic power for peaceful purposes.

Antibiotics are powerful drugs that kill bacteria that enter our bodies and make us sick. In 1928, **ALEXANDER FLEMING** discovered the first antibiotic, penicillin. It was made from a mold that grew in his lab. Without antibiotics, infections like strep throat could be deadly.

On February 28, 1953, **JAMES WATSON** of the United States and **FRANCIS CRICK** of England made one of the greatest scientific discoveries in history. The two scientists found the double-helix structure of DNA. This molecule is made up of two strands that twist around each other and have an almost endless variety of chemical patterns that create instructions for the human body to follow. Our genes are made of DNA and determine things like what color

hair and eyes we'll have. In 1962, Watson and Crick were awarded the Nobel Prize for their work. The discovery has helped doctors understand diseases and may someday prevent some illnesses like heart disease and cancer.

THE ELEMENTS

Elements are the building blocks of nature. Water, for example, is created from two basic ingredients: the element hydrogen and the element oxygen. Each element is a substance made up of only one type of **atom.** For example, all the atoms in a bar of pure gold are the same. Elements cannot be split up into any simpler substances. (When elements combine, they form substances called **compounds.** Water is a compound.)

An atom, however, is made up of even smaller particles. These are known as subatomic particles. The most important are:

- **protons, which have positive electrical charges.**
- **electrons, which have negative electrical charges.**
- **neutrons, which are electrically neutral.**

The **atomic number** of an element is the number of protons in one atom of the element. Each element has a different atomic number. For example, the atomic number of hydrogen is 1, and the atomic number of oxygen is 8.

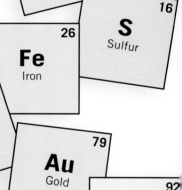

Types of Elements

As of 2004, scientists have discovered at least 112 different elements.

- Elements with atomic numbers 1 (hydrogen) to 92 (uranium) are found naturally on Earth.

- Those with atomic numbers 94 (plutonium) or greater are artificial elements. They have to be synthesized—that is, created by scientists in a high-tech laboratory.

- Elements with atomic numbers 101 or greater are known as the transfermium elements. They are also known as heavy elements because their atoms have very large masses compared with atoms of hydrogen, the lightest of all elements.

Did You Know?

In February 2004, researchers in Russia discovered two new chemical elements. They are Element 113, called Ununtrium, and Element 115, called Ununpentium. They are the newest additions to the Periodic Table of Elements.

How the Elements Are Named

Names for new elements are approved by the International Union of Pure and Applied Chemistry (IUPAC) in Geneva, Switzerland. They are often named for scientists, places or Greek or Latin words. For example, krypton (atomic number 36) is from the Greek word kryptos, meaning hidden, because it is colorless and odorless.

Periodic Table of Elements

Key:
- Number
- Period
- Weight
- Group
- Symbol
- Name

Example: 1 / 1 / H / Hydrogen / 1.00794

Period	1	2	3	4	5	6	7	8	9	10	11	12	13	14	15	16	17	18
1	1 H Hydrogen 1.00794																	2 He Helium 4.002602
2	3 Li Lithium 6.941	4 Be Beryllium 9.012182											5 B Boron 10.811	6 C Carbon 12.0107	7 N Nitrogen 14.0067	8 O Oxygen 15.9994	9 F Flourine 18.9984032	10 Ne Neon 20.1797
3	11 Na Sodium 22.98977	12 Mg Magnesium 24.305											13 Al Aluminium 26.981538	14 Si Silicon 28.0855	15 P Phosphorus 30.973761	16 S Sulfur 32.065	17 Cl Chlorine 35.453	18 Ar Argon 39.948
4	19 K Potassium 39.0983	20 Ca Calcium 40.078	21 Sc Scandium 44.95591	22 Ti Titanium 47.867	23 V Vanadium 50.9415	24 Cr Chromium 51.9961	25 Mn Manganese 54.938049	26 Fe Iron 55.845	27 Co Cobalt 58.9332	28 Ni Nickel 58.6934	29 Cu Copper 63.546	30 Zn Zinc 65.39	31 Ga Gallium 69.723	32 Ge Germanium 72.64	33 As Arsenic 74.9216	34 Se Selenium 78.96	35 Br Bromine 79.904	36 Kr Krypton 83.8
5	37 Rb Rubidium 85.4678	38 Sr Strontium 87.62	39 Y Yttrium 88.90585	40 Zr Zirconium 91.224	41 Nb Niobium 92.90638	42 Mo Molybdenum 95.94	43 Tc Technetium 98[1]	44 Ru Ruthenium 101.07	45 Rh Rhodium 102.9055	46 Pd Palladium 106.42	47 Ag Silver 107.8682	48 Cd Cadmium 112.411	49 In Indium 114.818	50 Sn Tin 118.71	51 Sb Antimony 121.76	52 Te Tellurium 127.60	53 I Iodine 126.90447	54 Xe Xenon 131.293
6	55 Cs Cesium 132.90545	56 Ba Barium 137.327	57 La Lanthanum 138.9055 *	72 Hf Hafnium 178.49	73 Ta Tantalum 180.9479	74 W Tungsten 183.84	75 Re Rhenium 186.207	76 Os Osmium 190.23	77 Ir Iridium 192.217	78 Pt Platinum 195.078	79 Au Gold 196.96655	80 Hg Mercury 200.59	81 Tl Thallium 204.3833	82 Pb Lead 207.2	83 Bi Bismuth 208.98038	84 Po Polonium 209[1]	85 At Astatine 210[1]	86 Rn Radon 222[1]
7	87 Fr Francium 223[1]	88 Ra Radium 226[1]	89 Ac Actinium 227[1] **	104 Rf Rutherfordium 261[1]	105 Db Dubnium 262[1]	106 Sg Seaborgium 266[1]	107 Bh Bohrium 264[1]	108 Hs Hassium 277[1]	109 Mt Meitnerium 268[1]	110 Ds Darmstadtium 269[1]	111 Rg Roentgenium 272[1]	112 Uub Ununbium 285[1]	113 Uut Ununtrium 284[1]	114 Uuq Ununquadium 289[1]	115 Uup Ununpentium 288[1]	116 (−)	117 (−)	118 (−)

Lanthanide Series 6 *

57 La Lanthanum 138.9055	58 Ce Cerium 140.116	59 Pr Praseodymium 140.90765	60 Nd Neodymium 144.24	61 Pm Promethium 145[1]	62 Sm Samarium 150.36	63 Eu Europium 151.964	64 Gd Gadolinium 157.25	65 Tb Terbium 158.92534	66 Dy Dysprosium 162.5	67 Ho Holmium 164.93032	68 Er Erbium 167.259	69 Tm Thulium 168.93421	70 Yb Ytterbium 173.04	71 Lu Lutetium 174.967

Actinide Series 7 **

89 Ac Actinium 227[1]	90 Th Thorium 232.0381	91 Pa Protactinium 231.03588	92 U Uranium 238.02891	93 Np Neptunium 237[1]	94 Pu Plutonium 244[1]	95 Am Americium 243[1]	96 Cm Curium 247[1]	97 Bk Berkelium 247[1]	98 Cf Californium 251[1]	99 Es Einsteinium 252[1]	100 Fm Fermium 257[1]	101 Md Mendelevium 258[1]	102 No Nobelium 259[1]	103 Lr Lawrencium 262[1]

Legend:
- Alkali Metals
- Alkaline Earth Metals
- Transition Metals
- Other Metals
- Non-Metals
- Noble Gases

Notes: Elements 112, 113, 114, and 115 are under review. A temporary system of naming recommended by J. Chatt has been used above. 1. Mass number of the longest-lived isotope that is known.
Source: International Union of Pure and Applied Chemistry (IUPAC). Web: http://www.chem.qmw.ac.uk/iupac/AtWt/

Plants

Without plants, nearly all life on Earth would end. Plants provide not only oxygen for humans and animals to breathe but also food for many animals to eat. There are about 260,000 plant species in the world today. They are found on land, in oceans and in fresh water. They were among the first living things on Earth.

Plants and animals are organisms, or living things. Three features distinguish plants from animals: plants have chlorophyll, a green pigment necessary for photosynthesis; they are fixed in one place (they don't move); and their cell walls are made sturdy by a material called cellulose.

Plants are broadly divided into two groups: flower- and fruit-producing plants, and those that do not produce flowers or fruits. Flowering and fruiting plants include all garden flowers, agricultural crops, grasses, shrubs and most leaf trees. Nonflowering plants include pines, ferns, mosses and conifers (evergreen trees and shrubs that produce cones).

Photosynthesis

Photosynthesis is a process by which green plants (and some bacteria) use **energy** from the Sun, **carbon dioxide** from the air and **water** from the ground to make **oxygen** and **glucose.** Glucose is a sugar that plants use for energy and growth.

Chlorophyll is what makes the process of photosynthesis work. Chlorophyll, a green pigment, traps the energy from the Sun and helps to change it into glucose.

Photosynthesis is one example of how people and plants depend on each other. It provides us with most of the oxygen we need in order to breathe. We, in turn, exhale the carbon dioxide needed by plants.

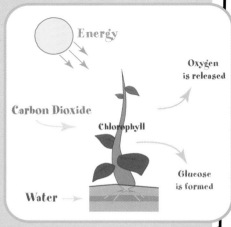

Energy

Oxygen is released

Carbon Dioxide

Chlorophyll

Glucose is formed

Water

TFK Puzzles & Games

FLOWER POWER

The flowers on the right hold all the answers. At least they hold the answers to the clues on the left. To find each answer, cross off some letters in the name of the flower to its right. The leftover letters will spell out the answer, reading from left to right. **Example:** Some advice T̶U̶LIP̶

1. Covers food	DAFFODIL	
2. Bear's home	GARDENIA	
3. Hump back	CAMELLIA	
4. Tube of light	DANDELION	
5. Period of time	GERANIUM	
6. Fungus among us	MARIGOLD	
7. Opposite of borrow	LAVENDER	
8. Backstroke	SWEET WILLIAM	
9. Scary movie	TOUCH-ME-NOT	
10. Penny	COLUMBINE	

(See Answer Key that begins on page 342.)

ROCKS

Rocks are classified in **three** categories, based on how they are formed.

IGNEOUS ROCKS are formed when molten rock (magma) from within the Earth cools and solidifies. There are two kinds: intrusive igneous rocks solidify beneath the Earth's surface; extrusive igneous rocks solidify at the surface. **Examples:** granite, basalt, obsidian

METAMORPHIC ROCKS are sedimentary or igneous rocks that have been transformed by heat, pressure or both. Metamorphic rocks are usually formed deep within the Earth, during a process such as mountain building. **Examples:** schist, marble, slate

SEDIMENTARY ROCKS are formed when sediment (bits of rock plus material such as shells and sand) gets packed together. These rocks can take millions of years to form. Most rocks that you see on the ground are sedimentary. **Examples:** limestone, sandstone, shale

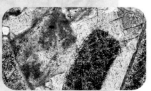

Minerals and Gems

MINERALS are solid, inorganic (not living) substances that are found in and on Earth. Most are chemical compounds, which means they are made up of two or more elements. For example, the mineral sapphire is made up of aluminum and oxygen. A few minerals, such as gold, silver and copper, are made from a single element. Minerals are considered the building blocks of rocks. Rocks can be made up of as many as six minerals.

Many minerals, such as gold and platinum, are very valuable because they are beautiful and rare. Limestone, clay and quartz are other examples of minerals. Quartz is the most common mineral.

GEMS are minerals or other organic substances that have been cut and polished. Pearls are gems, but they're not minerals. Gems are used as ornaments, like jewelry. Precious stones are the most valuable gems. They include diamonds, rubies and emeralds.

TFK Mystery Person

CLUE 1: I have been called a a groundbreaking scientist. I was born in Brooklyn, New York, in 1902.

CLUE 2: As a biologist in the 1950s, I came up with a theory that genes can move around and between chromosomes. However, I couldn't prove this idea.

CLUE 3: Years later, new technology proved my theory correct, and in 1983 I won a Nobel Prize in Biology. I was also awarded the National Medal of Science, the U.S. government's highest science prize.

WHO AM I?

(See Answer Key that begins on page 342.)

Our Solar System

MERCURY

VENUS

EARTH

MARS

JUPITER

SATURN

NEPTUNE

URANUS

PLUTO

The Sun

The solar system is made up of the **Sun** (*solar* means Sun) at its center, nine planets and the various moons, asteroids, comets and meteors controlled primarily by the Sun's gravitational pull.

The Sun, our closest star, is thought to be about 4.6 billion years old. This fiery ball measures 870,000 miles (1,392,000 km) across and its temperature is estimated to be more than 27,000,000°F (15,000,000°C) at its core. Did you know that more than a million Earth-size planets could fit inside the Sun? The Sun's great mass exerts a powerful gravitational pull on everything in our solar system, including Earth.

The Planets

Our solar system has nine planets: **Mercury, Venus, Earth, Mars, Jupiter, Saturn, Uranus, Neptune** and **Pluto.** The planets travel around the Sun in an oval-shaped path called an **orbit.** One **revolution** around the Sun is called a year. As the planets orbit the Sun, they also spin on their axes.

Galaxies

Astronomers think that the universe could contain 40 billion to 50 billion galaxies—huge systems with billions of stars. Our own galaxy is the **Milky Way.** It contains about 200 billion stars.

New Moon

Crescent Moon

First Quarter

Full Moon

Last Quarter

Crescent Moon

New Moon

The Moon

The Moon travels around Earth in an oval orbit at 22,900 miles (36,800 km) per hour. Temperatures range from -299°F (-184°C) during its night to 417°F (214°C) during its day, except at the poles, where the temperature is a constant -141°F (-96°C). The Moon's gravity affects our planet's ocean tides. The closer the Moon is to Earth, the greater the effect. The time between high tides is about 12 hours 25 minutes.

Space

THE PLANETS

MERCURY

Named for a Roman god, a winged messenger, this planet zooms around the Sun at 30 miles per second!

Size

Two-fifths the size of Earth

Diameter

3,032.4 miles (4,880 km)

Surface

Covered by a dusty layer of minerals, the surface is made up of plains, cliffs and craters.

Atmosphere

A thin mixture of helium (95%) and hydrogen

Temperature

The sunlit side reaches 950°F (510°C). The dark side drops to -346°F (-210°C).

Mean Distance from the Sun

36 million miles (57.9 million km)

Revolution Time (in Earth days or years)

88 Earth days

**Moons: 0
Rings: 0**

VENUS

Named after the Roman goddess of love and beauty, Venus is also known as the "morning star" and "evening star" since it is visible at these times.

Size

Slightly smaller than Earth

Diameter

7,519 miles (12,100 km)

Surface

A rocky, dusty expanse of mountains, canyons and plains, with a 200-mile river of hardened lava

Atmosphere

Carbon dioxide (95%), nitrogen, sulfuric acid and traces of other elements

Temperature

Ranges from 55°F (13°C) to 396°F (202°C) at the surface

Mean Distance from the Sun

67.24 million miles (108.2 million km)

Revolution Time (in Earth days or years)

243.1 Earth days

**Moons: 0
Rings: 0**

EARTH

Our planet is not perfectly round. It bulges at the equator and is flatter at the poles.

Size

Four planets in our solar system are larger and four are smaller than Earth.

Diameter

7,926.2 miles (12,756 km)

Surface

Earth is made up of water (70%) and solid ground.

Atmosphere

Nitrogen (78%), oxygen (20%), other gases

Temperature

Averages 59°F (15°C) at sea level

Mean Distance from the Sun

92.9 million miles (149.6 million km)

Revolution Time (in Earth days or years)

365 days, 5 hours, 46 seconds

**Moons: 1
Rings: 0**

TURN THE PAGE FOR MORE PLANETS ➞ **219**

THE GREAT RED SPOT Jupiter's Great Red Spot is a raging storm of gases, mainly red phosphorus. The storm is larger in size than Earth and has continued for centuries with no sign of dying down.

MARS

Because of its blood-red color (which comes from iron-rich dust), this planet was named for the Roman god of war.

Size
About one-quarter the size of Earth

Diameter
4,194 miles (6,794 km)

Surface
Canyons, dunes, volcanoes and polar caps of water ice and carbon dioxide ice

Atmosphere
Carbon dioxide (95%)

Temperature
As low as -305°F (-187°C)

Mean Distance from the Sun
141.71 million miles (227.9 million km)

Revolution Time
(in Earth days or years)
687 Earth days

Moons: 2
Rings: 0

JUPITER

The largest planet in our solar system was named for the most important Roman god.

Size
11 times the diameter of Earth

Diameter
88,736 miles (142,800 km)

Surface
A hot ball of gas and liquid

Atmosphere
Whirling clouds of colored dust, hydrogen, helium, methane, water and ammonia

Temperature
-234°F (-148°C) average

Mean Distance from the Sun
483.88 million miles (778.3 million km)

Revolution Time
(in Earth days or years)
11.9 Earth years

Moons: 63
Rings: 3

SATURN

Named for the Roman god of farming, the second-largest planet has many majestic rings surrounding it.

Size
About 10 times larger than Earth

Diameter
74,978 miles (120,660 km)

Surface
Liquid and gas

Atmosphere
Hydrogen and helium

Temperature
-288°F (-178°C) average

Mean Distance from the Sun
887.14 million miles (1,427 million km)

Revolution Time
(in Earth days or years)
29.5 Earth years

Moons: 33
Rings: 1,000?

URANUS

This greenish-blue planet is named for an ancient Greek sky god.

Size
About four times larger than Earth

Diameter
32,193 miles (51,810 km)

Surface
Little is known.

Atmosphere
Hydrogen, helium and methane

Temperature
Uniform temperature of -353°F (-214°C)

Mean Distance from the Sun
1,783,980,000 miles (2,870,000,000 km)

Revolution Time
(in Earth days or years)

84 Earth years

Moons: 27
Rings: 11

NEPTUNE

This stormy blue planet is named for an ancient Roman sea god.

Size
About four times the size of Earth

Diameter
30,775 miles (49,528 km)

Surface
A liquid layer covered with thick clouds and raging storms

Atmosphere
Hydrogen, helium, methane and ammonia

Temperature
-353°F (-214°C)

Mean Distance from the Sun
2,796,460,000 miles (4,497, 000,000 km)

Revolution Time
(in Earth days or years)

164.8 Earth years

Moons: 13
Rings: 4

PLUTO

Named for the Roman god of the underworld, Pluto is the coldest and smallest planet. Some astronomers think it is actually a large comet orbiting the Sun.

Size
Less than one-fifth the size of Earth

Diameter
1,423 miles? (2,290 km?)

Surface
A giant snowball of methane and water mixed with rock

Atmosphere
Methane

Temperature
Between -369° and -387°F (-223° and -233°C)

Mean Distance from the Sun
3,666,000,000 miles (5,900,000,000 km)

Revolution Time
(in Earth days or years)

248.5 Earth years

Moons: 1
Rings: ?

The Constellations

For more than 5,000 years, people have looked into the night sky and seen the same stars we see today. They noticed groups of stars that stayed in the same shape and connected them with imaginary lines. These groups are known as **constellations.** They help astronomers quickly locate other objects in the sky. There are 88 recognized constellations. The constellations on this page appear in the sky in North America during the summer.

LIBRA
(THE SCALES)

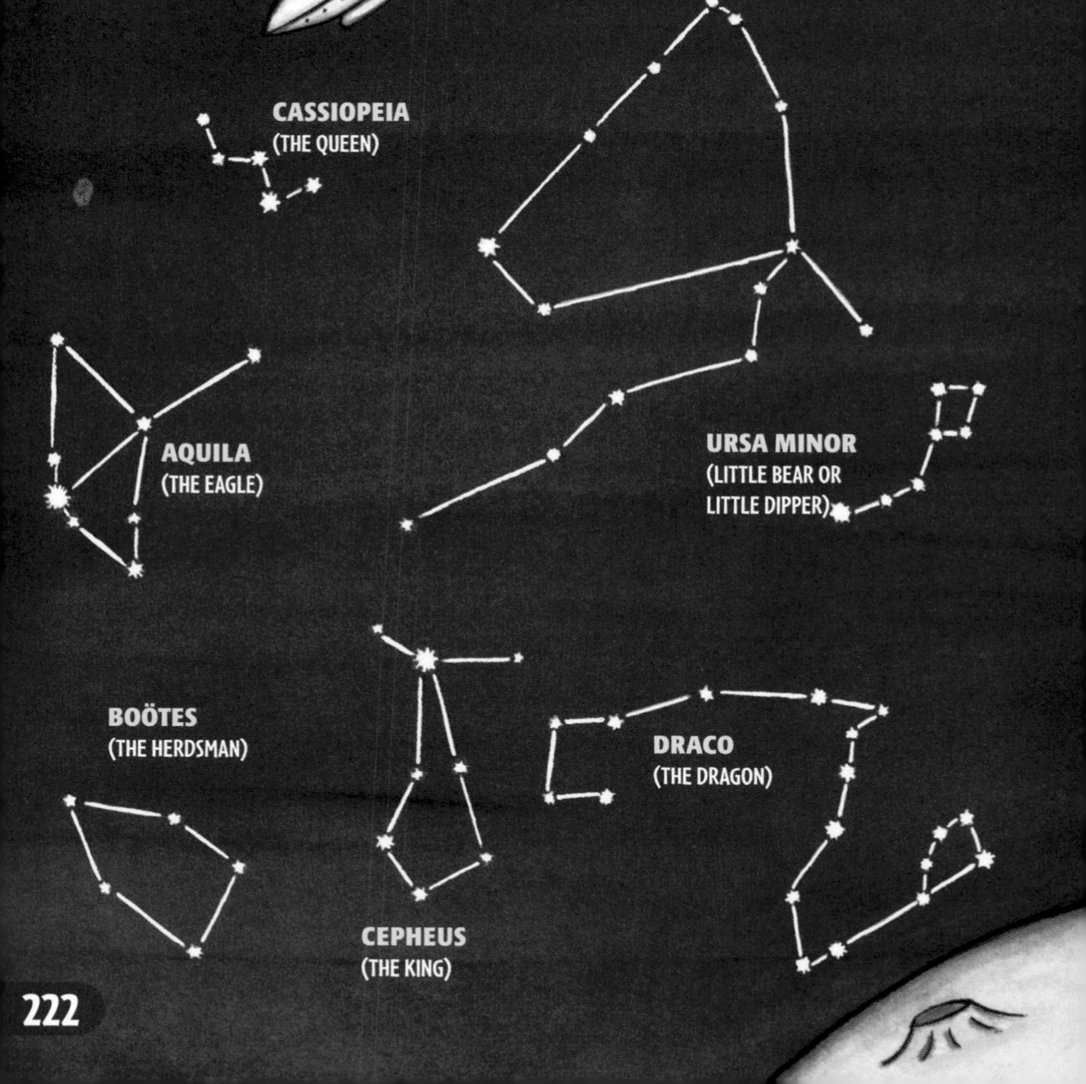

OPHIUCHUS
(THE SERPENT BEARER)

CASSIOPEIA
(THE QUEEN)

AQUILA
(THE EAGLE)

URSA MINOR
(LITTLE BEAR OR
LITTLE DIPPER)

BOÖTES
(THE HERDSMAN)

DRACO
(THE DRAGON)

CEPHEUS
(THE KING)

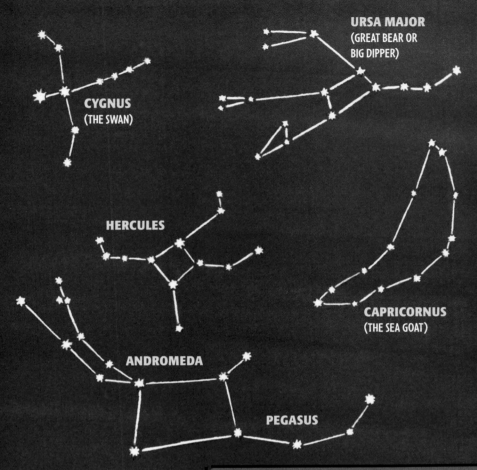

CYGNUS
(THE SWAN)

URSA MAJOR
(GREAT BEAR OR
BIG DIPPER)

HERCULES

CAPRICORNUS
(THE SEA GOAT)

ANDROMEDA

PEGASUS

The Zodiac

As Earth revolves around the Sun, a different part of the sky becomes visible. The dates below show when the constellations can be seen on the horizon.

AQUARIUS	**WATER BEARER**	**JAN. 20–FEB. 19**
PISCES	**FISH**	**FEB. 20–MARCH 20**
ARIES	**RAM**	**MARCH 21–APRIL 19**
TAURUS	**BULL**	**APRIL 20–MAY 20**
GEMINI	**TWINS**	**MAY 21–JUNE 20**
CANCER	**CRAB**	**JUNE 21–JULY 22**
LEO	**LION**	**JULY 23–AUG. 22**
VIRGO	**VIRGIN**	**AUG. 23–SEPT. 22**
LIBRA	**SCALES**	**SEPT. 23–OCT. 22**
SCORPIO	**SCORPION**	**OCT. 23–NOV. 21**
SAGITTARIUS	**ARCHER**	**NOV. 22–DEC. 21**
CAPRICORN	**SEA GOAT**	**DEC. 22–JAN. 19**

TFK News

Discovering New Worlds

Geoffrey Marcy helped discover the exoplanets.

Scientists have long wondered whether Earth is one of a kind. Could planets the size of our own exist anywhere outside our solar system? In 2004, NASA officials announced that they are one step closer to an answer.

Using telescopes in Hawaii and Texas, teams of veteran astronomers discovered two medium-size planets outside our solar system. Scientists call such planets exoplanets. A team of European scientists announced that they, too, had found a new exoplanet earlier in the year.

The recently discovered planets give researchers reason to believe that smaller, Earth-like planets may be found in distant solar systems.

To spot exoplanets, scientists use a technique that measures how much a distant star wobbles. The wobble measurement helps determine whether there are planets orbiting the star and, if so, how large they are.

Since 1995, scientists have found more than 110 exoplanets. Until now, however, all of those planets have been large. Most are about the size of Jupiter and around 300 times as heavy as Earth. And like Jupiter, they are giant balls of gas that lack a solid surface.

The newly discovered planets are closer in size to our solar system's icy Neptune or Uranus. They are only about 15 times as heavy as Earth. Scientists believe that these smaller exoplanets might be made of rock, ice and gas rather than gas alone.

"We can't quite see the Earth-like planets yet, but we are seeing their big brothers," says astronomer Geoffrey Marcy, who announced one of the discoveries. Marcy is a professional planet hunter. He and his colleagues helped find many of the exoplanets that have been discovered in the last 10 years.

Charles Beichman, the head of NASA's mission to find Earth-size planets, says scientists will continue to search for exoplanets for the next decade. By around 2014, an official space mission to find Earth-size exoplanets is scheduled to be launched. "One of the oldest questions people have asked is, 'Are we alone in the universe?' " says Beichman. "Scientists may one day find some answers."

This drawing shows an exoplanet named 55 Cancrie with the star that it orbits.

—By Jeremy Caplan

1957	The Soviet Union launches *Sputnik*, the first satellite.
1961	Soviet Yuri Gagarin is the first space traveler. Less than a month later, Alan Shepard Jr. becomes the first American in space.
1962	John Glenn is the first American to orbit Earth.
1963	Soviet Valentina Tereshkova becomes the first woman in space.
1965	Soviet cosmonaut Alexei Leonov makes the first space walk.
1969	*Apollo 11* astronaut Neil Armstrong becomes the first human to walk on the Moon.
1971	The Soviet Union launches the world's first space station, *Salyut 1*.
1973	The United States sends its first space station, *Skylab*, into orbit.
1976	*Viking I* is the first spacecraft to land on Mars.
1981	U.S. space shuttle *Columbia*, the world's first reusable spacecraft, is launched.
1986	The space shuttle *Challenger* explodes 73 seconds after liftoff. Six astronauts and civilian Christa McAuliffe die.
1990	The Hubble Space Telescope is put into orbit.
1995	American Eileen Collins becomes the first woman to pilot a space shuttle.
1998	The Russian *Proton* rocket makes the first flight to the International Space Station. The U.S. space shuttle *Endeavor* follows.
2000	The first crew reaches the International Space Station.
2003	The space shuttle *Columbia* breaks up over Texas during re-entry; seven astronauts die.
	An image taken by a powerful satellite confirms that the universe is 13.7 billion years old and supports the theory that the universe formed in a giant burst of energy called the Big Bang.
2004	The Mars rovers *Spirit* and *Opportunity* send detailed color images of the surface of Mars back to Earth.
	President George W. Bush unveils plans to send astronauts on missions to the Moon and Mars.

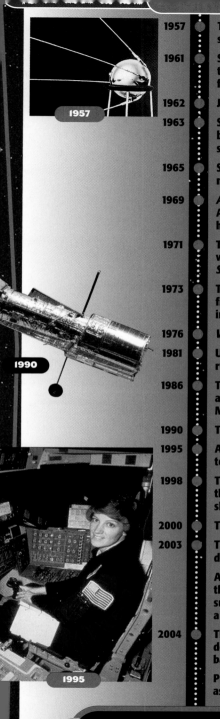

1957

1990

1995

1969

go Find out how astronauts suit up for space at timeforkids.com/spacesuit

Eclipses

A **SOLAR ECLIPSE** occurs when the Moon is in its new phase and it moves between the Sun and the Earth, blocking the Sun's light from a small part of the Earth. In a **TOTAL SOLAR ECLIPSE,** the Moon completely obscures the Sun.

During an **ANNULAR ECLIPSE** (annular means "ring"), the Moon blocks out most of the Sun's disk, leaving just a ring of light that is still visible around the edge. In a **LUNAR ECLIPSE,** the Earth blocks the Sun's light from the Moon.

Here are the dates for lunar and solar eclipses in 2005 and 2006. Check the newspaper to see if any eclipses are visible where you live.

2005 OCTOBER 3 Annular eclipse of the Sun
OCTOBER 17 Partial eclipse of the Moon

2006 MARCH 29 Total eclipse of the Sun
SEPTEMBER 7 Partial eclipse of the Moon
SEPTEMBER 22 Annular eclipse of the Moon

Your Turn · How Much Would You Weigh on Mercury?

To figure out how much you'd weigh on another planet, multiply your weight on Earth by the gravitational pull listed in the table below.

Example: I weigh 90 pounds on Earth.
On Mercury, I would weigh:
90 pounds x 0.38 = 34.2 pounds

PLANET	GRAVITATIONAL PULL (COMPARED TO EARTH)
MERCURY	0.38
VENUS	0.91
EARTH	1.00
MARS	0.38
JUPITER	2.54
SATURN	0.93
URANUS	0.80
NEPTUNE	1.20
PLUTO	NOT AVAILABLE

Source: National Aeronautics and Space Administration (NASA)

Astronomical Terms

Between the orbits of Mars and Jupiter are an estimated 30,000 pieces of rocky debris, known collectively as the **ASTEROIDS,** or planetoids (small planets). **CERES** was the first asteroid discovered, on New Year's night in 1801.

A **BLACK HOLE** is a mysterious dense object with a gravity so strong that even light cannot escape from it. That's why black holes are almost impossible to see.

The Hale-Bopp comet

A **COMET** is an enormous "snowball" of frozen gases (mostly carbon dioxide, methane and water vapor). Comets originate in the outer solar system. As comets move toward the Sun, heat from the Sun turns some of the snow into gas, which begins to glow and is seen as the comet's tail.

A **GALAXY** is a collection of gas and millions of stars held together by gravity. Almost everything you see in the sky belongs to our galaxy, the Milky Way.

A spiraling galaxy

GRAVITY is the force that draws objects to each other. On Earth, gravity pulls things down, toward the center of the planet. That's why things fall down.

A **LIGHT YEAR** is the distance light travels in one year. It equals 5.88 trillion miles.

A **METEOROID** is a small piece of cosmic matter. When a meteoroid enters our atmosphere, it is called a **METEOR.** It is also known as a shooting star, because it burns while passing through the air. Larger meteors that survive the journey through the atmosphere and land on Earth are called **METEORITES.**

TFK Puzzles & Games

Jumping Jupiter!
Jupiter is a ball mostly of gas, which swirls in beautiful colors and patterns. Can you find the two identical Jupiters in this group?

(See Answer Key that begins on page 342.)

TFK Mystery Person

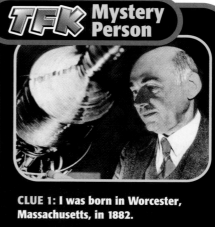

CLUE 1: I was born in Worcester, Massachusetts, in 1882.

CLUE 2: When I was 17, my biggest wish was to one day fly humans to Mars. In 1926, I launched the first liquid-fuel rocket.

CLUE 3: My inventions helped later space exploration get off the ground. I am sometimes called the father of space flight.

WHO AM I?

(See Answer Key that begins on page 342.)

BASEBALL'S NEW MATH

Teams count on formulas for winning

Oakland A's general manager Billy Beane (far right) thinks solid hitters like Scott Hatteberg (right) are more valuable than home-run kings.

Look around a major league baseball clubhouse. You'll find bats, balls, mitts and calculators. That's right, calculators. Old-time managers used to rely on hunches, guesswork and some statistics. But now, a new strategy is sweeping the major leagues. Many owners and managers believe that using mathematical formulas can help them decide which players have the right skills to help the team win. The idea is catching on with the speed of a blazing fastball!

HE'S A BASEBALL WIZARD

Billy Beane, the general manager for the Oakland Athletics (A's), gets much of the credit for the new approach to winning. Beane has a novel way of combining math with America's favorite pastime. By using a complex set of statistics and equations, Beane claims he can figure out exactly how much a player will help his team. For example, he rates a player who gets on base much higher than one who wallops a lot of homers *(see box)*.

Beane won't reveal his formula. But a book about his methods— *Moneyball*, written by Michael Lewis—

was published in 2003. Now other teams are borrowing his equations.

With Beane's help, the A's have become one of the best teams in the American League. In the past seven years, Beane has managed to put together a top team without blowing the team owners' budget. The A's spend far less on their players' salaries than many other teams do. Yet they have the best record in baseball over the past four seasons.

So far, Beane's winning ways have not carried the A's to a World Series. But Oakland fans hope that the new strategy will soon add up to victory in October. —*By Jeremy Caplan*

A WHOLE NEW BALL GAME

Using computer software, Billy Beane and his followers are changing the way baseball is played. Here's how the new approach differs from the old ball game.

OLD: Bunting, or hitting a ball softly into the infield, sacrifices one player's chance to get a hit but helps another base runner score.

NEW: Letting players try for a hit will score runs more often.

OLD: Stealing bases allows fast runners to improve a team's opportunity to score.

NEW: Statistics show that stealing bases is too risky for even the fastest runners.

OLD: Teams should seek out power hitters— players who can win a game with one big swing.

NEW: Hitters who consistently get on base but rarely hit homers contribute more to a team's success.

The Wide World of Sports

Baseball, football and basketball are big hits in the U.S., but in other countries, different sports are just as popular. Here are a few of them.

Hurling This rough game is played mainly in Ireland. Players use their hands, feet and a curved wooden stick called a hurley to advance a ball. Points are scored when the ball is either swatted between goalposts or past the goalkeeper and under the crossbar.

Rugby is a rough sport.

Rugby The rugby ball looks like an American football, and the object is to cross the goal line with the ball or kick it between goalposts. Popular in Great Britain, Australia, New Zealand, France and South Africa, this brutal sport is actually a lot different from our brand of football. Rugby players can kick the ball forward or run with it, but they can only pass it to teammates sideways or backwards. Tackling is a big part of the game, but rugby players wear almost no protective equipment.

Petanque This French game is similar to bocce, an Italian game. The object is to toss a metal ball (boule) as close as possible to a small wooden ball (jack). You get a point when your ball is closer to the jack than an opponent's ball. Knocking away an opponent's ball with your own is good strategy. Games can be set up on almost any flat stretch of ground.

Cricket It started in England, but now cricket is popular in many of the former British colonies, especially in the West Indies and India. Like baseball, a batsman must hit a ball tossed by a pitcher (bowler)—except the ball must be hit on a bounce. Games are usually four innings long. An innings ends when 10 batsmen make an out; then the fielding team gets to bat. Hundreds of runs are often scored in one game, which can take days to complete.

Jai alai baskets are made of wicker.

Jai alai First played in the Basque region of Spain, it has spread to Mexico, France and Italy. In jai alai, a very fast-moving game, players use a two-foot-long curved basket to catch and throw a small hard ball against a 40-foot-high wall. The court, called a fronton, has three sides. Players must catch the ball on the fly or on one bounce as it caroms off any of the three walls. The ball moves at up to 188 miles per hour!

229

Baseball

Many people believe that **BASEBALL** was invented in 1839 by Abner Doubleday at Cooperstown, New York, the site of the Hall of Fame and National Museum of Baseball. But research has proved that a game called "base ball" was played in the U.S. and in England before 1839. In fact, Jane Austen mentioned the game in her 1817 novel *Northanger Abbey*.

The first baseball game as we know it was played at Elysian Fields, Hoboken, New Jersey, on June 19, 1846, between the Knickerbockers and the New York Nine.

The Little League World Series

The Little League World Series—the sport's annual world-championship tournament—has been played in Williamsport, Pennsylvania, every year since 1947. Willemstad, Curaçao (in the Netherlands Antilles), won the 2004 honors with a 5–2 victory over Thousand Oaks, California. Taiwan has won 16 times, more than any other foreign country.

Teams representing towns in the U.S. have won 27 times. California has five championship wins; Connecticut, New Jersey and Pennsylvania each have four wins, and New York and Texas have two each.

2004 World Series

The **Boston Red Sox** appeared to be on their way to another disappointing season before they snatched the American League Championship from the New York Yankees. The Sox made history when they swept the final four games of the series, a great comeback after losing the first three games.

The Sox went on to beat the St. Louis Cardinals in a four-game sweep to win their first World Series since 1918. After 86 years, the "Curse of the Bambino" was broken!

The Negro Leagues

From the 1920s through the 1940s, black professional ballplayers could play only for the segregated teams of the legendary Negro Leagues. The leagues included such Hall of Famers as Josh Gibson, Cool Papa Bell and Satchel Paige. The color barrier was broken when African-American baseball player Jackie Robinson joined the Brooklyn Dodgers in 1947.

Top Players of 2004

Most Valuable Player
A.L.–**Vladimir Guerrero,** Anaheim Angels
N.L.–**Barry Bonds,** San Francisco Giants

Cy Young Award (Best Pitcher)
A.L.–**Johan Santana,** Minnesota Twins
N.L.–**Roger Clemens,** Houston Astros

Rookie of the Year
A.L.–**Bobby Crosby,** Oakland Athletics
N.L.–**Jason Bay,** Pittsburgh Pirates

Home-Run Champions
A.L.–**Manny Ramirez,** Boston Red Sox, 43 home runs
N.L.–**Adrian Beltre,** Los Angeles Dodgers, 48 home runs

Batting Champions
A.L.–**Ichiru Suzuki,** Seattle Mariners, .372 batting average
N.L.–**Barry Bonds,** San Francisco Giants, .362 batting average

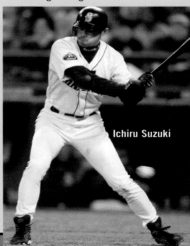

Ichiru Suzuki

Basketball

In 1891, Dr. James Naismith invented **BASKETBALL** in Springfield, Massachusetts. The game was originally played with a soccer ball and two peach bushel baskets, which is how the game got its name. Twelve of the 13 rules Naismith created are still part of the game. One thing has changed: originally there were nine players on each team, now there are only five. The Basketball Hall of Fame is named in Naismith's honor.

Top 5 Career NBA Scorers

PLAYER	AVERAGE POINTS PER GAME
MICHAEL JORDAN	30.1
WILT CHAMBERLAIN	30.1
ELGIN BAYLOR	27.4
SHAQUILLE O'NEAL	27.1
JERRY WEST	27.0

Ben Wallace (left) of the Detroit Pistons

Lauren Jackson of the Seattle Storm

2004 Basketball Championships

NBA (National Basketball Association)
Detroit Pistons beat the Los Angeles Lakers, 4 games to 1.

WNBA (Women's National Basketball Association)
Seattle Storm beat the Connecticut Sun, 2 games to 1.

TFK Top 5

Sports Kids Play

Do you play hoops, baseball, tennis? A poll of more than 1,000 kids reveals what their favorite sports to play are.

1. Basketball — 30%
2. Baseball — 20.9%
3. Football — 20.8%
4. Hockey — 9.8%
5. Soccer — 9.1%

Source: *Sports Illustrated for Kids*

WNBA Hot Shots

2004 SCORING LEADERS

PLAYER	GAMES	POINTS	AVERAGE
Lauren Jackson, Seattle	31	634	20.5
Tina Thompson, Houston	26	520	20.0
Lisa Leslie, Los Angeles	34	598	17.6

PRO Football

The Patriots celebrate

Originally a game played by colleges, professional **FOOTBALL** became popular in America in the 1920s. The National Football League (NFL) was established in 1922 and merged with the American Football League in 1970 to form a 26-team league. With the addition of the Houston Texans in 2002, the NFL consists of 32 teams.

Super Bowl Déjà Vu

Super Bowl XXXIX (39) was super for the New England Patriots. They beat the Philadelphia Eagles 24–21 to win their second straight Super Bowl and their third in four years. New England is the seventh team to win back-to-back Super Bowls. Tom Brady became the youngest quarterback to win three titles. Patriots receiver Deion Branch was named the game's Most Valuable Player.

Top Players 2004 NFL Season

PASSING LEADER
Duante Culpepper, Minnesota Vikings (4,717 yards)

RUSHING LEADER
Curtis Martin, New York Jets (1,697 yards)

RECEIVING LEADER
Muhsin Muhammad, Carolina Panthers (1,405 yards)

RUSHING TOUCHDOWNS
LaDainian Tomlinson, San Diego Chargers (17)

INTERCEPTIONS
Ed Reed, Baltimore Ravens (9)

SACKS
Dwight Freeney, Indianapolis Colts (16)

Daunte Culpepper

Football Phenomena

Most points scored in a game:
● The Washington Redskins beat the New York Giants, 72–41, on November 27, 1966.

Longest field goal: 63 yards (tie)
● Tom Dempsey, New Orleans Saints vs. Detroit Lions, November 8, 1970
● Jason Elam, Denver Broncos vs. Jacksonville Jaguars, October 25, 1998

Longest touchdown run: 99 yards
● Tony Dorsett, Dallas Cowboys vs. Minnesota Vikings, January 3, 1983

Upcoming Super Bowl Sites

2006	Super Bowl XL (40)	Detroit, Michigan
2007	Super Bowl XLI (41)	Miami, Florida
2008	Super Bowl XLII (42)	Glendale, Arizona

Did You Know?

America's first pro-football dynasty was also the first franchise to take advantage of corporate sponsorship. In 1919, the Indian Packing Company gave the Green Bay, Wisconsin, team $500 for gear. From then on the team was called the Packers.

Super Stars

These teams have won the most Super Bowls.

5 Dallas Cowboys and San Francisco 49ers

4 Pittsburgh Steelers

3 Green Bay Packers, New England Patriots, Oakland/Los Angeles Raiders and Washington Redskins

COLLEGE Basketball

March Madness

Fans describe the end of college-basketball season as March Madness. That's because the men's and women's championship tournaments are held in March and feature more than 100 of the best teams in the country.

Tennessee holds the most women's titles (six), but the 2004 women's champ, the University of Connecticut, is catching up, with five titles. UCLA has won the most men's championships (11).

In 2005, the North Carolina Tar Heels won its fourth NCAA men's championship, beating the Fighting Illini of Illinois 75-70. In the women's tournament, the Lady Bears of Baylor defeated the Michigan State Spartans 84-62.

Sports

COLLEGE Football

Trojans Triumph!

The University of Southern California Trojans trounced the University of Oklahoma Sooners 55–19 in the 2005 FedEx Orange Bowl to claim the national championship. Before 1998, polls of writers and coaches named the unofficial champ. Now the BCS (Bowl Championship Series) decides who is No. 1. The championship game rotates among the major bowls. In 2006, the Rose Bowl will determine the best college football team in the country.

TOP Dog

The Heisman Trophy is an annual award given since 1935 to the most outstanding college-football player in the country. Several Heisman winners have gone on to success in the NFL and been elected to the Pro Football Hall of Fame after retiring. Current NFL stars Eddie George (1995), Charles Woodson (1997) and Carson Palmer (2002) are recent winners. In 2004, quarterback Matt Leinart of the University of Southern California won the award.

Other 2005 Bowl Games

ROSE BOWL (Pasadena, California) Texas 38, Michigan 37

FIESTA BOWL (Tempe, Arizona) Utah 35, Pittsburgh, 7

SUGAR BOWL (New Orleans, Louisiana) Auburn 16, Virginia Tech 13

COTTON BOWL (Dallas, Texas) Tennessee 38, Texas A&M 7

OUTBACK BOWL (Tampa, Florida) Georgia 24, Wisconsin 21

GATOR BOWL (Jacksonville, Florida) Florida State 30, West Virginia 18

For sports superstitions:
www.factmonster.com/spot/superstitions

233

Soccer

SOCCER is the world's most popular sport. Known as football throughout the rest of the world, soccer is played by boys, girls, men and women of nearly all ages. Hundreds of millions of people play the game.

The World Cup

The world's biggest soccer tournament is called the World Cup. It's played every four years by teams made up of each country's best players.

Germany won the women's World Cup in 2003, while Brazil was the winner of the men's World Cup in 2002.

The next men's World Cup tournament will be held in 2006 in Germany. China will host the women's World Cup in 2007.

World Cup Champions

Men		Women	
1930	Uruguay	1991	U.S.A.
1934	Italy	1995	Norway
1938	Italy	1999	U.S.A.
1942, 1946	not held	2003	Germany
1950	Uruguay		
1954	West Germany		
1958	Brazil		
1962	Brazil		
1966	England		
1970	Brazil		
1974	West Germany		
1978	Argentina		
1982	Italy		
1986	Argentina		
1990	West Germany		
1994	Brazil		
1998	France		
2002	Brazil		

TFK Spotlight

Hamm Bows Out

Mia Hamm's career was complete. On a clear night in Athens, Greece, the U.S. women's soccer team won the 2004 Olympic gold medal by defeating Brazil, 2-1, in overtime. The most famous player in the history of women's team sports could retire—at the top.

"I can't believe this moment is finally here," the forward said after the game, her smile streaked with tears of joy. "You just couldn't have scripted it any better."

The same might be said of Hamm's remarkable 18-year career. She was only 15 when she joined the U.S. national team, in 1987. Since then, Hamm has racked up a list of accomplishments that will be difficult to match: soccer's all-time scoring record for men and women (153 goals), two World Cup titles (1991, 1999), two Olympic gold medals (1996, 2004) ... the list goes on.

But Hamm's place in sports history is about much more than numbers and trophies. As the face of women's soccer, she has worked tirelessly to increase respect and recognition for her sport. Hamm's influence can be seen in the millions of soccer-playing girls across America who wear her No. 9 jersey, plaster her picture on their bedroom walls and yell her name from the stands.

—By Grant Wahl

Hockey

ICE HOCKEY, by birth and upbringing a Canadian game, is an offshoot of field hockey. Some historians say that the first ice-hockey game was played in Montreal in December 1879 between two teams composed almost exclusively of McGill University students. But others believe that earlier hockey games took place in Kingston, Ontario, or Halifax, Nova Scotia.

In the Montreal game of 1879, there were 15 players on a side. The players used an assortment of sticks to keep the puck in motion. Early rules allowed nine men on a side, but the number was reduced to seven in 1886 and later to six.

In the winter of 1894–1895, a group of college students from the United States visited Canada and saw hockey played. Enthusiastic about the game, they introduced it as a winter sport when they returned home.

NHL All-Time Career Point Scorers

PLAYER	GOALS	ASSISTS	POINTS
1. WAYNE GRETZKY	894	1,963	2,857
2. MARK MESSIER	694	1,193	1,887
3. GORDIE HOWE	801	1,049	1,850
4. RON FRANCIS	549	1,249	1,798
5. MARCEL DIONNE	731	1,040	1,771

(Through 2003–2004 season)

Top Goalies

These goaltenders have won the most games.

PLAYER	GAMES	WINS	LOSSES	TIES
1. PATRICK ROY	1,029	551	315	131
2. TERRY SAWCHUK	971	447	330	172
3. JACQUES PLANTE	837	435	247	146
4. ED BELFOUR	856	435	281	111
5. TONY ESPOSITO	886	423	306	152

(Through 2003–2004 season)

Patrick Roy

TFK News

A Frozen Season

Not a single goal was scored in the 2004–2005 National Hockey League season. The labor contract between players and team owners expired on September 15, 2004. After months of meetings, players and owners could not agree on a new contract, and the season was cancelled.

The owners wanted to limit how much players earn by creating a salary cap. The players didn't want a cap. The two sides couldn't compromise, and the owners staged a "lockout." In a lockout, games are canceled until a new contract has been signed.

To find work, many NHL players joined professional hockey leagues across Europe, including those in Germany, Finland and Russia.

The Stanley Cup

Each player on the team that wins the NHL championship gets his name engraved on the STANLEY CUP, along with all the previous winners. The original cup was only seven inches high; now it stands about three feet tall. The Montreal Canadiens have won the most titles with 23. The Tampa Bay Lightning won the 2004 Stanley Cup.

Golf

It may be that **GOLF** originated in Holland—historians believe it did—but certainly Scotland developed the game and is famous for it. Formal competition began in 1860 with the British Open championship.

Tee Time

The four major events in men's professional golf (the Grand Slam) are:

> The Masters
> British Open
> U.S. Open
> PGA Championship

The four major events in women's professional golf (the Women's Grand Slam) are:

> LPGA Championship
> U.S. Women's Open
> Nabisco Championship
> Women's British Open

The **RYDER CUP** is the most prestigious team golf event in the world. It is played every two years between a team of American golfers and a team of European golfers.

Winners of 2004's Major Tournaments

Men:
The Masters: Phil Mickelson
British Open: Todd Hamilton
U.S. Open: Retief Goosen
PGA Championship: Vijay Singh

2004 U.S. Amateur Champion:
Ryan Moore

Women:
LPGA Championship: Annika Sorenstam
U.S. Women's Open: Meg Mallon
Nabisco Championship: Grace Park
Women's British Open: Karen Stupples

2004 U.S. Women's Amateur Champion:
Jane Park

Annika Sorenstam

Cycling

In 2004, **LANCE ARMSTRONG** won his sixth consecutive Tour de France and became the first person ever to win six times. The Tour is the world's most famous bike race. It was first run in 1903. Armstrong breezed to the finish line of the 2,109-mile course. His next closest competitor was 6 minutes 19 seconds behind him! This was amazing because in 1996 Armstrong had been diagnosed with cancer and was given only a 50% chance to live.

Olympics

The very first **OLYMPICS** was held in Greece in 776 B.C. In 1896, more than 2,000 years later, Athens was the site of the first Modern Olympics, as 245 athletes from 14 nations came together to compete.

In August 2004, the Olympics returned to their roots. More than 11,000 athletes from 202 nations competed in 28 sports at the 28th Olympic Games.

Women's wrestling debuted at the 2004 games. Japanese athletes won medals in each of the four weight categories.

Carly Patterson brought home gold.

2004 Summer Olympics: Top Overall Medal Winners

COUNTRY	GOLD	SILVER	BRONZE	TOTAL
UNITED STATES	35	39	29	103
RUSSIA	27	27	38	92
CHINA	32	17	14	63
AUSTRALIA	17	16	16	49
GERMANY	14	16	18	48
JAPAN	16	9	12	37
FRANCE	11	9	13	33
ITALY	10	11	11	32
SOUTH KOREA	9	12	9	30
GREAT BRITAIN	9	9	12	30
CUBA	9	7	11	27
UKRAINE	9	5	9	23
NETHERLANDS	4	9	9	22
ROMANIA	8	5	6	19
SPAIN	3	11	5	19
HUNGARY	8	6	3	17
GREECE	6	6	4	16
BELARUS	2	6	7	15
CANADA	3	6	3	12
BULGARIA	2	1	9	12

Upcoming Olympic Games

2006	(WINTER)	Turin, Italy
2008	(SUMMER)	Beijing, China
2010	(WINTER)	Vancouver, British Columbia

Gymnastics

GYMNASTICS is one of the most physically demanding sports, not to mention one of the most popular at the Summer Olympics.

The Fédération Internationale de Gymnastique (FIG) is the organization that oversees gymnastics throughout the world. The FIG recognizes seven gymnastic areas: men's artistic gymnastics, women's artistic gymnastics, rhythmic gymnastics, trampoline, sports aerobics, sports acrobatics and noncompetitive general gymnastics. Artistic, rhythmic and trampoline gymnasts competed in the 2004 Olympics in Athens.

Courtney Kupets on a balance beam

Here's a look at some of the most popular events.

Artistic Gymnastics

MEN & WOMEN

FLOOR EXERCISE Gymnasts should use the entire 40-foot by 40-foot mat. The men's exercises require strength, flexibility and balance. Women combine dance movements, tumbling and acrobatics and use music in their routines.

VAULT After a running start onto a springboard, the gymnast performs a handspring off the vaulting table

MEN

POMMEL HORSE The gymnast performs a series of circular and scissor movements over the "horse." Only the gymnast's powerful hands should touch the apparatus.

Paul Hamm on the pommel horse

RINGS He performs backward and forward swings and holds while keeping the rings as still as possible. Tremendous balance and an acrobatic dismount are important.

PARALLEL BARS The athlete works along the bars and swings above and below them.

HORIZONTAL (HIGH) BAR He performs several swinging movements and grip changes. It's important that the body does not touch the bar. Spectacular dismounts rate high.

WOMEN

BALANCE BEAM Gymnasts do leaps, turns, jumps and more on a beam 16 feet long and only four inches wide!

UNEVEN BARS The athletes perform continuous swinging movements in both directions, above and below the bars. Twists, somersaults, high flight and smooth dismounts will help to earn a high score.

Rhythmic Gymnastics

Rhythmic gymnasts combine sport and artistic interpretation. They use ropes, hoops, balls, clubs and ribbons, which must be kept in constant motion.

Gymnastic Stars

Olga Korbut, a Soviet gymnast, inspired many girls to take up gymnastics after she won three gold medals at the 1972 Olympics in Munich. Romanian gymnast **Nadia Comaneci** became the first woman to score a perfect 10, at the 1976 summer games in Montreal, Canada. **Kerri Strug** provided one of the most exciting events of the 1996 Olympics—and gymnastics history—when she nailed her vault on an injured ankle to ensure a gold medal for the U.S. team.

Olga Korl

At the 2004 Olympics in Athens, Paul Hamm and Carly Patterson of the United States earned gold in the all-around competition. The U.S. team won a total of nine gymnastic medals in Athens.

Extreme Sports

The **X GAMES** were dreamed up by the sports television network ESPN. They debuted during the summer of 1994 in Newport and Providence, Rhode Island. The games were supposed to take place every two years. But the first games were so popular, organizers made it an annual competition.

The summer games include bicycle stunts, Moto X, skateboarding, surfing, inline skating and wakeboarding. Dave Mirra won first place in two bike-stunt events at the 2004 Summer Extreme Games in Los Angeles, mirroring Ryan Nyquist's 2003 double first.

Probably the most famous "extreme" athlete is skateboarder Tony Hawk. He was the first skateboarder to land a 900 trick in the half-pipe competition. A 900 is 2½ complete midair rotations on the skateboard. It's called a 900 because one complete spin is 360 degrees around (like a circle) and 2½ × 360 = 900.

The winter games include snowboarding, skiing, snowmobiling and Moto X. At the 2005 Winter Games in Aspen, Colorado, Canadian Charles Gagnier dashed American Tanner Hall's quest for a fourth gold in ski slopestyle. American Gretchen Bleiler came back from an injury to take the women's superpipe honors.

Swimming

Making a Splash

MICHAEL PHELPS entered the 2004 Summer Olympics poised to tie or break Mark Spitz's record of seven gold medals. While he didn't accomplish the Olympian feat, he did bring home eight medals (six were gold). That tied him with Russian gymnast Aleksandr Dityatin as the winningest athlete at a single Olympic Games.

239

Tennis

The four biggest tournaments in **TENNIS** make up the Grand Slam. Here are the recent winners.

Marat Safin

AUSTRALIAN OPEN (2005):
Men: Marat Safin
Women: Serena Williams

FRENCH OPEN (2004):
Men: Gaston Gaudio **Women:** Anastasia Myskina

WIMBLEDON (2004):
Men: Roger Federer **Women:** Maria Sharapova

U.S. OPEN (2004):
Men: Roger Federer **Women:** Svetlana Kuznetsova

Surfing

TFK Spotlight

Meet Bethany Hamilton

Bethany Hamilton is a teenage star surfer from Hawaii who has become an international hero. In October 2003, Bethany was surfing when a shark attacked and bit off her left arm. Not only did she survive, but Bethany has also since returned to surfing.

TFK: Do you have any fear of going into the water now?
Hamilton: I don't feel differently about the water, but I think of sharks more often.

TFK: What's been the most difficult thing in adapting?
Hamilton: The most difficult thing is that I used to play guitar and now I can't play. Maybe if I get a new prosthetic arm I'll be able to, but it's kind of hard, because that was one of my favorite things to do.

TFK: What's tricky about surfing now?

Hamilton: Getting up and paddling up. Say you're trying to do a pushup and you only have one arm. Pushups are hard with one arm. Getting up on a board is kind of like that.

TFK: What advice or guidance would you give someone feeling a big loss?
Hamilton: If they've had a bad situation, they should try to be thankful that they have a life. They should look at the surrounding beauty that they're in.

—By Jeremy Caplan

Racing

AUTOMOBILE RACING originated in France in 1894 and appeared in the U.S. the next year.

Racing, Anyone?

The National Association for Stock Car Racing's **Nextel Cup Series** is the most popular auto-racing series in the U.S. The NASCAR season runs from February to November. The biggest Nextel Cup race of the year is the **Daytona 500.** Jeff Gordon won the 2005 Daytona 500. Kurt Busch was the 2004 **NASCAR** points champion.

Jeff Gordon

What Do the Flags Mean?

Race officials use flags to instruct drivers during a race. Here's what they mean.

GREEN: Go!

YELLOW: Caution. There is a problem on the track, and drivers must go slowly and not pass.

RED: Stop. Something has made the track unusable (maybe an accident or bad weather).

WHITE: Last lap

CHECKERED: Finish. The race is over.

World Champions

Germany's Michael Schumacher won his seventh Formula One driver's world championship in 2004, giving him two more titles than his nearest competitor on the all-time list, Argentina's Juan-Manuel Fangio.

Top Formula One Title Winners

7 – **Michael Schumacher** (Germany)
5 – **Juan-Manuel Fangio** (Argentina)
4 – **Alain Prost** (France)
3 – **Jack Brabham** (Australia)
    Niki Lauda (Austria)
    Nelson Piquet (Brazil)
    Ayrton Senna (Brazil)
    Jackie Stewart (Britain)

Our Need for Speed

The biggest and oldest race held in the U.S. is the **Indianapolis 500.** It's held every year at the oval-shaped Indianapolis Motor Speedway in Indiana. Buddy Rice was the 2004 Indy 500 winner.

TFK Mystery Person

CLUE 1: One of greatest boxers of all time, I was born Cassius Clay in 1942, in Louisville, Kentucky.

CLUE 2: I became the world heavy-weight champion in 1964, and recited little rhymes before my fights. When I became a Muslim I changed my name, causing great controversy.

CLUE 3: A three-time heavyweight champ, I was honored to light the Olympic flame at the 1996 Summer Games in Atlanta, Georgia.

WHO AM I?

(See Answer Key that begins on page 342.)

FROM TFK MAGAZINE

The Fight Against Poverty

Volunteers build a house in Tallahassee, Florida (above). A food program for low-income people helps a Chicago family (left).

More kids are poor, but caring Americans are trying to help

For John, 11, being poor in New York City means never having enough to eat. For Shannon, 9, from rural Mississippi, poverty means squinting at the blackboard because eyeglasses are too costly. For every one of the 12.7 million American children living in poverty, growing up poor means something different.

From 1993 to 2000, the percentage of poor American children fell steadily. But since then, it has been on the rise. One out of every six children in the U.S. lives in poverty. These families often can't afford food, clothing, medical care or housing.

Organizations around the country are working hard to fight child poverty. For example, America's Second Harvest is a network of more than 200 food banks that provide free groceries for needy children.

"We live in the wealthiest country in the world, but we still have a very high child-poverty rate," says William O'Hare, who works for the Annie E. Casey Foundation, in Baltimore, Maryland, which researches the roots of poverty. Why is poverty on the rise now? Says O'Hare: There are too many "parents who don't have enough work or whose work doesn't pay enough."

MAKING A DIFFERENCE

Many students at Carver Upper Elementary School in Indianola, Mississippi, come from low-income families. Mississippi is one of the poorest states in the U.S. Silento Thomas, 9, says he enjoys eating breakfast and lunch at school. For many kids, free school meals help ensure they get enough to eat.

Geoffrey Canada runs the Harlem Children's Zone (HCZ) in New York City. The program provides a network of support to strengthen families. HCZ helps more than 8,000 kids with health care, education and nutrition.

"If kids fall behind early, life gets harder and harder. We want to help them succeed," Canada says.

—By Jeremy Caplan

Roadside Attractions

Going on a road trip? If you prefer offbeat destinations, check out these roadside attractions and odd museums.

World's Largest Ball of Paint
Alexandria, Indiana

In 1977, Michael Carmichael starting painting over a baseball, adding layers of paint, day after day, year after year. After more than 20,000 coats of paint, the ball weighs more than 1,300 pounds. Visitors can paint the ball themselves and become part of ball-of-paint history.

Dinosaur Park
Rapid City, South Dakota

The land that time forgot can be found outside Rapid City. On a hill overlooking the city, dinosaurs made out of brightly painted concrete stand guard. The park was built as a work project in 1936, during the Depression. The five dinos, which include a *triceratops* and a *T. rex,* are life size and can be seen for miles.

Scale Model of the Solar System
Peoria, Illinois

The Lakeview Museum Community Solar System is home to the biggest little solar system in the world. The planets and their orbits are in scale (42 feet equals 1 million miles). The museum's planetarium, a big yellow dome 36 feet in diameter, stands in for the Sun. Forty miles away, astronaut-tourists can find Pluto, with a diameter of one inch. Distant comets are located as far away as the South Pole!

Watts Towers
Los Angeles, California

These amazing towers are located in an area of Los Angeles called Watts. Simon Rodia began work on them in 1921 and finished the project 33 years later. He built the structures out of steel rods covered by concrete. Embedded in the concrete are stones, glass, broken tiles and other materials. The tallest tower stands nearly 100 feet.

Barney Smith's Toilet Seat Art Museum
San Antonio, Texas

Nearly 700 toilet seats—all painted or engraved by Barney Smith—are on display at this unusual museum. Many have objects glued on them, such as model trains, dog licenses and Boy Scout badges. Smith sees himself as an artist who just happens to use a different type of canvas.

The Museum of Dirt
Boston, Massachusetts

The museum is the brainchild of Glenn Johanson. Labeled glass bottles contain such treasures as dirt from the Great Wall of China, sand from a desert in Saudi Arabia, lava from Mount Fuji in Japan and shells from the Great Barrier Reef in Australia. Best of all, the cost of seeing this museum is dirt cheap: it's free.

A Look at the U.S. Population*

U.S. Population: 281,421,906

Males: 138,053,563
(49.1% of population)
Females: 143,368,343
(50.9% of population)
Number of kids ages 5 to 9: 20,549,505
Number of kids ages 10 to 14: 20,528,072
**Number of centenarians
(people over age 100):** 50,454
It's estimated that by the year 2050, there will be about 834,000 Americans over the age of 100!

Number of families: 71,787,347
Average family size: 3.14 people
Median age of the population: 35.3

Race

75.1% of Americans are white.
12.5% are of Hispanic origin (they may be of any race).
12.3% are black.
3.6% are Asian, Native Hawaiian or Pacific Islander.
0.9% are Native American or Alaskan Native.
*Figures based on Census 200.

Life Expectancy

When the nation was founded, the average American could expect to live to age 35. By 1900, life expectancy had increased to 47.3. In 2001, the life expectancy for men was 74.4 years and 79.8 years for women.

Kids at Home

About 71% of kids live with two parents.
About 25% live with one parent.
Nearly 4% live with neither parent.
About 5.5% live in a home maintained by a grandparent.

A Look Back at the U.S. Population*

1790	3,929,214	**1900**	75,994,575
1800	5,308,483	**1920**	105,710,620
1820	9,638,453	**1950**	150,697,361
1850	23,191,876	**1980**	226,545,805
1880	50,155,783	**1990**	248,709,873

*Figures do not include armed forces overseas.

Ancestry of the U.S. Population

The United States is indeed a big melting pot, made up of people of different ethnicities and cultures. Here are the top ancestries of U.S. citizens, according to the U.S. Census Bureau.

1. **German**
2. **Irish**
3. **African American**
4. **English**
5. **American**
6. **Mexican**
7. **Italian**
8. **Polish**
9. **French**
10. **American Indian**

Did You Know?

In 2003, there were 96.8 males for every 100 females in the United States. For kids age 14 and under, there were 104.8 boys for every 100 girls.

Foreign-Born Americans

The term "foreign born" refers to Americans who were not born in this country. Below is a list of the top 10 places where these Americans were born.

1. Mexico
2. China
3. Philippines
4. India
5. Cuba
6. Vietnam
7. El Salvador
8. Korea
9. Dominican Republic
10. Canada

Source: Immigration and Naturalization Service

International Adoptions

Each year, thousands of American families adopt infants and young children from countries all over the world. Here's a look at where children were born who were adopted from foreign countries in 2003.

Rank	Country of Birth	Number
1.	CHINA	6,859
2.	RUSSIA	5,209
3.	GUATEMALA	2,328
4.	SOUTH KOREA	1,790
5.	KAZAKHSTAN	825
6.	UKRAINE	702
7.	INDIA	472
8.	VIETNAM	382
9.	COLOMBIA	272
10.	HAITI	250

Source: U.S. State Department

African Americans in the United States

In 1790, when the first census was taken, African Americans in the U.S. numbered about 760,000—about 19% of the population. In 1860, at the start of the Civil War, the African-American population increased to 4.4 million, about 14% of the overall population. Most were slaves, with only 488,000 counted as "freemen." By 1900, the black population had reached 8.8 million.

In 1910, about 90% of African Americans lived in the South, but large numbers began migrating north to look for better opportunities and to escape racial violence. By 2000, the African-American population reached nearly 35 million—more than 12% of the population.

African American Population

Year	Population	% of U.S. Population
1790	800,000	19.3
1800	1,000,000	18.9
1850	3,600,000	15.7
1900	8,800,000	11.6
1910	9,800,000	10.7
1920	10,500,000	9.9
1930	11,900,000	9.7
1940	12,900,000	9.8
1950	15,000,000	10.0
1960	18,900,000	10.5
1970	22,600,000	11.1
1980	26,500,000	11.7
1990	30,000,000	12.1
2000	34,600,000	12.3

The Great Seal of the United States

Benjamin Franklin, John Adams and Thomas Jefferson began designing the Great Seal in 1776. The Great Seal is printed on the back of the $1 bill and is used on certain government documents, such as foreign treaties.

The bald eagle, our national bird, is at the center of the seal. It holds a banner in its beak. The motto says *E pluribus unum*, which is Latin for "out of many, one." This refers to the colonies that united to make a nation. In one claw, the eagle holds an olive branch for peace; in the other claw, it carries arrows for war.

Other Symbols of the United States

The **bald eagle** has been our national bird since 1782. The Founding Fathers had been unable to agree on which native bird should have the honor—Benjamin Franklin strongly preferred the turkey! Besides appearing on the Great Seal, the bald eagle is also pictured on coins, the $1 bill, all official U.S. seals and the President's flag.

The image of **Uncle Sam,** with his white hair and top hat, first became famous on World War I recruiting posters. The artist, James Montgomery Flagg, used himself as a model. But the term dates back to the War of 1812, when a meat packer nicknamed Uncle Sam supplied beef to the troops. The initials for his nickname were quite appropriate!

The U.S. Flag

In 1777 the Continental Congress decided that the flag would have 13 alternating red and white stripes, for the 13 colonies, and 13 white stars on a blue background. A new star has been added for every new state. Today the flag has 50 stars.

The Pledge of Allegiance to the Flag

The original pledge was published in the September 8, 1892, issue of *The Youth's Companion* in Boston. For years, there was a dispute over who should get credit for writing the pledge, James B. Upham or Francis Bellamy, both members of the magazine's staff. In 1939, the United States Flag Association decided that Bellamy deserved the credit.

Here's the original version of the pledge:

I pledge allegiance to my Flag and the Republic for which it stands—one nation indivisible—with liberty and justice for all.

American Indians

There are more than 550 federally recognized American Indian tribes in the United States, including 223 village groups in Alaska. "Federally recognized" means these tribes and groups have a special legal relationship with the U.S. government.

Largest American Indian Tribes

1. Cherokee
2. Navajo
3. Latin American Indian
4. Choctaw
5. Sioux
6. Chippewa
7. Apache
8. Blackfeet
9. Iroquois
10. Pueblo

Source: U.S. Census Bureau

American Indian Population by State

Here are the states with the highest American Indian populations.

	STATE	POPULATION
1.	Oklahoma	252,420
2.	California	242,164
3.	Arizona	203,527
4.	New Mexico	134,355
5.	Washington	81,483
6.	North Carolina	80,155
7.	Texas	65,877
8.	New York	62,651
9.	Michigan	55,638
10.	South Dakota	50,575

Source: U.S. Census Bureau

Homework Tip!

On group projects, meet several days before the deadline. This way you can make sure that each member has completed the work and the project will be completed on time.

TFK Puzzles & Games

BUMPER CROP

Honk if you think these bumper stickers are misspelled! Cross out the extra letter in each one to get the correct spelling of the drivers' hometowns.

Lap Crosse, Wisconsin

Lost Angeles, California

Newt Orleans, Louisiana

Lost Alamos, New Mexico

Sand Diego, California

Forty Collins, Colorado

Desk Moines, Iowa

St. Louise, Missouri

Little Rocky, Arkansas

News Haven, Connecticut

NEWARK, KNEW JERSEY

Butter, Montana

(See Answer Key that begins on page 342.)

247

Most COMMON FIRST NAMES in the United States

Is your name Jacob or Michael, Sarah or Olivia? If it is, you have one of the most popular names in the country! Here's a list of the most popular first names.

Hello, my name is Emily.

Hi, my name is Jacob.

GIRLS

1. Emily
2. Madison
3. Hannah
4. Emma
5. Alexis
6. Ashley
7. Abigail
8. Sarah
9. Samantha
10. Olivia

BOYS

1. Jacob
2. Michael
3. Joshua
4. Matthew
5. Ethan
6. Joseph
7. Andrew
8. Christopher
9. Daniel
10. Nicholas

EXTREME Points of the U.S.

Extreme Points (from the geographic center of the U.S. in Castle Rock, South Dakota)	Latitude	Longitude	Distance
Northernmost: Point Barrow, Alaska	71°23' N	156°29' W	2,507 miles (4,034 km)
Easternmost: West Quoddy Head, Maine	44°49' N	66°57' W	1,788 miles (2,997 km)
Southernmost: Ka Lae (South Cape), Hawaii	18°55' N	155°41' W	3,463 miles (5,573 km)
Westernmost: Cape Wrangell, Alaska (Attu Island)	52°55' N	172°27' E	3,625 miles (5,833 km)

Minutes   Degrees   Direction

Largest Cities in the U.S.

RANK	CITY	POPULATION*
1.	New York, New York	8,008,278
2.	Los Angeles, California	3,694,820
3.	Chicago, Illinois	2,896,016
4.	Houston, Texas	1,953,631
5.	Philadelphia, Pennsylvania	1,517,550
6.	Phoenix, Arizona	1,321,045
7.	San Diego, California	1,223,400
8.	Dallas, Texas	1,188,580
9.	San Antonio, Texas	1,144,646
10.	Detroit, Michigan	951,270

*Figures based on Census 2000

Park It Here!

There are 388 parks, monuments and recreation areas in the National Park System. Here are a few sites that are less well known but fascinating.

Biscayne National Park
Biscayne, Florida
This park in eastern Florida covers 270 square miles, and 95% of it is underwater. Divers and snorkelers hit the ocean to explore shipwrecks and a bright coral reef.

Women's Rights National Historical Park
Seneca Falls, New York
The Wesleyan Chapel, site of the first Women's Rights Convention in 1848, is part of this historical park. So is the home of women's rights leader Elizabeth Cady Stanton.

Cape Cod National Seashore
Wellfleet, Massachusetts
With its 40-mile stretch of beach and historic lighthouses, including Nauset Light and Highland Light, this park is a great place to swim in the Atlantic, explore nature trails and learn about our nation's seafaring past and present.

Hawaii Volcanoes National Park
near Hilo, Hawaii
Visitors will find the Earth's most massive volcano, 13,677-foot Mauna Loa, and watch bubbling lava flow from the world's most active volcano, Kilauea.

Alcatraz Island
San Francisco, California
Sitting in the middle of San Francisco Bay, "the Rock" was the home of America's most famous federal prison.

Florissant Fossil Beds National Monument
Florissant, Colorado
Located near Pike's Peak, this mountain valley holds giant petrified redwoods and fossils of ancient insects and plants.

Lower East Side Tenement Museum
New York City, New York
See what life was like for immigrants in this tenement building in which people lived between 1863 and 1935.

Brown vs. Board of Education National Historic Site
Topeka, Kansas
The Supreme Court case that ended segregation in public schools originated in Topeka, Kansas. This site honors the decision. On view is a segregated elementary school once reserved for African-American kids.

go For more National Parks:
www.factmonster.com/nationalparks

PACIFIC
OCEAN

• Seattle
Tacoma
Olympia ○
Portland
• Spokane

Washington

○ Salem

Eugene

Oregon

• Great Falls

Ro
ck
y

Montana

Helena ○

Billings •

Missouri River

Bismar

California

Boise ○

Idaho

Yellowstone
National
Park

M
o
u
n
t
a
i
n
s

Gre
at
Pla
in
s

Rapid City •

Pie

Reno •

Nevada

Great
Salt
Lake

Wyoming

Santa Rosa •
Sacramento ○ ○ Carson City
San Francisco •
Modesto •
San José •

Yosemite
National
Park

Fresno •

Salt Lake City
•

Cheyenne
○

Utah

Colorado

Denver
○

Colorado Springs
•

Death
Valley

Las Vegas
•

Grand
Canyon

Pueblo
•

Los Angeles
•

Escondido •

San Diego •

Phoenix
○

Flagstaff
•

Santa Fe
○

• Albuquerque

Arizona

Tucson
•

New Mexico

Amarillo
•

Lubbock
•

Abil

• El Paso

Texas

<table>
<tr><td>Kauai</td></tr>
<tr><td>Oahu</td><td>Hawaii</td></tr>
</table>

Kauai
Oahu
Honolulu ○

Hawaii

Maui

Hawaii

PACIFIC
OCEAN

ARCTIC OCEAN

RUSSIA

CANADA

Alaska

MEXICO

La

**BERING
SEA**

Anchorage
•

Juneau
•

A l e u t i a n   I s l a n d s

0 mi.   300 mi.   600 mi.

0 km   400 km   800 km

PACIFIC OCEAN

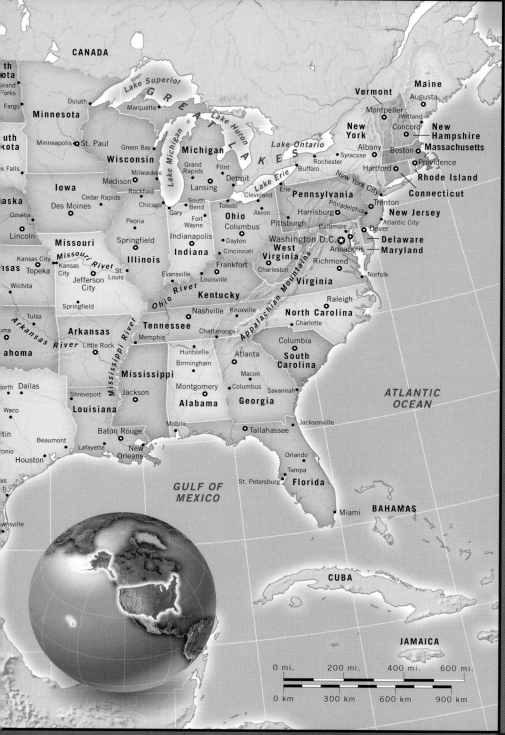

CANADA

Lake Superior

GREAT LAKES

Lake Huron

Lake Michigan

Lake Ontario

Lake Erie

th ota
rand Forks
Fargo
Duluth
Marquette

Minnesota

uth ota
Minneapolis • St. Paul
k Falls

aska
Omaha
Lincoln

Iowa
Des Moines
Cedar Rapids
Rockford

Wisconsin
Green Bay
Madison
Milwaukee

Michigan
Grand Rapids
Flint
Lansing
Detroit

Vermont
Montpelier

Maine
Augusta

New York
Albany
Syracuse
Rochester
Buffalo

New Hampshire
Concord
Portland
Boston

Massachusetts
Providence

Rhode Island
Hartford
Connecticut

New York City

sa
Kansas City
Topeka
Wichita

Missouri
Missouri River
Kansas City
Jefferson City
St. Louis
Springfield

Illinois
Peoria
Springfield
Chicago

Indiana
Indianapolis
Gary
South Bend
Fort Wayne

Ohio
Columbus
Toledo
Dayton
Cincinnati
Akron
Cleveland

Pennsylvania
Harrisburg
Pittsburgh
Philadelphia

New Jersey
Trenton
Atlantic City

Delaware
Dover
Maryland
Annapolis

Washington D.C.

West Virginia
Charleston

Virginia
Richmond
Norfolk

Ohio River

Evansville
Louisville
Frankfort

Kentucky
Nashville
Knoxville
Chattanooga

Tennessee
Memphis

North Carolina
Raleigh
Charlotte

Appalachian Mountains

ahoma
Tulsa
ma

Arkansas River
Arkansas
Little Rock

Mississippi River
Mississippi
Jackson

Huntsville
Birmingham

Alabama
Montgomery
Mobile

Atlanta
Macon
Columbus

Georgia
Savannah

Columbia
South Carolina

ATLANTIC OCEAN

orth Dallas
Waco
tin
Beaumont
Lafayette
onio
Houston

Louisiana
Shreveport
Baton Rouge
New Orleans

Tallahassee

Jacksonville

Florida
Orlando
Tampa
St. Petersburg
Miami

GULF OF MEXICO

BAHAMAS

nsville
ti

CUBA

JAMAICA

0 mi.   200 mi.   400 mi.   600 mi.

0 km   300 km   600 km   900 km

251

ALABAMA

Capital: Montgomery
Largest City: Birmingham
Abbreviation: Ala.
Postal Code: AL

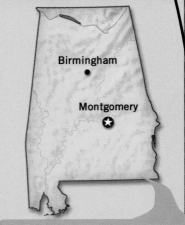

Origin of name: May come from a Choctaw word meaning "thicket-clearers"

Entered union (rank): December 14, 1819 (22)

Motto: *Audemus jura nostra defendere* (We dare defend our rights)

Tree: southern longleaf pine

Flower: camellia

Bird: yellowhammer (yellow-shafted flicker)

Other: dance: square dance; nut: pecan

Song: "Alabama"

Nickname: Yellowhammer State

Residents: Alabamian, Alabaman

Land area: 50,750 square miles (131,443 sq km)

Population (2004): 4,530,182

Did You Know?
The Confederacy was founded in Montgomery in 1861.

Home of: George Washington Carver, who discovered more than 300 uses for peanuts

---

ALASKA

Capital: Juneau
Largest City: Anchorage
Abbreviation: Alaska
Postal Code: AK

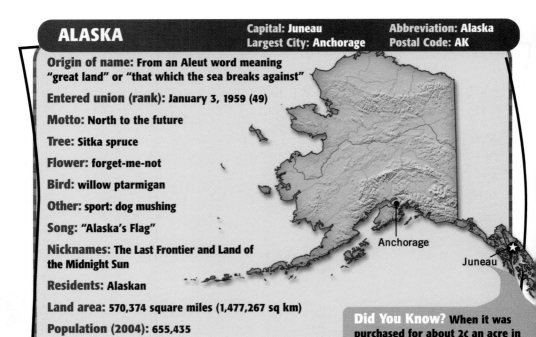

Origin of name: From an Aleut word meaning "great land" or "that which the sea breaks against"

Entered union (rank): January 3, 1959 (49)

Motto: North to the future

Tree: Sitka spruce

Flower: forget-me-not

Bird: willow ptarmigan

Other: sport: dog mushing

Song: "Alaska's Flag"

Nicknames: The Last Frontier and Land of the Midnight Sun

Residents: Alaskan

Land area: 570,374 square miles (1,477,267 sq km)

Population (2004): 655,435

Home of: The longest coastline in the U.S., 6,640 miles, which is greater than that of all other states combined

Did You Know? When it was purchased for about 2¢ an acre in 1867, Alaska was called "Seward's Folly."

ARIZONA

Capital: Phoenix
Largest City: Phoenix

Abbreviation: Ariz.
Postal Code: AZ

Phoenix

Origin of name: From the Native American *Arizonac*, meaning "little spring"

Entered union (rank): February 14, 1912 (48)

Motto: *Ditat deus* (God enriches)

Tree: palo verde

Flower: flower of saguaro cactus

Bird: cactus wren

Other: gemstone: turquoise; neckwear: bolo tie

Song: "Arizona"

Nickname: Grand Canyon State

Residents: Arizonan, Arizonian

Land area: 113,642 square miles (296,400 sq km)

Population (2004): 5,743,834

Home of: The most telescopes in the world, in Tucson

Did You Know? London Bridge was shipped to Lake Havasu City and rebuilt there stone-by-stone.

ARKANSAS

Capital: Little Rock
Largest City: Little Rock

Abbreviation: Ark.
Postal Code: AR

Little Rock

Origin of name: From the Quapaw Indians

Entered union (rank): June 15, 1836 (25)

Motto: *Regnat populus* (The people rule)

Tree: pine

Flower: apple blossom

Bird: mockingbird

Other: fruit and vegetable: pink tomato; insect: honeybee

Song: "Arkansas"

Nickname: Land of Opportunity

Residents: Arkansan

Land area: 52,075 square miles (134,874 sq km)

Population (2004): 2,752,629

Home of: The only active diamond mine in the U.S.

Did You Know? Arkansas's Hattie Caraway was the first woman elected to the U.S. Senate.

CALIFORNIA

Capital: Sacramento
Largest City: Los Angeles
Abbreviation: Calif.
Postal Code: CA

Origin of name: From a book, *Las Sergas de Esplandián,* by Garcia Ordóñez de Montalvo, circa 1500

Entered union (rank): September 9, 1850 (31)

Motto: *Eureka* (I have found it)

Tree: California redwood

Flower: golden poppy

Bird: California valley quail

Other: dance: West Coast swing dance; prehistoric artifact: chipped-stone bear

Song: "I Love You, California"

Nickname: Golden State

Residents: Californian

Land area: 155,973 square miles (403,970 sq km)

Population (2004): 35,893,799

Home of: "General Sherman," a 2,500-year-old sequoia

Did You Know? More immigrants settle in California than in any other state.

COLORADO

Capital: Denver
Largest City: Denver
Abbreviation: Colo.
Postal Code: CO

Origin of name: From the Spanish, "ruddy" or "red"

Entered union (rank): August 1, 1876 (38)

Motto: *Nil sine numine* (Nothing without providence)

Tree: Colorado blue spruce

Flower: Rocky Mountain columbine

Bird: lark bunting

Other: fossil: *Stegosaurus;* gemstone: aquamarine

Song: "Where the Columbines Grow"

Nickname: Centennial State

Residents: Coloradan, Coloradoan

Land area: 103,730 square miles (268,660 sq km)

Population (2004): 4,601,403

Home of: The world's largest silver nugget (1,840 pounds), found in 1894 near Aspen

Did You Know? There are 54 peaks in the Rocky Mountains that rise above 14,000 feet.

CONNECTICUT

Capital: Hartford
Largest City: Bridgeport
Abbreviation: Conn.
Postal Code: CT

Origin of name: From a Quinnehtukqut Indian word meaning "beside the long tidal river"

Entered union (rank): January 9, 1788 (5)

Motto: *Qui transtulit sustinet* (He who transplanted still sustains)

Tree: white oak

Flower: mountain laurel

Bird: American robin

Other: hero: Nathan Hale; heroine: Prudence Crandall

Song: "Yankee Doodle"

Nickname: Nutmeg State

Residents: Nutmegger

Land area: 4,845 square miles (12,550 sq km)

Population (2004): 3,503,604

Home of: The first American cookbook—*American Cookery* by Amelia Simmons—published in Hartford in 1796

Did You Know? The U.S. Constitution was modeled after Connecticut's colonial laws.

DELAWARE

Capital: Dover
Largest City: Wilmington
Abbreviation: Del.
Postal Code: DE

Origin of name: From Delaware River and Bay, named for Sir Thomas West, Baron De La Warr

Entered union (rank): December 7, 1787 (1)

Motto: Liberty and independence

Tree: American holly

Flower: peach blossom

Bird: blue hen chicken

Other: colors: colonial blue and buff; insect: ladybug

Song: "Our Delaware"

Nicknames: Diamond State, First State and Small Wonder

Residents: Delawarean

Land area: 1,955 square miles (5,153 sq km)

Population (2004): 830,364

Home of: The first log cabins in North America, built in 1683 by Swedish immigrants

Did You Know? Delaware was the first of the original 13 colonies to ratify the Constitution.

Show what you know about America's 50 states at www.timeforkids.com/staterace

255

FLORIDA

Capital: Tallahassee
Largest City: Jacksonville
Abbreviation: Fla.
Postal Code: FL

Origin of name: From the Spanish, meaning "feast of flowers"

Entered union (rank): March 3, 1845 (27)

Motto: In God we trust

Tree: Sabal palm

Flower: orange blossom

Bird: mockingbird

Other: shell: horse conch; soil: Myakka fine sand

Song: "The Sewanee River"

Nickname: Sunshine State

Residents: Floridian, Floridan

Land area: 54,153 square miles (140,256 sq km)

Population (2004): 17,397,161

Home of: U.S. spacecraft launchings from Cape Canaveral, formerly Cape Kennedy

Jacksonville

Tallahassee

Did You Know? There are two rivers in Florida with the name Withlacoochee.

GEORGIA

Capital: Atlanta
Largest City: Atlanta
Abbreviation: Ga.
Postal Code: GA

Origin of name: In honor of George II of England

Entered union (rank): January 2, 1788 (4)

Motto: Wisdom, justice and moderation

Tree: live oak

Flower: Cherokee rose

Bird: brown thrasher

Other: crop: peanut; fossil: shark tooth

Song: "Georgia on My Mind"

Nicknames: Peach State and Empire State of the South

Residents: Georgian

Land area: 57,919 square miles (150,010 sq km)

Population (2004): 8,829,383

Home of: One of the world's largest college campuses, Berry College, in Rome

Atlanta

Did You Know? During the Civil War, Atlanta was burned and nearly destroyed by Union troops.

HAWAII

Capital: Honolulu (on Oahu) **Abbreviation:** Hawaii
Largest City: Honolulu **Postal Code:** HI

Origin of name: Probably from a Polynesian word meaning "ancestral home"

Entered union (rank): August 21, 1959 (50)

Motto: *Ua mau ke ea o ka aina i ka pono* (The life of the land is perpetuated in righteousness)

Tree: kukui (candlenut)

Flower: yellow hibiscus

Bird: nene (Hawaiian goose)

Other: gem: black coral; marine mammal: humpback whale

Song: "Hawaii Ponoi"

Nickname: Aloha State

Residents: Hawaiian

Land area: 6,423 square miles (16,637 sq km)

Population (2004): 1,262,840

Home of: The only royal palace in the U.S. (Iolani)

Did You Know? Hawaii was formed by undersea volcanoes.

IDAHO

Capital: Boise **Abbreviation:** Idaho
Largest City: Boise **Postal Code:** ID

Origin of name: Although popularly believed to be a Native American word, it is an invented name whose meaning is unknown.

Entered union (rank): July 3, 1890 (43)

Motto: *Esto perpetua* (It is forever)

Tree: white pine

Flower: lilac

Bird: mountain bluebird

Other: fish: cutthroat trout; horse: Appaloosa

Song: "Here We Have Idaho"

Nickname: Gem State

Residents: Idahoan

Land area: 82,751 square miles (214,325 sq km)

Population (2004): 1,393,262

Home of: The longest Main Street in America, 33 miles, in Island Park

Did You Know? Idaho produces about 25% of the country's potato crop.

257

ILLINOIS

Capital: Springfield
Largest City: Chicago

Abbreviation: Ill.
Postal Code: IL

Origin of name: Algonquian for "tribe of superior men"

Entered union (rank): December 3, 1818 (21)

Motto: State sovereignty, national union

Tree: white oak

Flower: violet

Bird: cardinal

Other: animal: white-tailed deer; prairie grass: big bluestem

Song: "Illinois"

Nickname: Prairie State

Residents: Illinoisan

Land area: 55,593 square miles (143,987 sq km)

Population (2004): 12,713,634

Home of: The tallest building in the country, Sears Tower, in Chicago

Did You Know? The country's first skyscraper was built in Chicago in 1885.

INDIANA

Capital: Indianapolis
Largest City: Indianapolis

Abbreviation: Ind.
Postal Code: IN

Origin of name: Means "land of Indians"

Entered union (rank): December 11, 1816 (19)

Motto: The crossroads of America

Tree: tulip tree

Flower: peony

Bird: cardinal

Other: river: Wabash; stone: limestone

Song: "On the Banks of the Wabash, Far Away"

Nickname: Hoosier State

Residents: Indianan, Indianian

Land area: 35,870 sq miles (92,904 sq km)

Population (2004): 6,237,569

Home of: The famous car race, the Indianapolis 500

Did You Know? Wabash, Indiana, was the first U.S. city to be lighted by electricity.

IOWA

Capital: Des Moines
Largest City: Des Moines
Abbreviation: Iowa
Postal Code: IA

Origin of name: Probably from an Indian word meaning "this is the place"

Entered union (rank): December 28, 1846 (29)

Motto: Our liberties we prize and our rights we will maintain

Tree: oak

Flower: wild rose

Bird: eastern goldfinch

Other: fossil: crinoid; rock: geode

Song: "Song of Iowa"

Nickname: Hawkeye State

Residents: Iowan

Land area: 55,875 square miles (144,716 sq km)

Population (2004): 2,954,451

Home of: The shortest and steepest railroad in the U.S., in Dubuque: 296 feet, 60° incline

Des Moines ☆

Did You Know? The Eskimo Pie, the first chocolate-covered ice cream bar, was invented in Onawa in 1921.

KANSAS

Capital: Topeka
Largest City: Wichita
Abbreviation: Kans.
Postal Code: KS

Origin of name: From a Sioux word meaning "people of the south wind"

Entered union (rank): January 29, 1861 (34)

Motto: *Ad astra per aspera* (To the stars through difficulties)

Tree: cottonwood

Flower: sunflower

Bird: western meadowlark

Other: animal: buffalo; reptile: ornate box turtle

Song: "Home on the Range"

Nicknames: Sunflower State and Jayhawk State

Residents: Kansan

Land area: 81,823 square miles (211,922 sq km)

Population (2004): 2,735,502

Home of: Helium, discovered by scientists in 1905 at the University of Kansas

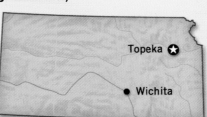
Topeka ☆
● Wichita

Did You Know? The world's largest ball of twine is in Cawker City.

KENTUCKY

Capital: Frankfort
Largest City: Louisville

Abbreviation: Ky.
Postal Code: KY

Origin of name: From an Iroquoian word (Kentahten) meaning "land of tomorrow"

Entered union (rank): June 1, 1792 (15)

Motto: United we stand, divided we fall

Tree: tulip poplar

Flower: goldenrod

Bird: Kentucky cardinal

Other: bluegrass song: "Blue Moon of Kentucky"; horse: Thoroughbred

Song: "My Old Kentucky Home"

Nickname: Bluegrass State

Residents: Kentuckian

Land area: 39,732 square miles (102,907 sq km)

Population (2004): 4,145,922

Home of: The largest underground cave in the world, the Mammoth-Flint Cave system, over 300 miles long

Louisville ● ✪ Frankfort

Did You Know? "Happy Birthday to You" was written by two Louisville teachers.

LOUISIANA

Capital: Baton Rouge
Largest City: New Orleans

Abbreviation: La.
Postal Code: LA

Origin of name: In honor of Louis XIV of France

Entered union (rank): April 30, 1812 (18)

Motto: Union, justice and confidence

Tree: bald cypress

Flower: magnolia

Bird: eastern brown pelican

Other: crustacean: crawfish; dog: Catahoula leopard hound

Songs: "Give Me Louisiana" and "You Are My Sunshine"

Nickname: Pelican State

Residents: Louisianan, Louisianian

Land area: 43,566 square miles (112,836 sq km)

Population (2004): 4,515,770

Home of: About 98% of the world's crawfish

New Orleans

Baton Rouge ✪

Did You Know? Tourists have been flocking to New Orleans for Mardi Gras since 1838.

MAINE

Capital: Augusta
Largest City: Portland
Abbreviation: Maine
Postal Code: ME

Origin of name: First used to distinguish the mainland from the coastal islands

Entered union (rank): March 15, 1820 (23)

Motto: *Dirigo* (I lead)

Tree: white pine tree

Flower: white pine cone and tassel

Bird: chickadee

Other: animal: moose; cat: Maine coon cat

Song: "State of Maine Song"

Nickname: Pine Tree State

Residents: Mainer

Land area: 30,865 square miles (79,939 sq km)

Population (2004): 1,317,253

Home of: The most easterly point in the U.S., West Quoddy Head

Did You Know? Maine is the world's largest producer of blueberries.

MARYLAND

Capital: Annapolis
Largest City: Baltimore
Abbreviation: Md.
Postal Code: MD

Origin of name: In honor of Henrietta Maria (queen of Charles I of England)

Entered union (rank): April 28, 1788 (7)

Motto: *Fatti maschii, parole femine* (Manly deeds, womanly words)

Tree: white oak

Flower: black-eyed Susan

Bird: Baltimore oriole

Other: crustacean: Maryland blue crab; sport: jousting

Song: "Maryland! My Maryland!"

Nicknames: Free State and Old Line State

Residents: Marylander

Land area: 9,775 square miles (25,316 sq km)

Population (2004): 5,558,058

Home of: The first umbrella factory in the U.S., opened in 1928, in Baltimore

Did You Know? During the Civil War, Maryland was a slave state but part of the Union.

 For fun facts and trivia on all the states: www.factmonster.com/states

MASSACHUSETTS

Capital: Boston **Abbreviation: Mass.**
Largest City: Boston **Postal Code: MA**

Origin of name: From the Massachusett Indian tribe, meaning "at or about the great hill"

Entered union (rank): February 6, 1788 (6)

Motto: *Ense petit placidam sub libertate quietem* (By the sword we seek peace, but peace only under liberty)

Tree: American elm

Flower: mayflower

Bird: chickadee

Other: beverage: cranberry juice; dessert: Boston cream pie

Song: "All Hail to Massachusetts"

Nicknames: Bay State and Old Colony State

Residents: Bay Stater

Land area: 7,838 square miles (20,300 sq km)

Population (2004): 6,416,505

Home of: The first World Series, played between the Boston Pilgrims and the Pittsburgh Pirates in 1903

Boston ✪

Did You Know? The first basketball game was played in Springfield, Massachusetts, in 1891.

MICHIGAN

Capital: Lansing **Abbreviation: Mich.**
Largest City: Detroit **Postal Code: MI**

Origin of name: From an Indian word (Michigana) meaning "great or large lake"

Entered union (rank): January 26, 1837 (26)

Motto: *Si quaeris peninsulam amoenam circumspice* (If you seek a pleasant peninsula, look around you)

Tree: white pine

Flower: apple blossom

Bird: robin

Other: reptile: painted turtle; wildflower: Dwarf Lake iris

Song: "Michigan, My Michigan"

Nickname: Wolverine State

Residents: Michigander, Michiganian

Land area: 56,809 square miles (147,135 sq km)

Population (2004): 10,112,620

Home of: Battle Creek, "Cereal City," producer of most of the breakfast cereal in the U.S.

Lansing ✪

Detroit ●

Did You Know? Michigan is the country's top producer of automobiles and auto parts.

MINNESOTA

Capital: St. Paul
Largest City: Minneapolis
Abbreviation: Minn.
Postal Code: MN

Origin of name: From a Dakota Indian word meaning "sky-tinted water"

Entered union (rank): May 11, 1858 (32)

Motto: *L'Étoile du nord* (The north star)

Tree: red (or Norway) pine

Flower: lady slipper

Bird: common loon

Other: drink: milk; mushroom: morel

Song: "Hail Minnesota"

Nicknames: North Star State, Gopher State and Land of 10,000 Lakes

Residents: Minnesotan

Land area: 79,617 square miles (206,207 sq km)

Population (2004): 5,100,958

Home of: One of the world's oldest rocks, 3.8 billion years old

Minneapolis

St. Paul

Did You Know? Although it's called "Land of 10,000 Lakes," Minnesota has more than 15,000 lakes.

MISSISSIPPI

Capital: Jackson
Largest City: Jackson
Abbreviation: Miss.
Postal Code: MS

Origin of name: From an Indian word meaning "Father of Waters"

Entered union (rank): December 10, 1817 (20)

Motto: *Virtute et armis* (By valor and arms)

Tree: magnolia

Flower: magnolia

Bird: mockingbird

Other: stone: petrified wood; water mammal: bottlenose dolphin

Song: "Go, Mississippi"

Nickname: Magnolia State

Residents: Mississippian

Land area: 46,914 square miles (121,506 sq km)

Population (2004): 2,902,966

Home of: Coca-Cola, first bottled in 1894 in Vicksburg

Jackson

Did You Know? Hernando de Soto discovered the Mississippi River in 1540.

263

MISSOURI

Capital: Jefferson City
Largest City: Kansas City
Abbreviation: Mo.
Postal Code: MO

Origin of name: Named after the Missouri Indian tribe; means "town of the large canoes"

Entered union (rank): August 10, 1821 (24)

Motto: *Salus populi suprema lex esto*
(The welfare of the people shall be the supreme law)

Tree: flowering dogwood

Flower: hawthorn

Bird: bluebird

Other: musical instrument: fiddle; tree nut: eastern black walnut

Song: "Missouri Waltz"

Nickname: Show-Me State

Residents: Missourian

Land area: 68,898 square miles (178,446 sq km)

Population (2004): 5,754,618

Home of: Mark Twain and some of his characters, such as Tom Sawyer and Huckleberry Finn

Did You Know? The strongest earthquake in U.S. history was centered in New Madrid in 1811.

MONTANA

Capital: Helena
Largest City: Billings
Abbreviation: Mont.
Postal Code: MT

Origin of name: The Latin form of a Spanish word meaning "mountainous"

Entered union (rank): November 8, 1889 (41)

Motto: *Oro y plata* (Gold and silver)

Tree: ponderosa pine

Flower: bitterroot

Bird: western meadowlark

Other: animal: grizzly bear; stones: sapphire and agate

Song: "Montana"

Nickname: Treasure State

Residents: Montanan

Land area: 145,556 square miles (376,991 sq km)

Population (2004): 926,865

Home of: Grasshopper Glacier, named for the grasshoppers that can be seen frozen in ice

Did You Know? Glacier National Park has 60 glaciers, 200 lakes and countless streams.

NEBRASKA

Capital: Lincoln
Largest City: Omaha
Abbreviation: Neb.
Postal Code: NE

Origin of name: From an Oto Indian word meaning "flat water"

Entered union (rank): March 1, 1867 (37)

Motto: Equality before the law

Tree: cottonwood

Flower: goldenrod

Bird: western meadowlark

Other: ballad: "A Place Like Nebraska";
soft drink: Kool-Aid

Song: "Beautiful Nebraska"

Nicknames: Cornhusker State and Beef State

Residents: Nebraskan

Land area: 76,878 square miles (199,113 sq km)

Population (2004): 1,747,214

Home of: The only roller-skating museum in the world, in Lincoln

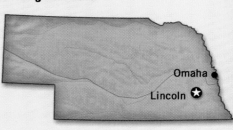

Omaha
Lincoln

Did You Know? A favorite summer drink, Kool-Aid, was invented in Hastings.

NEVADA

Capital: Carson City
Largest City: Las Vegas
Abbreviation: Nev.
Postal Code: NV

Origin of name: From the Spanish, "snowcapped"

Entered union (rank): October 31, 1864 (36)

Motto: All for our country

Trees: single-leaf piñon and bristlecone pine

Flower: sagebrush

Bird: mountain bluebird

Other: metal: silver; reptile: desert tortoise

Song: "Home Means Nevada"

Nicknames: Sagebrush State, Silver State and Battle Born State

Residents: Nevadan, Nevadian

Land area: 109,806 square miles (284,397 sq km)

Population (2004): 2,334,771

Home of: The Devil's Hole pupfish, found only in Devil's Hole, an underground pool near Death Valley

Carson City

Las Vegas

Did You Know? Nevada is the driest state in the country, with about seven inches of rainfall each year.

NEW HAMPSHIRE

Capital: Concord   **Abbreviation: N.H.**
Largest City: Manchester   **Postal Code: NH**

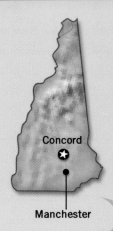

Origin of name: From the English county of Hampshire

Entered union (rank): June 21, 1788 (9)

Motto: Live free or die

Tree: white birch

Flower: purple lilac

Bird: purple finch

Other: amphibian: spotted newt; sport: skiing

Songs: "Old New Hampshire" and "New Hampshire, My New Hampshire"

Nickname: Granite State

Residents: New Hampshirite

Land area: 8,969 square miles (23,231 sq km)

Population (2004): 1,299,500

Home of: Artificial rain, first used near Concord in 1947 to fight a forest fire

Concord ✪

Manchester

Did You Know? The world's highest wind speed, 231 m.p.h., was recorded on top of Mount Washington.

NEW JERSEY

Capital: Trenton   **Abbreviation: N.J.**
Largest City: Newark   **Postal Code: NJ**

Origin of name: From the Isle of Jersey in the English Channel

Entered union (rank): December 18, 1787 (3)

Motto: Liberty and prosperity

Tree: red oak

Flower: purple violet

Bird: eastern goldfinch

Other: folk dance: square dance; shell: knobbed whelk

Song: "I'm from New Jersey"

Nickname: Garden State

Residents: New Jerseyite, New Jerseyan

Land area: 7,419 square miles (19,215 sq km)

Population (2004): 8,698,879

Home of: The world's first drive-in movie theater, built in 1933 near Camden

Newark

Trenton ✪

Did You Know? The street names in the game of Monopoly were named after streets in Atlantic City, New Jersey.

NEW MEXICO

Capital: Santa Fe
Largest City: Albuquerque
Abbreviation: N.M.
Postal Code: NM

Origin of name: From Mexico

Entered union (rank): January 6, 1912 (47)

Motto: *Crescit eundo* (It grows as it goes)

Tree: piñon

Flower: yucca

Bird: roadrunner

Other: cookie: biscochito; vegetables: chilies and beans

Song: "O Fair New Mexico"

Nickname: Land of Enchantment

Residents: New Mexican

Land area: 121,365 square miles (314,334 sq km)

Population (2004): 1,903,289

Home of: Smokey Bear, a cub orphaned by fire in 1950, buried in Smokey Bear Historical State Park in 1976

Did You Know? Each night thousands of bats swarm out of Carlsbad Caverns to eat insects.

NEW YORK

Capital: Albany
Largest City: New York
Abbreviation: N.Y.
Postal Code: NY

Origin of name: In honor of the Duke of York

Entered union (rank): July 26, 1788 (11)

Motto: *Excelsior* (Ever upward)

Tree: sugar maple

Flower: rose

Bird: bluebird

Other: animal: beaver; muffin: apple

Song: "I Love New York"

Nickname: Empire State

Residents: New Yorker

Land area: 47,224 square miles (122,310 sq km)

Population (2004): 19,227,088

Home of: The first presidential Inauguration. George Washington took the oath of office in New York City on April 30, 1789.

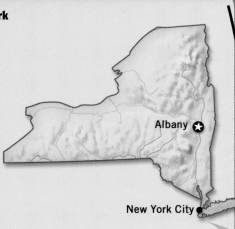

Did You Know? New York City was one of the nation's first capitals. Congress met there from 1785 to 1790.

NORTH CAROLINA

Capital: Raleigh
Largest City: Charlotte
Abbreviation: N.C.
Postal Code: NC

Origin of name: In honor of Charles I of England

Entered union (rank): November 21, 1789 (12)

Motto: *Esse quam videri* (To be rather than to seem)

Tree: pine

Flower: dogwood

Bird: cardinal

Other: dog: plott hound; historic boat: shad boat

Song: "The Old North State"

Nickname: Tar Heel State

Residents: North Carolinian

Land area: 48,718 square miles (126,180 sq km)

Population (2004): 8,541,221

Did You Know? Although the state was pro-Union and antislavery, it joined the Confederacy.

Home of: Virginia Dare, the first English child born in America, on Roanoke Island around 1587

NORTH DAKOTA

Capital: Bismarck
Largest City: Fargo
Abbreviation: N.D.
Postal Code: ND

Origin of name: From the Sioux word, meaning "allies"

Entered union (rank): November 2, 1889 (39)

Motto: Liberty and union, now and forever: one and inseparable

Tree: American elm

Flower: wild prairie rose

Bird: western meadowlark

Other: equine: Nokota horse; grass: western wheatgrass

Song: "North Dakota Hymn"

Nicknames: Sioux State, Flickertail State, Peace Garden State and Rough Rider State

Residents: North Dakotan

Land area: 70,704 square miles (183,123 sq km)

Population (2004): 634,366

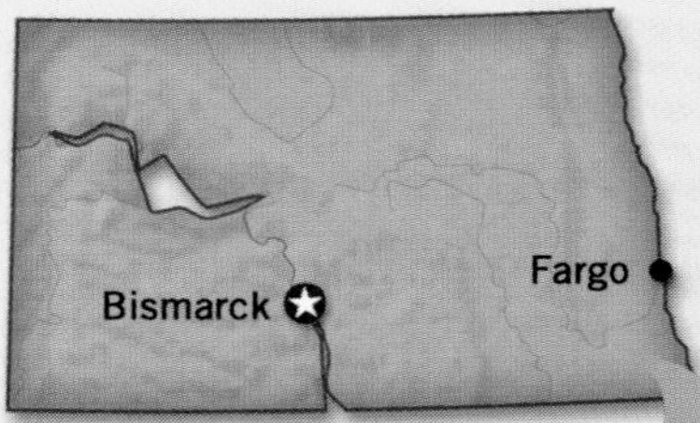

Did You Know? Farms cover more than 90% of North Dakota's land.

Home of: The "World's Largest Buffalo," a 26-foot-high, 60-ton concrete monument

OHIO

Capital: Columbus
Largest City: Columbus
Abbreviation: Ohio
Postal Code: OH

Origin of name: From an Iroquoian word meaning "great river"

Entered union (rank): March 1, 1803 (17)

Motto: With God all things are possible

Tree: buckeye

Flower: scarlet carnation

Bird: cardinal

Other: beverage: tomato juice; fossil: trilobite

Song: "Beautiful Ohio"

Nickname: Buckeye State

Residents: Ohioan

Land area: 40,953 square miles (106,067 sq km)

Population (2004): 11,459,011

Home of: The first electric traffic lights, invented and installed in Cleveland in 1914

Columbus

Did You Know? The Cincinnati Reds were the world's first professional baseball team.

OKLAHOMA

Capital: Oklahoma City
Largest City: Oklahoma City
Abbreviation: Okla.
Postal Code: OK

Origin of name: From two Choctaw Indian words meaning "red people"

Entered union (rank): November 16, 1907 (46)

Motto: *Labor omnia vincit* (Labor conquers all things)

Tree: redbud

Flower: mistletoe

Bird: scissor-tailed flycatcher

Other: furbearer: raccoon; waltz: "Oklahoma Wind"

Song: "Oklahoma!"

Nickname: Sooner State

Residents: Oklahoman

Land area: 68,679 square miles (177,880 sq km)

Population (2004): 3,523,553

Home of: The first parking meter, installed in Oklahoma City in 1935

Oklahoma City

Did You Know? Oklahoma City's state capitol building is the only capitol in the world with an oil well (it's dry) under it.

OREGON

Capital: Salem
Largest City: Portland
Abbreviation: Ore.
Postal Code: OR

Origin of name: Unknown

Entered union (rank): February 14, 1859 (33)

Motto: *Alis volat propriis* **(She flies with her own wings)**

Tree: Douglas fir

Flower: Oregon grape

Bird: western meadowlark

Other: fish: Chinook salmon; nut: hazelnut

Song: "Oregon, My Oregon"

Nickname: Beaver State

Residents: Oregonian

Land area: 96,003 square miles (248,647 sq km)

Population (2004): 3,594,586

Home of: The world's smallest park, totaling 452 square inches, created in Portland in 1948 for snail races

Did You Know? Oregon's state flag is the only one with designs on both sides.

PENNSYLVANIA

Capital: Harrisburg
Largest City: Philadelphia
Abbreviation: Pa.
Postal Code: PA

Origin of name: In honor of Sir William Penn, father of state founder William Penn. It means "Penn's Woodland."

Entered union (rank): December 12, 1787 (2)

Motto: Virtue, liberty and independence

Tree: hemlock

Flower: mountain laurel

Bird: ruffed grouse

Other: dog: Great Dane; insect: firefly

Song: "Pennsylvania"

Nickname: Keystone State

Residents: Pennsylvanian

Land area: 44,820 square miles (116,083 sq km)

Population (2004): 12,406,292

Home of: The first magazine in America, the *American Magazine,* **published in Philadelphia for three months in 1741**

Did You Know? The first baseball stadium in the U.S., Pittsburgh's Forbes Field, was built in 1909.

RHODE ISLAND

Capital: Providence
Largest City: Providence
Abbreviation: R.I.
Postal Code: RI

Origin of name: From the Greek Island of Rhodes

Entered union (rank): May 29, 1790 (13)

Motto: Hope

Tree: red maple

Flower: violet

Bird: Rhode Island Red hen

Other: shellfish: quahog; stone: cumberlandite

Song: "Rhode Island"

Nickname: Ocean State

Residents: Rhode Islander

Land area: 1,045 square miles (2,706 sq km)

Population (2004): 1,080,632

Home of: Rhode Island Red chickens, first bred in 1854; the start of poultry as a major American industry

Providence

Did You Know? Rhode Island is the smallest of the 50 U.S. states.

SOUTH CAROLINA

Capital: Columbia
Largest City: Columbia
Abbreviation: S.C.
Postal Code: SC

Origin of name: In honor of Charles I of England

Entered union (rank): May 23, 1788 (8)

Mottoes: *Animis opibusque parati* (Prepared in mind and resources) and *Dum spiro spero* (While I breathe, I hope)

Tree: palmetto

Flower: yellow jessamine

Bird: Carolina wren

Other: hospitality beverage: tea; music: the spiritual

Song: "Carolina"

Nickname: Palmetto State

Residents: South Carolinian

Land area: 30,111 square miles (77,988 sq km)

Population (2004): 4,198,068

Home of: The first tea farm in the U.S., created in 1890 near Summerville

Columbia

Did You Know? South Carolina was the first state to secede from the Union. The Civil War started here.

SOUTH DAKOTA

Capital: Pierre
Largest City: Sioux Falls
Abbreviation: S.D.
Postal Code: SD

Origin of name: From the Sioux word, meaning "allies"

Entered union (rank): November 2, 1889 (40)

Motto: Under God the people rule

Tree: black hills spruce

Flower: American pasqueflower

Bird: ring-necked pheasant

Other: dessert: kuchen; jewelry: Black Hills gold

Song: "Hail! South Dakota"

Nicknames: Mount Rushmore State and Coyote State

Residents: South Dakotan

Land area: 75,898 square miles (196,575 sq km)

Population (2004): 770,883

Home of: The world's largest natural indoor warm-water pool, Evans' Plunge, in Hot Springs

Did You Know? It took Gutzon Borglum 14 years to carve Mount Rushmore.

TENNESSEE

Capital: Nashville
Largest City: Memphis
Abbreviation: Tenn.
Postal Code: TN

Origin of name: Of Cherokee origin; the exact meaning is unknown

Entered union (rank): June 1, 1796 (16)

Motto: Agriculture and commerce

Tree: tulip poplar

Flower: iris

Bird: mockingbird

Other: amphibian: Tennessee cave salamander; animal: raccoon

Songs: "Tennessee Waltz," "My Homeland, Tennessee," "When It's Iris Time in Tennessee" and "My Tennessee"

Nickname: Volunteer State

Residents: Tennessean, Tennesseean

Land area: 41,220 square miles (106,759 sq km)

Population (2004): 5,900,962

Home of: Graceland, the estate and grave site of Elvis Presley

Did You Know? Nashville, site of the Grand Ole Opry, is considered the country-music capital of the world.

TEXAS

Capital: Austin
Largest City: Houston
Abbreviation: Tex.
Postal Code: TX

Origin of name: From a Native American word meaning "friends"

Entered union (rank): December 29, 1845 (28)

Motto: Friendship

Tree: pecan

Flower: bluebonnet

Bird: mockingbird

Other: fiber and fabric: cotton; small mammal: armadillo

Song: "Texas, Our Texas"

Nickname: Lone Star State

Residents: Texan

Land area: 261,914 square miles (678,358 sq km)

Population (2004): 22,490,022

Home of: NASA, in Houston, the headquarters for all piloted U.S. space projects

Austin ⭐ Houston ●

Did You Know? Texans fought the Mexican Army at the Alamo, known now as the "cradle of Texas liberty."

UTAH

Capital: Salt Lake City
Largest City: Salt Lake City
Abbreviation: Utah
Postal Code: UT

Origin of name: From the Ute tribe, meaning "people of the mountains"

Entered union (rank): January 4, 1896 (45)

Motto: Industry

Tree: blue spruce

Flower: sego lily

Bird: California gull

Other: cooking pot: Dutch oven; fruit: cherry

Song: "Utah, We Love Thee"

Nickname: Beehive State

Residents: Utahan, Utahn

Land area: 82,168 square miles (212,816 sq km)

Population (2004): 2,389,039

Home of: Rainbow Bridge, the largest natural stone bridge in the world, 290 feet high, 275 feet across

Salt Lake City ⭐

Did You Know? Driving the "golden spike" at Promontory Point in 1869 completed the transcontinental railroad.

273

VERMONT

Capital: Montpelier
Largest City: Burlington
Abbreviation: Vt.
Postal Code: VT

Burlington

Montpelier

Origin of name: From the French *vert mont,* meaning "green mountain"

Entered union (rank): March 4, 1791 (14)

Motto: Vermont, freedom and unity

Tree: sugar maple

Flower: red clover

Bird: hermit thrush

Other: animal: Morgan horse; insect: honeybee

Song: "Hail, Vermont!"

Nickname: Green Mountain State

Residents: Vermonter

Land area: 9,249 square miles (23,956 sq km)

Population (2004): 621,394

Home of: The largest production of maple syrup in the U.S.

Did You Know? Montpelier, with just over 8,000 residents, is the smallest state capital in the United States.

VIRGINIA

Capital: Richmond
Largest City: Virginia Beach
Abbreviation: Va.
Postal Code: VA

Origin of name: In honor of Elizabeth I, "Virgin Queen" of England

Entered union (rank): June 25, 1788 (10)

Motto: *Sic semper tyrannis* (Thus always to tyrants)

Tree: dogwood

Flower: American dogwood

Bird: cardinal

Other: dog: American foxhound; shell: oyster shell

Song: "Carry Me Back to Old Virginia"

Nicknames: The Old Dominion and Mother of Presidents

Residents: Virginian

Land area: 39,598 square miles (102,558 sq km)

Population (2004): 7,459,827

Home of: The only full-length statue of George Washington

Richmond

Virginia Beach

Did You Know? Jamestown was the first permanent English settlement in North America.

WASHINGTON

Capital: Olympia
Largest City: Seattle
Abbreviation: Wash.
Postal Code: WA

Origin of name: In honor of George Washington

Entered union (rank): November 11, 1889 (42)

Motto: *Al-ki* (Indian word meaning "by and by")

Tree: western hemlock

Flower: coast rhododendron

Bird: willow goldfinch

Other: fossil: Columbian mammoth; fruit: apple

Song: "Washington, My Home"

Nickname: Evergreen State

Residents: Washingtonian

Land area: 66,582 square miles (17,447 sq km)

Population (2004): 6,203,788

Home of: The Lunar Rover, the vehicle used by astronauts on the Moon in 1971. Boeing, in Seattle, makes aircraft and spacecraft.

Seattle
Olympia

Did You Know? The Grand Coulee dam, on the Columbia River, is the largest concrete structure in the U.S.

WEST VIRGINIA

Capital: Charleston
Largest City: Charleston
Abbreviation: W.Va.
Postal Code: WV

Origin of name: In honor of Elizabeth I, "Virgin Queen" of England

Entered union (rank): June 20, 1863 (35)

Motto: *Montani semper liberi* (Mountaineers are always free)

Tree: sugar maple

Flower: rhododendron

Bird: cardinal

Other: animal: black bear; fruit: golden delicious apple

Songs: "West Virginia," "My Home Sweet Home," "The West Virginia Hills" and "This Is My West Virginia"

Nickname: Mountain State

Residents: West Virginian

Land area: 24,087 square miles (62,384 sq km)

Population (2004): 1,815,354

Home of: Marbles. Most of the country's glass marbles are made around Parkersburg.

Charleston

Did You Know? Mother's Day was first celebrated in Grafton in 1908.

WISCONSIN

Capital: Madison
Largest City: Milwaukee
Abbreviation: Wis.
Postal Code: WI

Origin of name: French corruption of an Indian word whose meaning is disputed

Entered union (rank): May 29, 1848 (30)

Motto: Forward

Tree: sugar maple

Flower: wood violet

Bird: robin

Other: dance: polka; symbol of peace: mourning dove

Song: "On, Wisconsin"

Nickname: Badger State

Residents: Wisconsinite

Land area: 54,314 square miles (140,673 sq km)

Population (2004): 5,509,026

Home of: The typewriter, invented in Milwaukee in 1867

Did You Know? Wisconsin produced a 17-ton cheddar cheese for the 1964 New York World's Fair.

WYOMING

Capital: Cheyenne
Largest City: Cheyenne
Abbreviation: Wyo.
Postal Code: WY

Origin of name: From a Delaware Indian word meaning "mountains and valleys alternating"

Entered union (rank): July 10, 1890 (44)

Motto: Equal rights

Tree: cottonwood

Flower: Indian paintbrush

Bird: meadowlark

Other: dinosaur: *Triceratops;* gemstone: jade

Song: "Wyoming"

Nickname: Equality State

Residents: Wyomingite

Land area: 97,105 square miles (251,501 sq km)

Population (2004): 506,529

Home of: Independence Rock, a huge granite boulder that covers 27 acres and has the names of 5,000 early pioneers carved on it

Did You Know? Wyoming, with just over 500,000 people, ranks 50th in state populations.

WASHINGTON, D.C.

The **District of Columbia**, which covers the same area as the city of Washington, is the capital of the United States. It is located between Virginia and Maryland on the Potomac River. The district is named after Columbus. The Federal Government and tourism are the mainstays of its economy. Many labor unions as well as business, professional and nonprofit organizations have headquarters there.

D.C. history began in 1790 when Congress took charge of organizing a new site for the capital. George Washington chose the spot, midway between the northern and southern states on the Potomac River. The seat of government was transferred from Philadelphia, Pennsylvania, to Washington, D.C., on December 1, 1800, and President John Adams became the first resident of the White House.

A petition asking for the district's admission to the Union as the 51st state was filed in Congress on September 9, 1983. The district is continuing this drive for statehood.

Motto: *Justitia omnibus* (Justice to all)

Flower: American Beauty rose

Tree: scarlet oak

Land area: 68.25 square miles (177 sq km)

Population (2004): 553,523

Smithsonian National Air and Space Museum

WASHINGTON, D.C., LANDMARKS

In addition to the White House, several architectural masterpieces and symbolic landmarks are found in our nation's capital. Here are some of them.

Capitol Building
This is where Congress meets and conducts business.

Jefferson Memorial
This memorial to Thomas Jefferson is modeled on the Roman Pantheon.

Jefferson Memorial

Lincoln Memorial
Lincoln's Gettysburg Address is carved into the walls of the south chamber, and his famous Second Inaugural Address is on the north-chamber wall.

National Archives
The records of the three branches of government, including the Declaration of Independence, are kept here.

Smithsonian Institution
The Smithsonian is a network of 14 museums, art galleries and research centers.

U.S. Holocaust Memorial Museum
This is America's national institution for the documentation, study and interpretation of Holocaust history.

Vietnam Veterans Memorial
This V-shaped monument lists the names of the 58,000 veterans who died during the Vietnam War.

Washington Monument
This monument to our first President stands just over 555 feet high. Stones from the 50 states and several foreign countries line the inside walls.

277

The U.S. Territories

Aterritory is a region that belongs to the U.S. but is not one of the 50 states. Although territories govern themselves to a limited extent, they are really governed by the U.S. Sometimes territories become states; Alaska and Hawaii were the last two territories admitted to the Union as states.

The Commonwealth of Puerto Rico

Puerto Rico is located in the Caribbean Sea, about 1,000 miles east-southeast of Miami, Florida. A U.S. possession since 1898, it consists of the island of Puerto Rico plus the adjacent islets of Vieques, Culebra and Mona.

Capital: San Juan
Land area: 3,459 square miles (8,959 sq km)
Population estimate (2004): 3,894,855
Languages: Spanish and English

Guam

Guam, the largest and southernmost island in the Mariana Island chain *(see "Commonwealth of the Northern Mariana Islands," below)*, became a U.S. territory in 1898.

Capital: Agana
Land area: 212 square miles (549 sq km)
Population estimate (2004): 166,090
Languages: English and Chamorro; Japanese is also widely spoken

The Commonwealth of the Northern Mariana Islands (CNMI)

The Northern Mariana Islands, east of the Philippines and south of Japan, have been part of the U.S. since 1986. They include the islands of Rota, Saipan, Tinian, Pagan, Guguan, Agrihan and Aguijan.

Capital: Chalan Kanoa (on Saipan)
Total area: 184.17 square miles (477 sq km)
Population estimate (2004): 78,252
Languages: English, Chamorro, Carolinian

The U.S. Virgin Islands

The Virgin Islands consist of nine main islands and some 75 islets. Since 1666, Britain has ruled six of the main islands; the remaining three (St. Croix, St. Thomas and St. John), as well as about 50 of the islets, were acquired by Denmark and then purchased by the U.S in 1917.

Capital: Charlotte Amalie (on St. Thomas)
Land area: 140 square miles (363 sq km):
St. Croix, 84 square miles (218 sq km);
St. Thomas, 32 square miles (83 sq km);
St. John, 20 square miles (52 sq km)
Population estimate (2004): 108,775
Languages: Mostly English, but Spanish and French are also spoken

American Samoa

American Samoa is a group of five volcanic islands and two coral atolls. It is located some 2,600 miles south of Hawaii in the South Pacific. It includes the eastern Samoan islands of Tutuila, Aunu'u and Rose; three islands (Ta'u, Olosega and Ofu) of the Manu'a group; and Swains Island. The territory became part of the U.S. in 1900, except for Swains Island, which was acquired in 1925.

Capital: Pago Pago
Land area: 77 square miles (199 sq km)
Population estimate (2004): 57,902
Languages: Samoan (closely related to Hawaiian) and English

The Midway Islands

The Midway Islands lie about 1,150 miles west-northwest of Hawaii. They became part of the U.S. in 1867.

Total area: 2 square miles (5.2 sq km)
Population estimate (2004): no indigenous inhabitants; about 40 people make up the staff of the U.S. Fish and Wildlife Service.

Wake Island

Wake Island, between Midway and Guam, is an atoll consisting of the three islets of Wilkes, Peale and Wake. It was annexed by Hawaii in 1899.

Total area: 2.5 square miles (6.5 sq km)
Population estimate (2004): no indigenous inhabitants; 200 U.S. military personnel and civilian contractors

Johnston Atoll

Johnston is a coral atoll about 700 miles southwest of Hawaii. It consists of four small islands—Johnston Island, Sand Island, Hikina Island and Akau Island—which lie on a 9-mile-long reef. It was claimed by Hawaii in 1858.

Land area: 1.08 square miles (2.8 sq km)
Population estimate (2004): No indigenous inhabitants; about 800 U.S. military and civilian contractors.

Baker, Howland and Jarvis Islands

These Pacific islands were claimed by the U.S. in 1936. **Baker Island** is an atoll of approximately 1 square mile (2.6 sq km) located about 1,650 miles from Hawaii. **Howland Island,** 36 miles to the northwest, is 1 mile long. Tiny **Jarvis Island** is several hundred miles to the east.

Kingman Reef

Kingman Reef, located about 1,000 miles south of Hawaii, has been a U.S. possession since 1922. Triangular in shape, it is about 9.5 miles long.

Navassa Island

Navassa Island is located in the Caribbean Sea, between Cuba, Haiti and Jamaica. It has an area of 2 square miles (5.2 sq km) and was claimed for the U.S. in 1857.

Palmyra Atoll

Palmyra Atoll has a total area of 4.6 square miles (11.9 sq km) and is located 994 miles (1,600 km) southwest of Honolulu.

Did You Know?

An atoll is a coral island made up of a reef surrounding a lagoon (shallow pool).

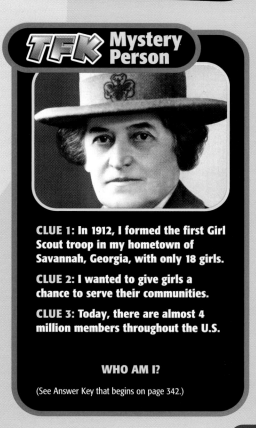

TFK Mystery Person

CLUE 1: In 1912, I formed the first Girl Scout troop in my hometown of Savannah, Georgia, with only 18 girls.

CLUE 2: I wanted to give girls a chance to serve their communities.

CLUE 3: Today, there are almost 4 million members throughout the U.S.

WHO AM I?

(See Answer Key that begins on page 342.)

Kids Lend a Hand

Young fund-raisers help those hurt by the tsunami

Fourth-graders from Johnson City, Tennessee, display some of the thousands of coins they have collected to benefit survivors of the 2004 tragedy.

Can you imagine collecting 75,000 coins in just five days? That is what a class of fourth-graders did at Woodland Elementary School in Johnson City, Tennessee. They are just a few of the many kids around the country who are finding ways to help the victims of the tsunami that hit South Asia on December 26, 2004.

Woodland's Give Change, Change Lives project started on the first day the students returned from their winter vacation. Chris Miller, 10, wanted his class to help. "I had never seen a tsunami," Chris told TFK. "The amount of damage surprised me."

With guidance from their teacher, Mary Nell McIntyre, Chris and his classmates decided to gather a coin to honor each person who had died in the disaster. (More than 280,000 people lost their lives.) Parents, kids and neighbors chipped in coins. Within a week, the class had collected $1,695.68! The students planned to send the money to UNICEF and Interchurch Medical Assistance.

Some other aid projects were huge, others were smaller. Eighth-graders in Wenatchee, Washington, had been raising money for a class trip for more than a year. They voted to give it to the Red Cross. In Lincoln, Nebraska, Kyle Sinagra, 8, sold cupcakes and donated $62.12 in earnings to relief funds. In Sammamish, Washington, Stephen McClure, 12, raised money by selling hot chocolate.

Roshan Baddeliyanage, who was born in Sri Lanka and now lives in Silver Spring, Maryland, built a website to encourage contributions. "Our basement is so full of clothes, you can barely walk," Roshan told TFK. "I'd like to go to Sri Lanka so I can hand out the clothes myself." —By Jeremy Caplan

go Read about kids' tsunami relief efforts at timeforkids.com/kidshelp

Volunteering

Calling All Volunteers

Robbie and Brittany Bergquist want your cell phones! Don't worry, they won't be using up your minutes. The brother and sister from Norwell, Massachusetts, are on a mission to help men and women serving overseas in the armed forces stay connected with their families.

Brittany, 13, and Robbie, 12, decided to take action after learning about the plight of U.S. Army Reserve Sergeant Bryan Fletcher. While serving in Iraq, Fletcher had rung up a $7,600 cell-phone bill.

Brittany and Robbie started a group called Cell Phones for Soldiers. Their group has raised more than $150,000, purchased 6,500 calling cards and sent thousands of phones to troops in Afghanistan, Iraq and Kuwait. Brittany and Robbie's goal is to raise $9 million and give 150,000 soldiers access to prepaid phones. "We hope to help soldiers by making their lives easier," Robbie said.

Find out how you can help Brittany and Robbie at *cellphonesforsoldiers.com*.
—By Claudia Atticot

A LITTLE BIT Goes a LONG WAY

Your service project can be as complex as helping to build a home or as simple as collecting coins for charity. Here are some ways kids can make a difference.

- Visit a local retirement or nursing home. Sing songs, recite poems or read for the elderly people.

- Donate toys, clothing and toiletries to families in need.

- Have a bake sale. Choose an organization or a cause to support.

- Pick up papers, cans and litter.

- Help the hungry and homeless. Cook or serve a meal at a shelter.

- Help people with special needs. Volunteer to help at a Special Olympics event. Bring books and toys to kids at local hospitals.

Former Secretary of State Colin Powell helps a clean-up drive in Philadelphia.

- Get involved in government. Find out what you can do to encourage people to register to vote. Identify a local problem and write to officials with your ideas for how to solve it.

TRICK-OR-TREAT FOR UNICEF

Kids in the United States have been taking part in "Trick-or-Treat for UNICEF" since the program began in 1950. They have raised $115 million! The chart below shows how UNICEF helps the world's children with the money you raise. If you want to get involved, go to *www.unicef.org/young*.

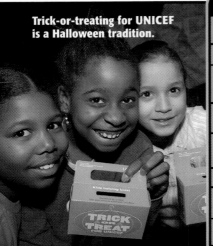

Trick-or-treating for UNICEF is a Halloween tradition.

AMOUNT	WHAT IT BUYS
4¢	**Two vitamin A capsules to protect a child against blindness**
36¢	**Penicillin to treat a child's infection**
$1	**Polio vaccine for one child (lifetime protection) or 120 water-purification tablets, each making one gallon of water drinkable**
$2	**40 packets of rehydration salts, used to treat dehydration**
$7	**School supplies for three children, including chalk, a slate, colored pencils and a plastic schoolbag**
$20	**A first-aid kit**
$150	**A hand pump and pipes for a well that will serve 250 people**
$220	**One large cold-storage box to maintain vaccines**

TFK Spotlight

Helping Our Land

SPHS 2003

Lily Dong, 16, is on a mission to save the planet, one tree at a time. In 2004, Lily's efforts took root in South Pasadena, California. The Arroyo Seco Woodland and Wildlife Park was opened. The area holds some of the last remaining undeveloped land in South Pasadena. Lily's hard work and determination helped city officials set it aside as parkland.

Lily fell in love with the tree-filled canyon in 2000, a year after her family moved to the U.S. from China. She visited Arroyo Seco with her school's science club and decided that the area needed protection. Lily started a campaign to save the four-acre site, writing letters to local leaders. Her message? "This land represents a certain kind of beauty and magnificence that the buildings and the streets in the city lack." —*By Claudia*

go Learn about volunteering and how you can help others at timeforkids.com/fixtheworld

Help Wanted

These organizations give kids opportunities to make a difference.

- **American Society for the Prevention of Cruelty to Animals (ASPCA)**
  424 E. 92nd St.
  New York, NY 10128
  212-876-7700 *www.aspca.org*
  Kids can hold fund-raisers, and collect blankets, towels and toys for animals in shelters.

- **Do Something**
  423 W. 55th St., 8th Floor
  New York, NY 10019
  212-523-1175 *www.dosomething.org*
  Works with kids to identify important issues and create community projects

- **Family Cares**
  1400 I St., NW, Suite 800
  Washington, D.C. 20005
  800-865-8683 *www.familycares.org*
  Encourages families to work together to help those in their community

- **Habitat for Humanity**
  121 Habitat St.
  Americus, GA 31709-3498
  229-924-6935 *www.habitat.org*
  Kids help build homes for people in need around the world.

- **Make-A-Wish Foundation of America**
  3550 N. Central Ave.
  Suite 300
  Phoenix, AZ 85012-2127
  800-722-WISH (9474) *www.wish.org*
  Kids help raise money to grant the wishes of children with life-threatening illnesses.

- **National Park Service Jr. Ranger Programs**
  1849 C St., NW
  Washington, D.C. 20240
  202-208-6843
  www.nps.gov/learn/juniorranger.htm
  Kids can participate in Jr. Ranger programs to help protect our national parks.

- **Youth Volunteer Network**
  2000 M St., NW, Suite 500
  Washington, D.C. 20036
  415-346-4433
  www.networkforgood.youthnoise.com
  Voice an opinion on how to fight poverty in the U.S. or learn how to make a difference.

- **Special Olympics**
  1325 G St., NW, Suite 500
  Washington, D.C. 20005
  800-700-8585 *www.specialolympics.org*
  Kids can volunteer to help raise money and run the events.

- **Toys For Tots**
  Marine Toys For Tots Foundation
  P.O. Box 1947
  Quantico, VA 22134
  703-640-9433 *www.toysfortots.org*
  Kids can donate holiday presents to other children.

TIPS FOR PLANNING a SERVICE PROJECT

Organizing a service project takes thought and planning. Here are some tips to help you get started.

- **Identify a problem that exists in your community.**
- **Learn more about the problem and think about ways to solve it.**
- **Set a goal for the project.**
- **Decide what supplies and help you'll need.**
- **Get the whole school involved! Encourage other classes to help you with your project. Parents can also lend a helping hand.**
- **Have fun! Knowing that you are helping to make a difference in your community should bring you enjoyment.**

TFK Mystery Person

CLUE 1: Although born to rich English parents in 1820, I spent my life helping the sick, especially the poor.

CLUE 2: I became a nurse and earned renown for treating wounded soldiers in the Crimean War. I helped create the modern nursing profession.

CLUE 3: My work to improve the sanitary conditions in hospitals saved many lives.

WHO AM I?

(See Answer Key that begins on page 342.)

FROM
TFK MAGAZINE

IVAN THE TERRIBLE!

As many storms hit Florida, experts predict that more will come

In 2004, hurricanes Ivan, Charley and Frances slammed into the U.S.

Hurricane Ivan stormed ashore in September 2004, toppling trees, ripping off roofs and flooding neighborhoods. Ivan hit land along the Gulf of Mexico. Winds of up to 130 miles per hour lashed the Gulf Coast. Communities in southeast Louisiana, southern Mississippi and Alabama and northwest Florida felt the storm's fury. "We have never seen a hurricane of this size come into Alabama," said Governor Bob Riley.

Tornadoes spun off from the storm, causing even more damage. More than 1.5 million homes and businesses in the Gulf states lost power. As many as 33 people in the United States died as a result of Ivan.

In Hartford, Alabama, a man lends a hand to a hound.

A FLURRY OF HURRICANES

When Ivan hit, Florida was still struggling to recover from Hurricanes Charley and Frances. Ivan had been the third hurricane to pound the area in five weeks.

Residents reeled from the back-to-back blows. But scientists had been expecting an especially stormy season, says Stanley Goldenberg, a research meteorologist in Miami, Florida. "I'm in shock over the damage and the deaths, but I am not surprised," he told TIME.

Ten years ago, scientists began warning residents in coastal areas that big hurricanes were headed their way. Why? One factor is higher ocean-surface temperatures. In the 1990s, Atlantic surface temperatures increased by 1°F to 1.5°F. Scientists say that naturally shifting ocean currents and patterns caused the increase.

Such a change may seem slight, but it is significant. The last time the Atlantic Ocean warmed, between 1926 and 1970, a slew of severe storms hit the coastal U.S. We may be in for another stretch of deadly tropical weather. The risk to Americans is greater now, because the coastlines are much more heavily populated. More than 50% of the U.S. population lives along the coast. And they may be battered by many more Ivans.

—By Kathyrn R. Satterfield

WEATHER WORDS

BLIZZARD A major snowstorm with strong winds of 35 m.p.h. or more.

CLOUDS Little drops of water hanging in the atmosphere. The major types of clouds are cirrus (thin, feathery), cirrocumulus (small patches of white), cirrostratus (thin, white sheets), stratus (a low, gray blanket), cumulus (flat-bottomed, white, puffy) and cumulonimbus (mountains of dark, heavy clouds).

DROUGHT A long period of no rainfall in a region. Droughts can destroy crops, dry up water supplies and sometimes lead to widespread hunger or famine.

HAIL Pellets of ice and snow created within clouds that then fall to Earth. Hailstones can sometimes be quite large and can cause major damage.

HURRICANE Violent storms in the Atlantic with strong winds from 40 to 150 m.p.h. They are called typhoons in the Pacific.

LIGHTNING Flashes of electrical discharges moving through the atmosphere during thunderstorms.

SNOW When clouds become too heavy with humidity, water falls from them. In colder clouds, this water forms ice crystals that fall as snow.

SLEET A mixture of falling rain and snow, or rain and ice pellets.

THUNDER The loud noise that follows lightning. Lightning is seen before thunder is heard because light travels faster than sound.

TORNADO *See page 289.*

WIND CHILL The wind-chill temperature indicates how cold people feel when the wind blows during cold weather. Wind draws heat from the body, and makes the temperature feel much colder than the thermometer reading.

TFK Puzzles & Games — Winter Wonderland

Maybe you've seen winter cover the ground with snow. But never like this! Artist Joan Steiner built this snowy scene with at least 45 objects. Can you find a dog bone, a notebook, a paper clip, a pencil, a crayon, a marshmallow and a comb? Bonus: Find 10 other tiny objects used to create the scene.

(See Answer Key that begins on page 342.)

LOWEST Recorded Temperatures

	PLACE	DATE	°F*	°C**
Antarctica	Vostok	July 21, 1983	-129°	-89°
Asia	Oimekon, Russia	February 6, 1933	-90°	-68°
	Verkhoyansk, Russia	February 7, 1892	-90°	-68°
Greenland	Northice	January 9, 1954	-87°	-66°
North America (excluding Greenland)	Snag, Yukon, Canada	February 3 1947	-81°	-63°
United States	Prospect Creek, Alaska	January 23, 1971	-80°	-62°
U.S. (excluding Alaska)	Rogers Pass, Montana	January 20, 1954	-70°	-56.5°
Europe	Ust'Shchugor, Russia	Exact date unknown[1]	-67°	-55°
South America	Sarmiento, Argentina	June 1, 1907	-27°	-33°
Africa	Ifrane, Morocco	February 11, 1935	-11°	-24°
Australia	Charlotte Pass, N.S.W.	June 29, 1994	-9°	-22°
Oceania	Mauna Kea, Hawaii	May 17, 1979	12°	-11°

[1] Lowest in 15-year period. *degrees Fahrenheit **degrees Celsius   Source: U.S. Army Corps of Engineers

Did You Know?

The longest hot spell ever recorded was in Marble Bar, West Australia. The temperature was 100°F (37.8°C) or above for 162 consecutive days (October 30, 1923 to April 7, 1924).

HIGHEST Recorded Temperatures

	PLACE	DATE	°F*	°C**
Africa	El Azizia, Libya	September 13, 1922	136°	58°
North America	Death Valley, California	July 10, 1913	134°	57°
Asia	Tirat Tsvi, Israel	June 21, 1942	129°	54°
Australia	Cloncurry, Queensland	January 16, 1889	128°	53°
Europe	Seville, Spain	August 4, 1881	122°	50°
South America	Rivadavia, Argentina	December 11, 1905	120°	49°
Canada	Midale and Yellow Grass, Saskatchewan	July 5, 1937	113°	45°
Oceania	Tuguegarao, Philippines	April 29, 1912	108°	42°
Persian Gulf (sea-surface)		August 5, 1924	96°	36°
Antarctica	Vanda Station, Scott Coast	January 5, 1974	59°	15°
South Pole		December 27, 1978	7.5°	-14°

*degrees Fahrenheit **degrees Celsius   Source: U.S. Army Corps of Engineers

go **Track weather changes in your area at timeforkids.com/weathertracker**

GREATEST Snowfalls in North America

Duration	Place	Date	Inches
24 hours	Silver Lake, Colorado	April 14–15, 1921	76
1 month	Tamarack, California	January 1911	390
1 storm	Mt. Shasta Ski Bowl, California	February 13–19, 1959	189
1 season	Mt. Baker, Washington	1998–1999	1,140

GREATEST Rainfalls in the World

Duration	Place	Date	Inches
1 minute	Unionville, Maryland	July 4, 1956	1.23
20 minutes	Curtea-de-Arges, Romania	July 7, 1889	8.1
12 hours	Grand Ilet, La Réunion	January 26, 1980	46
24 hours	Foc-Foc, La Réunion	January 7–8, 1966	72
12 months	Cherrapunji, India	August 1860–August 1861	1,042

How's the WEATHER?

Temperature

Did You Know?
The world's driest place is the Atacama Desert in Chile, South America. During a 59-year period, its annual rainfall was only 3/100 of an inch of rain!

AIR TEMPERATURE is measured by a mercury thermometer. When the temperature rises, the mercury expands and rises in the thermometer tube. When the temperature falls, the mercury contracts and falls.

In the U.S., the **FAHRENHEIT** scale is used most often. On this scale, 32° is the freezing point of water, and 212° is the boiling point.

The **CELSIUS,** or centigrade, scale is used by the World Meteorological Organization and most countries in the world. On this scale, 0° is freezing, and 100° is boiling.

To convert Fahrenheit to Celsius, subtract 32, multiply by 5, and divide the result by 9.

EXAMPLE: To convert 50°F to °C:
50 – 32 = 18;
18 x 5 = 90; 90 ÷ 9 = 10°C

To convert Celsius to Fahrenheit, multiply by 9, divide by 5, and add 32.

EXAMPLE: To convert 10°C to °F:
10 x 9 = 90; 90 ÷ 5 = 18; 18 + 32 = 50°F

CELSIUS	FAHRENHEIT
−50	−58
−40	−40
−30	−22
−20	−4
−10	14
0	32
5	41
10	50
15	59
20	68
25	77
30	86
35	95
40	104
45	113
50	122

A LIGHTNING-FAST History of Lightning

Zeus, the Greek king of the gods, was said to have punished mortals and gods he was angry with by hurling thunderbolts at them. Sky deities from many world cultures, including Zeus's Roman counterpart Jupiter, Germany's Thor and the Mayans' Chac, used the thunderbolt as a sign of their power.

Dead Ringers

During the Middle Ages, people believed that ringing church bells would get rid of lightning. Many church bells were engraved with the Latin words, *Fulgura frango* ("I break up the lightning"). One medieval scholar decided to put this theory to a test. He found that being anywhere near church bells during a thunderstorm was extremely dangerous. Over a 33-year period, there were 386 lightning strikes on church towers and 103 deaths among bell ringers.

Lightning Strikes Seven Times!

The person who is believed to have been struck by lightning the most times is Roy C. Sullivan. This former park ranger survived seven different lightning strikes! According to *Guinness World Records*, Sullivan was first hit by lightning in 1942, which caused him to lose his big toenail. Over the next 35 years, lightning burned off Sullivan's eyebrows, seared his left shoulder, set his hair on fire, struck his legs, injured his ankle and burned his stomach and chest.

Homework Tip!

Make homework part of your daily schedule. If you don't get any homework one night, take that extra time to read books, newspapers, magazines or write for pleasure.

288

IT'S A TWISTER!

A **TORNADO** is a dark, funnel-shaped cloud made up of violently churning winds that can reach speeds of up to 300 m.p.h. A tornado can measure from a few feet to a mile wide, and its track can extend from less than a mile to several hundred miles. Tornadoes generally travel in a northeast direction at speeds ranging from 20 to 60 m.p.h.

Tornadoes are most often caused by giant thunderstorms that are called "supercells." These highly powerful storms form when warm, moist air along the ground rushes upward, meeting cooler, drier air. As the rising warm air cools, the moisture it carries condenses, forming a massive thundercloud, sometimes growing to as much as 50,000 feet in height. Winds at different levels of the atmosphere feed the updraft and cause the formation of the tornado's characteristic funnel shape.

The Fujita scale classifies tornadoes according to the damage they cause. Almost half of all tornadoes fall into the F1, or "moderate damage" category. These tornadoes reach speeds of 73 to 112 m.p.h. and can overturn automobiles and uproot trees.

Only about 1% of tornadoes are classified as F5, causing "incredible damage." With wind speeds in excess of 261 m.p.h., these storms can hurl houses and cars far and wide.

DEADLIEST Tornadoes in the United States

Date	Location	Deaths
1. March 18, 1925	Tri-State (Missouri, Illinois and Indiana)	689
2. May 6, 1840	Natchez, Mississippi	317
3. May 27, 1896	St. Louis, Missouri	255
4. April 5, 1936	Tupelo, Mississippi	216
5. April 6, 1936	Gainesville, Georgia	203

Did You Know?

More tornadoes occur in the lowland areas between the Rocky and Appalachian Mountains (especially from Central Texas to Nebraska) than anywhere else in the world, earning the region the nickname "tornado alley."

TFK Mystery Person

CLUE 1: I was born in Ireland in 1774. Today, my name is well known to meterologists.

CLUE 2: As an Admiral in the British Navy, I devised a scale to describe the force of the wind. The scale was based on the visible effects of wind on water and ships' sails.

CLUE 3: Used internationally, a slightly different version of this wind scale bears my name.

WHO AM I?

(See Answer Key that begins on page 342.)

CAN SUDAN BE

Violence, starvation and disease are killing thousands of people

Halima was working in her family's field in Darfur, a region of Sudan, in Africa, when she heard "the voice of guns." "The attackers wanted to kill us," she told TIME for Kids. "We had to hide and walk at night. We had nothing to eat." It took Halima, 30, and her young daughter three weeks to reach the Abu Shouk refugee camp.

Darfur is full of stories like Halima's. Aid workers say the violence that began in February 2003 has killed tens of thousands and forced some 1.5 million people from their homes. Many people have sought shelter in crowded refugee camps. At least half of the refugees cannot get enough food and clean water.

The United Nations World Health Organization (WHO) reported that within six months, at least 70,000 refugees died because of poor conditions in the camps. United Nations (U.N.) officials called Darfur's situation the world's worst

Refugees line up outside an aid center in western Darfur.

\$AVED?

humanitarian crisis.

The recent fighting began with an uprising of black Africans against what they viewed as discrimination by the predominately Arab government. In response, Sudanese President Omar al-Bashir called on local tribes to crush the rebellion. Some Arab nomads saw the President's call as a chance to grab land and livestock from the farmers. Armed Arab bandits began attacking African farmers.

WHAT CAN BE DONE?
Human-rights groups say the world needs to impose economic and military punishments against Sudan. If nothing is done, many more people will die, either at the hands of bandits or from starvation and disease.

At a meeting, the Presidents of Sudan, Chad, Egypt, Libya and Nigeria stressed that they would reject any foreign intervention in Sudan. They called the crisis in Sudan a "purely African" issue. It seems that much of the world agrees.
—By Nelida Gonzalez Cutler

Most Livable & Least Livable Countries

The U.N.'s Human Development Index ranks nations according to their citizens' quality of life. The rankings are based on life expectancy, amount of education received and income.

MOST LIVABLE	LEAST LIVABLE
1. NORWAY	1. SIERRA LEONE
2. SWEDEN	2. NIGER
3. AUSTRALIA	3. BURKINA FASO
4. CANADA	4. MALI
5. THE NETHERLANDS	5. BURUNDI
6. BELGIUM	6. GUINEA-BISSAU
7. ICELAND	7. MOZAMBIQUE
8. UNITED STATES	8. ETHIOPIA
9. JAPAN	9. CENTRAL AFRICAN REPUBLIC
10. IRELAND	10. DEMOCRATIC REPUBLIC OF THE CONGO

Source: Human Development Report, 2004, United Nations

Travel Papers

Your bags are packed and you're ready for a cool vacation abroad (to a foreign country). Do you have all the documents you need?

PASSPORT
A passport is an official document that proves a person's identity and citizenship. U.S. citizens need a passport to leave the country and to enter the U.S. from a foreign country. You also need one to enter most foreign countries.

You can apply for a passport at a passport agency, many federal and state courts, some county and city offices and some post offices. Kids ages 14 and up must apply for a passport in person. For children ages 13 and under, a parent or legal guardian should apply for them.

For more information on what you need to apply for a passport, go to the State Department's website: http://travel.state.gov.

VISA
In addition to a passport, some countries require travelers to present a visa before they can enter the country. You must apply for this additional document of identification through the foreign consulate of the country you plan to visit. Most foreign consular representatives have offices in major cities. In most cases, however, you can apply for a visa by mail.

Learn how you can help refugees in Sudan at timeforkids.com/sudan

First Nations to Allow Women to Vote

Women in the U.S. won the right to vote in 1920. But in South Africa, some women were not allowed to vote until 1994. And in some countries, women still can't vote. Here are the first countries where women gained voting rights.

COUNTRY	YEAR VOTING RIGHTS WERE WON
1. New Zealand	1893
2. Australia	1902
3. Finland	1906
4. Norway	1907
5. Denmark and Iceland (tie)	1915

Source: *Top 10 of Everything*, DK

TFK Puzzles & Games

Going in Circles

This dartboard was made by a mapmaker. Here's how her dart game works: For every country you identify, you earn the points listed on it. Score a perfect 15 and you're King Cartographer. Score 8 to 14 and you're a Map Expert. Score below 8 and you're a Geography Goof-Off.

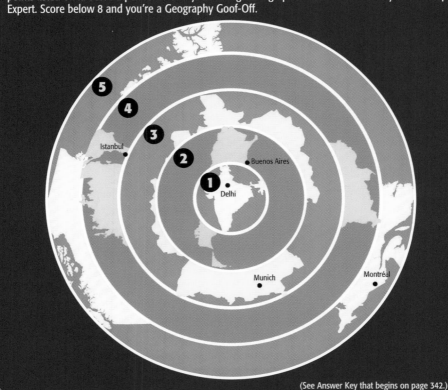

Istanbul

Buenos Aires

Delhi

Munich

Montréal

(See Answer Key that begins on page 342.)

The World's Nations from A to Z

On the following pages you will find information about the world's nations. Here's an example.

If you divide the population by the area, you can find out the population density—how many people there are per square mile.

This tells the main languages and the official languages (if any) spoken in a nation. In this case, most people in the nation speak Icelandic.

This is the type of money used in the nation.

This tells an interesting fact about the country.

Iceland

Where? Europe
Capital: Reykjavik
Area: 39,768 sq mi (103,000 sq km)
Population estimate (2005): 296,737
Government: Constitutional republic
Language: Icelandic
Monetary unit: Icelandic króna
Life expectancy: 80.2
Literacy rate: 100%
Did You Know? Iceland boasts the world's oldest constitution, drafted around 930.

Life expectancy is the number of years a person can expect to live. It's affected by heredity, a person's health and nutrition, the health care and wealth of a nation, and a person's occupation.

This tells the percentage of people who can read and write.

Afghanistan

Where? Asia
Capital: Kabul
Area: 251,737 sq mi (647,500 sq km)
Population estimate (2005): 29,928,987
Government: Transitional
Languages: Pushtu, Dari Persian, other Turkic and minor languages
Monetary unit: Afghani
Life expectancy: 42.5
Literacy rate: 36%
Did You Know? Islam is Afghanistan's official religion.

Albania

Where? Europe
Capital: Tirana
Area: 11,100 sq mi (28,750 sq km)
Population estimate (2005): 3,563,112
Government: Emerging democracy
Languages: Albanian (Tosk is the official dialect), Greek
Monetary unit: Lek
Life expectancy: 77.1
Literacy rate: 87%
Did You Know? This former communist country is now a struggling democracy.

Algeria

Where? Africa
Capital: Algiers
Area: 919,590 sq mi (2,381,740 sq km)
Population estimate (2005): 32,531,853
Government: Republic
Languages: Arabic (official), French, Berber dialects
Monetary unit: Dinar
Life expectancy: 72.7
Literacy rate: 70%
Did You Know? The Sahara Desert covers about 85% of Algeria.

Andorra

Where? Europe
Capital: Andorra la Vella
Area: 181 sq mi (468 sq km)
Population estimate (2005): 70,549
Government: Parliamentary democracy
Languages: Catalán (official), French, Spanish
Monetary units: French franc and Spanish peseta
Life expectancy: 83.5
Literacy rate: 100%
Did You Know? This country has the world's highest life expectancy.

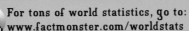

Angola

Where? Africa
Capital: Luanda
Area: 481,350 sq mi
(1,246,700 sq km)
Population estimate (2005):
11,190,786
Government: Republic
Languages: Bantu, Portuguese (official)
Monetary unit: Kwanza
Life expectancy: 36.8
Literacy rate: 42%
Did You Know? In 2002, Angola ended a decades-long civil war.

Antigua and Barbuda

Where? North America
Capital: St. John's
Area: 171 sq mi
(443 sq km)
Population estimate (2005): 68,722
Government: Constitutional monarchy
Language: English
Monetary unit: East Caribbean dollar
Life expectancy: 71.6
Literacy rate: 89%
Did You Know? The Bird family has controlled the islands since the 1940s.

Argentina

Where? South America
Capital: Buenos Aires
Area: 1,068,296 sq mi
(2,766,890 sq km)
Population estimate (2005): 39,537,943
Government: Republic
Languages: Spanish (official), English, Italian, German, French
Monetary unit: Peso
Life expectancy: 75.7
Literacy rate: 96%
Did You Know? Most Argentineans are of Spanish or Italian descent.

Armenia

Where? Asia
Capital: Yerevan
Area: 11,500 sq mi
(29,800 sq km)
Population estimate (2005): 2,982,904
Government: Republic
Language: Armenian
Monetary unit: Dram
Life expectancy: 71.2
Literacy rate: 99%
Did You Know? About 60% of the world's 8 million Armenians live outside Armenia.

Australia

Where? Pacific Islands
Capital: Canberra
Area: 2,967,893 sq mi
(7,686,850 sq km)
Population estimate (2005): 20,090,437
Government: Democracy
Language: English
Monetary unit: Australian dollar
Life expectancy: 80.3
Literacy rate: 100%
Did You Know? Australia's Great Barrier Reef is the largest coral reef in the world.

Austria

Where? Europe
Capital: Vienna
Area: 32,375 sq mi
(83,850 sq km)
Population estimate (2005): 8,184,691
Government: Federal Republic
Language: German
Monetary unit: Euro (formerly schilling)
Life expectancy: 78.9
Literacy rate: 98%
Did You Know? Three-quarters of Austria is covered by the Alps.

Azerbaijan

Where? Asia
Capital: Baku
Area: 33,400 sq mi
(86,600 sq km)
Population estimate (2005): 7,911,974
Government: Republic
Languages: Azerbaijani Turkic, Russian, Armenian
Monetary unit: Manat
Life expectancy: 63.2
Literacy rate: 97%
Did You Know? Oil recently discovered in Azerbaijan may improve its economy.

Bahamas

Where? North America
Capital: Nassau
Area: 5,380 sq mi
(13,940 sq km)
Population estimate (2005): 301,790
Government: Parliamentary democracy
Language: English
Monetary unit: Bahamian dollar
Life expectancy: 65.6
Literacy rate: 96%
Did You Know? The Bahamas is made up of more than 700 islands.

Bahrain

Where? Asia
Capital: Manamah
Area: 257 sq mi
(665 sq km)
Population estimate (2005): 688,345
Government: Constitutional monarchy
Languages: Arabic (official), English, Farsi, Urdu
Monetary unit: Bahrain dinar
Life expectancy: 74
Literacy rate: 89%
Did You Know? Bahrain is an archipelago in the Persian Gulf.

Bangladesh

Where? Asia
Capital: Dhaka
Area: 55,598 sq mi
(144,000 sq km)
Population estimate (2005): 144,319,628
Government: Parliamentary democracy
Languages: Bangla (official), English
Monetary unit: Taka
Life expectancy: 61.7
Literacy rate: 43%
Did You Know? Until 1971, Bangladesh was part of Pakistan.

Barbados

Where? North America
Capital: Bridgetown
Area: 166 sq mi
(431 sq km)
Population estimate (2005): 279,254
Government: Parliamentary democracy
Language: English
Monetary unit: Barbados dollar
Life expectancy: 71.6
Literacy rate: 97%
Did You Know? Barbados was a British colony before its independence in 1966.

Belarus

Where? Europe
Capital: Minsk
Area: 80,154 sq mi
(207,600 sq km)
Population estimate (2005): 10,300,483
Government: Republic
Language: Belarussian
Monetary unit: Belarussian ruble
Life expectancy: 68.6
Literacy rate: 100%
Did You Know? Belarus was part of the Soviet Union until it became independent in 1991.

Belgium

Where? Europe
Capital: Brussels
Area: 11,781 sq mi
(30,510 sq km)
Population estimate (2005): 10,364,388
Government: Constitutional monarchy
Languages: Dutch (Flemish), French,
German (all official)
Monetary unit: Euro (formerly Belgian franc)
Life expectancy: 78.4
Literacy rate: 98%
Did You Know? Nuclear power generates
more than 75% of Belgium's electricity.

Belize

Where? Central America
Capital: Belmopan
Area: 8,865 sq mi
(22,960 sq km)
Population estimate (2005): 279,457
Government: Parliamentary democracy
Languages: English (official), Creole,
Spanish, Garifuna, Mayan
Monetary unit: Belize dollar
Life expectancy: 67.4
Literacy rate: 94%
Did You Know? Belize is the only English-
speaking country in Central America.

Benin

Where? Africa
Capital: Porto-Novo
Area: 43,483 sq mi
(112,620 sq km)
Population estimate (2005): 7,460,025
Government: Multiparty democracy
Languages: French (official), African
languages
Monetary unit: CFA franc
Life expectancy: 50.8
Literacy rate: 41%
Did You Know? Benin's pottery, masks
and bronze statues are world renowned.

Bhutan

Where? Asia
Capital: Thimphu
Area: 18,147 sq mi
(47,000 sq km)
Population estimate (2005): 2,232,291
Government: Monarchy
Language: Dzongkha
Monetary unit: Ngultrum
Life expectancy: 54
Literacy rate: 42%
Did You Know? About 75% of
Bhutanese are Buddhists.

Bolivia

Where? South America
Capital: La Paz (seat of
government), Sucre
(legal capital)
Area: 424,162 sq mi (1,098,580 sq km)
Population estimate (2005): 8,857,870
Government: Republic
Languages: Spanish (official), Quechua,
Aymara, Guarani
Monetary unit: Boliviano
Life expectancy: 65.1
Literacy rate: 87%
Did You Know? Bolivia has had more than
190 revolutions and coups since 1825.

Bosnia and Herzegovina

Where? Europe
Capital: Sarajevo
Area: 19,741 sq mi
(51,129 sq km)
Population estimate (2005): 4,025,476
Government: Emerging democracy
Languages: The language is called
Serbian, Croatian or Bosnian depending
on the speaker.
Monetary unit: Dinar
Life expectancy: 72.6
Literacy rate: Not available
Did You Know? This country was a part
of Yugoslavia until 1992.

Botswana

Where? Africa
Capital: Gaborone
Area: 231,800 sq mi
(600,370 sq km)
Population estimate (2005): 1,640,115
Government: Parliamentary republic
Languages: English (official), Setswana
Monetary unit: Pula
Life expectancy: 34.2
Literacy rate: 80%
Did You Know? The Kalahari desert
is located in this southern African country.

Brazil

Where? South America
Capital: Brasília
Area: 3,286,470 sq mi
(8,511,965 sq km)
Population estimate (2005): 186,112,794
Government: Federative republic
Language: Portuguese
Monetary unit: Real
Life expectancy: 71.4
Literacy rate: 86%
Did You Know? Brazil is the largest
country in South America.

Brunei

Where? Asia
Capital: Bandar
Seri Begawan
Area: 2,228 sq mi (5,770 sq km)
Population estimate (2005): 372,361
Government: Constitutional sultanate
Languages: Malay (official), Chinese, English
Monetary unit: Brunei dollar
Life expectancy: 74.5
Literacy rate: 92%
Did You Know? This tiny country is ruled
by a sultan who is one of the richest men
in the world.

Bulgaria

Where? Europe
Capital: Sofia
Area: 48,822 sq mi
(110,910 sq km)
Population estimate (2005): 7,450,349
Government: Parliamentary democracy
Language: Bulgarian
Monetary unit: Lev
Life expectancy: 71.8
Literacy rate: 99%
Did You Know? Bulgaria was a
communist country until 1991.

Burkina Faso

Where? Africa
Capital: Ouagadougou
Area: 105,870 sq mi
(274,200 sq km)
Population estimate (2005): 13,925,313
Government: Parliamentary republic
Languages: French (official), tribal languages
Monetary unit: CFA franc
Life expectancy: 44.2
Literacy rate: 27%
Did You Know? This country was
formerly named Upper Volta.

Burundi

Where? Africa
Capital: Bujumbura
Area: 10,745 sq mi
(27,830 sq km)
Population estimate (2005): 6,370,609
Government: Republic
Languages: Kirundi and French
(both official), Swahili
Monetary unit: Burundi franc
Life expectancy: 43.4
Literacy rate: 52%
Did You Know? Burundi was once a
German colony.

Cambodia

Where? Asia
Capital: Phnom Penh
Area: 69,900 sq mi
(181,040 sq km)
Population estimate (2005): 13,607,069
Government: Democracy under a constitutional monarchy
Languages: Khmer (official), French, English
Monetary unit: Riel
Life expectancy: 58.4
Literacy rate: 70%
Did You Know? Cambodia's Angkor Wat temple is one of the world's wonders.

Cameroon

Where? Africa
Capital: Yaoundé
Area: 183,567 sq mi
(475,440 sq km)
Population estimate (2005): 16,380,005
Government: Unitary republic
Languages: French and English (both official), African languages
Monetary unit: CFA franc
Life expectancy: 48
Literacy rate: 79%
Did You Know? Germany, France and Britain once controlled Cameroon.

Canada

Where? North America
Capital: Ottawa, Ontario
Area: 3,851,788 sq mi
(9,976,140 sq km)
Population estimate (2005): 32,805,041
Government: Parliamentary democracy
Languages: English and French (both official)
Monetary unit: Canadian dollar
Life expectancy: 80
Literacy rate: 97%
Did You Know? Canada is the world's second largest country.

Cape Verde

Where? Africa
Capital: Praia
Area: 1,557 sq mi
(4,033 sq km)
Population estimate (2005): 418,224
Government: Republic
Languages: Portuguese, Crioulo
Monetary unit: Cape Verdean escudo
Life expectancy: 70.1
Literacy rate: 77%
Did You Know? Off the northwest coast of Africa, Cape Verde is made up of 10 islands and five islets.

Central African Republic

Where? Africa
Capital: Bangui
Area: 240,534 sq mi
(622,984 sq km)
Population estimate (2005): 3,799,897
Government: Republic
Languages: French (official), Sangho, Arabic, Hansa, Swahili
Monetary unit: CFA franc
Life expectancy: 41.4
Literacy rate: 51%
Did You Know? This country was called the Central African Empire from 1976 to 1979.

Chad

Where? Africa
Capital: N'Djamena
Area: 495,752 sq mi
(1,284,000 sq km)
Population estimate (2005): 9,826,419
Government: Republic
Languages: French (official), Sangho, Arabic, Hansa, Swahili
Monetary unit: CFA franc
Life expectancy: 48.2
Literacy rate: 48%
Did You Know? The country is named for its largest lake, Lake Chad.

 Go Places with TFK! Take a country tour at timeforkids.com/goplaces

Chile

Where? South America
Capital: Santiago
Area: 292,258 sq mi
(756,950 sq km)
Population estimate (2005): 15,980,912
Government: Republic
Language: Spanish
Monetary unit: Peso
Life expectancy: 76.4
Literacy rate: 96%
Did You Know? Chile's Atacama Desert is
the driest place on earth.

China

Where? Asia
Capital: Beijing
Area: 3,705,386 sq mi
(9,596,960 sq km)
Population estimate (2005): 1,306,313,812
Government: Communist state
Languages: Chinese (Mandarin), local
dialects
Monetary unit: Yuan
Life expectancy: 72
Literacy rate: 86%
Did You Know? China is the most
populous country in the world.

Colombia

Where? South America
Capital: Bogotá
Area: 439,733 sq mi
(1,138,910 sq km)
Population estimate (2005):
42,954,279
Government: Republic
Language: Spanish
Monetary unit: Peso
Life expectancy: 71.4
Literacy rate: 93%
Did You Know? Coffee is Colombia's
major crop.

Comoros

Where? Africa
Capital: Moroni
Area: 838 sq mi
(2,170 sq km)
Population estimate (2005): 671,247
Government: Republic
Languages: French and Arabic (both official),
Shaafi Islam (Swahili dialect), Malagasu
Monetary unit: CFA franc
Life expectancy: 61.6
Literacy rate: 57%
Did You Know? Comoros is made up of
three tiny islands off the East African coast.

Congo, Democratic Republic of the

Where? Africa
Capital: Kinshasa
Area: 905,562 sq mi
(2,345,410 sq km)
Population estimate (2005): 60,085,004
Government: Dictatorship
Languages: French (official), Swahili,
Lingala, Ishiluba, Kikongo, others
Monetary unit: Congolese franc
Life expectancy: 49.1
Literacy rate: 66%
Did You Know? This country was
formerly named Zaïre.

Congo, Republic of the

Where? Africa
Capital: Brazzaville
Area: 132,046 sq mi
(342,000 sq km)
Population estimate (2005): 3,039,126
Government: Dictatorship
Languages: French (official), Lingala,
Kikongo, others
Monetary unit: CFA franc
Life expectancy: 49.5
Literacy rate: 84%
Did You Know? Petroleum production
provides 90% of the country's revenues
and exports.

Costa Rica

Where? Central America
Capital: San José
Area: 19,730 sq mi
(51,100 sq km)
Population estimate (2005): 4,016,173
Government: Republic
Language: Spanish
Monetary unit: Colón
Life expectancy: 76.6
Literacy rate: 96%
Did You Know? This country's name means "rich coast."

Côte d'Ivoire

Where? Africa
Capital: Yamoussoukro
Area: 124,502 sq mi
(322,460 sq km)
Population estimate (2005): 17,298,040
Government: Republic
Languages: French (official), African languages
Monetary unit: CFA franc
Life expectancy: 48.4
Literacy rate: 51%
Did You Know? More than 60 distinct tribes are represented in Côte d'Ivoire.

Croatia

Where? Europe
Capital: Zagreb
Area: 21,829 sq mi
(56,538 sq km)
Population estimate (2005): 4,495,904
Government: Parliamentary democracy
Language: Croatian
Monetary unit: Kuna
Life expectancy: 74.1
Literacy rate: 99%
Did You Know? Croatia was part of Yugoslavia until it declared independence in 1991.

Cuba

Where? North America
Capital: Havana
Area: 42,803 sq mi
(110,860 sq km)
Population estimate (2005): 11,346,670
Government: Communist state
Language: Spanish
Monetary unit: Peso
Life expectancy: 77
Literacy rate: 97%
Did You Know? Fidel Castro has ruled Cuba since 1959.

Cyprus

Where? Middle East
Capital: Nicosia
Area: 3,572 sq mi (9,250 sq km)
Population estimate (2005): 780,133
Government: Republic
Languages: Greek, Turkish
Monetary unit: Cypriot pound, Turkish lira
Life expectancy: 77.5
Literacy rate: 98%
Did You Know? This nation is divided by a long-standing conflict between its Greek and Turkish populations.

Czech Republic

Where? Europe
Capital: Prague
Area: 30,450 sq mi
(78,866 sq km)
Population estimate (2005): 10,241,138
Government: Parliamentary democracy
Language: Czech
Monetary unit: Koruna
Life expectancy: 75.8
Literacy rate: 100%
Did You Know? Until 1993, the country was part of Czechoslovakia, which no longer exists.

Denmark

Where? Europe
Capital: Copenhagen
Area: 16,639 sq mi
(43,094 sq km)
Population estimate (2005): 5,432,335
Government: Constitutional monarchy
Languages: Danish, Faeroese,
Greenlandic, German
Monetary unit: Krone
Life expectancy: 77.4
Literacy rate: 100%
Did You Know? One of Denmark's territories,
Greenland, is the world's largest island.

Djibouti

Where? Africa
Capital: Djibouti
Area: 8,800 sq mi
(23,000 sq km)
Population estimate (2005): 476,703
Government: Republic
Languages: Arabic and French (both
official), Afar, Somali
Monetary unit: Djibouti franc
Life expectancy: 43.1
Literacy rate: 68%
Did You Know? Djibouti's capital is
one of Africa's major seaports.

Dominica

Where? North America
Capital: Roseau
Area: 290 sq mi
(750 sq km)
Population estimate (2005): 69,029
Government: Parliamentary democracy
Languages: English (official), French patois
Monetary unit: East Caribbean dollar
Life expectancy: 74.4
Literacy rate: 94%
Did You Know? This mountainous
Caribbean island nation was explored by
Columbus in 1493.

Dominican Republic

Where? North America
Capital: Santo Domingo
Area: 18,815 sq mi
(48,730 sq km)
Population estimate (2005): 8,950,034
Government: Representative democracy
Languages: Spanish
Monetary unit: Peso
Life expectancy: 67.6
Literacy rate: 85%
Did You Know? This country, along with
Haiti, makes up the island of Hispaniola
in the Caribbean.

East Timor

Where? Asia
Capital: Dili
Area: 5,814 sq mi
(15,057 sq km)
Population estimate (2005): 1,040,880
Government: Republic
Languages: Tetum, Portuguese (official),
Bahasa Indonesia, English
Monetary unit: U.S. dollar
Life expectancy: 65.6
Literacy rate: 48%
Did You Know? East Timor is the world's
newest country, formed in 2002.

Ecuador

Where? South America
Capital: Quito
Area: 109,483 sq mi
(283,560 sq km)
Population estimate (2005): 13,363,593
Government: Republic
Languages: Spanish (official), Quechua
Monetary unit: U.S. dollar
Life expectancy: 76
Literacy rate: 93%
Did You Know? The country takes its
name from the equator, which runs
through it.

Egypt

Where? Africa
Capital: Cairo
Area: 386,660 sq mi
(1,001,450 sq km)
Population estimate (2005): 77,505,756
Government: Republic
Language: Arabic
Monetary unit: Egyptian pound
Life expectancy: 70.7
Literacy rate: 58%
Did You Know? Almost 95% of Egypt is desert.

El Salvador

Where? Central America
Capital: San Salvador
Area: 8,124 sq mi
(21,040 sq km)
Population estimate (2005): 6,704,932
Government: Republic
Language: Spanish
Monetary unit: U.S. dollar
Life expectancy: 70.9
Literacy rate: 80%
Did You Know? El Salvador is the smallest country in Central America.

Equatorial Guinea

Where? Africa
Capital: Malabo
Area: 10,830 sq mi
(28,050 sq km)
Population estimate (2005): 535,881
Government: Republic
Languages: Spanish (official), French (second official), pidgin English, Fang, Bubi, Creole
Monetary unit: CFA franc
Life expectancy: 55.1
Literacy rate: 86%
Did You Know? This is Africa's only Spanish-speaking country.

Eritrea

Where? Africa
Capital: Asmara
Area: 46,842 sq mi
(121,320 sq km)
Population estimate (2005): 4,561,599
Government: Transitional
Languages: Afar, Bilen, Kunama, Nara, Arabic, Tobedawi, Saho, Tigre, Tigrinya
Monetary unit: Nakfa
Life expectancy: 52.7
Literacy rate: 59%
Did You Know? Once a part of Ethiopia, Eritrea became independent in 1993.

Estonia

Where? Europe
Capital: Tallinn
Area: 17,462 sq mi
(45,226 sq km)
Population estimate (2005): 1,332,893
Government: Parliamentary democracy
Languages: Estonian (official), Russian, Finnish, English
Monetary unit: Kroon
Life expectancy: 71.4
Literacy rate: 100%
Did You Know? Estonia is one of the three Baltic countries.

Ethiopia

Where? Africa
Capital: Addis Ababa
Area: 485,184 sq mi
(1,127,127 sq km)
Population estimate (2005): 73,053,286
Government: Federal republic
Languages: Amharic (official), English, Orominga, Tigrigna, others
Monetary unit: Birr
Life expectancy: 48.6
Literacy rate: 43%
Did You Know? Remains of the oldest-known human ancestors have been found in Ethiopia.

Fiji

Where? Oceania
Capital: Suva
Area: 7,054 sq mi (18,270 sq km)
Population estimate (2005): 893,354
Government: Republic
Languages: Fijian, Hindustani, English (official)
Monetary unit: Fiji dollar
Life expectancy: 69.2
Literacy rate: 94%
Did You Know? Fiji is made up of 332 islands in the South Pacific.

Finland

Where? Europe
Capital: Helsinki
Area: 130,127 sq mi (337,030 sq km)
Population estimate (2005): 5,223,442
Government: Republic
Languages: Finnish and Swedish (both official)
Monetary unit: Euro (formerly markka)
Life expectancy: 78.2
Literacy rate: 100%
Did You Know? Laplanders live in the north of Finland, above the Arctic Circle.

France

Where? Europe
Capital: Paris
Area: 211,208 sq mi (547,030 sq km)
Population estimate (2005): 60,656,178
Government: Republic
Language: French
Monetary unit: Euro (formerly French franc)
Life expectancy: 79.4
Literacy rate: 99%
Did You Know? France is the world's top travel destination.

Gabon

Where? Africa
Capital: Libreville
Area: 103,347 sq mi (267,670 sq km)
Population estimate (2005): 1,389,201
Government: Republic
Languages: French (official), Fang, Myene, Bateke, Bapounou/Eschira, Bandjabi
Monetary unit: CFA franc
Life expectancy: 56.5
Literacy rate: 63%
Did You Know? Most of Gabon is covered by a dense tropical forest.

The Gambia

Where? Africa
Capital: Banjul
Area: 4,363 sq mi (11,300 sq km)
Population estimate (2005): 1,593,256
Government: Republic
Languages: English (official), native tongues
Monetary unit: Dalasi
Life expectancy: 54.8
Literacy rate: 40%
Did You Know? Gambia is Africa's smallest country.

Georgia

Where? Asia
Capital: T'bilisi
Area: 26,911 sq mi (69,700 sq km)
Population estimate (2005): 4,677,401
Government: Republic
Languages: Georgian (official), Russian, Armenian, Azerbaijani
Monetary unit: Lari
Life expectancy: 75.6
Literacy rate: 99%
Did You Know? Georgia was part of the Soviet Union before its breakup in 1991.

Germany

Where? Europe
Capital: Berlin
Area: 137,846 sq mi
(357,021 sq km)
Population estimate (2005): 82,431,390
Government: Federal republic
Language: German
Monetary unit: Euro (formerly Deutsche mark)
Life expectancy: 78.5
Literacy rate: 99%
Did You Know? The German name for the country is Deutschland.

Ghana

Where? Africa
Capital: Accra
Area: 92,456 sq mi
(239,460 sq km)
Population estimate (2005): 21,029,853
Government: Constitutional democracy
Languages: English (official), native tongues
Monetary unit: Cedi
Life expectancy: 56.3
Literacy rate: 75%
Did You Know? Ghana was formerly a British colony called the Gold Coast.

Greece

Where? Europe
Capital: Athens
Area: 50,942 sq mi
(131,940 sq km)
Population estimate (2005): 10,668,354
Government: Parliamentary republic
Language: Greek
Monetary unit: Euro (formerly drachma)
Life expectancy: 78.9
Literacy rate: 98%
Did You Know? Greece is known for its magnificent ancient temples, particularly the world-renowned Parthenon.

Grenada

Where? North America
Capital: Saint George's
Area: 133 sq mi
(344 sq km)
Population estimate (2005): 89,502
Government: Constitutional monarchy
Language: English
Monetary unit: East Caribbean dollar
Life expectancy: 64.5
Literacy rate: 90%
Did You Know? This Caribbean island was explored by Columbus in 1498.

Guatemala

Where? Central America
Capital: Guatemala City
Area: 42,042 sq mi
(108,890 sq km)
Population estimate (2005): 14,655,189
Government: Republic
Languages: Spanish (official), Indian languages
Monetary unit: Quetzal
Life expectancy: 65.2
Literacy rate: 71%
Did You Know? Most Guatemalans are of Mayan or Spanish descent.

Guinea

Where? Africa
Capital: Conakry
Area: 94,925 sq mi
(245,860 sq km)
Population estimate (2005): 9,467,866
Government: Republic
Languages: French (official), native tongues
Monetary unit: Guinean franc
Life expectancy: 49.7
Literacy rate: 36%
Did You Know? Guinea's chief exports are agricultural products and minerals, especially bauxite.

Guinea-Bissau

Where? Africa
Capital: Bissau
Area: 13,946 sq mi
(36,120 sq km)
Population estimate (2005): 1,416,027
Government: Republic
Languages: Portuguese (official),
African languages
Monetary unit: CFA franc
Life expectancy: 47
Literacy rate: 42%
Did You Know? This country was once a
Portuguese colony.

Guyana

Where? South America
Capital: Georgetown
Area: 83,000 sq mi
(214,970 sq km)
Population estimate (2005): 765,283
Government: Republic
Languages: English (official),
Amerindian dialects
Monetary unit: Guyana dollar
Life expectancy: 65.1
Literacy rate: 99%
Did You Know? Guyana's people are
primarily of East Indian and African
descent.

Haiti

Where? North America
Capital: Port-au-Prince
Area: 10,714 sq mi
(27,750 sq km)
Population estimate (2005): 8,121,622
Government: Elected government
Languages: Creole and French (both
official)
Monetary unit: Gourde
Life expectancy: 52.6
Literacy rate: 53%
Did You Know? This country, along with
the Dominican Republic, makes up the
island of Hispaniola in the Caribbean.

Honduras

Where? Central America
Capital: Tegucigalpa
Area: 43,278 sq mi
(112,090 sq km)
Population estimate (2005): 6,975,204
Government: Republic
Languages: Spanish, Amerindian
dialects
Monetary unit: Lempira
Life expectancy: 66.2
Literacy rate: 76%
Did You Know? About 80% of Honduras
is mountainous.

Hungary

Where? Europe
Capital: Budapest
Area: 35,919 sq mi
(93,030 sq km)
Population estimate (2005): 10,006,835
Government: Parliamentary democracy
Language: Magyar (Hungarian)
Monetary unit: Forint
Life expectancy: 72.2
Literacy rate: 99%
Did You Know? Magyar is the Hungarian
name for the country's people.

Iceland

Where? Europe
Capital: Reykjavik
Area: 39,768 sq mi
(103,000 sq km)
Population estimate (2005): 296,737
Government: Constitutional republic
Language: Icelandic
Monetary unit: Icelandic krona
Life expectancy: 80.2
Literacy rate: 100%
Did You Know? Iceland boasts the
world's oldest constitution, drafted
around 930.

India

Where? Asia
Capital: New Delhi
**Area: 1,269,338 sq mi
(3,287,590 sq km)**
Population estimate (2005): 1,080,264,388
Government: Republic
**Languages: Hindi (national), English;
24 major languages plus more than 1,600
dialects**
Monetary unit: Rupee
Life expectancy: 64
Literacy rate: 60%
**Did You Know? India is the world's
second most populous country.**

Indonesia

Where? Asia
Capital: Jakarta
**Area: 741,096 sq mi
(1,919,440 sq km)**
Population estimate (2005): 241,973,879
Government: Republic
**Languages: Bahasa Indonesia (official),
Dutch, English; more than 500 languages
and dialects**
Monetary unit: Rupiah
Life expectancy: 69.3
Literacy rate: 89%
**Did You Know? Indonesia has the largest
number of active volcanoes in the world.**

Iran

Where? Middle East
Capital: Tehran
**Area: 636,293 sq mi
(1,648,000 sq km)**
Population estimate (2005): 68,017,860
Government: Theocratic republic
**Languages: Farsi (Persian), Azari,
Kurdish, Arabic**
Monetary unit: Rial
Life expectancy: 69.7
Literacy rate: 79%
**Did You Know? Iran was once known
as Persia.**

Iraq

Where? Middle East
Capital: Baghdad
**Area: 168,753 sq mi
(437,072 sq km)**
Population estimate (2005): 26,074,906
Government: Transitional
Languages: Arabic, Kurdish
Monetary unit: Iraqi dinar
Life expectancy: 68.3
Literacy rate: 40%
**Did You Know? The ancient civilization
of Mesopotamia was located in what is
today called Iraq.**

Ireland

Where? Europe
Capital: Dublin
**Area: 27,136 sq mi
(70,280 sq km)**
Population estimate (2005): 4,015,676
Government: Republic
Languages: English, Irish Gaelic
**Monetary units: Euro (formerly Irish
pound, or punt)**
Life expectancy: 77.4
Literacy rate: 98%
**Did You Know? The name for Ireland in
Gaelic (the Irish language) is Eire.**

Israel

Where? Middle East
Capital: Jerusalem
**Area: 8,020 sq mi
(20,770 sq km)**
Population estimate (2005): 6,276,883
Government: Parliamentary democracy
**Languages: Hebrew (official), Arabic,
English**
Monetary unit: Shekel
Life expectancy: 79.2
Literacy rate: 95%
**Did You Know? Modern Israel became
a country in 1948.**

Italy

Where? Europe
Capital: Rome
Area: 116,305 sq mi
(301,230 sq km)
Population estimate (2005): 58,103,033
Government: Republic
Language: Italian
Monetary unit: Euro (formerly lira)
Life expectancy: 79.5
Literacy rate: 99%
Did You Know? Italy is known for its magnificent art treasures and architecture.

Jamaica

Where? North America
Capital: Kingston
Area: 4,244 sq mi
(10,991 sq km)
Population estimate (2005): 2,731,832
Government: Parliamentary democracy
Languages: English, patois English
Monetary unit: Jamaican dollar
Life expectancy: 76.1
Literacy rate: 88%
Did You Know? Jamaica once had a large slave population that worked on sugar-cane plantations.

Japan

Where? Asia
Capital: Tokyo
Area: 145,882 sq mi
(377,835 sq km)
Population estimate (2005): 127,417,244
Government: Constitutional monarchy
Language: Japanese
Monetary unit: Yen
Life expectancy: 81
Literacy rate: 99%
Did You Know? The Japanese name for the country is Nippon.

Jordan

Where? Middle East
Capital: Amman
Area: 34,445 sq mi
(89,213 sq km)
Population estimate (2005): 5,759,732
Government: Constitutional monarchy
Languages: Arabic (official), English
Monetary unit: Jordanian dinar
Life expectancy: 78.1
Literacy rate: 91%
Did You Know? Jordan is a kingdom ruled by the Hashemite dynasty.

Kazakhstan

Where? Asia
Capital: Astana
Area: 1,049,150 sq mi
(2,717,300 sq km)
Population estimate (2005): 15,185,844
Government: Republic
Languages: Kazak (Qazaq) and Russian (both official)
Monetary unit: Tenge
Life expectancy: 66.1
Literacy rate: 98%
Did You Know? Oil was discovered in Kazakhstan in 2000. It was the largest oil find in 30 years.

Kenya

Where? Africa
Capital: Nairobi
Area: 224,960 sq mi
(582,650 sq km)
Population estimate (2005): 33,829,590
Government: Republic
Languages: English (official), Swahili, several others
Monetary unit: Kenyan shilling
Life expectancy: 47.2
Literacy rate: 85%
Did You Know? About 40 different ethnic groups live in Kenya.

Kiribati

Where? Pacific Islands
Capital: Tarawa
Area: 313 sq mi (811 sq km)
Population estimate (2005): 103,092
Government: Republic
Languages: English (official), I-Kiribati (Gilbertese)
Monetary unit: Australian dollar
Life expectancy: 61.3
Literacy rate: Not available
Did You Know? This nation is made up of three widely separated island groups in the South Pacific.

Korea, North

Where? Asia
Capital: Pyongyang
Area: 46,540 sq mi (120,540 sq km)
Population estimate (2005): 22,912,177
Government: Communist dictatorship
Language: Korean
Monetary unit: Won
Life expectancy: 71.1
Literacy rate: 99%
Did You Know? North Korea is one of the world's last hard-line communist countries.

Korea, South

Where? Asia
Capital: Seoul
Area: 38,023 sq mi (98,480 sq km)
Population estimate (2005): 48,422,644
Government: Republic
Language: Korean
Monetary unit: Won
Life expectancy: 75.6
Literacy rate: 98%
Did You Know? About half of South Korea's people are Christian; the other half are Buddhist.

Kuwait

Where? Middle East
Capital: Kuwait
Area: 6,880 sq mi (17,820 sq km)
Population estimate (2005): 2,335,648
Government: Constitutional monarchy
Languages: Arabic (official), English
Monetary unit: Kuwaiti dinar
Life expectancy: 76.8
Literacy rate: 84%
Did You Know? This small country has the fourth largest oil reserves in the world.

Kyrgyzstan

Where? Asia
Capital: Bishkek
Area: 76,641 sq mi (198,500 sq km)
Population estimate (2005): 5,146,281
Government: Republic
Languages: Kyrgyz (official), Russian
Monetary unit: Som
Life expectancy: 67.8
Literacy rate: 97%
Did You Know? The Tien Shan mountain range covers about 95% of the country.

Laos

Where? Asia
Capital: Vientiane
Area: 91,429 sq mi (236,800 sq km)
Population estimate (2005): 6,217,141
Government: Communist state
Languages: Lao (official), French, English
Monetary unit: Kip
Life expectancy: 54.7
Literacy rate: 53%
Did You Know? Laos is one of the 10 poorest countries in the world.

Latvia

Where? Europe
Capital: Riga
Area: 24,938 sq mi
(64,589 sq km)
Population estimate (2005): 2,290,237
Government: Parliamentary democracy
Language: Latvian
Monetary unit: Lats
Life expectancy: 70.9
Literacy rate: 100%
Did You Know? One of the three Baltic countries, Latvia is located in the far north of Europe.

Lebanon

Where? Middle East
Capital: Beirut
Area: 4,015 sq mi
(10,400 sq km)
Population estimate (2005): 3,826,018
Government: Republic
Languages: Arabic (official), French, English
Monetary unit: Lebanese pound
Life expectancy: 72.3
Literacy rate: 87%
Did You Know? About 60% of Lebanese are Muslim and 30% are Christian.

Lesotho

Where? Africa
Capital: Maseru
Area: 11,720 sq mi
(30,350 sq km)
Population estimate (2005): 1,867,035
Government: Monarchy
Languages: English and Sesotho (both official), Zulu, Xhosa
Monetary unit: Loti
Life expectancy: 36.8
Literacy rate: 85%
Did You Know? This small African kingdom is surrounded on all sides by South Africa.

Liberia

Where? Africa
Capital: Monrovia
Area: 43,000 sq mi
(111,370 sq km)
Population estimate (2005): 3,482,211
Government: Republic
Languages: English (official), tribal dialects
Monetary unit: Liberian dollar
Life expectancy: 47.9
Literacy rate: 58%
Did You Know? Liberia was founded by freed American slaves in 1847.

Libya

Where? Africa
Capital: Tripoli
Area: 679,358 sq mi
(1,759,540 sq km)
Population estimate (2005): 5,765,563
Government: Military dictatorship
Languages: Arabic, Italian, English
Monetary unit: Libyan dinar
Life expectancy: 76.3
Literacy rate: 83%
Did You Know? The world's highest temperature ever recorded (136°F) was in Al Azizyah, Libya, in 1922.

Liechtenstein

Where? Europe
Capital: Vaduz
Area: 62 sq mi
(160 sq km)
Population estimate (2005): 33,717
Government: Constitutional monarchy
Languages: German (official), Alemannic dialect
Monetary unit: Swiss franc
Life expectancy: 79.4
Literacy rate: 100%
Did You Know? This tiny kingdom borders Austria and Switzerland.

309

Lithuania

Where? **Europe**
Capital: **Vilnius**
Area: **25,174 sq mi (65,200 sq km)**
Population estimate (2005): **3,596,617**
Government: **Parliamentary democracy**
Languages: **Lithuanian (official), Polish, Russian**
Monetary unit: **Litas**
Life expectancy: **73.5**
Literacy rate: **100%**
Did You Know? **One of the three Baltic countries, Lithuania is located in northern Europe.**

Luxembourg

Where? **Europe**
Capital: **Luxembourg**
Area: **999 sq mi (2,586 sq km)**
Population estimate (2005): **468,571**
Government: **Constitutional monarchy**
Languages: **Luxembourgian, French, German**
Monetary unit: **Euro (formerly Luxembourg franc)**
Life expectancy: **78.6**
Literacy rate: **100%**
Did You Know? **This tiny kingdom is located in central Europe.**

Macedonia

Where? **Europe**
Capital: **Skopje**
Area: **9,781 sq mi (25,333 sq km)**
Population estimate (2005): **2,045,262**
Government: **Emerging democracy**
Languages: **Macedonian, Albanian**
Monetary unit: **Denar**
Life expectancy: **73.5**
Literacy rate: **Not available**
Did You Know? **Until Macedonia declared independence in 1991, it was part of Yugoslavia.**

Madagascar

Where? **Africa**
Capital: **Antananarivo**
Area: **226,660 sq mi (587,040 sq km)**
Population estimate (2005): **18,040,341**
Government: **Republic**
Languages: **Malagasy and French (both official)**
Monetary unit: **Malagasy franc**
Life expectancy: **56.5**
Literacy rate: **69%**
Did You Know? **Madagascar is the world's fourth largest island.**

Malawi

Where? **Africa**
Capital: **Lilongwe**
Area: **45,745 sq mi (118,480 sq km)**
Population estimate (2005): **12,158,924**
Government: **Multiparty democracy**
Languages: **English and Chichewa (both official)**
Monetary unit: **Kwacha**
Life expectancy: **37.5**
Literacy rate: **63%**
Did You Know? **About 20% of Malawi is made up of a large lake named Nyasa.**

Malaysia

Where? **Asia**
Capital: **Kuala Lumpur**
Area: **127,316 sq mi (329,750 sq km)**
Population estimate (2005): **23,953,136**
Government: **Constitutional monarchy**
Languages: **Malay (official), Chinese, Tamil, English**
Monetary unit: **Ringgit**
Life expectancy: **72**
Literacy rate: **89%**
Did You Know? **Most of Malaysia is located in Southeast Asia; a smaller portion is located on the island of Borneo.**

Maldives

Where? Asia
Capital: Male
Area: 116 sq mi
(300 sq km)
Population estimate (2005): 349,106
Government: Republic
Languages: Dhivehi (official), Arabic,
Hindi, English
Monetary unit: Maldivian rufiyaa
Life expectancy: 63.7
Literacy rate: 97%
Did You Know? This group of islands
lies off the southern coast of India.

Mali

Where? Africa
Capital: Bamako
Area: 478,764 sq mi (1,240,000 sq km)
Population estimate (2005): 12,291,529
Government: Republic
Languages: French (official), African
languages
Monetary unit: CFA franc
Life expectancy: 45.3
Literacy rate: 46%
Did You Know? The fabled, ancient city
of Timbuktu is located in Mali.

Malta

Where? Europe
Capital: Valletta
Area: 122 sq mi
(316 sq km)
Population estimate (2005): 398,534
Government: Republic
Languages: Maltese and English (both
official)
Monetary unit: Maltese lira
Life expectancy: 78.7
Literacy rate: 93%
Did You Know? The country is made up of
five small islands in the Mediterranean.

Marshall Islands

Where? Pacific Islands
Capital: Majuro
Area: 70 sq mi
(181.3 sq km)
Population estimate (2005): 59,071
Government: Constitutional government
Languages: Marshallese and English
(both official)
Monetary unit: U.S. dollar
Life expectancy: 69.7
Literacy rate: 94%
Did You Know? The Marshall Islands
were once a dependency of the U.S.

Mauritania

Where? Africa
Capital: Nouakchott
Area: 397,953 sq mi
(1,030,700 sq km)
Population estimate (2005): 3,086,859
Government: Republic
Languages: Arabic (official), French
Monetary unit: Ouguiya
Life expectancy: 52.3
Literacy rate: 42%
Did You Know? This northern African
country is primarily desert.

Mauritius

Where? Africa
Capital: Port Louis
Area: 788 sq mi
(2,040 sq km)
Population estimate (2005): 1,230,602
Government: Parliamentary democracy
Languages: English (official), French,
Creole, Hindi, Urdu, Hakka, Bojpoori
Monetary unit: Mauritian rupee
Life expectancy: 72.1
Literacy rate: 86%
Did You Know? Most of this island's
population is of African or Indian descent.

Mexico

Where? North America
Capital: Mexico City
Area: 761,600 sq mi
(1,972,550 sq km)
Population estimate (2005): 106,202,903
Government: Republic
Languages: Spanish, Indian languages
Monetary unit: Peso
Life expectancy: 74.9
Literacy rate: 92%
Did You Know? Teotihuacán (circa 300–900) was once the largest city in the Americas.

Micronesia

Where? Pacific Islands
Capital: Palikir
Area: 271 sq mi
(702 sq km)
Population estimate (2005): 108,105
Government: Constitutional government
Languages: English (official), native languages
Monetary unit: U.S. dollar
Life expectancy: 69.4
Literacy rate: 89%
Did You Know? Four different island groups make up this country.

Moldova

Where? Europe
Capital: Chisinau
Area: 13,067 sq mi
(33,843 sq km)
Population estimate (2005): 4,455,421
Government: Republic
Languages: Moldovan (official), Russian, Gagauz
Monetary unit: Moldovan leu
Life expectancy: 65
Literacy rate: 99%
Did You Know? This eastern European country was once a part of the Soviet Union.

Monaco

Where? Europe
Capital: Monaco
Area: 0.75 sq mi
(1.95 sq km)
Population estimate (2005): 32,409
Government: Constitutional monarchy
Languages: French (official), English, Italian, Monégasque
Monetary unit: French franc
Life expectancy: 79.4
Literacy rate: 99%
Did You Know? Bordering France, this tiny nation is famous for its casinos.

Mongolia

Where? Asia
Capital: Ulaanbaatar
Area: 604,250 sq mi
(1,565,000 sq km)
Population estimate (2005): 2,791,272
Government: Parliamentary republic
Languages: Mongolian (official), Turkic, Russian, Chinese
Monetary unit: Tugrik
Life expectancy: 64.2
Literacy rate: 99%
Did You Know? Mongolia is Asia's most sparsely populated country.

Morocco

Where? Africa
Capital: Rabat
Area: 172,413 sq mi
(446,550 sq km)
Population estimate (2005): 32,725,847
Government: Constitutional monarchy
Languages: Arabic (official), French, Berber dialects, Spanish
Monetary unit: Dirham
Life expectancy: 70.3
Literacy rate: 52%
Did You Know? About 99% of Moroccans are of Arab-Berber descent.

Mozambique

Where? Africa
Capital: Maputo
Area: 309,494 sq mi
(801,590 sq km)
Population estimate (2005): 19,406,703
Government: Republic
Languages: Portuguese (official), Bantu languages
Monetary unit: Metical
Life expectancy: 40.9
Literacy rate: 48%
Did You Know? In 1992, Mozambique endured a devastating drought.

Myanmar (Burma)

Where? Asia
Capital: Rangoon
Area: 261,969 sq mi
(678,500 sq km)
Population estimate (2005): 42,909,464
Government: Military regime
Languages: Burmese, minority languages
Monetary unit: Kyat
Life expectancy: 56
Literacy rate: 83%
Did You Know? In 1989, the government changed the name of Burma to Myanmar.

Namibia

Where? Africa
Capital: Windhoek
Area: 318,694 sq mi
(825,418 sq km)
Population estimate (2005): 2,030,692
Government: Republic
Languages: Afrikaans, German, English (official), native languages
Monetary unit: Namibian dollar
Life expectancy: 44.8
Literacy rate: 84%
Did You Know? Namibia achieved independence from South Africa in 1990.

Nauru

Where? Pacific Islands
Capital: Yaren District (unofficial)
Area: 8.2 sq mi (21 sq km)
Population estimate (2005): 13,048
Government: Republic
Languages: Nauruan (official), English
Monetary unit: Australian dollar
Life expectancy: 62.3
Literacy rate: Not available
Did You Know? Nauru is the smallest island nation in the world.

Nepal

Where? Asia
Capital: Kathmandu
Area: 54,363 sq mi
(140,800 sq km)
Population estimate (2005): 27,676,547
Government: Constitutional monarchy
Languages: Nepali (official), Newari, Bhutia, Maithali
Monetary unit: Nepalese rupee
Life expectancy: 59.4
Literacy rate: 45%
Did You Know? Mount Everest, on Nepal's border, is the world's highest mountain.

The Netherlands

Where? Europe
Capital: Amsterdam
Area: 16,036 sq mi
(41,532 sq km)
Population estimate (2005): 16,407,491
Government: Constitutional monarchy
Language: Dutch
Monetary unit: Euro (formerly guilder)
Life expectancy: 78.7
Literacy rate: 99%
Did You Know? About 40% of the Netherlands is land reclaimed from the sea.

New Zealand

Where? Pacific Islands
Capital: Wellington
Area: 103,737 sq mi (268,680 sq km)
Population estimate (2005): 4,035,461
Government: Parliamentary democracy
Languages: English (official), Maori
Monetary unit: New Zealand dollar
Life expectancy: 78.5
Literacy rate: 99%
Did You Know? The first people to inhabit New Zealand were the Maoris, who settled there about 1,200 years ago.

Nicaragua

Where? Central America
Capital: Managua
Area: 49,998 sq mi (129,494 sq km)
Population estimate (2005): 5,465,100
Government: Republic
Language: Spanish
Monetary unit: Cordoba
Life expectancy: 70
Literacy rate: 68%
Did You Know? Nicaragua is the largest but most sparsely populated Central American country.

Niger

Where? Africa
Capital: Niamey
Area: 489,189 sq mi (1,267,000 sq km)
Population estimate (2005): 11,665,937
Government: Republic
Languages: French (official), Hausa, Songhai, Arabic
Monetary unit: CFA franc
Life expectancy: 42.2
Literacy rate: 18%
Did You Know? Most of Niger is situated in the Sahara Desert.

Nigeria

Where? Africa
Capital: Abuja
Area: 356,700 sq mi (923,770 sq km)
Population estimate (2005): 128,771,988
Government: Republic
Languages: English (official), Hausa, Yoruba, Ibo, more than 200 others
Monetary unit: Naira
Life expectancy: 46.5
Literacy rate: 68%
Did You Know? Nigeria is Africa's most populous country.

Norway

Where? Europe
Capital: Oslo
Area: 125,181 sq mi (324,220 sq km)
Population estimate (2005): 4,593,041
Government: Constitutional monarchy
Languages: Two official forms of Norwegian, Bokmål and Nynorsk
Monetary unit: Krone
Life expectancy: 79.2
Literacy rate: 100%
Did You Know? Norway has won the most winter Olympic medals of any nation.

Oman

Where? Middle East
Capital: Muscat
Area: 82,030 sq mi (212,460 sq km)
Population estimate (2005): 3,001,583
Government: Monarchy
Languages: Arabic (official), English, Indian languages
Monetary unit: Omani rial
Life expectancy: 72.8
Literacy rate: 76%
Did You Know? Oman's major product is oil.

go Hear different languages and learn about different cultures at timeforkids.com/goplaces

Pakistan

Where? Asia
Capital: Islamabad
Area: 310,400 sq mi (803,940 sq km)
Population estimate (2005): 162,419,946
Government: Republic
Languages: Punjabi, Sindhi, Siraiki, Pashtu, Urdu (official), others
Monetary unit: Pakistan rupee
Life expectancy: 62.6
Literacy rate: 46%
Did You Know? K2, the world's second highest mountain, is in Pakistan.

Palau

Where? Pacific Islands
Capital: Koror
Area: 177 sq mi (458 sq km)
Population estimate (2005): 20,303
Government: Constitutional government
Languages: Palauan, English (official)
Monetary unit: U.S. dollar
Life expectancy: 69.8
Literacy rate: 92%
Did You Know? Palau is made up of 200 islands.

Panama

Where? Central America
Capital: Panama City
Area: 30,193 sq mi (78,200 sq km)
Population estimate (2005): 3,039,150
Government: Constitutional democracy
Languages: Spanish (official), English
Monetary unit: Balboa
Life expectancy: 72.1
Literacy rate: 93%
Did You Know? The Panama Canal links the Atlantic and Pacific oceans and is one of the world's most vital waterways.

Papua New Guinea

Where? Pacific Islands
Capital: Port Moresby
Area: 178,703 sq mi (462,840 sq km)
Population estimate (2005): 5,545,268
Government: Constitutional monarchy
Languages: English, Tok Pisin, Hiri Motu, 717 native languages
Monetary unit: Kina
Life expectancy: 64.6
Literacy rate: 66%
Did You Know? More languages (800) are spoken in this country than in any other.

Paraguay

Where? South America
Capital: Asunción
Area: 157,046 sq mi (406,750 sq km)
Population estimate (2005): 6,347,884
Government: Republic
Languages: Spanish (official), Guaraní
Monetary unit: Guaraní
Life expectancy: 74.6
Literacy rate: 94%
Did You Know? More than half of Paraguay's workers are employed in either agriculture or forestry.

Peru

Where? South America
Capital: Lima
Area: 496,223 sq mi (1,285,220 sq km)
Population estimate (2005): 27,925,628
Government: Republic
Languages: Spanish and Quechua (both official), Aymara, other native languages
Monetary unit: Nuevo sol
Life expectancy: 69.2
Literacy rate: 91%
Did You Know? Peru's Machu Picchu is a magnificent ancient Incan fortress in the Andes mountains.

The Philippines

Where? Asia
Capital: Manila
Area: 115,830 sq mi
(300,000 sq km)
Population estimate (2005): 87,857,473
Government: Republic
Languages: Filipino (based on Tagalog) and English (both official), regional languages
Monetary unit: Peso
Life expectancy: 69.6
Literacy rate: 96%
Did You Know? The country is made up of more than 7,000 tropical islands.

Poland

Where? Europe
Capital: Warsaw
Area: 120,727 sq mi
(312,683 sq km)
Population estimate (2005): 38,635,144
Government: Republic
Language: Polish
Monetary unit: Zloty
Life expectancy: 74.2
Literacy rate: 100%
Did You Know? The Polish name for the country is Polska.

Portugal

Where? Europe
Capital: Lisbon
Area: 35,672 sq mi
(92,391 sq km)
Population estimate (2005): 10,566,212
Government: Parliamentary democracy
Language: Portuguese
Monetary unit: Euro (formerly escudo)
Life expectancy: 77.3
Literacy rate: 93%
Did You Know? Many of the world's famous explorers were Portuguese, including Magellan and Vasco de Gama.

Qatar

Where? Middle East
Capital: Doha
Area: 4,416 sq mi
(11,439 sq km)
Population estimate (2005): 863,051
Government: Traditional monarchy
Languages: Arabic (official), English
Monetary unit: Qatari riyal
Life expectancy: 73.4
Literacy rate: 83%
Did You Know? This country is a small peninsula extending into the Persian Gulf.

Romania

Where? Europe
Capital: Bucharest
Area: 91,700 sq mi
(237,500 sq km)
Population estimate (2005): 22,329,977
Government: Republic
Languages: Romanian (official), Hungarian, German
Monetary unit: Leu
Life expectancy: 71.1
Literacy rate: 98%
Did You Know? Romania was once a Roman province known as Dacia.

Russia

Where?
Europe and Asia
Capital: Moscow
Area: 6,592,735 sq mi
(17,075,200 sq km)
Population estimate (2005): 143,420,309
Government: Federation
Languages: Russian, others
Monetary unit: Ruble
Life expectancy: 66.8
Literacy rate: 100%
Did You Know? Russia is the world's largest country.

Rwanda

Where? Africa
Capital: Kigali
Area: 10,169 sq mi
(26,338 sq km)
Population estimate (2005): 8,440,820
Government: Republic
Languages: Kinyarwanda, French, English
(all official)
Monetary unit: Rwandan franc
Life expectancy: 46.6
Literacy rate: 70%
Did You Know? Ethnic violence led to the
deaths of about 800,000 Rwandans in 1994.

Saint Kitts and Nevis

Where? North America
Capital: Basseterre
Area: 101 sq mi
(261 sq km)
Population estimate (2005): 38,958
Government: Constitutional monarchy
Language: English
Monetary unit: East Caribbean dollar
Life expectancy: 71.9
Literacy rate: 97%
Did You Know? Nevis is almost entirely
a single mountain, Nevis Peak.

Saint Lucia

Where? North America
Capital: Castries
Area: 239 sq mi
(620 sq km)
Population estimate (2005): 166,312
Government: Parliamentary democracy
Languages: English (official), patois
Monetary unit: East Caribbean dollar
Life expectancy: 73.3
Literacy rate: 67%
Did You Know? The major crop of this
Caribbean island is bananas.

Saint Vincent and the Grenadines

Where? North America
Capital: Kingstown
Area: 150 sq mi
(389 sq km)
Population estimate (2005): 117,534
Government: Parliamentary democracy
Languages: English (official),
French patois
Monetary unit: East Caribbean dollar
Life expectancy: 73.3
Literacy rate: 96%
Did You Know? This country's highest
point is the active volcano Soufrière.

Samoa

Where? Pacific Islands
Capital: Apia
Area: 1,104 sq mi
(2,860 sq km)
Population estimate (2005): 177,287
Government: Constitutional monarchy
Languages: Samoan, English
Monetary unit: Tala
Life expectancy: 70.4
Literacy rate: 100%
Did You Know? Samoa, now independent,
was once ruled by Germany and
New Zealand.

San Marino

Where? Europe
Capital: San Marino
Area: 24 sq mi
(61 sq km)
Population estimate (2005): 28,880
Government: Republic
Language: Italian
Monetary unit: Italian lira
Life expectancy: 81.5
Literacy rate: 96%
Did You Know? Tiny San Marino is
part of the Italian peninsula.

São Tomé and Príncipe

Where? Africa
Capital: São Tomé
Area: 386 sq mi
(1,001 sq km)
Population estimate (2005): 187,410
Government: Republic
Language: Portuguese
Monetary unit: Dobra
Life expectancy: 66.6
Literacy rate: 79%
Did You Know? The recent discovery of oil may bring wealth to this poor nation.

Saudi Arabia

Where? Middle East
Capital: Riyadh
Area: 756,981 sq mi
(1,960,582 sq km)
Population estimate (2005): 26,417,599
Government: Monarchy
Language: Arabic
Monetary unit: Riyal
Life expectancy: 75.2
Literacy rate: 79%
Did You Know? This country contains two of Islam's holiest cities, Mecca and Medina.

Senegal

Where? Africa
Capital: Dakar
Area: 75,749 sq mi
(196,190 sq km)
Population estimate (2005): 11,126,832
Government: Republic
Languages: French (official), Wolof, Serer, other dialects
Monetary unit: CFA franc
Life expectancy: 56.6
Literacy rate: 40%
Did You Know? Senegal's capital, Dakar, is the westernmost point of Africa.

Serbia and Montenegro

Where? Europe
Capital: Belgrade
Area: 39,517 sq mi
(102,350 sq km)
Population estimate (2005): 10,829,175
Government: Republic
Languages: Serbian, Albanian
Monetary unit: Yugoslav new dinar
Life expectancy: 74.4
Literacy rate: 93%
Did You Know? In 2003, the country changed its name from Yugoslavia.

Seychelles

Where? Africa
Capital: Victoria
Area: 176 sq mi
(455 sq km)
Population estimate (2005): 81,188
Government: Republic
Languages: English and French (both official), Seselwa
Monetary unit: Seychelles rupee
Life expectancy: 71.5
Literacy rate: 58%
Did You Know? This island nation is located in the Indian Ocean.

Sierra Leone

Where? Africa
Capital: Freetown
Area: 27,699 sq mi
(71,740 sq km)
Population estimate (2005): 6,017,643
Government: Constitutional democracy
Languages: English (official), Mende, Temne, Krio
Monetary unit: Leone
Life expectancy: 42.7
Literacy rate: 31%
Did You Know? This nation is one of the poorest countries in the world.

Singapore

Where? Asia
Capital: Singapore
Area: 267 sq mi
(692.7 sq km)
Population estimate (2005): 4,425,720
Government: Parliamentary republic
Languages: Malay, Chinese (Mandarin), Tamil, English (all official)
Monetary unit: Singapore dollar
Life expectancy: 81.5
Literacy rate: 93%
Did You Know? Singapore is the second most densely populated country in the world.

Slovakia

Where? Europe
Capital: Bratislava
Area: 18,859 sq mi
(48,845 sq km)
Population estimate (2005): 5,431,363
Government: Parliamentary democracy
Languages: Slovak (official), Hungarian
Monetary unit: Koruna
Life expectancy: 74.2
Literacy rate: Not available
Did You Know? Until 1993, the country was part of Czechoslovakia, which now no longer exists.

Slovenia

Where? Europe
Capital: Ljubljana
Area: 7,820 sq mi
(20,253 sq km)
Population estimate (2005): 2,011,070
Government: Parliamentary republic
Languages: Slovenian, Serbo-Croatian
Monetary unit: Slovenian tolar
Life expectancy: 75.9
Literacy rate: 100%
Did You Know? Slovenia was part of Yugoslavia until it declared independence in 1991.

Solomon Islands

Where?
Pacific Islands
Capital: Honiara
Area: 10,985 sq mi
(28,450 sq km)
Population estimate (2005): 538,032
Government: Parliamentary democracy
Languages: English, Solomon pidgin, more than 60 Melanesian languages
Monetary unit: Solomon Islands dollar
Life expectancy: 72.4
Literacy rate: Not available
Did You Know? This island nation was recently ravaged by civil unrest.

Somalia

Where? Africa
Capital: Mogadishu
Area: 246,199 sq mi
(637,657 sq km)
Population estimate (2005): 8,591,629
Government: Transitional government
Languages: Somali (official), Arabic, English, Italian
Monetary unit: Somali shilling
Life expectancy: 47.7
Literacy rate: 38%
Did You Know? Between January 1991 and August 2000, Somalia had no working government.

South Africa

Where? Africa
Capital (administrative):
Pretoria
Area: 471,008 sq mi (1,219,912 sq km)
Population estimate (2005): 44,344,136
Government: Republic
Languages: 11 official languages: Afrikaans, English, Ndebele, Pedi, Sotho, Swazi, Tsonga, Tswana, Venda, Xhosa, Zulu
Monetary unit: Rand
Life expectancy: 44.1
Literacy rate: 86%
Did You Know? South Africa is the world's largest producer of gold.

Spain

Where? Europe
Capital: Madrid
Area: 194,896 sq mi
(504,782 sq km)
Population estimate (2005): 40,341,462
Government: Parliamentary monarchy
Languages: Castilian Spanish (official),
Catalan, Galician, Basque
Monetary unit: Euro (formerly peseta)
Life expectancy: 79.4
Literacy rate: 98%
Did You Know? Spain is the closest
European country to Africa.

Sri Lanka

Where? Asia
Capital: Colombo
Area: 25,332 sq mi
(65,610 sq km)
Population estimate (2005): 20,064,776
Government: Republic
Languages: Sinhala (official), Tamil,
English
Monetary unit: Sri Lankan rupee
Life expectancy: 72.9
Literacy rate: 92%
Did You Know? Sri Lanka was once
called Ceylon.

Sudan

Where? Africa
Capital: Khartoum
Area: 967,493 sq mi
(2,505,810 sq km)
Population estimate (2005): 40,187,486
Government: Authoritarian regime
Languages: Arabic (official), English,
tribal dialects
Monetary unit: Sudanese dinar
Life expectancy: 58.1
Literacy rate: 61%
Did You Know? Sudan is Africa's largest
country.

Suriname

Where? South America
Capital: Paramaribo
Area: 63,039 sq mi
(163,270 sq km)
Population estimate (2005): 438,144
Government: Constitutional democracy
Languages: Dutch (official),
Surinamese, English
Monetary unit: Suriname guilder
Life expectancy: 69.1
Literacy rate: 93%
Did You Know? Suriname is named
after its earliest inhabitants,
the Surinen Indians.

Swaziland

Where? Africa
Capital: Mbabane
Area: 6,704 sq mi
(17,360 sq km)
Population estimate (2005): 1,173,900
Government: Monarchy
Languages: Swazi (official), English
Monetary unit: Lilangeni
Life expectancy: 37.5
Literacy rate: 82%
Did You Know? The nation's King is one
of the world's last absolute monarchs.

Sweden

Where? Europe
Capital: Stockholm
Area: 173,731 sq mi
(449,964 sq km)
Population estimate (2005): 9,001,774
Government: Constitutional monarchy
Language: Swedish
Monetary unit: Krona
Life expectancy: 80.3
Literacy rate: 99%
Did You Know? The Nobel Prizes
(except the Peace Prize) are awarded
each year in Sweden.

Switzerland

Where? Europe
Capital: Bern
Area: 15,942 sq mi
(41,290 sq km)
Population estimate (2005): 7,489,370
Government: Federal republic
Languages: German, French, Italian (all official), Romansch
Monetary unit: Swiss franc
Life expectancy: 80.3
Literacy rate: 99%
Did You Know? Switzerland, in central Europe, is the land of the Alps.

Syria

Where? Middle East
Capital: Damascus
Area: 71,498 sq mi
(185,180 sq km)
Population estimate (2005): 18,448,752
Government: Republic
Languages: Arabic (official), French, English
Monetary unit: Syrian pound
Life expectancy: 69.7
Literacy rate: 77%
Did You Know? Damascus is considered the oldest capital city in the world.

Taiwan

Where? Asia
Capital: Taipei
Area: 13,892 sq mi
(35,980 sq km)
Population estimate (2005): 22,894,384
Government: Multiparty democracy
Language: Chinese (Mandarin)
Monetary unit: New Taiwan dollar
Life expectancy: 77.1
Literacy rate: 86%
Did You Know? The nation was once called Formosa. The name, meaning "the beautiful," was given by Portuguese explorers.

Tajikistan

Where? Asia
Capital: Dushanbe
Area: 55,251 sq mi
(143,100 sq km)
Population estimate (2005): 7,163,506
Government: Republic
Language: Tajik
Monetary unit: Somoni
Life expectancy: 64.5
Literacy rate: 99%
Did You Know? Once part of the Soviet Union, its name means "Land of the Tajiks."

Tanzania

Where? Africa
Capital: Dar es Salaam
Area: 364,898 sq mi
(945,087 sq km)
Population estimate (2005): 36,766,356
Government: Republic
Languages: Swahili and English (both official), local languages
Monetary unit: Tanzanian shilling
Life expectancy: 44.9
Literacy rate: 78%
Did You Know? Mount Kilimanjaro, in Tanzania, is the highest mountain in Africa.

Thailand

Where? Asia
Capital: Bangkok
Area: 198,455 sq mi
(514,000 sq km)
Population estimate (2005): 65,444,371
Government: Constitutional monarchy
Languages: Thai (Siamese), Chinese, English
Monetary unit: Baht
Life expectancy: 71.4
Literacy rate: 96%
Did You Know? Thailand was once known as Siam.

Togo

Where? Africa
Capital: Lomé
Area: 21,925 sq mi (56,790 sq km)
Population estimate (2005): 5,681,519
Government: Republic
Languages: French (official), Éwé, Mina, Kabyé, Cotocoli
Monetary unit: CFA franc
Life expectancy: 53
Literacy rate: 61%
Did You Know? The Danish, Germans, British and French once ruled Togo.

Tonga

Where? Pacific Islands
Capital: Nuku'alofa
Area: 290 sq mi (748 sq km)
Population estimate (2005): 112,422
Government: Constitutional monarchy
Languages: Tongan, English
Monetary unit: Pa'anga
Life expectancy: 69.2
Literacy rate: 99%
Did You Know? Polynesians have lived on Tonga for at least 3,000 years.

Trinidad and Tobago

Where? North America
Capital: Port-of-Spain
Area: 1,980 sq mi (5,130 sq km)
Population estimate (2005): 1,088,644
Government: Parliamentary democracy
Languages: English (official), Hindi, French, Spanish
Monetary unit: Trinidad and Tobago dollar
Life expectancy: 69.3
Literacy rate: 99%
Did You Know? Columbus explored Trinidad in 1498.

Tunisia

Where? Africa
Capital: Tunis
Area: 63,170 sq mi (163,610 sq km)
Population estimate (2005): 10,074,951
Government: Republic
Languages: Arabic (official), French
Monetary unit: Tunisian dinar
Life expectancy: 74.7
Literacy rate: 74%
Did You Know? Bordering the Mediterranean, Tunisia stretches south into the Sahara Desert.

Turkey

Where? Europe and Asia
Capital: Ankara
Area: 301,388 sq mi (780,580 sq km)
Population estimate (2005): 69,660,559
Government: Parliamentary democracy
Language: Turkish
Monetary unit: Turkish lira
Life expectancy: 72.1
Literacy rate: 87%
Did You Know? Turkey was once the home of the Byzantine and the Ottoman empires.

Turkmenistan

Where? Asia
Capital: Ashgabat
Area: 188,455 sq mi (488,100 sq km)
Population estimate (2005): 4,952,081
Government: Republic
Languages: Turkmen, Russian, Uzbek
Monetary unit: Manat
Life expectancy: 61.3
Literacy rate: 98%
Did You Know? About nine-tenths of the country is desert, mainly the Kara-Kum.

Tuvalu

Where? Pacific Islands
Capital: Funafuti
Area: 10 sq mi
(26 sq km)
Population estimate (2005): 11,636
Government: Constitutional monarchy
Languages: Tuvaluan, English
Monetary unit: Tuvaluan dollar
Life expectancy: 67.7
Literacy rate: Not available
Did You Know? Tuvalu was formerly named the Ellice Islands.

Uganda

Where? Africa
Capital: Kampala
Area: 91,135 sq mi
(236,040 sq km)
Population estimate (2005): 27,269,482
Government: Republic
Languages: English (official), Swahili, Luganda, Ateso, Luo
Monetary unit: Ugandan shilling
Life expectancy: 50.4
Literacy rate: 70%
Did You Know? Uganda's brutal former dictator, Idi Amin, died in 2003.

Ukraine

Where? Europe
Capital: Kyiv (Kiev)
Area: 233,089 sq mi
(603,700 sq km)
Population estimate (2005): 47,425,336
Government: Republic
Language: Ukrainian
Monetary unit: Hryvnia
Life expectancy: 66.7
Literacy rate: 100%
Did You Know? In 1986, a nuclear reactor blew at Chernobyl, causing the worst such accident in history.

United Arab Emirates

Where? Middle East
Capital: Abu Dhabi
Area: 32,000 sq mi
(82,880 sq km)
Population estimate (2005): 2,563,212
Government: Federation
Languages: Arabic (official), English
Monetary unit: U.A.E. dirham
Life expectancy: 75
Literacy rate: 78%
Did You Know? This country is made up of seven Gulf states.

United Kingdom

Where? Europe
Capital: London
Area: 94,525 sq mi
(244,820 sq km)
Population estimate (2005): 60,441,457
Government: Constitutional monarchy
Languages: English, Welsh, Scots, Gaelic
Monetary unit: British pound
Life expectancy: 78.3
Literacy rate: 99%
Did You Know? The United Kingdom is made up of England, Wales, Scotland and Northern Ireland.

United States

Where? North America
Capital: Washington, D.C.
Area: 3,717,792 sq mi
(9,629,091 sq km)
Population estimate (2005): 295,734,134
Government: Republic
Languages: English, Spanish (spoken by a sizable minority)
Monetary unit: U.S. dollar
Life expectancy: 77.4
Literacy rate: 97%
Did You Know? The U.S. is the world's third largest country and the world's third most populous country.

Uruguay

Where? South America
Capital: Montevideo
Area: 68,040 sq mi
(176,220 sq km)
Population estimate (2005): 3,415,920
Government: Republic
Language: Spanish
Monetary unit: Peso
Life expectancy: 75.9
Literacy rate: 98%
Did You Know? The first inhabitants of Uruguay were a people called the Charrúas.

Uzbekistan

Where? Asia
Capital: Tashkent
Area: 172,741 sq mi
(447,400 sq km)
Population estimate (2005): 26,851,195
Government: Republic
Languages: Uzbek, Russian, Tajik
Monetary unit: Uzbekistani som
Life expectancy: 64.1
Literacy rate: 99%
Did You Know? In 2001, Uzbekistan gave the U.S. a base to fight the Taliban and al-Qaeda in Afghanistan.

Vanuatu

Where? Pacific Islands
Capital: Port Vila
Area: 5,700 sq mi
(14,760 sq km)
Population estimate (2005): 205,754
Government: Republic
Languages: English and French (both official), Bislama
Monetary unit: Vatu
Life expectancy: 62.1
Literacy rate: 53%
Did You Know? Vanuatu is an archipelago of 83 islands.

Vatican City (Holy See)

Where? Europe
Capital: none
Area: 0.17 sq mi
(0.44 sq km)
Population estimate (2005): 890
Government: Ecclesiastical
Languages: Latin, Italian, various others
Monetary unit: Italian lira
Life expectancy: Not available
Literacy rate: 100%
Did You Know? This nation is the world's smallest country.

Venezuela

Where? South America
Capital: Caracas
Area: 352,143 sq mi
(912,050 sq km)
Population estimate (2005): 25,375,281
Government: Republic
Languages: Spanish (official), native languages
Monetary unit: Bolivar
Life expectancy: 74.1
Literacy rate: 93%
Did You Know? Venezuela's Angel Falls is the world's highest waterfall.

Vietnam

Where? Asia
Capital: Hanoi
Area: 127,243 sq mi
(329,560 sq km)
Population estimate (2005): 83,535,576
Government: Communist state
Languages: Vietnamese (official), French, English, Khmer, Chinese
Monetary unit: Dong
Life expectancy: 70.4
Literacy rate: 94%
Did You Know? The country was divided into North and South Vietnam in 1954, and reunified in 1976.

Yemen

Where? Middle East
Capital: Sanaa
Area: 203,850 sq mi
(527,970 sq km)
Population estimate (2005): 20,727,063
Government: Republic
Language: Arabic
Monetary unit: Rial
Life expectancy: 61.4
Literacy rate: 50%
Did You Know? In 1990, North and South Yemen joined to form the Republic of Yemen.

Zambia

Where? Africa
Capital: Lusaka
Area: 290,584 sq mi
(752,610 sq km)
Population estimate (2005): 11,261,795
Government: Republic
Languages: English (official), local dialects
Monetary unit: Kwacha
Life expectancy: 39.4
Literacy rate: 81%
Did You Know? Zambia changed its name from Northern Rhodesia after it gained independence in 1964.

Zimbabwe

Where? Africa
Capital: Harare
Area: 150,803 sq mi
(390,580 sq km)
Population estimate (2005): 12,746,990
Government: Parliamentary democracy
Languages: English (official), Ndebele, Shona
Monetary unit: Zimbabwean dollar
Life expectancy: 37.8
Literacy rate: 91%
Did You Know? Before gaining independence in 1965, this country was called Rhodesia.

The Security Council can send U.N. troops to help settle disputes.

The United Nations

The **United Nations (U.N.)** was created after World War II to provide a meeting place to help develop good relations between countries, promote peace and security around the world and encourage international cooperation in solving problems.

The major organizations of the U.N. are the Secretariat, the Security Council and the General Assembly.

The **Secretariat** is the management center of U.N. operations and is headed by the Secretary-General, who is the director of the U.N.

The **Security Council** is responsible for making and keeping international peace. Its main purpose is to prevent war by settling disputes between nations. The Security Council has 15 members. There are five permanent members: the U.S., the Russian Federation, Britain, France and China. There are also 10 temporary members that serve two-year terms.

The **General Assembly** is the world's forum for discussing matters that affect world peace and security and for making recommendations concerning both. It has no power of its own to enforce decisions. Including the 51 original member nations, it is made up of a total of 191 countries.

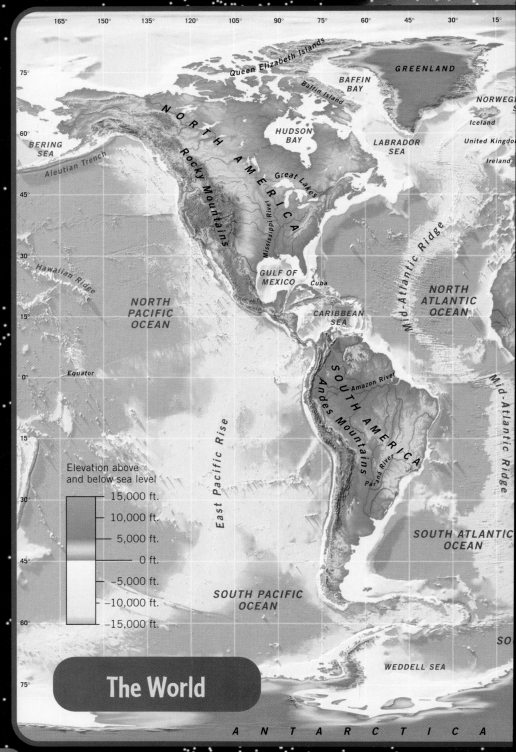

The World

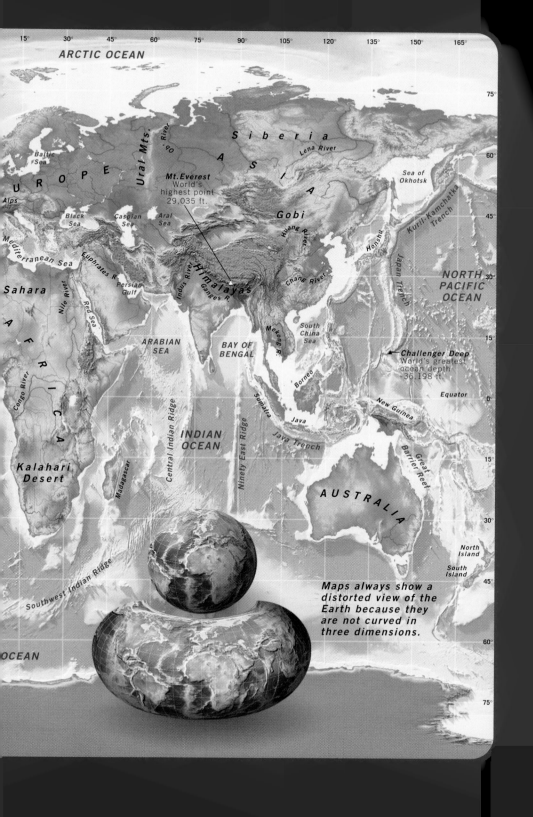

ARCTIC OCEAN

15° 30° 45° 60° 75° 90° 105° 120° 135° 150° 165°

75°

EUROPE

Baltic Sea

Alps

Ural Mts.

River

90

S i b e r i a

Lena River

A S I A

60°

Sea of Okhotsk

45°

Mediterranean Sea

Black Sea

Caspian Sea

Aral Sea

Gobi

Kuril-Kamchatka Trench

Sahara

Nile River

Euphrates R.

Red Sea

Persian Gulf

Indus River

Himalayas

Ganges R.

Huang River

Chang River

Honshu

Japan Trench

NORTH PACIFIC OCEAN

30°

Mt. Everest
World's
highest point
29,035 ft.

AFRICA

ARABIAN SEA

BAY OF BENGAL

Mekong R.

South China Sea

Challenger Deep
World's greatest
ocean depth
-36,198 ft.

15°

Congo River

Borneo

Equator

0°

Kalahari Desert

Madagascar

Central Indian Ridge

INDIAN OCEAN

Ninety East Ridge

Sumatra

Java

Java Trench

New Guinea

Great Barrier Reef

15°

AUSTRALIA

30°

North Island

45°

Southwest Indian Ridge

South Island

Maps always show a
distorted view of the
Earth because they
are not curved in
three dimensions.

60°

OCEAN

75°

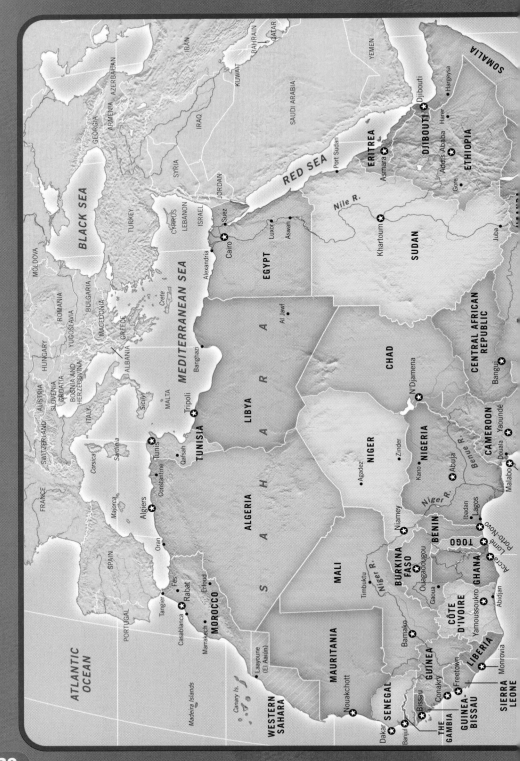

ATLANTIC
OCEAN

BLACK SEA

MEDITERRANEAN SEA

RED SEA

Nile R.

MOLDOVA

GEORGIA
ARMENIA
AZERBAIJAN
BAHRAIN
QATAR
YEMEN

SOMALIA

ROMANIA
BULGARIA
YUGOSLAVIA
MACEDONIA
ALBANIA
GREECE
TURKEY
CYPRUS
LEBANON
ISRAEL
JORDAN
SYRIA
IRAQ
IRAN
KUWAIT
SAUDI ARABIA

HUNGARY
AUSTRIA
SLOVENIA
CROATIA
BOSNIA AND
HERZEGOVINA
ITALY
SWITZERLAND
FRANCE

Crete
Malta
Sicily
Sardinia
Corsica
Majorca

SPAIN
PORTUGAL

Madeira Islands

Canary Is.

WESTERN
SAHARA

MOROCCO

Tangier
Casablanca
Marrakech
Fès
Rabat
Erfoud
Oran

Laayoune
(El Aaiún)

MAURITANIA

Nouakchott

SENEGAL

Dakar
Banjul

THE
GAMBIA

GUINEA-
BISSAU

Bissau
Conakry

GUINEA

SIERRA
LEONE

Freetown

LIBERIA

Monrovia

Abidjan

CÔTE
D'IVOIRE

Yamoussoukro

Bamako

MALI

Timbuktu

Gaoua

BURKINA
FASO

Ouagadougou

GHANA

Accra

TOGO

Lomé

BENIN

Porto-Novo

Niamey

NIGER

Agadez
Zinder

Niger R.

Niger R.

Niger R.

Benue R.

NIGERIA

Kano
Abuja
Ibadan
Lagos

CAMEROON

Douala
Malabo
Yaoundé

Bangui

CENTRAL AFRICAN
REPUBLIC

CHAD

N'Djamena

LIBYA

Tripoli
Benghazi

TUNISIA

Tunis
Constantine
Gafsa

ALGERIA

Algiers

S A H A R A

EGYPT

Cairo
Alexandria
Suez
Luxor
Aswan
Al Jawf

SUDAN

Khartoum
Juba
Port Sudan

ERITREA

Asmara

DJIBOUTI

Djibouti

ETHIOPIA

Addis Ababa
Harer
Gore

Hargeysa

328

INDIAN
OCEAN

Antananarivo

MADAGASCAR

Moroni

COMOROS

Mombasa

Dar es Salaam

Zanzibar

TANZANIA

Cidade
de Nacala

MALAWI

Lilongwe

Blantyre

Lake
Nyasa

MOZAMBIQUE

Beira

RWANDA

BURUNDI

Kigoma

Bukavu

Lake
Tanganyika

Bujumbura

Harare

ZIMBABWE

Maputo

SWAZILAND

Mbabane

Durban

Lubumbashi

Kitwe

Lusaka

Pretoria

DEMOCRATIC
REPUBLIC OF
THE CONGO

Kananga

ZAMBIA

Johannesburg

LESOTHO

Maseru

Port Elizabeth

Kinshasa

Brazzaville

BOTSWANA

Gaborone

SOUTH
AFRICA

ANGOLA

NAMIBIA

Windhoek

Cape Town

Pointe-Noire

Luanda

Lubango

Namibe

Walvis Bay

(EQUATORIAL GUINEA)

ATLANTIC
OCEAN

Africa

1,000 mi.

500 mi.

1,000 km

0 mi.

500 km

0 km

Mozambique Channel

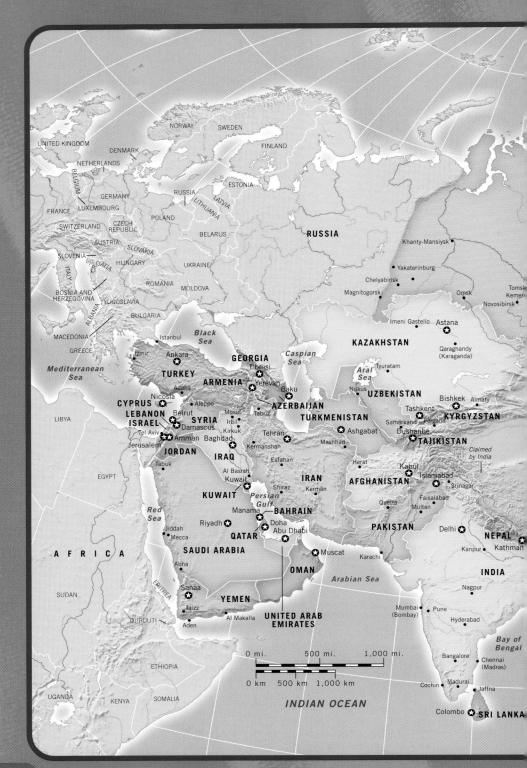

UNITED KINGDOM

NORWAY   SWEDEN

DENMARK   FINLAND

NETHERLANDS
BELGIUM   GERMANY   RUSSIA   ESTONIA
FRANCE LUXEMBOURG   LATVIA
        SWITZERLAND CZECH   LITHUANIA
                     REPUBLIC POLAND
        AUSTRIA   SLOVAKIA   RUSSIA   Khanty-Mansiysk
SLOVENIA   HUNGARY   UKRAINE   Yakaterinburg
ITALY   CROATIA   Chelyabinsk
        BOSNIA AND   ROMANIA   MOLDOVA   Magnitogorsk   Omsk   Tomsk
        HERZEGOVINA YUGOSLAVIA   Kemer
ALBANIA   BULGARIA   Imeni Gastello   Astana   Novosibirsk
MACEDONIA   Black
GREECE   Istanbul   Sea   KAZAKHSTAN   Qaraghandy
Mediterranean   Caspian   (Karaganda)
    Sea   Izmir   Ankara   Sea   Aral
                              GEORGIA   Tbilisi   Sea   Tyuratam
             Adana ARMENIA Yerevan Baku   Nukus   UZBEKISTAN   Bishkek Almaty
CYPRUS   Nicosia   Aleppo   AZERBAIJAN   Tashkent   KYRGYZSTAN
LEBANON Beirut   Mosul   Tabriz TURKMENISTAN   Samarkand Fergana
ISRAEL   Damascus SYRIA Irbil   Dushanbe   TAJIKISTAN
LIBYA   Tel Aviv   Kirkuk   Tehran   Ashgabat   Claimed
Jerusalem Amman Baghdad   Kermanshah   Mashhad   Kabul   by India
         JORDAN   IRAQ   Esfahan   Herat   AFGHANISTAN Islamabad
         Tabuk   Srinagar
EGYPT   Al Basrah   IRAN   Kerman   Quetta Faisalabad
         Kuwait Shiraz   Multan
         KUWAIT   Persian   PAKISTAN   Delhi
                  Gulf   Manama BAHRAIN   NEPAL
         Riyadh   Doha   Karachi   Kanpur Kathman
Red   QATAR Abu Dhabi   INDIA
Sea   Jiddah   Muscat
    Mecca   SAUDI ARABIA   Nagpur
AFRICA   OMAN   Arabian Sea
         Abha   Hyderabad
SUDAN   Sanaa   Mumbai   Pune
         Taizz YEMEN   UNITED ARAB   (Bombay)
ERITREA Aden   Al Makalla EMIRATES   Bay of
DJIBOUTI   Bengal
                                                              Bangalore Chennai
                  0 mi.   500 mi.   1,000 mi.   (Madras)
ETHIOPIA   Cochin Madurai
                  0 km   500 km 1,000 km   Jaffna
UGANDA KENYA SOMALIA   Colombo   SRI LANKA
                        INDIAN OCEAN

ARCTIC OCEAN

Cherskiy

Tiksi

Verkhoyansk

Bering
Sea

Magadan

Kamchatka
Peninsula

RUSSIA

Yakutsk

Petropavlovsk-
Kamchatskiy

Sea of
Okhotsk

S I B E R I A

arsk

Sakhalin

Irkutsk

Khabarovsk

Sapporo

Harbin

Ulaanbaatar

G o b i

Changchun

Vladivostok

MONGOLIA

Shenyang

JAPAN

Hohhot

Jinxi

N. KOREA

Tokyo

Beijing

P'yongyang

Nagoya

Tianjin

Seoul

Kyoto

Taiyuan

Jinan

Taegu

Kobe Osaka

Lanzhou

S. KOREA

Pusan

Hiroshima

Xi'an

Qingdao

Fukuoka

CHINA

Nagasaki

Hefei

Shanghai

Wuhan

Chengdu

Chongqing

Naha

PACIFIC
OCEAN

Fuzhou

Taipei

TAN

Xiamen

Liuzhou

TAIWAN

LADESH

Nanning

Guangzhou

Kao-hsiung

ka

Macau

Mandalay

Hong Kong

tagong

Hanoi

NMAR

LAOS

Luzon

RMA)

Vientiane

Baguio

Chiang Mai

Quezon City

angoon

Da Nang

Manila

THAILAND

PHILIPPINES

Bangkok

VIETNAM

Cebu

CAMBODIA

Phnom
Penh

Ho Chi Minh City

Phuket

Songkhla

Borneo

Asia and the Middle East

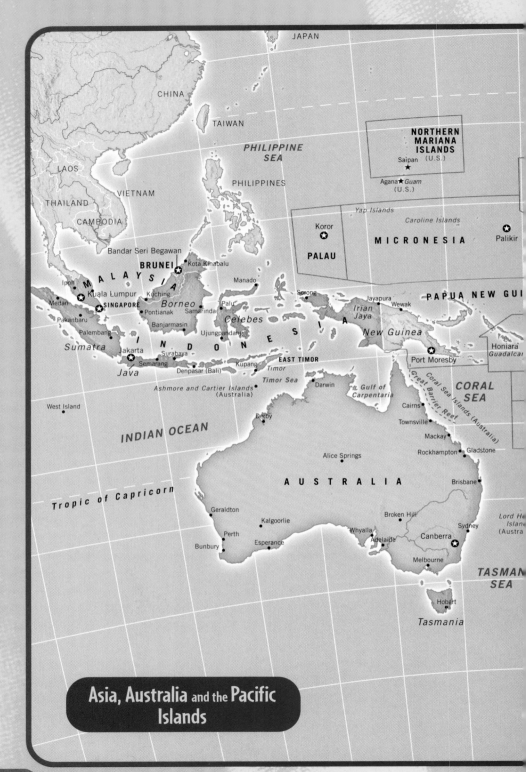

JAPAN

CHINA

TAIWAN

LAOS

VIETNAM

THAILAND

CAMBODIA

PHILIPPINE
SEA

PHILIPPINES

**NORTHERN
MARIANA
ISLANDS** (U.S.)

Saipan ★

Agana ★ *Guam*
(U.S.)

Yap Islands

Caroline Islands

Koror
✪

MICRONESIA

Palikir ✪

PALAU

Bandar Seri Begawan

BRUNEI

Kota Kinabalu

Manado

Ipoh

Kuala Lumpur

Kuching

Borneo

Palu

Sorong

Jayapura

PAPUA NEW GUI

Wewak

Medan

SINGAPORE

Pontianak

Samarinda

Celebes

*Irian
Jaya*

Pakanbaru

Banjarmasin

Ujungpandang

New Guinea

Palembang

I N D O N E S I A

Honiara
Guadalcar

Sumatra

Jakarta

Surabaya

Timor

EAST TIMOR

Port Moresby

Semarang

Kupang

Denpasar (Bali)

Java

Timor Sea

*Ashmore and Cartier Islands
(Australia)*

Darwin

*Gulf of
Carpentaria*

Great Barrier Reef

Coral Sea Islands (Australia)

**CORAL
SEA**

West Island

Derby

Cairns

INDIAN OCEAN

Townsville

Mackay

Alice Springs

Rockhampton

Gladstone

Tropic of Capricorn

A U S T R A L I A

Brisbane

Geraldton

Kalgoorlie

Broken Hill

*Lord He
Island
(Austra*

Perth

Whyalla

Sydney

Bunbury

Esperance

Adelaide

Canberra
✪

Melbourne

**TASMAN
SEA**

Hobart

Tasmania

Asia, Australia and the Pacific Islands

Tropic of Cancer

Honolulu

Johnston Atoll (U.S.)

Hilo

Hawaii
(U.S.)

PACIFIC OCEAN

MARSHALL ISLANDS

Majuro

Kingman Reef (U.S.)
Palmyra Atoll (U.S.)

Tarawa

Howland Island (U.S.)

Baker Island (U.S.)

Gilbert
Islands

K I R I B A T I

Jarvis
Island
(U.S.)

Equator

Phoenix Islands

**SOLOMON
ISLANDS**

Funafuti

TUVALU

TOKELAU (N.Z.)

Mata-Utu

SAMOA

**WALLIS AND
FUTUNA**
(FR.)

Apia

Pago
Pago

COOK ISLANDS
(N.Z.)

Marquesas
Islands

VANUATU

Port Vila

Suva

**AMERICAN
SAMOA**

Alofi

TONGA

Nuku'alofa

Papeete

Tuamotu Archipelago

Noumea

FIJI

NIUE
(N.Z.)

Avarua

Society
Islands

Tahiti

**NEW
CALEDONIA**
(France)

Norfork Island
gston
tralia)

FRENCH POLYNESIA (France)

Kermadec Islands
(N.Z.)

Adamstown

**PITCAIRN
ISLANDS**
(U.K.)

NEW ZEALAND

Auckland

Hastings

Wellington

Christchurch

Chatham Islands

Dunedin

Invercargill

Stewart Island

0 mi.   500 mi.   1,000 mi.

0 km   1,000 km

Europe

0 mi.   300 mi.   600 mi.

0 km   300 km   600 km

Reykjavik

ICELAND

Arctic Circle

FAROE ISLANDS
(Denmark)
Torshavn

Trondheim

SHETLAND ISLANDS

ORKNEY
ISLANDS

HEBRIDES

Bergen

NORWAY

Oslo

Gävle

Stavanger

SWEDEN

Göteborg

Aberdeen

DENMARK

Ålborg

Glasgow
Edinburgh

NORTH
SEA

Copenhagen

Malmö

Belfast

UNITED
KINGDOM

Dublin

Liverpool   Leeds

IRELAND

Manchester
Sheffield

NETHERLANDS

Hamburg

Bremen

Berlin

Poznan

Birmingham

London

Amsterdam
The Hague
Rotterdam

GERMANY

GUERNSEY (U.K.)

Calais   Lille

Antwerp

Essen
Dusseldorf
Cologne

Wroclaw

JERSEY (U.K.)

Le Havre

Brussels

BELGIUM

Bonn   Frankfurt

LUXEMBOURG

Paris

Prague

Luxembourg

CZECH
REPUBLIC

Brno

ATLANTIC OCEAN

Nantes

Strasbourg

Stuttgart

Bratislava

FRANCE

Dijon

LIECHTENSTEIN   Munich

Vienna

Zurich   Vaduz

BAY OF
BISCAY

Bern

AUSTRIA

HUNG

Geneva

SWITZERLAND

Ljubljana

SLOVENIA

Bordeaux

Lyon

Turin   Milan

Trieste

Zagreb

Porto

Bilbao

Genoa

CROATIA

Toulouse

SAN
MARINO

BOSNIA AN
HERZEGOVIN

Lisbon

Madrid

Andorra
la Vella

Marseille

Bastia

Florence

Sarajevo

MONACO

ITALY

ADRIATIC SE

PORTUGAL

SPAIN

ANDORRA

Vatican
City

Rome

Barcelona

Corsica

Bari

Seville

Valencia

Majorca

Naples

Faro

Málaga

Palma

Sardinia

Cagliari

Gibraltar

MEDITERRANEAN SEA

Palermo   Messina

Sicily

MOROCCO

ALGERIA

Valletta

MALTA

A F R I C A

TUNISIA

Murmansk

Pechora

ASIA

Arkhangel'sk

Oulu

FINLAND

RUSSIA

Tampere

Izhevsk

Helsinki
St. Petersburg

Tallinn

ESTONIA

Nizhniy Novgorod

Kazan

Riga

LATVIA

Moscow

Samara

HUANIA

Smolensk

Vilnius

Lipetsk

Saratov

Minsk

Voronezh

KAZAKHSTAN

D

BELARUS

Homyel'

Brest

Kiev

Kharkiv

Volgograd

L'viv

Derazhnya

Voroshilovgrad

UKRAINE

Gorlovka

Makeyevka

Zhdanov

Rostov

Chisinau

Iasi

Odessa

Mykolavia

Kerch'

Groznyy

MOLDOVA

Simferopol'

ROMANIA

Sevastopol'

Bucharest

Craiova

Constanta

BLACK SEA

EGRO

Varna

Sofia

BULGARIA

opje

EDONIA

Istanbul

essaloniki

T U R K E Y

Volos

IRAN

Izmir

ECE

SYRIA

Athens

IRAQ

Crete

CYPRUS

LEBANON

Greenland Sea

ICELAND

Tasiilaq
(Ammassalik)

Narssuaq

GREENLAND
(Denmark)

Labrador
Sea

*Island of
Newfoundland*

St. John's

Happy Valley
Goose Bay

Nuuk (Godthab)

Davis Strait

Baffin Bay

Qaanaaq (Thule)

Iqaluit

Baffin Island

Chisasibi
(Fort George)

CANADA

Alert

**HUDSON
BAY**

Moosonee

Queen Elizabeth Islands

Kangiqtugaapik (Clyde River)

Churchill

Arctic Circle

Winnipeg

**ARCTIC
OCEAN**

Banks Island

Victoria Island

Echo Bay

Yellowknife

Saskatoon

Regina

*Beaufort
Sea*

Inuvik

Whitehorse

Edmonton

Calgary

Helena

RUSSIA

Barrow

Prudhoe Bay

Juneau

Vancouver

Seattle

Boise

Alaska (U.S.)

Fairbanks

Anchorage

Valdez

Victoria

Olympia

Portland

Nome

Bethel

Kodiak

Salem

*Bering
Sea*

Aleutian Islands

North America and Central America

ATLANTIC OCEAN

BERMUDA (U.K.)
Hamilton ★

0 mi.   500 mi.   1,000 mi.
0 km   500 km   1,000 km

TURKS AND CAICOS ISLANDS (U.K.)
Grand Turk ★

SAINT MAARTEN/ SAINT MARTIN (Neth. Antilles)/(Guad.)
ANGUILLA (U.K.)
SAINT BARTHÉLEMY (Guad.)
ANTIGUA AND BARBUDA
VIRGIN ISLANDS (U.S.-U.K.)
SAINT KITTS AND NEVIS
MONTSERRAT (U.K.)
GUADELOUPE (Fr.)
DOMINICA
MARTINIQUE (Fr.)
SAINT LUCIA
BARBADOS
SAINT VINCENT AND THE GRENADINES
GRENADA
NETHERLANDS ANTILLES (Neth.)
ARUBA (Neth.)
TRINIDAD AND TOBAGO

GUYANA

VENEZUELA

COLOMBIA

PUERTO RICO (U.S.)
San Juan
DOMINICAN REPUBLIC
Santiago ★
Santo Domingo
HAITI
Port-au-Prince

BAHAMAS
Nassau ★
Freeport
Miami

CUBA
Havana ★
Camagüey
Camaguey
Guantánamo
Guantanamo Bay
Montego Bay
JAMAICA
Kingston
CAYMAN ISLANDS (U.K.) ★
George Town

CARIBBEAN SEA

Jacksonville
Savannah
Columbia
Raleigh
Charleston
Richmond

Augusta
Concord
Boston
Providence
Albany
Hartford
New York
Philadelphia
Dover
Baltimore
Washington, DC
Norfolk
Harrisburg
Pittsburgh
Buffalo
Toronto
Cleveland
Frankfort
Detroit
Toledo
Cincinnati
Columbus
Nashville
Louisville
Indianapolis
Chicago
Milwaukee
Madison
Springfield
Saint Louis
Jefferson City
Des Moines
Omaha
Lincoln
Kansas City
Topeka
Memphis
Little Rock
Jackson
Birmingham
Atlanta
Montgomery
Tallahassee
Baton Rouge
New Orleans

ATLANTIC OCEAN

UNITED STATES

Denver
Santa Fe
Oklahoma City
Dallas
Austin
San Antonio
Houston
Ciudad Juárez
El Paso
Hermosillo
Phoenix
Los Angeles
San Diego
Tijuana

GULF OF MEXICO

Tampico
Veracruz
Mérida
Cancún
Belize City
BELIZE
Belmopan
Guatemala City
GUATEMALA
San Salvador
EL SALVADOR
Tegucigalpa
HONDURAS
Managua
NICARAGUA
San José
COSTA RICA
Panama City
PANAMA

Puebla
Oaxaca
Mexico City
Acapulco
MEXICO
León
Guadalajara
Monterrey
Puerto Vallarta
Mazatlán
La Paz

Gulf of California

Tropic of Cancer

PACIFIC OCEAN

North America and Central America

PACIFIC OCEAN

ATLANTIC OCEAN

Brazilian
Highlands

Belo Horizonte

Rio de Janeiro

São Paulo

Curitiba

Porto Alegre

Paraná River

Paraguay River

PARAGUAY

Asunción

Ciudad
del Este

Encarnación

Formosa

Resistencia

Paraná River

Rosario

Salto

URUGUAY

Montevideo

Río de la Plat

Mar del Plata

Buenos Aires

ARGENTINA

Córdoba

San Miguel
de Tucumán

Bahía Blanca

Santa Cruz

Sucre

Andes Mts.

Arica

Iquique

Antofagasta

CHILE

Santiago

Valparaíso

Concepción

Puerto Montt

Comodoro Rivadavia

Strait of
Magellan

Río Gallegos

Punta Arenas

Ushuaia

Stanley

Falkland Is.
(Islas Malvinas)
(Administered by U.K.;
claimed by Argentina)

Cape Horn

South America

0 mi.   500 mi.   1,000 mi.

0 km   500 km   1,000 km

500 mi.

1,000 km

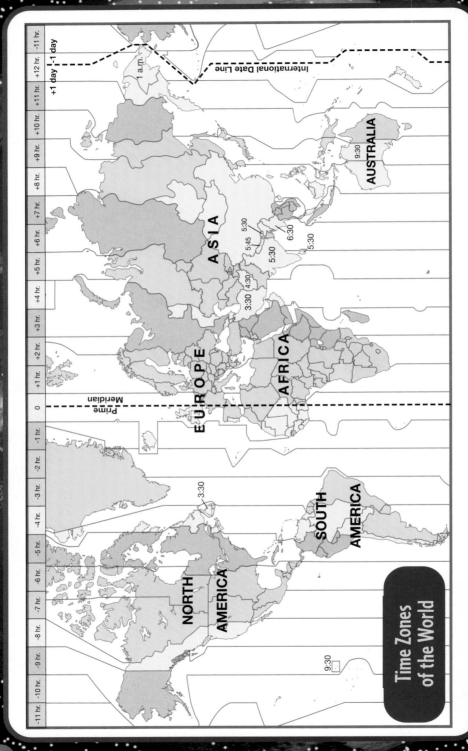

Time Zones
of the World

-11 hr. -10 hr. -9 hr. -8 hr. -7 hr. -6 hr. -5 hr. -4 hr. -3 hr. -2 hr. -1 hr. 0 +1 hr. +2 hr. +3 hr. +4 hr. +5 hr. +6 hr. +7 hr. +8 hr. +9 hr. +10 hr. +11 hr. +12 hr. -11 hr.

+1 day -1 day

1 a.m.

International Date Line

Prime Meridian

ASIA

EUROPE

AFRICA

AUSTRALIA

NORTH
AMERICA

SOUTH
AMERICA

3:30

9:30

3:30 4:30

5:45

5:30

5:30

5:30

6:30

9:30

340

Did You Know?

These countries have admitted they have nuclear weapons: **Britain, China, France, India, North Korea, Pakistan, Russia** and the **United States. Israel** is believed to have them but hasn't acknowledged the fact. **Iran** has been working toward acquiring nuclear weapons.

WORLD POPULATION MILESTONES

1 billion in 1804	
2 billion in 1927	**123 years later**
3 billion in 1960	**33 years later**
4 billion in 1974	**14 years later**
5 billion in 1987	**13 years later**
6 billion in 1999	**12 years later**

Source: United Nations Population Division

Countries with the Largest Military Budgets

These countries spend the most money each year on their military. The figures are given in U.S. dollars.

COUNTRY	BUDGET
1. **UNITED STATES**	**$417,400,000,000**
2. **JAPAN**	**46,900,000,000**
3. **UNITED KINGDOM**	**37,100,000,000**
4. **FRANCE**	**35,000,000,000**
5. **CHINA**	**32,800,000,000**
6. **GERMANY**	**27,200,000,000**
7. **ITALY**	**20,800,000,000**
8. **IRAN**	**19,200,000,000**
9. **SAUDI ARABIA**	**19,100,000,000**
10. **SOUTH KOREA**	**13,900,000,000**

Source: *SIPRI Yearbook 2004*, Stockholm International Peace Research Institute.

TFK Mystery Person

CLUE 1: I have fought for human rights in Iran, where I was born in 1947.

CLUE 2: One of Iran's first female judges, I have defended the rights of women and children and helped those who oppose Iran's government.

CLUE 3: In 2003, I became the first Iranian and first Muslim woman to win the Nobel Peace Prize.

WHO AM I?

(See Answer Key that begins on page 342.)

Where the World's Refugees Come From

Refugees are people who flee their native lands for safety, usually during war or political upheaval. Here's a list of the regions that people flee from most often.

1. **WEST BANK AND GAZA STRIP**
2. **AFGHANISTAN**
3. **SUDAN**
4. **MYANMAR (BURMA)**
5. **DEMOCRATIC REPUBLIC OF THE CONGO**
6. **LIBERIA**
7. **BURUNDI**
8. **ANGOLA**
9. **VIETNAM**
10. **IRAQ**

A Vietnamese refugee seeks safety in Hong Kong.

Source: World Refugee Survey 2004, U.S. Committee on Refugees

go — Take a quiz about the world's most famous landmarks at **timeforkids.com/worldtrivia**

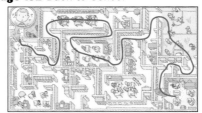
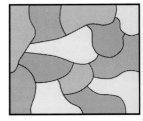
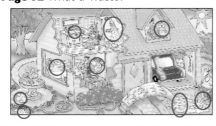

Answers

5. THE, HE, HER, HERE, I, THERE, IN, HEREIN. (Bonus points for getting ERE, RE, REIN.) 6. There is a MILE between the first and last letters.
Page 157 Mystery Person: Peter Mark Roget

MATH
Page 169
Computing Pie

Page 16 Mystery Person: John Nash

MILITARY & WAR
Page 175 Mystery Person: Alexander the Great

MONEY
Page 178 Brand News:

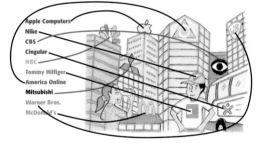

Page 179 Mystery Person: Oprah Winfrey

MOVIES & TV
Page 183 Made in Hollywood: 1. B; 2. E; 3. D; 4. C; 5. A
Page 185 Mystery Person: George Lucas

MUSIC & DANCE
Page 189 Mystery Person: Maria Tallchief

MYTHOLOGY
Page 193 Mystery Person: Venetia Burney

PRESIDENTS
Page 203 Mystery Person: George Gallup

RELIGION
Page 207 Mystery Person: Joseph Smith

SCIENCE
Page 216 Flower Power: 1. Foil; 2. Den; 3. Camel; 4. Neon; 5. Era; 6. Mold; 7. Lend; 8. Swim; 9. Omen; 10. Coin
Page 217 Mystery Person: Barbara McClintock

SPACE
Page 227 Jumping Jupiter: 3 and 4.
Page 227 Mystery Person: Robert Goddard

SPORTS
Page 241 Mystery Person: Muhammad Ali

UNITED STATES
Page 247 Bumper Crop: La Crosse, Wisconsin; Los Angeles, California; New Orleans, Louisiana; Los Alamos, New Mexico; San Diego, California; Fort Collins, Colorado; Des Moines, Iowa; Little Rock, Arkansas; St. Louis, Missouri; New Haven, Connecticut; Newark, New Jersey; Butte, Montana
Page 279 Mystery Person: Juliette Gordon Low

VOLUNTEERING
Page 283 Mystery Person: Florence Nightingale

WEATHER
Page 285 Winter Wonderland:

Page 289
Mystery Person: Sir Francis Beaufort

WORLD
Page 292 Going in Circles: The countries are (from the center to the outermost ring) India, Argentina, Germany, Turkey, Canada
Page 341 Mystery Person: Shirin Ebadi

INNER FRONT COVER Mathamazing:
A: 34; B: 3; C: 1; D: 103; E: 17; F: 7; G: 8; H: 3; I: 7; J: 1; K: 6; L: 2; M: 10; N: 10; O: 2.

INNER BACK COVER Riddle Wrecker:
Riddle 1: A screwdriver. Riddle 2: The second President. Riddle 3: The letter g.

344

Index

357

McCurry/Magnum Photos; Bruno Barbey/Magnum Photos

Language: 152: Courtesy Dawn van Ryckeghem; Robert Rosamillio/New York Daily News; David Lassman/The Post Standard; Jeff Greenberg/Photo Edit; George Walker IV/The Tennessean. 153: Felipe Galindo. 155: Felipe Galindo. 156: PD; Felipe Galindo. 157: The Granger Collection; Jane Sanders.

Math: 160: Felipe Galindo. 161: Felipe Galindo. 169: Punchstock; Reuters/Newscom

Military & War: 170: Bettmann/Corbis; Northwind Picture Archive/Northwind Production. 171: The Granger Collection. 172: Time-Life Pictures/Getty Images; The Granger Collection. 173: Yuri Kovyrev; Max Becherer/Polaris. 174: Library of Congress; Veterans History Project (2). 175: AP Photo/U.S. Airforce; AP Photo/U.S. Marines, Justin Watkins; The Granger Collection

Money: 176: The U.S. Mint. 177: AP Photo/Treasury Department; AP Photo/Dan Loh; PD. 178: Charles O'Rear/Corbis; Charles & Josette Lenars/Corbis; Felipe Galindo. 179: AP Photo/Amy Sussman; Felipe Galindo

Movies & TV: 180: Warner Bros. (4). 182: John Springer Collection/Corbis; Bettmann/Corbis. 183: Felipe Galindo. 184: Felipe Galindo. 185: AP Photo/Kevork Djansezian; Monty Brinton/CBS; Nickelodeon Movies and Parmount; Nikeledeon; CBS/Cobal Collection; AP Photo/Mark Lenniham

Music & Dance: 186: AP Photo/Harry Scull Jr.; AP Photo/Rob Griffith. 187: PD; Punchstock. 189: AP Photo/Jim Slosiarey; Reuters/Newscom; AP Photo

Mythology: 190: Swim Inc./Corbis; Time-Life Pictures/Getty Images. 191: Archivo Iconografico, S.A./Corbis; The Granger Collection. 192: Joe Lertola; Roger Wood/Corbis; Free Agents Limited/Corbis. 193: Felipe Galindo; Bettmann/Corbis

Presidents: 194-201: Christie's Images/Corbis (Washington); John Trumbull/NPG/SI (Adams); Mather Brown/NPG/SI beq. of Charles Francis Adams (Jefferson); Chester Harding/NPG/SI (Madison); John Vanderlyn/NPG/SI (Monroe) George Caleb Bingham/NPG/SI (Adams); Ralph Eleaser Whiteside Earl/NPG/SI gift of Andrew W. Mellon (Jackson); Mathew B. Brady/NPG/SI (Van Buren); Albert Gallatin Hoit/NPG/SI (Harrison); LOC (Tyler); Max Westfield/NPG/SI (Polk); James Reid Lambdin/ NPG/SI gift of Barry Bingham Sr. (Taylor); NPG/SI (Fillmore); George Peter Healy/NPG/SI gift of Andrew W. Mellon (Pierce); George Peter Healy/NPG/SI gift of Andrew W. Mellon (Buchanan); William Judkins Thomson); George Peter Healy/NPG/SI (Lincoln); Washington Bogart Cooper/NPG/SI; Thomas Le Clear/NPG/SI gift of Mrs. Grant (Grant); Bettmann/Corbis (Hayes); Ole Peter Hansen Balling/NPG/SI gift of IBM; Ole Peter Hansen Balling/NPG/SI gift of Mrs. H.N. Blue; Anders Zorn/NPG/SI (Cleveland); LOC (Harrison); LOC (Cleveland); Adolfo Muller-Ury/NPG/SI (McKinley); Adrian Lamb/NPG/SI gift of T.R. Assoc. (Roosevelt); William Valentine Schevill/NPG/SI gift of W.E. Schevill (Taft); Edmund Tarbell/ NPG/SI (Wilson); Margaret Lindsay Williams/NPG/SI (Harding). Joseph E. Burgess/NPG/SI gift of Phi Gamma Delta (Coolidge); Douglas Chandor/NPG/SI (Hoover); Oscar White/Corbis (FDR); Greta Kempton/NPG/SI (Truman); Thomas Edgar Stephens/NPG/SI gift of Ailsa Mellon Bruce (Eisenhower); JFK Presidential Library (Kennedy); Peter Hurd/NPG/SI gift of the artist (Johnson); Norman Rockwell/NPG/SI gift of Nixon Foundation (Nixon); Everett R. Kinstler/NPG/SI gift of Ford Foundation (Ford); Jimmy Carter Presidential Library (Carter); Ronald Reagan Presidential Library (Reagan); Ronald N.

Sherr/NPG/SI gift of Mr. & Mrs. R.E. Krueger (Bush); Bettmann/Corbis (Clinton); Eric Draper/White House (G.W. Bush). 201: Royalty-Free/Getty Images; Michael Simpson/Getty Images. 202: Katheryn Hewitt. 203: Jason Reed/Reuters/Corbis; AP Photo

Religion: 204: Punchstock (2). 205: AP Photo; Royalty-Free Corbis (2). 206: Pascal Le Segretain/Getty Images. 207: Reuters/Corbis; AP Photo/Dita Alangkara; Punchstock; Bettmann/Corbis

Science: 208: Courtesy Peter Brown (2); EPA Agency. 210: AP Photo/Ted S. Warren; Punchstock. 211: Punchstock; Felipe Galindo. 212: The Granger Collection (2). 213: The Granger Collection (2); Ted Spiegel/Corbis. 216: Jane Sanders. 217: Royalty-Free/Getty Images (3); Punchstock; AP Photo/Ron Frehm

Space: 218-221: Punchstock (background). 218: NASA; Antonio Cidadao (Moon). 219: NASA (Mercury, Venus); Punchstock (Earth); Punchstock (Mars); University of Arizona/JPL/NASA (Jupiter); NASA (Saturn); Punchstock (2). 222-223: Felipe Galindo. 224: Renee Bouchard/ NASA; NASA. 225: Corbis; AP Photo/NASA; Bettmann/ Corbis; NASA. 226: Reuters/David Gray; Felipe Galindo. 227: AP Photo/The Daily Ledger, Paula Albert, Kelly Huff; NASA; Stock Trek/Corbis; The Granger Collection. Dr. Albrecht, ESA/ESO/NASA

Sports: 228: Lew Dematieis/Reuters; Nick Lammers/Tribune Sports; PD. 229: AFP/Getty Images; Scott Halloran/Getty Images. 230: PD; Reuters/Newscom; AP Photo/HMB; AP Photo/John Froschauer. 231: PD; Anthony Causi/Newscom; AP Photo/Elaine Thompson. 232: David Drapkin/Getty Images; AP Photo/Ann Heisenfelt; Bettmann/Corbis. 233: AP Photo/Chris Graythen; AP Photo/Chris O'Meara. 234: PD; Lisa Blumenfeld/Getty Images; AP Photo/Mark J. Terril. 235: PD; Royalty-Free/Getty Images; AP Photo/David Zalubowski; PD. 236: AP Photo/Steve Mitchell; Martin Bureau/Getty Images. 237: AP Photo/Amy Sancetta; AP Photo/Paul Chiasson. 238: AP Photo/Kevork Djansezian; AP Photo/Morry Gash; AP Photo. 239: AP Photo/Paul Sakuma; Tim Clary/Newscom. 240: AP Photo/Lionel Cironneau; Noah Hamilton. 241: PD; AP Photo/Alan Marlin; AP Photo/Richard Drew

U.S.: 242: Stefan Hacker/Habitat for Humanity; Charlie Westerman/Greater Chicago Food Depository. 243: Bettmann/Corbis; AP Photo/Rapid City Journal; Courtesy Barney Smith Toilet Seat Museum. 244: Felipe Galindo. 245: Johnny Hernandez/Getty Images; Felipe Galindo. 246: The Granger Collection; AP Photo/Charles Rex Arbogast. 248: Felipe Galindo; Bill Ross/Corbis. 249: AP Photo/Eric Risberg; AP Photo/Don Ryan; AP Photo/Beth A. Keiser; AP Photo/David Jordan. 250-276: Joe Lertola (maps). 277: AP Photo/J. Scott Applewhite; Royalty-Free/Getty Images. 279: AP Photo

Volunteering: 280: Sam Watson/Johnson City Press/AP. 281: Courtesy Bob Bergquist; AP Photo/George Widman. 282: UNICEF; Courtesy Brower Youth Awards. 283: The Granger Collection

Weather: 284: Jennifer Kraemer-Smith; Danny Tindell-Dothan Eagle/AP. 285: AP Photo/Poul Ranal; AP Photo/ Steve Gooch; AP Photo/Gregory Bull; Ogden Gigli. 286: Eastcott Momatiuk/Getty Images; Royalty-Free/Getty Images. 288: PD; Brad Holland; Richard Hamilton Smith/Corbis; PD. 289: PD; The Granger Collection

World: 290: AP Photo/Ben Curtis; Nic Bothma/EPA. 291: Ed Gabel; Royalty-Free/Getty Images. 292: Dave Klug; Joe LeMonnier. 294: Punchstock. 293-340: Joe Lertola (maps). 325: Corbis. 341: John Schults/Reuters; Peter Turnley/Corbis

TIME FOR KIDS online

Check out TimeForKids.com, your online news, homework-helper and exploration destination!

→ **Look for daily news and polls, stories and interviews by TFK Kid Reporters, games and interactive features.**

→ **Go Places with TFK online to hear languages from around the world, send E-Cards and see amazing sites.**

→ **Search the best kid-recommended homework sites on the Web.**

→ **Give your writing a boost with our step-by-step guides to writing nonfiction papers, along with sample papers, idea organizers and checklists.**

Millions of kids each week go to **FACTMONSTER.COM** for tons of facts, puzzles and games, cool features and homework help!

■ **Get the facts**
on animals, the planets, presidents, movies and more.

■ **Tips and ideas**
for creating a spectacular science project.

■ **How smart are you?**
Take a quiz on flags, ice cream, Harry Potter or Lemony Snicket.

■ **Your opinion counts!**
Vote in our fun polls and see what other kids think.

Webby Award Winner for Best Kids' Site

www.FactMonster.com
a Pearson Education Company